P9-CMV-484

WORKING VICE

WORKING VICE

THE GRITTY TRUE STORY
OF LT. LUCIE J. DUVALL

TAMAR HOSANSKY
AND PAT SPARLING

HarperCollins*Publishers*

Photographs follow page 168.

WORKING VICE. Copyright © 1992 by Tamar Hosansky and Pat Sparling. All rights reserved. Printed in the United States of America. No part of this book may be used or reproduced in any manner whatsoever without written permission except in the case of brief quotations embodied in critical articles and reviews. For information address HarperCollins Publishers, Inc., 10 East 53rd Street, New York, NY 10022.

HarperCollins books may be purchased for educational, business, or sales promotional use. For information, please write: Special Markets Department, HarperCollins Publishers, Inc., 10 East 53rd Street, New York, NY 10022.

FIRST EDITION

Designed by George J. McKeon

Library of Congress Cataloging-in-Publication Data
Hosansky, Tamar.
    Working vice: the gritty true story of Lt. Lucie J. Duvall / Tamar Hosansky and Pat Spar
    ling.—1st ed.
    p.   cm
    Includes index.
    ISBN 0-06-016679-7
    1. Duvall, Lucie J., 1944– . 2. Police—Ohio—Cleveland—Biography. 3. Policewomen—
Ohio—Cleveland—Biography. 4. Vice control—Ohio—Cleveland. I. Sparling, Pat, 1949–
.II.Title HV7911.D98H67 1992
363.2′092—dc20
[B]   91-59930

92 93 94 95 96 ❖/HC 10 9 8 7 6 5 4 3 2 1

To Seda Aronian Sparling, M.D.,

Sandra Elkin,

and the women and men

of the Cleveland Police Department

for daring to take the risk

WORKING VICE

Authors' Note

This book is about real people and real events. We conducted over 120 interviews, read court and police records and utilized our own observations to write this book. We also read newspaper accounts and viewed television footage. All dialogue comes directly from these interviews and records. In four instances, we took liberties with time frame and sequence; however, all events are portrayed as they actually happened.

Although Lucie J. Duvall checked the manuscript for factual accuracy, we controlled the book's content and Lucie J. Duvall is not responsible for the views expressed in this book.

Certain names have been changed to protect privacy. Each pseudonym has been italicized the first time it appears.

PROLOGUE

Lieutenant Lucie J. Duvall raises her long-barreled .38, her wrist locked in line with her arm. She aims toward the stairwell of the schoolyard. The sound, like the roar of a DC-7's cockpit, fills her ears. "Police officers—freeze."

The drug dealer caught in her sights rushes toward her, the stiff flat metal of his 9mm pistol flashing. He fires three shots and pivots back to a stairway rising along the side of the building. Lucie unloads her six rounds. He spins and falls against the concrete sidewalk. His sandy blond hair flops over his arm, his pale yellow checkered shirt goes white in the glare of the sun, his body shudders from the impact. His gun is still clutched in his hand.

Without warning a second man appears. Heavyset, with curly dark hair. He leaps from the shadowy stairwell onto the walkway. He sprints up the stairs, brandishing his automatic assault rifle as he runs for escape. A burst of gunfire sputters from his weapon.

"OK. Relax, Lieutenant Duvall. Put your gun in your holster." Sergeant Thomas R. Gaul's voice is soothing within the roar of the firearms training room. He walks over and switches on the fluorescent lights.

Lucie has just satisfied her yearly Chapter Ten firearms training, rules of the Cleveland, Ohio police department on the use of deadly force. The high-tech FATS (Firearms Training Systems) produces life-size video reenactments of actual police scenarios from Los Angeles. Faced with armed criminals, panicking hostages, and suspects who pretended they were surrendering while reaching for their weapons, Lucie had to decide in a split second when to shoot.

The thick black belt and holster strapped about her tan slacks holds a specially designed gun, a Smith and Wesson .38 with a primer cap inside. Adapted for the FATS machine, it converts energy so that a laser hits the screen where a bullet was aimed.

"You know it's really amazing. Almost everyone who comes down here gets killed. Definitely fun." Sergeant Gaul enjoys teaching. A lock from his full head of gray hair falls centered on his forehead.

"The recruits get so excited during the scenarios that sometimes I have to stop them from going right at the screen," Gaul explains.

Lucie replaces her sunglasses to the top of her head, her dark red hair falls loosely over her forehead. Her smile reaches wide until her eyes and cheeks are full of laughter. Lucie's laugh fills the room. She remembers a rookie eighteen years ago. There was no FATS then, but she understands the enthusiasm of the recruits.

"Their judgment isn't tempered," Gaul continues. "They beat themselves up over mistakes. 'I'm dead' they say, and they start getting depressed. I don't know if this is done intentionally, or just maybe accidentally, Lieutenant, but they give them the routine at the academy about how many different times and ways you can be sued for shooting someone. Then, they come in here, and they're getting shot at."

Lucie agrees. "They have to learn that, but the problem is they get so afraid. They may jeopardize their own life." Lucie unbuckles the training weapon and hands it to Sergeant Gaul.

"How's the nine-millimeter training? When will the whole department get them?" Lucie asks. She slips on her fuchsia jacket.

"The whole department?" Gaul shakes his head. "After I'm retired."

"I will be too," Lucie says with a smile as she opens the thin metal door of the trailer and steps out onto the wooden deck.

"I'm not even fond of guns." Gaul remembers shooting a rabbit once and never hunting again.

"No. I'm not either." They chat on the way out. The fresh air smells good. Lucie walks across the graveled grounds toward her car. She is on her way back to the Justice Center, where, as lieutenant in charge of Cleveland's citywide sex crime and child abuse unit, she supervises about sixteen hundred felony investigations a year and fifteen detectives who work two shifts a day under her command.

Back in her office, Lucie read the computer printouts of the day's crime reports. *Debby,* a nineteen-year-old Cleveland State University student, accused Roy Z. Williams of rape. Williams, a basketball player on a full athletic scholarship, was also a student at CSU, recruited from California's Compton Community College where he had been named Most Inspirational Player.

Lucie saw no reason not to take the case seriously, even though it was a contaminated investigation—Debby had waited to report. Instead she had met with Williams to talk to him about the rape.

Lucie's attitude about date rape was simple: under the Ohio Revised Code forced sexual conduct was a felony. In some police departments around the country, victims were discouraged from making date rape reports, but in Lucie's sex crimes unit, every report was investigated. She sent them all to the prosecutor. She assigned the Williams case to Detective Mike Cipo. There were some investigations that led Lucie and the detectives to think the victim might be lying. But Debby stuck to her story. She never wavered. She wanted to prosecute.

Force or threat of force was needed for a rape charge. Williams's size alone—he is six feet eight inches—could constitute force, Lucie thought. The facts were presented to the municipal court prosecutor, who determined that the elements of a crime were present. An arrest warrant was issued. Lucie called Cleveland State University and suggested Williams turn himself in voluntarily, which he did. But Lucie was concerned. She felt some of the prosecutors considered it a bullshit case. Debby had attended a fraternity party. She drank too much and passed out. Williams, she said, then carried her upstairs and raped her.

Outside the sex crimes unit's main office, *Kathy* waited for Detective Patrick Evans. *Douglas Brecht,* her mother's landlord, had molested her for years. Now she was eighteen years old, married, and out on her own, away from Douglas Brecht.

Kathy's husband, seated in one of the blue plastic chairs, was holding their infant. He waited for her with a somber look on his face. Kathy walked down the hall, past Lucie's office and into the interview room. Kathy was afraid for her eleven-year-old sister. What if Brecht was doing the same thing to her?

Detective Pat Evans consoled her. He knew what it meant to worry about a sibling. His adoptive sister had been abused by her natural parents. They were involved in the occult and had used her in ritual rapes. Evans was seventeen when she was adopted into his family. His chin still quivered when he thought about her.

At six foot two and 225 pounds Evans cut an imposing figure. But now, he spoke softly and listened to Kathy's fears. He wrote down the facts. Kathy told Evans that Brecht had taken sexually explicit pictures of her.

Detective Evans was eager to learn. Though a cop for nine years, he'd only been in the sex crimes unit for two years. But his partner, Mark

Hastings, had been working with Lucie since 1982. Hastings had watched Lucie develop an expertise in the investigation of child pornography and had accompanied her on many pornography raids. In his opinion, "Lucie wrote the book on child pornography."

Hastings went out to interview Kathy's eleven-year-old sister at her school. She told him a little, but not that much. Hastings didn't really expect her to. "They don't tell you everything the first time." His manner with her was easy, relaxed. He would talk to her again.

Lucie studied the case. She had a victim, Kathy, who was saying Brecht had sexually abused her the whole time she was a teenager—but there was no evidence to support any of that, except for her statement. No medical evidence. And the eleven-year-old hadn't corroborated the story. But the judges usually gave a little more leeway with child pornography search warrants—the implications were so awful. Besides, they trusted Lucie. She had a good track record.

Lucie had detectives Evans and Hastings get the information to issue the search warrant: the location and description of Brecht's house, a statement of the crimes involved, and a list specifying the smallest item they would search for—photographs or negatives. Lucie always went out on search warrants with her detectives. She didn't like it when supervisors backed off. It could come back to haunt them. People could sue. If her commander wouldn't agree to give her overtime, she would execute the warrant at Brecht's on her own time. Lucie waited for Mark Hastings to come back with the warrant for the child pornography raid.

Over two thousand miles away, in California, civil attorney Richard Caplan read about Cleveland State University student Roy Z. Williams's arrest for rape in Cleveland. Caplan thought it was pretty clear Roy Williams was the murderer of his client's granddaughter, Lina Aldridge.

Lina Aldridge, a nineteen-year-old Compton Community College prelaw honors student, had disappeared in July of 1989. Roy Williams had been hired by the college as a counselor in its National Youth Sports Program, and Lina Aldridge was one of his four female co-workers. She had given Williams a ride to San Diego, and then Lina Aldridge had been found dead, her body stuffed in the trunk of her car, nude from the waist down. Roy Williams was the chief suspect.

But Lina's case had never made it to the district attorney's office. It had gotten stalled at the police department level. Williams gave police several conflicting versions of what had happened the night Lina disappeared. He was arrested but released without being charged.

By the time Lina's body was found, it had been in the trunk at least eighteen hours and had begun to decompose. The medical examiners were unable to determine how she died, even after conducting twelve weeks of tests. Without a homicide ruling from the medical examiner, the police believed they were powerless to make an arrest.

"A healthy nineteen-year-old found dead in the trunk of a car," civil attorney Caplan concluded, "it's strongly suspicious. It's just a matter of time before some other poor girl is found dead."

Caplan was trying to get Lina Aldridge's case reopened. He had the forensic evidence reexamined by a Texas medical examiner. He did some of his own legal research into how charges might be brought against Williams without a homicide ruling. He filed a civil suit against Williams for her murder. The Aldridge family wanted justice. They felt other students had to be protected from Williams.

Caplan called Lucie. "Are you going to pursue the rape investigation?" he asked her.

"Of course," Lucie responded. "I think we'll get an indictment."

Now, Caplan had more ammunition. He went to the San Diego County district attorney and said: Roy Williams is still out there. He's raped somebody in Cleveland.

Next door to Lucie's office, in the homicide unit, Lieutenant John C. James had more information for Lucie about Roy Williams. James told Lucie that his unit had assisted police in Long Beach, California, in executing a court order to obtain a blood sample from Williams for a DNA match. Williams was a suspect in a second homicide. About a year before Lina Aldridge's death, nineteen-year-old Trina Denise Young had been found raped, stabbed, and strangled in her mother's home, an electrical cord knotted around her neck.

And there was more. Ohio's Willoughby *News Herald* ran a story on Williams: as a juvenile, he had been convicted of first-degree murder and committed to the California Youth Authority.

The bullshit date rape case had assumed very serious proportions.

Long Beach *Press-Telegram* reporter Susan Pack called Lucie for information.

"I can't compromise the investigation ... we're in the middle of it.... I can't discuss the details." Lucie pulled on her red bangs as she talked. "Women in these situations, they are embarrassed. They're frightened. They see these people around every day." She explained Cleveland's court system—the arraignment procedure, the grand jury.

Then Lucie called the Long Beach police department for more information. Williams was scheduled for a hearing in Cleveland's municipal court on December 24, 1990. Lucie firmly believed Roy Williams was a serial killer. She didn't want to take any chances. The Cleveland rape case wasn't a strong one. She knew it might fall apart, but she wanted to help in any way she could to force California to act. She wanted to ensure that Williams would not slip through the system.

Her magenta heels clicking on the floor, Lucie walked into the outer office to talk to Detective Cipo. "Make sure the prosecutors get her a rape shield attorney. I can see the classic fraternity house defense shaping up here, where they bring in the whole fraternity house and they all say they slept with her."

Lucie decried the California laws. In Cleveland, at least they could have arrested Williams for something on the Aldridge case—abuse of a corpse, failure to report a possible felony, tampering with evidence. Something.

At home, Lucie changed into jeans and sneakers, strapped on her leather shoulder holster, checked her .38, and thought, What else do I need—badge, gun, pencil, notebook—right. She tied her red hair back with a silk twister, slipped her notebook into her blue denim coat pocket, and waited for detectives Hastings and Evans to swing by. It was five o'clock in the afternoon.

The pornography raid was in the Second District, where Lucie lived. Detectives Hastings and Evans drove with Lucie to the parking lot of a Chinese restaurant near Douglas Brecht's house.

Lucie hoped that using her car, 8-1-7-0, the boss's car, would get a faster response from radio. They waited for zone car backup in the empty dirt lot. Neighborhood dogs were barking.

"I'm glad to see the canine unit is here." Lucie delivered the line straight-faced except for a slight raise of her eyebrows.

"Eight-one-seven-zero. Go ahead." Mark Hastings keyed in the mike. "Need in reference to a search." His deep voice was monotone.

Mark Hastings was older than Pat Evans. He was as low-key as Evans was gregarious. Only a reddening of his cheeks when embarrassed and his low under-the-breath chuckle revealed any of his reactions.

"Two-two-three is supposedly on its way," Mark told Lucie. He stretched his thick legs outside the car.

It was getting dark. The street was still visible as Brecht drove up in the white van Kathy had described. They watched as Brecht parked in front of his house.

Zone car 2-2-3 pulled into the lot. The patrolmen followed Lucie's lead and drove over to Brecht's street. Clevelanders heading home for dinner drove past as Lucie and her team parked across from the Brecht house. The lady next door peered out of her large kitchen window. She was talking rapidly on the telephone. Every so often her face turned toward the Brecht house. Her expression became animated. What is going on?

The patrol officers led the way to the Brecht's back door, with Hastings, Evans, and Lucie right behind. They knocked. "We have a search warrant. Police. Open the door."

Douglas Brecht answered the door and stepped out onto the porch, leaving the door ajar. Mark informed him of the warrant and read him his rights. The patrolmen led Brecht to the zone car at the front of the house. They cuffed him and drove him to jail.

"There's a search warrant," Mark reiterated. He tried to open the door.

Just behind the door was *Mrs. Brecht,* barring their way. She was in her forties, not a large woman, but she looked formidable.

"You're not coming in," Mrs. Brecht said.

"Ho, yes we are—" Mark kicked at the door. He was over six feet tall, heftily built, but his movements were lightning fast. He flew into the house, gun drawn, with Evans and Lucie following.

The door pushed Mrs. Brecht backward. She fell against the refrigerator and the counter. Mark rushed in and tried to grab her to break her fall. He took one look at the place. She wouldn't be hurt if she'd hit the floor—that was for sure. There was no room to fall.

Places like the Brechts' scared Lucie to death. The kitchen was totally dark inside, the dimmer switch turned way down low. And it was stifling, kerosene fumes filling the air.

"Is anybody else in this house, Mrs. Brecht?" Lucie demanded, her chin tight, her voice stern. She had Mrs. Brecht by the arm.

The kitchen was narrow, clogged with boxes leaving only a pathway from the back door, past the counters, between the kerosene heater, the sink, and range. Five large red cans of kerosene were lined up on the floor in front of the heater.

Lucie moved Mrs. Brecht past the dining room, which was also a jumble, and into the bathroom.

Hastings and Evans, weapons drawn, searched for lights. They were all vulnerable until the scene could be secured.

Lucie talked to Mrs. Brecht, taking control with the tone of her voice, the direct expression in her clear blue eyes. "I don't want to have to take you to jail, too."

Mrs. Brecht bristled, her body puffed up in the excitement, her dark brown eyes frantic with concern, worry, confusion—fear.

Mrs. Brecht was entitled to stay, but if she gave them any trouble she'd be obstructing. Lucie cautioned her. "Look, here's what we're gonna do ..." Lucie explained what was expected of her and that she had to cooperate if she wanted to remain in the house. Lucie had seen situations fall apart. She was careful. She didn't want to abuse anyone. This woman had rights. Lucie believed in that.

Hastings and Evans edged through the downstairs along the path to the living room, then back up the narrow wooden stairway to the second floor. They opened the door on the left. No one could get past the threshold. It looked like a Salvation Army truck had dumped a half-ton of clothes into the room and filled it up to the ceiling. They closed the door. Evans's face had turned red from the heat. His arms were raised, taut, hands clasped around his .38. He held it close to his face, just a few inches from the sweat that poured off his forehead and down his cheeks. The next room to the right was locked. There was no one in the master bedroom.

Hastings holstered his gun and called down to Lucie. "What about the locked door?"

It was her son's room, Mrs. Brecht told Lucie. He was away at work. "Can I call someone to come here?" she asked.

"No," Lucie informed her. "I'm allowing you a courtesy by letting you stay."

The phone rang. Mrs. Brecht grabbed the receiver. "It's my father-in-law," she announced to Lucie. "They arrested my husband," she told him, her voice was angry. "I'm going to sue … child pornography. They put him in handcuffs and put him in … are you there? I'm going to call *Herbie* and see if he can come over. Hold on."

Lucie went upstairs. "Get an inventory sheet," she told Mark. "Pat and I will do upstairs. You do downstairs. And get SIU over here."

Mark walked through the dining room and around the obstacle course in the living room. As he passed the living room heater, he kicked it, turning it off. The heat was unbearable, the smell nauseating. He headed for the TV, barely visible behind piles of clothes, boxes of Christmas decorations, boxes of half-knit projects. There was a couch against the back wall with a space to sit in front of the TV. Amidst the muddle were numerous video cassettes, a video player, photo albums, and a video camera in its case.

He immediately began collecting the tapes. Pedophiles slipped clips of child pornography in the middle of regular films. Mark groaned. He'd be spending many hours fast-forwarding through these, checking for clips.

The son's locked room could only be opened with the key. Lucie was not going to break down the door.

Mrs. Brecht was on the phone with her son. "Herbie, any way you can come home? The police are here. Kathy did this … charged with pornography."

The speakerphone broadcast her son's flat voice. "I got a lot of customers."

"Oh, Herbie, they'll break your door down," Mrs. Brecht pleaded.

"I'll be there in a little while," he said.

Upstairs, in the Brechts' bedroom, Lucie headed for the man's dresser to the right of the double bed. She had to wend her way around boxes of small lamps, ratty-looking stuffed animals, large wicker baskets full of smaller wicker baskets, boxes of clothes, housewares, and costume jewelry. A picture of Jesus was framed and hung on one wall.

Lucie worked quietly, methodically. She moved easily through the debris. She opened the drawer and looked through the mail. She opened the cabinet.

Pat Evans stood on the other side of the bed. He removed his dungaree jacket and searched under the bed.

"So many violations," Lucie said. "This place is a fire trap." She made a mental note to write up a report and call the fire and health departments. Then she found evidence. She pulled a batch of negatives from the bureau.

"You sure know where to look, Lieutenant," Evans commented. He didn't know for sure why Lucie had picked him to join the sex crimes unit, but he was glad she did. He had four years of college, a degree that was going to waste. He thought he didn't have a prayer getting into the unit. Sex crimes was up there with the homicide unit—really elite. It was prestigious, not moneywise, but he still considered it a promotion when Lucie picked him. He told her, "I'll give you a hundred and ten percent."

"This guy is a walking flea market," Lucie said, rolling her eyes. "We're talking clutter. Major clutter. We might be able to find a refrigerator." She laughed. "Probably haven't seen it since nineteen fifty-two." Her voice trailed off. Wisps of her deep red hair fell against her cheeks.

"Should I look in the other bureau?" Evans asked.

"No, there won't be stuff in there," Lucie said. There was no reason to believe the wife was involved in any of the crimes.

From under the bed came an eight-inch-high stack of magazines, *Nubile Nymphs*, *Young Buns*. Lucie would take them. They showed Brecht had an interest in young children, and that would help to substantiate the victim's story.

A small tool box under the bed was crammed full of photos, some loose, some in film envelopes. Lucie looked through them. There were old black-and-whites of young girls, teenagers having sex with a man. There were dozens of pictures of a thin, youthful Mrs. Brecht, naked, in different positions.

Technically, Lucie could have taken them. But she left all the photos of the wife. There was no question as to who the woman in the photos was—they were labeled on the back. The same principle applied to looking in Mrs. Brecht's bureau drawers. Lucie left them undisturbed out of deference to her. There was no need to put Mrs. Brecht through unnecessary embarrassment.

Lucie told Evans to start inventory on the items and not to bother with the attic. She took a few photos, the females were unidentified—there might be other victims. They might well tie into the investigation.

Downstairs, Mark was thinking that this had to be the worst mess he'd seen. Incredible. He shook his head. He looked at the photo albums. Brecht took quite a few self-portraits. He fancied himself quite the stud. Huh. Mark chuckled under his breath. What a guy.

The SIU runman arrived. Scientific investigation unit, crime scene analysis. He was dressed in a long black leather jacket and slacks. His silver Sherlock Holmes tie clip glimmered as he walked through the dining room.

"Hi," Lucie said. "This is about pandering sexually oriented matter involving a minor," she told him quietly.

"Is this necessary?" Mrs. Brecht asked, agitated at the sight of the SIU runman's Pentax camera.

"It is part of the court-ordered search warrant," Lucie answered. "I asked him to, it's for evidence."

"It's not for the newspaper," the runman added. He was already busy taking pictures, room by room. Lucie took him aside and told him why she had called him to the scene. Mrs. Brecht had accused the detectives of creating the disastrous condition in the house. He acknowledged her words with his eyes, but his manner never changed as he maneuvered through, flashing shots. He was all business. In and out.

Mrs. Brecht was on the phone again. "Taking pictures of the kids when they are little is pornography—do you believe it!" She was outraged. "Do you know what this is about? This is about Kathy. She's gonna be in trouble. Your father evicted her … I know … you're just going to let her get away with it!"

Mark called Mrs. Brecht to the living room to check the inventory list he and Evans had prepared. Everyone was packing up to leave. Outside, the December air was refreshing.

Lucie sat at the glass table in her dining room. A mirrored atrium with a pool and fountain extended through the three floors of her home; the sound of running water was soft in the air. *Carreras Domingo Pavarotti in Concert,* the three tenors, echoed from the tape deck in the kitchen. Lucie and Max shared some fried chicken from Sisters Chicken and Biscuits. Max was her sleek Manx. And fowl was his favorite. His stubby tail wiggled as he waited for his next piece. Lucie had called her commander and told him the raid had gone well. Then Mark called Lucie and said the negatives looked as if they might be of the victim, Kathy. Lucie smiled. She poured herself a glass of white zinfandel.

But when the photos came back from the lab, Hastings and Evans saw that the girl was not Kathy. The pictures were of Kathy's mother, taken when she was a teenager. A weak case and thin warrant had turned out to be a case of second-generation abuse. There were other photos that looked as though they had been taken at the same time as the mother's—with other teenage girls. How far did this extend?

Mark brought the mother in and showed her the pictures. He asked her if she could identify any of the other girls. She said no.

Brecht was indicted on sixteen counts. Then, out on bail, he began intimidating Kathy's eleven-year-old sister.

The girl hadn't talked much to Mark in their first interview. Now Mark brought her in as a victim of intimidation. She sat across from him, facing the red plastic Burger King clock on his desk.

"Are you sure you told me everything?" Hastings asked her.

She started talking. She told Hastings that Brecht had molested her and taken pictures of her.

Allegedly, the mother knew Brecht was abusing her two daughters. Lucie wanted any parent who was aware of such abuse to be charged with child endangering. She wanted to show the child there was support from the system. She wanted to give the child an unequivocal message: the abuse is not your fault.

Lucie knew women were caught in difficult situations, but they still had a responsibility to their children. If there were mitigating circumstances, the court would decide. Kathy's mother was charged with two counts of child endangering.

What would she do? Would she turn state's evidence against Brecht? Or did he have too strong a hold over her?

Kathy's mother decided to plead guilty. She was remanded to counseling. Brecht pled guilty to two counts of rape, one count on Kathy and one count on her eleven-year-old sister. He was sentenced to five to twenty-five years on each count, the sentences to run concurrently.

"Serious time," Lucie remarked. The cycle of abuse was finally broken.

On December 24, 1990, Detective Cipo went down to municipal courtroom D for CSU basketball player Roy Williams's preliminary hearing on the rape charge. Cipo made his way through the throng of bondsmen, lawyers, suspects, and worried family members clustered in the hall. The courtroom was packed with people waiting for their hearings and police waiting to testify.

Williams stood against the back wall, his face was thin, his ears small. He was lean and broad shouldered. He batted his chin with his right index finger as he waited. Television cameras lined up on the sides of the court; one camerawoman steadied a foot-long lens. When Williams walked to the front row to sit with his lawyer, the cameras turned in unison following him. There were many cases in front of his. A man pled no contest, paid ten dollars in costs. He had been driving with the hatch of his car open, a misdemeanor violation.

Eventually Williams's case was called. Judge Shirley Strickland Saffold tapped her gavel three times and called for the state's witnesses against him.

The prosecutor requested a continuance. The victim, Debby, hadn't shown up. Detective Cipo explained to Judge Saffold that she had been receiving harassing phone calls about the case. Williams was not making the calls, the victim had said. She didn't know who the caller was.

Judge Saffold was angry. Her voice pierced through the crowded courtroom as she stared into Williams's face. He stood eye level to the judge's bench. She told Williams that if he knew who was making the calls he was to tell them to stop. "I won't tolerate it," she added.

The defense attorney broke in. "My client hasn't made any phone calls."

"I don't care if he has made any phone calls or not," Saffold admonished sharply. "Victims have a right to appear in court to be fully heard without interference."

She issued a continuance until January 4 and went on to the next case. Detective Cipo left the court, the radio news reporters pressing around for an interview.

Though Debby had dropped out of school, she testified in January at the preliminary hearing. "There was nothing I could do." She described the assault to the court. "I was screaming inside my head."

In March 1991, Roy Williams was indicted on charges of rape and sexual battery. He pled not guilty. He was freed on a five-thousand-dollar bond.

Lucie called civil attorney Richard Caplan in California that day and told him the news of Williams's indictment. The next day, Caplan called her back. The San Diego County district attorney's office was reviewing Lina Aldridge's case. Caplan was excited. He felt strongly that Williams would be indicted for homicide. Lucie's willingness to take Debby's accusation of date rape seriously had been a key element in reopening the Lina Aldridge homicide investigation.

But in April, Roy Williams did not show up for his arraignment on the Cleveland rape charge. The alleged California serial killer and rapist had jumped his Cleveland bond and disappeared.

1

FIRECRACKER

The games Lucie invented as a child were of daring and adventure. She sat up on the drainboard of the sink at night, listening to the "Lone Ranger" on the radio. Playing alone, she made up cowgirl scenarios with different characters, writing down dialogue and stories.

Her father would find her notes. "My dad got the biggest charge out of them," Lucie remembered with a warm laugh. "He saved them and would carry them around. He always had a few in his wallet."

Lucie grew up in Towanda, a small, mountainside town in the northeast corner of Pennsylvania where Iroquois and other Indian nations lived for about fifteen thousand years before the Europeans arrived. Towanda means "Place of the Dead" in one of the Indian languages. Almost in front of Lucie's house there hung a sign: HERE OUR GREAT DEAD ARE BURIED.

Lucie was born on the Fourth of July, 1944. When her thirty-one-year-old mother, Jill, went into labor, she called the undertaker. The undertaker served as the town's ambulance driver. He drove Jill to the hospital in his car.

After the delivery, the nurse came into Jill's room, carrying a little bundle.

"You've got the cutest firecracker I have ever seen," the nurse said as she put the newborn girl in Jill's arms.

The baby was officially named Lucie Aline; the Lucie was after Jill's mother, Lucy, Aline after Jill's best friend. But Lucie was never called

Lucie or Aline in Towanda. The sobriquet given by the nurse stuck in a shortened form and the Fourth of July baby was known as "Cracker."

In Towanda, Jill said, no one had his or her own name. Her name was Mary Louise, but no one called her Mary, or Louise. She was called Jill. Jill's brother was Jack. They had a sense of humor.

Lucie's mother and father were living with Jill's parents. When Jill brought Lucie back to the twenty-two-room yellow home, the family was quite taken with its first granddaughter. "My brothers all kind of rattled over her—spoiled her," Jill said.

Lucie was bald until she was four years old. "We have pictures of me just like a bowling ball, a sugar bowl with big ears." Lucie laughed about it later, but she never laughed about the way her mother made fun of her ears. Jill called her Dumbo, and following advice, she taped Lucie's ears back.

When her parents bought their own home, Lucie's maternal grandmother, Lucy, lived with them. She was a seamstress and worked for a tailor in Towanda. She instilled in Lucie a love of fun and culture, taking her on excursions to New York to see the Rockettes at Radio City Music Hall.

For Lucie, Towanda was a sheltered environment. "At twelve we were still playing with dolls. Hell, maybe when we were juniors or seniors in high school we would sneak a cigarette."

Lucie had to go to catechism classes at a Catholic school a couple of times a week, so she could receive her First Communion and be confirmed, but she attended public school. Of Irish Catholic heritage, Jill had been sent to Catholic school—Mass each morning. But she broke with the church when she was thirty, to marry Lucie's father, who had been divorced. "I still think I'm a good woman, I go along with the Catholic religion, but I said, if it's against their religion for me to marry William, they don't want me in the church, so I just quit. He was more important to me than the church was."

Jill was the only girl in her family, and her brothers had watched her raised as "a china doll," Jill remembered. "They would squeal on me if I was running around and 'hoopin' and a hollerin'." Jill trained Lucie as she had been trained—to be a lady. She sent Lucie to ballet lessons "for the grace. That's the first thing you should do, especially with a girl." She tied Lucie's hands if she moved them too much; in that way Lucie was taught not to "wave her hands like an Indian."

Lucie didn't quite fit the mold. Her hands moved expressively as she talked. She was very close to her father, William Jayne, and felt that they shared an adventuresome spirit. When a new hospital, Towanda Memorial, was in the process of being built across the street from her home, she walked along the concrete walls a story and a half high. And she had a penchant for jumping off her garage roof with an umbrella.

Her father told her stories about the times before he was married, how he had taken wild trips out west with his friends. His hair was sandy blond, his skin a bit ruddy. Lucie's faintly freckled skin tone was more like his than her mother's. His company was located in Paterson, New Jersey, which meant he was away during the week and home on weekends. He was an electrical contractor and worked on industrial, commercial, and some government contracts. On one job, he traveled to the Dominican Republic. On another, he worked on the new lower level of the George Washington Bridge.

Lucie didn't know if he missed her while he was away at work, but she hoped he did, a little bit. When he came home on the weekends, he brought blueprints with him and let Lucie help him work. "See these marks on the blueprint," he explained. "Those are light poles. Count up how many there are." He was an extremely patient man. He had good insight into people and the ability to judge them accurately. If Lucie said anything critical about anybody, he would say, "Now, honey, there may be some things you don't know." The qualities he demonstrated were ones she valued.

He let her drive the car when she was eleven, and when she earned her driver's license, he immediately taught her how to do repairs, so she wouldn't be stranded if her car broke down. "He felt that everybody should know how to do these things—women being no exception."

He was a self-made man, the only one of his siblings not to receive a college education. He left home at fourteen, channeled his energy into his work, and did well for himself. When his sister's husband committed suicide, leaving her with five children, he was able to support her and her family. Lucie recalled, "My cousin said, 'We would have starved if your father hadn't helped us out.'"

The fortitude of her paternal grandmother, Rose, also made a deep impression on Lucie. Grandmother Rose lived to be almost one hundred years old. She was born in the Reconstruction South and was married at fifteen to an older man who died on their first wedding anniversary. The teenage widow taught school, saving money to go to college. She worked her way through college, graduating in the 1890s.

Lucie's grandparents Rose Richard Jayne and Lyman Bixby Jayne, or Bick, operated the Jayne farm, which stayed in the family for a hundred years, from 1847 to 1947. Lucie and her parents lived there when she was three years old, right before the farm was sold. The Jayne family had a pet pig named after Lucie's Uncle Tommy. Tommy came in at night and slept behind the kitchen stove. The family snapped pictures of Lucie on the pig. "She rode it just like you would a pony," Jill laughed in her rich, crackly voice. There were cows and workhorses. "Cracker could walk into that barn and walk under those cows, it never bothered her," Jill said.

Lucie was fascinated by the exciting history on her father's side of the family. The Jayne saga was collected by her relatives. The Jaynes traced their lineage back to Guido de Jeanne, a general in the service of the French Confederation who accompanied Henry II to England. Guido was knighted by Henry II and given the Manor of Kirkling in Cambridgeshire. He was made commander of the English Army.

One of Guido's descendants, William de Jeanne, was a Puritan who fled ecclesiastic persecution in 1658. He arrived in New York and changed his name from de Jeanne to Jayne. Lucie's Fourth of July birthday was a fitting one for a Jayne; it was said that there were fifty-nine Jaynes who served in the Revolution. Only eighteen survived. Captain Timothy Jayne was the fourth generation of Jaynes; Lucie was his direct descendant. He was taken prisoner in the battle of Flat Bush and held for over two years on a prison ship in New York Harbor, before being exchanged for Captain Swan of the British Army.

Timothy Jayne was said to be a large man, powerful, the leader of his brothers. He was described as "red haired and utterly fearless." Lucie was proud of that heritage.

Lucie followed traditional patterns for girls—she was a Girl Scout, a cheerleader. Her father encouraged her to get an education; he thought she might go to medical or law school. But her first career ambition was journalism. Her high school heartthrob was the local newspaper editor's son, and Lucie thought she would become a great reporter. She edited the school paper during her last two years of high school, writing feature articles about school events. Eventually she lost faith in her writing ability, and she didn't marry the newspaper editor's son. Instead when she was eighteen she married Terry Duvall, a boy from the same town whom she had known most of her life.

Lucie left Towanda when Terry was accepted at Thiel College, a conservative Lutheran school. By that time their son, Andrew Bradley Duvall IV, had been born. Lucie and Terry rented their own apartment. Lucie's father paid her tuition, and with his and her in-laws' assistance, Lucie was able to employ a sitter and attend classes. "I was going to major in philosophy, but everyone told me there were a lot of out-of-work philosophers." Lucie decided to major in sociology. Sensing that Terry wasn't going to stay in school, Lucie took as many courses as she could, doubling her class load and attending summer sessions.

When she studied, she propped Brad on her lap and entertained him by reading to him aloud from her textbooks. "I had to form a bond—and get the reading done. He had a whole education by the time he was a year old," Lucie said, smiling.

Terry didn't know what he wanted to do with his life. After two years at Thiel he quit and decided to go to Cleveland, where his uncle offered him a job.

Cleveland was called a three-sided city, Lake Erie forming its northern border. It was a city of bridges and iron mills; in the distance, at night, blue flares from steel company smoke stacks reared up through the dark. Salt mines operated beneath the lake. A blanket of sulfurlike smells hung heavily in the air. The Depression had hit Cleveland hard, some said it never recovered. The city held the desolate feel of a Bruce Springsteen song about working men and women.

Lucie was unhappy. She had done well at school, where she felt challenged. Interested. Now, living in one of Cleveland's suburbs, she wasn't working or attending school. Anything she needed was provided by Terry's family. Terry's mother selected Lucie's clothes in New York and sent them back to her. When Lucie and Terry went on vacations, they went with his parents. All she could see in front of her was a life of socializing. Although she enjoyed taking care of Brad, she wanted more. She grew restless and bored without a goal of her own.

To celebrate her twenty-first birthday, Lucie went home to Towanda for the July Fourth holiday weekend. Her family had planned a large party for her. In the middle of the night, her mother called her from the hospital. Jill was almost incoherent. All Lucie understood was, "Daddy might be dead."

Lucie's father had suffered a heart attack, and Jill had rushed him to the hospital, leaving the house in such a panic she didn't wake up Lucie.

After phoning an aunt and uncle and asking them to come right over to watch three-year-old Brad, who was still asleep, Lucie rushed to Towanda Memorial. Her father was already dead.

Lucie went into a state of shock. There had been no forewarning of his death. A girlfriend called all the people who had been invited to Lucie's birthday and canceled the plans. Now, during a holiday weekend, Lucie searched the stores for something to wear to the funeral home.

She stayed with her mother for a few days after the funeral, then she went back to Cleveland. She didn't realize yet how much she missed her father—but his death gave her the courage and determination to take charge of her life. It gave her the ability to cut the ties. Within a year she left Terry.

Lucie didn't want any money from Terry and his family. She was going to get a job. Her father-in-law helped her to buy a secondhand Volkswagen; that was all the help she would accept. She rented a small apartment in North Randall, a Cleveland suburb.

It seemed to Lucie that her mother and Terry's family thought she was just going through a phase and that they were humoring her until she got over it. They think I won't make it, Lucie suspected. They think I'll go back. They don't think I'll find a job. Lucie was afraid it was a ludicrous idea herself. She felt she had no skills. She had taken half a year of typing in high school, but that wasn't enough to be a secretary; she didn't even know how to file. She decided that she was virtually unemployable.

But she did get a job. At Bardons & Oliver, Inc., manufacturers of turret lathes and parts, special machinery, pipe and tube mill equipment. It was a family-owned business, which originally manufactured bicycle hubs and the machines to make them. Bardons & Oliver was located in Cleveland's warehouse district, in a dull red clapboard building on West Ninth Street. The main offices were on the second floor, level with the freeway. The third floor was production. The building crouched next to the Main Avenue Bridge, which crossed the Cuyahoga River. The river curled and twisted at almost right angles, cutting the city in two, an east side and a west side.

Lucie took a general intelligence and manual dexterity test and was given the position of personnel manager. Her job was hiring, firing, and interviewing the men who ran the machinery. Her boss was John Oliver, one of the company's owners.

It was Lucie's first job, but Oliver allowed her to take charge. He let her make mistakes and never browbeat her about them. He gave her advice that she would remember and apply to the rest of her life. "You are smarter than a lot of people," he told her. "If something doesn't seem right to you, chances are it isn't." Oliver's support and the job experience bolstered her confidence as she got on her own two feet.

Brad stayed with Lucie part of the time and then lived for a while in Towanda with Jill. Jill was thrilled to have her four-year-old grandson with her and fed him lobster for breakfast. Brad was surrounded by both sides of his family, there were lots of children to play with. Brad thought it would have been ideal, but he missed Lucie. She visited him on weekends. The drive was long as she traveled over the two lanes of Route 6 and Route 59 with nothing in sight for miles. Lucie was often tired and sometimes dozed while driving. It was a difficult time, a time she found herself going back "to a survival thing."

There were less than half a dozen women working at Bardons & Oliver. Lucie met Judy Cooke, who became a lifelong friend. Judy's long, dark blond hair was pulled back, showing a broad forehead above a fine-featured, smooth-skinned face. She worked on the second floor, "where they were keeping track of inventory and how many what's its were being made." Lucie worked way down in a little dark office that could be seen from the street. Judy and Lucie ate lunch together. They joked about their low salaries, and on Fridays, they went to May Company and cashed their ninety-seven-dollar checks, sticking the money in their boots when they walked back under the Main Avenue Bridge past the winos.

After a couple of years, Judy married and left her job. They kept track of each other through a woman at an employment agency. Judy was working for a company that made loudspeakers, and the agency woman mentioned to her that Lucie was working at a wig place down the street. They reconnected. "We sort of did this leapfrogging all through our lives," Judy said. "We weren't married. We were married. We got divorced, we got married; leapfrogging each other through. Basically it was a friendship between the two of us."

No matter what problems they were having in the rest of their lives, Judy and Lucie had fun doing projects together. They made their own clothes. Once, they went down to Coventry and bought a big bag of leather scraps. They were going to make themselves patchwork purses. It turned out to be a monumental project of cutting and pasting and sewing. They did finish one purse, and it became "the purse that got traded back and forth whenever somebody needed this fabulous leather bag," Judy remembered.

Lucie had also maintained a close friendship with Richard Davis, one of the first friends she had made in Cleveland. Richard thought of Lucie as the sister he never had. It was the hippie era, and Richard wore his wavy hair down to his shoulders. He taught drama, psychology, and algebra in Warrensville High School. Richard introduced Lucie to a friend of his, *Craig*. Lucie really liked Craig. He was personable, fun to be with. After a year of dating, Craig and Lucie were married. They moved into a condo.

Lucie was happy to have Brad return from Towanda and live with them. He entered kindergarten and joined the Cub Scouts. Lucie had missed him. She found Brad's sense of humor especially endearing; she thought he had been witty from the time he could talk, with a quirky, funny way of looking at things. Judy thought the flaxen-haired little boy was "really the neatest kid." He was both adult and child; Judy liked that.

Lucie and Brad both enjoyed living with animals. There were dogs and cats and birds and fish. The horny toad was named Chauncy. Brad owned two iguanas. He called them both George, so he would remember their names. This strategy of giving several pets the same name became a Lucie and Brad tradition.

But the happy life that seemed to be developing ended quickly. Although Craig was enjoyable to be with when Lucie and he were with friends, being at home alone with him was a whole different story. Soon after they were married, they were sitting at the dinner table one night when Lucie said something—afterward she would not be able to recall what she said—and Craig got up, walked around the table, and knocked her off her chair.

She was shocked. Her father would have died before ever laying a hand on her.

That was the beginning.

Sometimes Craig would grab her and shake her and hit her head against the wall. On her way home from work she never knew if Craig had locked her out of the house. When she would try to get in, he would start yelling.

The frightening part was she never could predict what would set off his temper. Once she gently nudged their cat out of the way with her foot. Craig went berserk.

Instinct told her not to fight back. He was stronger. If she fought, she'd lose. He would hit her once, and when she didn't respond, he stopped. She had bruises on her arms, but he never hit her in the face. He was even tempered with Brad and didn't hit him.

Lucie thought that if other people knew what he was doing, it would stop him temporarily. When he locked her out of the house, she went around the corner to her in-laws, called him, and told him where she was. After a while he would let her in. She just tried to get things "smoothed over for that moment."

Eventually, she told Richard what was happening. Richard talked to Craig, and Craig told Lucie he would never do it again. The first few times he promised her, she believed him.

She tried to think of someone who could exercise some control over him. She talked to Craig's best friend, *Jake,* who was a policeman in a suburban department where Craig worked as an auxiliary officer. Jake talked to Craig and the abuse stopped—for a short time.

She became convinced it was her own fault. She was functioning—she was a den mother, she belonged to the PTA, she was working, but she was emotionally immobilized. She reached the point where she stopped feeling anything.

She became afraid he would kill her. He liked guns, and there were guns in the house. Craig went shooting often. He never threatened her, but in the back of her mind she thought, He might shoot me.

Up until that point, though Judy was Lucie's best friend, she hadn't known what was happening. Lucie hid her distress well. When Judy realized Lucie was afraid for her life, Judy had a hard time dealing with the realization—someone she really cared about was being hurt, and she couldn't do anything, except listen and be supportive.

One day, Richard came over and found Lucie crying. "You've got to get out of this thing, Lucie," he told her. "You're just going to have to do it." He told her she was welcome to stay at his place.

Lucie was desperate. Finally, she got a good job at Huron Road Hospital, working in their personnel department, and began squirreling away money, so she could leave Craig. She didn't tell him her plans.

Lucie had been working at the hospital about seven months when a civil service test was scheduled. Craig said he was going to take it. He had wanted to be a police officer for years. Some of his friends were going to take the test, too.

"Why don't you sign up?" he suggested to Lucie.

She decided to give it a try. She wasn't sure why.

Thunderstorms threatened on Saturday morning, July 15, 1972, when Lucie entered the Cleveland Public Auditorium at East Sixth and Lakeside, across from Lake Erie. The auditorium building was Italian Renaissance, the lobby heavy with marble, tile, and decorative plaster. The Republican National Convention that nominated Calvin Coolidge had been held under the hall's curving arches in 1924.

The civil service exam held that summer morning in 1972 was not quite so momentous an event, but it would mark a turning point in the history of the 106-year-old Cleveland Police Department.

Several thousand men and women made their way inside the auditorium as 10 A.M. approached. Veterans returning from Vietnam were seeking jobs as firemen and policemen.

Maybe this is a dumb thing for me to do, Lucie thought. But it wasn't a big deal. She told herself she was taking it for a lark.

Three hundred and twelve women passed the test for patrolman (female). The results were on separate lists from those for patrolmen: the women's results were printed on white paper, the men's on yellow. Lucie scored number twenty-six. She heard they weren't even hiring women that year.

In the fall, Lucie heard rumblings about a lawsuit. Something to the effect that women should be allowed to go out on basic patrol. Lucie didn't follow Cleveland politics. She was just trying to raise her son and get out of a dangerous marriage. She had no idea she was stepping into a hornet's nest, no idea that the exam she took for a lark was going to alter the course of her life irrevocably.

2

PETTICOAT POLICEMEN

Attorney Jane M. Picker arrived in Cleveland in 1969, a few years after Lucie. Though they would never actually meet, Picker's work with policewomen would lay the stepping stones for Lucie's career. Picker and Lizabeth Moody, a friend and classmate from Yale Law School, sought private funding and established the Women's Law Fund in 1972. As a pilot project of the Ford Foundation, it was the first law firm in the country to focus solely on sex discrimination cases.

Picker embarked on a long road of lawsuits and complaints against the City of Cleveland concerning policewomen that would not end for a decade. A large woman, with simply cut brown hair streaked slightly with gray, Professor Picker speaks swiftly and with animation, pausing and punctuating with a cough that suggests her years of speaking in public. She sits in her office at Cleveland State University's Cleveland-Marshall School of Law, crammed in amidst books on international law and stacks of legal documents, the accumulations of long years of battling. Her eyebrows knit as she contemplates the policewomen's cases. "Where's my old docket book, it's got all the information on my old cases. I don't throw anything out." She coughs and rummages through cartons and files, peering through her thick glasses.

"The seventies," she summarizes, "was the era of police litigation."

Policewoman Jean Clayton became the organizing force behind the lawsuit that in 1973 propelled Lucie and fourteen other women into zone cars, changing the face of the Cleveland Police Department forever. Clayton, a handsome black woman with a deep-timbred voice, high cheekbones, and a keen eye, was sometimes called a troublemaker. The lawsuit never would have happened without Clayton, Picker said with admiration, observing that it seemed like Jean just didn't really care what kind of grief she suffered.

Jean Clayton joined the force in 1951 and worked in the Women's Bureau, handling crimes concerning women and children, rapes, juvenile delinquents, prostitution, runaways. She had no uniform, no nightstick, no gun. She arrested girls and brought them back to the station without benefit of handcuffs or a cruiser—she had to transport her prisoners on the street car and pay their fare.

If women did have a place in police work, it was said to be in the Women's Bureau, a separate but unequal entity under the auspices of the "real" police department. Cleveland's first policewoman, Elizabeth Metzger, had been appointed in 1923, and the Women's Bureau was created the following year, at the behest of the Women's City Club and the city council's first female member, Bryn Mawr graduate and suffragist Marie Remington Wing. "The officers resented us. One thought I was a spy," Metzger confided to a reporter from the *Plain Dealer*.

The chief, Jacob Graul, was not happy. "There is no place in police work for a woman," he declared. It was the era of Prohibition, and Graul sent the new policewomen into the Roaring Third, a hotbed of illicit activity. It was still a hotbed sixty years later when Lucie took over vice. Metzger said, "I had never been into a burlesque show before. We got a complaint that the show was indecent. It was, believe me. I nearly died."

For decades, policewomen did not go out on basic patrol, a cop's proving ground. Without that experience, they could never earn the kind of respect male officers had. They went directly into detective work, wearing soft clothes. This created resentment among the men, who might have to wait years to make it into the detective bureau and get out of uniform. But when conducting their investigations, the policewomen had to call male officers for backup. This inspired more resentment. The women were disparaged as nothing but a bunch of social workers. The *Plain Dealer* dubbed them "Petticoat Policemen."

Despite the odds, the women did gain a certain respect from some of the men. Lucie's future partner Booker Bledsoe said that Jean Clayton was a legend. If you wanted to know anything about a juvenile on the street, she was the Bible. The policewomen were renowned for their record keeping; they developed a system of "face sheets" that kept track of families, sometimes for three generations.

We took the same test as the men, Clayton said, but we had to wait until somebody died or retired to get promoted. That meant not only restricted job advancement but also limited salary increases. Women were detailed to narcotics and other units for undercover assignments but were not allowed to work anywhere but the Women's Bureau on a permanent basis. Clayton wanted to work in community relations.

Through the death of retired Policewoman Charlotte Clark Strode, Clayton discovered that pension benefits were limited to widows, children, and dependent parents. Mr. Strode could not collect. Clayton was appalled. What if something happened to her and her husband could not get the benefits? "She had money taken from her paycheck every week for her pension the same as the men did." Clayton fought for equal treatment on the pension issue, and the union, Fraternal Order of Police (FOP), backed the women. The problem was settled out of court, but Clayton remembered the opposing arguments distinctly. "It was in the wording, there was no she or he. The guys were trying to tell me when the wording was made up there were no policewomen. But I said you've had policewomen since nineteen twenty-two! So what are you talking about? I got very upset. I said wait a minute. Being a woman—nobody gives a doggone!"

In June of 1972, one month before Lucie would take the civil service test, Clayton testified about the policewomen's problems at civil service commission meetings. Two years earlier, the press had sensed a rumble and ran an item announcing that twelve black policewomen were getting restless.

Clayton was their organizer. She was financial secretary of the Shield Club, an organization for black and Hispanic officers. Frederick D. Johnson was the president of the Shield Club in 1972, and he fought for eight years, until his retirement, for minority officers' rights in hiring, promotion, transfers, and assignments. Johnson refused to use the term "colored" in his police reports. The Shield Club, with support from the NAACP and the Legal Aid Society, filed antidiscrimination suits beginning in 1972.

There was a long history of bias. Black men were not promoted as readily as the white officers. They were "detailed," never permanently assigned to certain units. The department used various methods to keep blacks out, said Jonathan McTier, Jr., who joined in 1969 and later worked with Lucie. "If you had a brother who was homosexual, if you had bad credit, they'd use it against us," he remembered. East Side police cars were ordered integrated in 1968, but there remained unwritten restrictions.

Judge William K. Thomas concurred with the Shield Club's charge, ruling in 1974 that there was discrimination in hiring. In 1976, he ruled there was discrimination in assignments and promotions. Finally, in 1977, the city signed a consent agreement in court in which it admitted that "there has been a history of race discrimination in the ... practices of the City of Cleveland's Police Department."

Jean Clayton was working with the Shield Club in this suit, but she found early on that it was not addressing issues pertinent to women. Attorney Edward R. Stege, Jr., head of the Law Reform Unit at Legal Aid, was working on the Shield Club case. His assistant, Attorney Isabelle Katz Pinzler, called Jane Picker and told her she had been meeting with some of the policewomen involved with the Shield Club case. She was afraid the men's suit, though not in conflict with the women's interests, was not going to address all their problems. Racial discrimination was based on unwritten rules. But the women were segregated by municipal ordinance. Even if racial bias was eliminated, black policewomen would have nowhere to go but the Women's Bureau.

"This was very much held under really quite close wraps," Picker later explained. Pinzler then asked Clayton if she was willing to let the Women's Law Fund represent her.

"I said sure!" Clayton declared. "I was mad. I was really mad."

In the sixties and seventies in the wake of the civil rights and women's movements, policewomen took action across the country. From Peoria, Illinois, to Honolulu, Hawaii, from Indianapolis to New York City, in municipal and state police departments across the nation, women gained the right to work out on patrol and receive promotions. Late in the sixties, the President's Commission on Law Enforcement recommended that women's roles be broadened. By 1972, Congress had amended Title VII of the 1964 Civil Rights Act to prohibit discrimination by public as well as private employers. For the first time, police departments were required by law to consider hiring women on an equal basis with men.

Between 1971 and 1974, the number of policewomen across the country on regular patrol would increase from twelve to one thousand. And the FBI graduated its first two female agents.

In October of 1972, the Women's Law Fund began taking depositions from policewomen and top-ranking male officers in order to file a class action suit against the City of Cleveland. They also took a statement from Chief Jerry Wilson of the Washington, D.C., Metropolitan Police Department, who early in 1973 had put about 160 policewomen on the street; by November, the women were in virtually every department there.

Wilson had anticipated the negative response. "Initially all the women were concentrated into two specific police districts, to ensure that the commanders had so many policewomen that they couldn't subtly hide them or protect them," he explained.

When asked why he instituted the program, he replied, "I thought it was required by law."

In October of 1972, three months after Lucie took the civil service exam, the Women's Law Fund sent a letter to Mayor Ralph J. Perk outlining the problems and their suggestions. They wanted women hired—and not just in token numbers. They wanted them allowed transfers into other departments, allowed to move beyond the Women's Bureau. The city ordinance that prohibited women from achieving rank higher than captain and severely limited women's promotional opportunities needed to be changed. They wanted all promotional vacancies available to the women on an equal basis. They wanted removed all discriminatory practices with regard to clothing allowances, fringe benefits, and disability, especially as it related to pregnancy.

"There is no justification for the assumption women are not able to handle patrol duties," Picker stated in an interview with the *Plain Dealer*.

That idea created the greatest controversy.

After five years of living in fear, Lucie was getting ready to leave her husband, Craig. She went to a bank and managed to secure a loan. She rented the second floor of a house that was owned by a Canadian couple, Carol and Jean Pierre Parent. She told Brad they were leaving, that they were moving to the East Side. Brad wasn't surprised. As an adult, he wouldn't remember much about Craig, except that he smoked, and Brad hated that.

Lucie didn't tell Craig she was leaving. She just picked up and moved one day. Although she still talked to him on the phone, she wouldn't see him. She was afraid of him, but she didn't hate him. He never bothered her again.

Lucie proved resilient. Her friends Judy and Richard noticed that after she left Craig she went right back to being the bouncy Lucie they had known. She put the marriage behind her. She forgot about it.

Until years later. Craig's second wife called Lucie for advice. Craig was abusing her. What should she do?

"Leave him," Lucie told her.

Lucie's new home was located on tree-lined DeSota Street in Cleveland Heights. A Canadian flag flew in front of the large bright red house. The floors all sloped to one corner. There was a big old-fashioned sink, and the house wasn't completely wired. Lucie ran her own 220 line by following the heating ducts down to the box in the basement.

Judy was divorced and living nearby. The single women did their first plumbing together. They went to the hardware store and asked for "a piece about this long and about that wide and it needs to do this," as the store clerks snickered. They almost set Judy's house on fire when they took the plumbing apart. "We had the blow torch and it started to catch, but it worked. Lucie was very good," Judy said. Lucie was small and could squeeze between the toilet and the bathtub. They put two showers together, running galvanized pipe around the top of the claw-footed bathtubs. They were successful in their home-improvement endeavors.

Challenging the city ordinance authorizing the size of the police force and limiting the number of policewomen to fifty meant negotiating with George L. Forbes, council majority leader. Forbes, who was born in Memphis, Tennessee, was the number one black leader in Cleveland, and his powerful tenure continued through most of Lucie's career and impacted in numerous ways on the police department.

George Forbes passed the bar in 1962 and ran successfully for councilman in 1963. Then he was on the campaign team for Carl B. Stokes, who was elected the first black mayor of a major American city. Forbes became city council president in 1973, the first black to hold that position. He was astute, sometimes crude, his political instinct sharp.

What instinct would Council President Forbes have on the police ordinance? Picker approached him and asked him for support. Forbes would not always be supportive of policewomen. In 1980, he called for a police officer to throw a disruptive man out of a city council meeting. Officer Gayle Smith answered the call. Forbes broke up the meeting, telling the audience, "I'm probably known as the greatest male chauvinist in the city, I sent for a policeman, and they sent me a woman."

Nevertheless, when Picker approached him, he wanted to increase the number of blacks on the police department. Enlarging the size of the authorized force was a practical move. So Forbes supported the women. After intensive negotiations, the ordinance was repealed by the city council, effective after January 10, 1973.

The quota limiting the number of policewomen was lifted, fifty years after Elizabeth Metzger became the city's first female officer.

Concurrent forces worked in the women's favor. In 1973, Congress passed the Crime Control Act which, among other things, banned sex discrimination in entities receiving federal aid for law enforcement agencies. The Law Enforcement Assistance Administration (LEAA), which managed the aid, required recipients to set up women's equal-opportunity plans.

Safety Director James T. Carney decided to hire policewomen only under threat of an impending lawsuit. If the city wanted the LEAA grant money, they would have to let women into the department.

The Women's Law Fund began a series of suits. Picker described the process. "The city's tactic was to refuse to settle any of these cases, then, on the first day of the trial to cave in and settle. The result is there are very few reported decisions in any of these litigations, because they were all settled. With the resolution of each type of problem another one would surface and we'd file another lawsuit." The initial cases were all on behalf of black women because they came from the Shield Club case. After that began, the white women joined.

About a month after Lucie left Craig, in December, the police department called and told her the date for her physical. She didn't show up. She already had plans to take off from work and drive back home with Brad for a Christmas visit with her mother. The job on the police department just didn't seem that important to her.

When she returned, the department called again. "You missed your physical."

"Yeah—I was out of town."

"No problem, we'll reschedule it."

"Oh, Okay, fine." Lucie thought they were being very accommodating. She had no idea why.

She decided to go. The medical unit was in the basement of the building on East Twenty-second. She walked in. There were policemen there on sick call. Dr. Ashby took her to the scales and weighed her in. The men were sniggering—something about women in zone cars.

"You don't weigh one hundred pounds." Dr. Ashby laughed, as the scale registered ninety-eight.

Next, he gave her the eye exam. The eyesight requirement was the ability to read 20/50 type with each eye separately, without the use of glasses or contact lenses. Lucie was nearsighted. Her glasses were so thick she called them "bug burners."

"I flunked," she told the doctor.

He concurred. "I'm going to pass you because they're not going to take you anyway. You don't weigh enough."

All recruits had to be at least twenty-one and not over thirty-one years of age. The physical requirements were different for women and men. Policewomen had to be proportional in height and weight. There were no other restrictions.

Lucie later realized that if Dr. Ashby had believed women were going out in zone cars she might not have made it on the force.

She returned to her job at Huron Road Hospital. A few weeks later, the department called again. It was time for the psychological test and polygraph. Once again, the scheduled times weren't convenient, and once again they offered to reschedule for her. I might as well do it, she thought. They are making all these special arrangements for me. She started to think she was destined for the job.

She made it through the polygraph and the written psychological test and then she went for the interview with the psychologist. She told Judy about it afterward.

The psychologist looked over her papers. "Don't you think there is something wrong with the fact that you have been married so many times at such a young age?" he asked.

If he was trying to unnerve her, it didn't work.

"I just figure I'm a bad picker," she replied.

Other women were having their own problems with the psychologists. Waiting for her interview, Maryanne Kingzett, a cop's daughter, an ex-nun, and one of Lucie's future partners, had watched women go in. They seemed furious as they came out. She found out one psychologist had asked a woman about her sexual preference, accusing her of being a homosexual. At first, Maryanne wondered if the women were making up the stories, but there were too many of them saying they were asked personal questions about their sex lives. It must be true. It seemed that some of the women had no problem at all and that others were bothered.

Sandra Ramsey thought it had to do with whether or not you had a policeman in the family. Sandra had wanted to be a cop back in high school, but when she went to the counselor's office and searched the file drawer, there was a file on policewomen—with nothing inside. She studied nursing instead. After being divorced in 1965, she was left with three children and no source of income. She worked at Kirby Distributors, as a key punch press operator on an assembly line, and she worked other jobs, but she still wanted to be a cop. She had taken the test in 1969, scoring twenty-four on the female list. They only hired eight women. She took the test in 1970, scoring number one, but they didn't hire any women at all. She took the test for the third time in 1972, and scored twenty-nine.

She went in for her interview. Dr. Parkhurst was an older man with gray hair. Sandra would never forget his name.

He reviewed the background investigation on her. "We can't have this," he shouted, hitting the papers he was reading with the back of his hand. "This is terrible." He seemed outraged. "We have a report here that says you have men in and out of your house all the time."

"That's not true," Sandra spoke up firmly. "Absolutely not. I belong to the PTA and the Cub Scouts. I have a boyfriend, but that's strictly my business. As far as having men overnight, I personally do not believe in doing that. My children are growing up." Sandra thought "uncles" in the house were not appropriate.

Parkhurst seemed to calm down suddenly. He looked at Sandra and said, "You're Lebanese; I really like Lebanese people." He laughed and shook her hand.

Wasn't that wild, she thought. She later talked with the other women about their experiences.

Dana Garcia had signed up because her mother told her to take the test. Never in a million years would she herself have thought of becoming a police officer. She had never seen a gun, let alone held one. Her sister and a friend took the test with her. She was the only one to make it. When she found out about the zone car idea she was shocked. She didn't think women ought to be in cars, but if she had to be, she wanted to be with someone with a lot of training. The interview with the psychologist rankled.

First, he verified her data. Her name. Age. Where she lived. Dana listened, waiting. Her long, dark hair touched her shoulders. Her heart-shaped face and soft brown eyes gave her a childlike quality.

The psychologist continued. "You're single. No children."

She broke in for the first time. "I have one child." Her daughter was three.

He raised himself back in his seat. He didn't look at her, but he said, "Tell me what it is about you women—"

"I beg your pardon?"

"What is it about you colored women, black women, whatever you want to call yourselves, that you go out there and screw all over the place and have all these little bastards running around?"

"Excuse me, I don't understand the question," Dana replied. She was stunned.

He repeated the question.

"I don't know about other women, but my daughter is very well adjusted," Dana said.

That was her interview. He never focused on anything else. She was so afraid he would fail her that she went to Jean Clayton. Jean put Dana in touch with the Women's Law Fund. They said, we'll wait and see. If, for some reason, you're rejected, we'll take it from there. She was appointed without any problem.

Karen Loy was given a negative evaluation based on her giggling and attitudes she had as a teenager. When she threatened to file suit with the Women's Law Fund, she was allowed on the force.

The first notice that indicated the women would be hired and put out on patrol came in mid-January. The Fraternal Order of Police (FOP) was all for doubling the quota on women but opposed sending them out in zone cars and opposed putting them on an equal footing with the male officers.

"They should be treated like women," said Richard J. Faragher, president of the Cleveland FOP lodge number eight. "There are some things women can't do. One of them is zone car work," he told the *Plain Dealer* reporter.

The city was now talking about hiring forty-five women over a period of three months. Some members of the city council joked about "Lady

Godivas" when they heard that women were thinking of going into the mounted unit. But despite pressure from the Women's Law Fund, only fifteen women would be hired in February.

The 1973 class was hired under the federally funded Impact Cities Program, which required that the rookies be sent to high-crime areas.

Lucie and the other women about to be appointed would not only be the first women in zone cars in Cleveland history, but they also would be sent to the three highest crime districts.

Reactions gathered steam. Not one policewoman had been sworn in, but opinions about them raged. The local FOP added to its earlier complaints: it would be a threat to marriages. Chief Gerald J. Rademaker was not enthusiastic about women in patrol cars. The issue caused him to blush.

"Couple Calls Zone Car No Place for a Lady Cop" announced one *Cleveland Press* headline. Michaeline Bakker of the Women's Bureau and her husband, Detective Bert Bakker, went to the FOP to try and block the hiring of the women. Michaeline felt women would not have the strength to subdue and arrest male suspects. A woman's place was in the Women's Bureau.

The bottom line was the all-around objection to the use of women in the zone cars. Anything else. But not that.

3

POLICE ACADEMY

T he official letter arrived, instructing Lucie to go to city hall for the swearing-in. She had passed the selection process, but she wasn't sure what she was going to do. It was Presidents' Day weekend, she had three days to make up her mind. Lucie offered to give her resignation, but her boss and friend at the hospital, Jan Dalton, said it was all right to wait and see.

"Either I'll be in Tuesday or I won't be in Tuesday, depending on what I decide," she told Jan. That's how they left it.

Lucie was sure all the other applicants had read their letters and decided immediately. Like Craig, they all knew that they wanted the job. As it turned out, Craig didn't end up joining the Cleveland force.

The media pressure and turmoil within the police department continued. On February 16 both the *Cleveland Press* and the *Plain Dealer* ran articles announcing that on February 20, ninety-four men and fifteen women would be sworn in by Mayor Perk. The women would be the first females trained for basic patrol.

Over the long weekend, Lucie thought, Do I want to do this? She had a good job, as benefits coordinator at the hospital. She had held many jobs, but none that really excited her. The pay on the police force was a little more than her current job. Plus—it sounded like fun.

Maybe this job with the police department would be a real career, as opposed to just a job. She didn't decide for certain until Tuesday morning. It's not the army, you can always quit and get another job, she told herself as she made her way downtown. I'll give it a try.

She arrived at city hall. The recruits were filing in, to the council chambers, as members of the personnel department checked off their names. Television crews were setting up lights and cameras, newspaper reporters were arriving. Lucie was directed toward the chairs in the front—where all the women recruits were to be seated.

Sandra Ramsey rushed to city hall at eight in the morning. She couldn't believe she'd been passed over again. Without so much as a letter or reason as to why. She asked to speak with Safety Director James Carney. Minutes passed. An hour. Then, it was nine-thirty. Only half an hour until the ceremony. Finally, Carney said he would see her.

"This is the third time I have taken this exam," she told him. "I've passed the age limit to take the next one. I want to know why I wasn't appointed."

Carney checked her file. Then he told her to get in line with the others. She was elated.

Smiling, Sandra sat down next to Lucie. They were waiting for the mayor. The media was in position. Lucie was wearing a long-sleeved, high-necked jersey dress, patterned in rust and navy blue. Her short red hair framed her face, her bangs hanging just an inch above her eyebrows. Behind her glasses, her eyes were a vibrant blue.

Mayor Perk took his place at the podium. The recruits raised their right hands. He began.

Women's Law Fund attorneys Jane Picker and Rita Page Reuss were standing toward the left side of council chambers. When Chief Rademaker saw them he visibly recoiled. Picker thought, He thinks we're vipers. Litigating these cases was considered radical, crazy. It was outrageous to say that women should be entitled to work in zone cars.

Mayor Perk continued, "Do you swear to uphold the laws of the State of Ohio and the United States ..."

Like Lucie, most of the women had no idea what they were getting themselves into when they took the exam. They weren't involved in the lawsuit. Maryanne Kingzett, her shoulder-length blond hair flipped at the ends and parted down the middle, wore a sweater and blouse outfit; her hand was raised, slightly tilted, as if waving "Hi." She thought, Everyone else is joining for noble reasons. They're not thinking of the money.

Maryanne had training in elementary education and was working as a secretary when she took the test. She wasn't making much money and she didn't like the work. Her father and cousin were policemen—it was a family thing. Her father kept telling her, Take the test. It's like social work, he said. You'll be working with women and kids. You'll be in plainclothes, you won't even have to carry a gun. It's right up your alley.

She thought, Why not, and took the exam. When she passed, she was thrilled to think she was going to work in the Women's Bureau. Everything happened so fast. She had no time to give notice on her secretarial job. Now, here she was, with all the lights and cameras. All her life she had been behind the scenes.

Marilyn Mason was two seats to the right. She stood, hand raised, in her fitted, scoop-necked dark dress, her light blond hair coiffed perfectly. She wasn't the least bit interested in the job. When she took the test, she was pregnant. She took it as a lark, supposing she would not have to work after she had her baby. Now her son was four months old. This was the time, she was taught, that a mother stayed home, taking care of her kids until they were in school. How could she have known her husband would become critically ill? It had just been a few months since the onset of his illness, and the bills were already stacking up. Now, she needed the job, just for the money. She was searching for something secure in case her husband died. Her husband was a cop, his father was a cop. Her father-in-law was dead set against her becoming a policewoman. "There's no way you want her on the job," he said to his son. "Start thinking for a change."

Phyllis Trappenberg's husband was a policeman. She had worked in an insurance office, then stopped when she had her two children. She talked on and off with her husband about becoming a policewoman. Finally, he said, "The only place you can go is the Women's Bureau. So, there really isn't any problem. You're not first on any assignments, it's all follow-up."

Michele Kratzer wanted to be a math teacher, but a run-in with a guidance counselor dissuaded her. She worked other jobs. Her father was a sergeant. He'd been nudging her to take the test since she was nineteen. When she turned twenty-one she took it just to shut him up. Now, she read the article in the newspaper. What happened to the idea of the Women's Bureau? Kratzer had three brothers. Her father had told them—never become policemen, because you'll go right to the East Side and it's so bad there you don't want to go there. None of them became policemen.

Lights flashed as photographers snapped each of the women's faces. Sandra Ramsey. Michele Kratzer. Stephanie Pilck. Marilyn Mason. Karen Mills. Lucie Duvall. Phyllis Trappenberg. Valerie Wilson. Margaret Novak. Dana Garcia. Sharon Caine. Karen Kilroy. Mary McGee. Maryanne Kingzett. Karen Loy would be sworn in the next day.

It was over. They had an hour and a half for lunch and then their classes at the police academy would begin.

Lucie looked around. It seemed to her that everyone else had family there. Lucie wished she could have shared this event with her father. She knew he believed women could do anything. She thought he would have been very excited.

Sandra Ramsey was also there alone. Sandra suggested they walk over to Top of the Town. Lucie agreed. "We have this great job, why not a fun lunch?"

Lieutenant Francis L. Reagan, in charge of the academy instruction, planned to give the women the same education as the men; that included twenty-six hours of firearms training, calisthenics, and self-defense techniques. The founder of Cleveland's police academy was the famed Eliot Ness, who, as safety director, began the academy in 1938 as part of his plan for raising the level of police professionalism, but women were not admitted until 1954.

The police academy was housed at the Amstan building on Lakeside Avenue. The recruits were divided into two classes, by last name. Sandra and Lucie ended up in different sections.

Lieutenant Reagan stood in front of the recruits, hands clasping the sides of the podium. He wore a long-sleeved white shirt and tie, and dark-rimmed glasses.

Here they would spend the next two months, Monday through Friday, from eight in the morning until four in the afternoon, learning what forms to fill out, what procedures to follow, the laws of the state. They were about to receive the 240 hours of training mandated in 1971 by the Ohio Police Officers Training Council.

The recruits took their places. The fifty men filled up five aisles of seats across the classroom, nine and ten rows deep.

There was one more line of seats, crammed against the left wall, separated by a large aisle from all the other rows. The women took their places.

Lucie was out shopping at a mall that night when Brad noticed the newspaper in the vending machine as they walked by. "Hey, Mom! There's you."

There was Lucie's picture. All the women's faces were splashed across the front page. "City Gets Fifteen Women in Blue," the *Cleveland Press* headline proclaimed. The photo caption stated that the women were going to be assigned to basic patrol zone cars. Brad took the article in to his fifth-grade class for show and tell.

The situation at Lucie's home on DeSota Street was perfect for a working mother because of her landlords, the Canadian couple. Carol did not work outside the home, she had a baby and a girl about Brad's age. Lucie took Brad to school, dropped him off, and was home within an hour of his return. He played with Carol and Jean Pierre's daughter. The house was set up in such a way that with the door open to the upstairs it was like one house. Brad thought Jean Pierre looked like a hockey player. But he actually was a chef. He cooked all the time, and the two families often ate together.

When Lucie returned home from the academy each day, she typed up her notes from her classes for inspection the next day. She and Brad talked about what she had learned. He helped her with her homework, giving her hints. He was excited. After all, he had volumes of the Hardy Boys under his belt. He must have read twenty-five or thirty of them. He was a ten-year-old expert. Lucie later said that she didn't learn surveillance at the academy—Brad taught her. He filled in her police academy curriculum drawing from the Hardy Boys' repertoire.

Lieutenant Reagan, Lucie decided, was a boring, put-you-to-sleep teacher. Other officers came in and told war stories. One wrote *assume* across the board—don't make an *ass* out of *u* and *me*. John T. Corrigan, chief county prosecutor, instructed them on search and seizure.

They were taught how to deliver a baby. They were given lessons in first aid—how to apply tourniquets, how to stop bleeding. Where the pressure points were. CPR. How to set a leg with pneumatic splints. Putting people on stretchers. They used one another for practice. The recruits were told: in Cleveland, you're never more than five minutes from a hospital. Keep them breathing, stop the bleeding. Drive like hell.

They viewed six- to eight-minute training films. One was a black-and-white film on childbirth. Lucie would see plenty of bloody scenes as she did police work, the gore didn't bother her, but the childbirth film made her queasy. She closed her eyes.

The first aid instructors were Nick Petries and his partner, Ernie Hayes. Petries had been on the street fifteen years. Lucie thought he was a wonderful man, and his commentary on how to survive police work became her credo.

"There's two things you need in the Cleveland Police Department," he told the class, "a strong stomach and a good sense of humor."

Lucie realized as time went on that if you don't have those qualities, you won't make it. She thought, They could have just told us that and sent us home.

She felt the undercurrents during the academy classes. Nobody really knew what was going to happen to the women. The instructors said, "Don't worry about it, you're going to end up in the Women's Bureau. They're not going to put you in a zone car." No one wanted to accept it. The way the teachers talked was almost threatening.

Sandra was apprehensive. How will the men accept us? What kind of trials and tribulations will they put us through. She was more concerned about her peers than being able to do the work.

Marilyn Mason shrugged her shoulders. Her husband was active in the patrolman's union, the CPPA, and he wasn't really familiar with the Women's Law Fund suits that were under way. They didn't know what it meant. She was just taking it one day at a time.

The press was there while Lucie and the other women learned how to fire shotguns at the outdoor range. Shooting wasn't anything new to Lucie. Her father had taught her to shoot a rifle when she was eleven or twelve. She had fired a shotgun. Craig and she had joined the trap league. The only problem was these shotguns had no nice kickpads.

They did handgun practice at the indoor range. Lucie had never shot a handgun. "I wasn't a great shooter," Lucie said. "But I passed with no problem."

Valerie Wilson, who would later work for Lucie, was a tall and attractive black woman whose eyes glowed with a dark gold light. She had been in the army for three years. She learned Teletype communications, to be an administrator—and to be a lady. The Women's Army Corps was not then what it later·became. "We're all soldiers now," Valerie said years later, flashing her warm smile. She had taken the 1972 civil service test for a city accounting job. But policework paid more. Plus, it was of interest to her. She had scored number one on the female list. Jean Clayton had contacted Valerie after the civil service exam and asked her if she would be a test case if there were any problems with appointing the fifteen women. Clayton was really the one who convinced Valerie to join the department.

Valerie's parents were proud of her when she was appointed, but her mother worried. Would she be out in a zone car? Valerie was all for it. Women didn't have to be limited. It was an adventure. She just wished she was shooting better. She hadn't been trained to use a gun in the army. Her hands were giving her problems. One of the men in the class suggested she squeeze a rubber ball to build up the strength in her wrists.

Marilyn Mason excelled. She was a great shot. Mary McGee was the top scorer in the academy class, Lieutenant Reagan noted in his deposition the following summer.

Three times a week the recruits had physical education training at the Kovacic Recreation Center at Sixty-fifth and St. Clair. They swam in the pool, played basketball, ran laps, did calisthenics, and learned self-defense. Lucie enjoyed the workouts.

Martial arts expert John Horvath taught the classes. Officer Horvath, dedicated to the idea of cops keeping fit, taught with fierceness and a humor extra dry, pushing people against their limits. Those who were disciplined, who worked hard, and then harder, gained his grudging respect. An athlete was his pride and pleasure.

He showed the recruits how to ward off blows with their nightsticks. He taught them where not to hit with a nightstick—so that they wouldn't cause too much damage. They learned wristlocks and arm-locks—techniques known as "come-alongs"—where painful pressure is exerted on someone's joints. They practiced escaping choke attacks—raising the right arm up and slamming it across the attacker's arm, breaking the hold.

They did sit-ups, leg raises, chin-ups and push-ups. They climbed ropes up to the top of the gym and back down. Donning headgear and mouthguards and sixteen-ounce gloves, they boxed for one minute rounds—if they volunteered. They ran as many laps as they could. Lucie noticed that some of the women couldn't keep up—but some of the men couldn't either.

Dana Garcia remembered Horvath going down the line during push-ups, saying, OK, guys, can you give me fifty on your knuckles. He asked the women for ten on their palms. He asked Dana for three. She said no. She grew up a tomboy, played softball and football, ran track and climbed mountains, but she had grown out of it. She wanted to use her head.

Maryanne Kingzett gave a quick laugh, she thought they would be lucky if they could defend themselves at all when they got out of the academy.

Michele Kratzer found some of the techniques Horvath described hard to believe. He made jumping in and somehow putting your hand between the cocked hammer of a gun look easy. She thought, I'm not going to remember this on the street. But some of the moves—where she learned to shift her weight, get the suspect off balance, break his elbow—impressed her. This could really work.

A reporter from the *Plain Dealer* arrived for one of their first work-outs. In "The Law's New Order," Horvath was quoted as saying he didn't know what all the "fuss" was about. He had been training women for five years.

The article led with Lucie—who "weighs in at ninety-eight pounds and measures five feet two"—throwing classmate Dave Lillash, six foot one and 180 pounds, onto the mats. A photograph caught her tossing another classmate, Greg Henderson. Lucie dealt with the press with off-hand humor. Asked about her expertise, she said, "If I can wake up tomorrow and get out of bed, then I'll know."

The joking stopped in the autopsy room. Lucie had seen dead bodies before at Huron Road Hospital. She worked in the bowels of the building, and the bodies were wheeled by her office on the way to the morgue.

But she had never seen an autopsy. She had never seen a morgue like the Cuyahoga County Morgue.

The students walked into the room. There was a smell of formaldehyde. Wooden seats bolted to the floor curved around the room in a half moon, facing a raised stainless steel table. Lucie sat in the front row.

Dr. Lester Adelson stood on the opposite side of the table, facing the students. His bow tie was accentuated by his knee-length white lab coat. His thick hair was combed back, and a lock fell forward as he worked, touching the edge of his dark-framed glasses. He had a pleasant yet somehow serious smile framed by his mustache. His voice was a smooth teacher's voice. He was comfortable in his role, a role that seemed inseparable from the rest of his life.

In front of him, on the autopsy table, lay an elderly woman. "Up until a few hours ago, this was a living person, who had a family and loved ones," Dr. Adelson said.

This is a very special man, Lucie thought.

He was born in Chelsea, Massachusetts, and was an honors student through high school, college, and Tufts College Medical School. He did his two-year internship and residency at John J. McCook Memorial Hospital. When he chose pathology as his specialty he worked for his three-year residency at Hartford Hospital, then took a fellowship in legal medicine at Harvard Medical School. Forensic medicine was called legal medicine at the time when Adelson came to Cleveland. He became the chief pathologist and chief deputy coroner in 1956 under Dr. Samuel Gerber. The morgue handled about fifteen hundred autopsies a year.

But Adelson saw the harsh realities of death not only from the streets of Cleveland, he had also seen battle casualties in the South Pacific during World War II. What is the feeling part of society going to do about it? he questioned.

"There is such a thing, without being trite," he told the recruits, "as the sanctity of all human life. Like Hamlet's mother said to him: thou knowest all that lives must die passing through nature to eternity."

Lucie was impressed that Dr. Adelson made no off-color or crude remarks. A few recruits squirmed as Adelson performed the autopsy. It was right after lunch. Adelson told them that if it became too emotionally traumatic, they should get some air. A few did leave the room.

He removed the woman's ovaries, showing how they had shriveled from age and gotten smaller after menopause.

"Not only do you see the gray hairs and the wrinkles and the things that show the aging externally, there are changes internally, what you might call fair wear and tear—arterial sclerosis," he explained.

He held the woman's heart in his hand. She had died from a heart attack. "How many times does the heart beat in a day? A normal heart beats seventy-two times a minute, sixty minutes an hour, twenty-four hours a day, that's over a hundred thousand times. It will beat for seventy-five or eighty years. That's the machinery we have. It will go eighty years. Think about that."

Lucie was fascinated. She didn't feel repulsed or queasy. It was incredible how much he could tell from this woman's body. Lucie always enjoyed watching anyone who was good at what they did—watching Adelson work was like watching an artist.

"When you're in the autopsy room you see people with their naked bodies," he relayed, his voice warm with feeling. "When the family comes in, you see people with their naked souls. Fright. Anger. Hostility. Grief."

Adelson wanted to teach the police officers. It was an important contribution. He looked at the recruits. If he could get across to them their role as an *amicus curiae*, a friend of the court . . . if the officer worked together with the coroner so that people who were wrongfully accused would not be prosecuted. . . .

"People are ambulatory masses of misinformation. An autopsy is cutting up dead people." He paused. "An autopsy is *not* cutting up dead people. What you can learn from it is respect for the dead. It is a careful anatomic dissection done with a very serious purpose. It's a very, very valuable laboratory medical test. It is the most expensive test done in medicine because every autopsy is done at the price of a human life.

"A homicide investigation is a team effort. A good team is a tight team. This is what we as forensic pathologists can learn in the laboratory and share with you to find the suspects, to interrogate them, to talk to witnesses, etc. Because there is no such thing as an unwitnessed murder. A dead body is a very eloquent witness—if you know how to interrogate it and interpret what it has to say. Does the victim corroborate what the suspect or other witnesses say? There are some people who intentionally, purposefully, maliciously, and with an evil heart try to deceive you. And the body says: she's a liar or he's trying to string you along. You know because you had a very informative witness.

"It's a very challenging and very responsible job, particularly if you get involved with the criminal side and the business of capital punishment. Somebody's life may be resting in your hands. Somebody's lifelong liberty. Somebody's good name." Adelson paraphrased from *Othello:* "He who steals my pocketbook steals trash—he who robbeth me of my good name taketh that which enricheth him not and leaveth me poor indeed."

Lucie had a lot to think about. The autopsy was done. She was glad she had attended. Some of the recruits missed it. She never forgot Adelson's words, his respect for life, his lack of crudity. Later, she would cross paths with him when they both served on the Task Force on Violent Crime.

Her two months of training were complete. Graduation day was April 20, 1973. Dana planned the party, with help from an officer who worked part-time security at the Statler on East Twelfth Street. The hotel was famed in organized crime circles as the meeting place of the first grand council of the Mafia, December 5, 1928.

Lucie drove to the party with her academy pal Sharon Caine. It was held in two adjoining suites, and the students opened the doors and partied back and forth. Someone brought in a record player. They danced and talked. It was a wild party. Somebody lost their gun. In the middle of it all the men called in and found out what districts they were assigned to and what shift they were starting on. Some had to be at work the next day at six in the morning.

Lucie had become close to her classmates. In the two months of schooling she learned that the profession of the police officer was not like any other. "I got on the job with him. That's the way we refer to it." A cohesive, almost expected camaraderie. The fraternalism of police was built from day one. It was very different from anything else she'd experienced. They stuck together. Being together in the same platoon was even different from the armed forces. After their tour, service buddies might never see one another again. This was different. This was for life. This might be the person who would save her life. Or she theirs.

But the women didn't get their district assignments as their male classmates did. It was another CPD tactic to keep the women separate from the men. Unlike the Washington, D.C., department with 160 women already integrated out on patrol, Cleveland was still bucking the tide. The Cleveland Police Department wasn't ready to send them out on patrol. The women were informed that they were going to the scientific investigation unit (SIU) for three weeks of additional training, to learn how to process the scene of a crime.

4

FINGERS OF THE DEAD

Lucie found her way downtown to the Central Police Station, in the Third District. It was an old, five-story granite and brick building. The once buff-colored brick had turned brownish red with years of wear. Two Colorado officers once visiting Cleveland to pick up prisoners at Central Station were quoted in the *Plain Dealer:* "We're glad we came. Now we can say we've seen where 'Barney Miller' is filmed for television."

Howie Filler and Larry Worz were two of the old-time detectives who were going to teach Lucie and the other women hands-on crime scene investigation. Howie was a tall, fair-skinned man with lanky, loose body movements. He had worked with women from the Women's Bureau. He thought they were tough and knew their job a lot more than people thought they did. "There's nobody could tell them beans about police work, because those girls really knew."

Howie had been on the job for twelve years when the female rookies were put in his care. He was determined to give the women a hard time. We are really getting the shaft, Howie thought. Hey, this department doesn't know what it's doing with these women, so it's sticking them with us.

"There's no bullshit. We tried to discourage them out of police work." They planned their strategy—they would talk like a "truck driver." And there were other ways to intimidate them: "Hey, your goddamn place is in the home having babies not out here with a gun at your side," Howie razzed. "What the hell's wrong with you."

42

After more time in a classroom, Lucie and the others drove all over the city processing crime scenes. Howie Filler and Larry Worz drove to the county morgue, with Sharon Caine and Lucie in the backseat. It was time to let the female rookies fingerprint their first body. No one was forced to do it. They had been shown fingerprinting, but not with a dead body. The day had already been busy. A safe job in the Sixth District and an HB and L (house break and larceny) in the Third. They drove over to Adelbert Road, the county morgue.

Lucie had already heard the speech from Howie about how you're here to learn.

"You watch. We're not going to hold your hand. So keep your mouths shut and your eyes and ears open for a while and some of this stuff might sink in." Howie was a real talker. He knew of no one who enjoyed fingerprinting the dead, the touch of a dead body. He wasn't about to give the women any tips on breaking the rig (rigor mortis) by bending and flexing the arm. Let them see for themselves. It would be fun to see if they could handle it.

It was ten-fifteen when they arrived. They entered the morgue through the back door, not the small auditorium where Lucie had watched Dr. Adelson. Worz and Filler took them past the seven-foot-long waist-high stainless steel body scales where corpses were weighed in and measured. Howie and Larry explained things as they walked—how clothing and the property of the deceased were inventoried. Everything was recorded exactly. It might be needed later in court.

To the left was the decomposition room. The stinker room, where they autopsied decomposed bodies and burn victims. They kept those bodies a little colder than the rest, almost frozen, until they could autopsy them. Adjacent to the large scales was the receiving desk where the fingerprint cards were kept for the scientific investigation unit (SIU) officers. The information was also recorded in a book at the morgue.

Howie explained the main reason they had to print the bodies was to purge police files. If the dead man's prints were on file at the department, the file would then be stamped deceased. If the body was unidentified, they might be able to locate the person's identity if the prints were on file.

The methods of fingerprinting the dead varied, depending on the amount of decomposition, the fragility of the skin. Sometimes the wrinkled finger was injected by needle and syringe with glycerine, to puff up the wrinkles until they were smooth. The fluid was kept taut by tying a string just below the area needed for printing. If the corpse's fingers were too puckered from immersion in water, someone at the morgue might have to amputate the fingers and send them bottled to the SIU office. Lucie watched as one of the detectives carefully cut around the finger and peeled the layers of skin off, then placed the skin over his own finger, like a glove. The detective could make the print with the smoothed out skin as if it were his own. This could only be done after softening the skin; Cleveland used Joy detergent.

Usually, these difficult jobs were from "floaters." Valerie had seen a floater on her trip to the morgue. She hadn't seen an autopsy like Lucie, so she was even less prepared for a floater. The man had been in water for an extended period of time. "He was bloated and busting. It was like a physical slap in the face," she recalled. She had to back out of the stinker room. She didn't throw up, but she thought, Wow, I have to deal with this.

Howie knew about stinkers. A lot of guys used different things to get away from the smell. He carried a small bottle of Mennen after-shave. If he got a bad one, he would open the after-shave and put it near his nose.

Lucie and Sharon in tow, Howie looked in the book at the receiving desk to see which drawer John Leroy Wilson was in. And where Eddie Robinson was. First, they would process the homicide. The information was needed as soon as possible.

An attendant wheeled a body through the hall on a gurney cart into the fluorescent-lit autopsy room. Lucie had never seen anything like this before. Rows of naked bodies being autopsied. Some covered, some not. Down the stairs, Sharon and Lucie followed the SIU men. And down a second short flight of cement stairs. The temperature grew slightly cooler as they descended. There was a moistness to the air. Around to the left was the storage area for the bodies. The attendant hovered in back of them as they looked for their homicide victim. In the walls on either side of the room were small, two-by-two-foot varnished oak doors with heavy metal levers for handles. They were three rows high and four or five across on both sides. Howie pulled the drawer open. Out rolled the slab with the enormous body of a black male. He was sixty-five years old and had been shot in the chest. At point blank range with a shotgun.

He was without a covering. Lucie remembered that part clearly. Independent Towel Supply doesn't come here, she thought.

He just seemed very big and very dead. The open lower berth placed him just about waist high to Lucie. She got ready. His hands had been bagged in plastic, preserving evidence for the chemical trace tests. His abdomen was sutured after the autopsy, leaving an unappealing hard edge around the incised area. The organs had been replaced, packaged in a blue material that poked out through the incision.

With the plastic hand bags removed, Lucie could see the fingers were cleaned after the trace evidence had been obtained. But the hands were in a clenched position.

The attendant wheeled him out. It was the first time policewomen had come to the morgue to print the bodies. The attendant gave them an odd look.

Larry and Howie said, "OK, girls, go ahead." They chuckled.

Sharon and Lucie looked at each other. They had been taught to do this in theory. The ink had to be evenly distributed. Too much ink would smudge. Too little and the ridges would not stand out enough to make a good classification. The fingers had to be held steadily as they were rolled or the print would blur on the card. This was one thing on a live subject, who could be told to relax while the officer rolled the finger against a stationary card holder. A light pressure was needed while making the 180-degree arc away from the officer.

The fingerprint card had room for the right hand and the left hand, and a space to write on the bottom. It was a little bigger than an index card, but the paper was thicker. Lucie folded the card in thirds like an accordion. Every detective developed their own method of how to obtain their prints. The problem was getting an acceptable print. That took practice.

Lucie was determined not to make a fool of herself. Her hand was minute compared to his. His open eye was looking right at her.

I've never touched a dead body before, Lucie thought. I've been to a funeral home a couple of times but—pick up his hand. Think of something else, she coaxed. Nothing is going to happen. What the hell am I going to do. It won't be so bad. I'll just do it.

She put the ink pad down on his chest with the shotgun hole in it. You'd think they'd come up with something better than this, she thought, as she worked around the hole and took the folded print card.

Lucie bent over the dead man. His hands were backward for the job. Of course, she thought, I could tell him, Roll your hand over, but it wasn't going to have any impact on him at this point. Lucie grabbed hold of his wrist with her left hand and tried to pull his fingers up with her right hand.

His hand snapped shut, catching her hand in its death grip. Howie and Larry roared. Sharon Caine said, "Oh my God," then she started to giggle. The attendant laughed. They were all in hysterics.

This is nuts, Lucie thought. Thank God I'm not a screamer. She tried to pry her hand out. She was stuck in his grasp. Just try to be cool. I'm cool. I don't want to act goofy. I'm a big-time big city policeman now. Albeit, I haven't done any police work yet. She started laughing, too.

They were all laughing so hard they were practically rolling around. Lucie was laughing so much she couldn't do anything at all. Eventually, she caught her breath. She tried to get her hand out. It wasn't working. She felt all tangled up. Oh my God, she thought. She felt so frustrated, yet found it funny.

Finally, she yanked his fingers back as hard as she could, muttering, "You bastard, let me go." The fingers went arrgh. Her hand was free.

The fingers were still too stiff to straighten out and roll. She took the fingers and inked them on the ink pad. She managed to get one hand printed, inking herself in the process.

It was Sharon's turn. Howie and Larry didn't say a word, they were still laughing.

Lucie helped Sharon with her prints as the detectives gave them some hints about breaking the "rig." Grab the wrist and bend the elbow. That movement stretched the tendons, which loosened up the fingers to print.

By the time they did the next body, Howie and Larry were helping them with the fingerprint cards and giving them clues on how to hold them. Two hours later they were on their way.

When Lucie returned three days later to print another body the morgue attendant said, "Honey, I'd never thought I'd see you back here again."

"Oh, it wasn't so bad," Lucie replied. She was hearing stories about the East Side districts, especially the Fourth District. Nothing could be as bad as the Fourth.

Fingerprinting bodies at the morgue was only one aspect of the SIU runman's job. Lucie processed cars for prints at the tow lot and collected evidence at the scenes of safe jobs, jewelry store break-ins, armed robberies, homicides, rapes, shootings, and a sodomy. Howie, Larry, Phyllis Trappenberg, and Lucie had just finished taking evidence from a burglary when the next call came from the other side of town. "There's a right and wrong way to drive a police car and to go to a crime scene," Howie said, as he zoomed off, careening through traffic, the old car rattling and bouncing. The fastest ride they ever had from the West Side to the East Side, he thought. He showed them how a runman drove.

There was only one SIU car for the whole city, and radio wanted them there in a hurry. It was a suicide of a young couple. They had asphyxiated themselves in a car garage. They had been there a couple of days. It was a warm day, and the garage was heavy with a putrid odor. Lucie and Phyllis seemed to take it in stride. Howie didn't know if it was a macho act or not.

He worked with them on fingerprinting, photography, dusting for fingerprints, and searching the crime scene for physical evidence. Once they got the first run they stayed out the whole day. If not on a run, they patroled. Howie would point out things about different characters on the street. He remembered having words with Lucie. "We got things straightened out between us and from that time on everything was all right. The girl stood her ground. There's no backing off from anybody with Lucie. As far as feelings being hurt or anything, she surely never showed that you could hurt her by words."

Howie found some of the women very aggressive. It was a "Hey, I don't give a shit if I get my ass kicked or not" attitude. "Lucie was psychologically aggressive. She could calm a person down. Somebody that's ready to tear your heart out, Lucie could calm them down, with conversation or intimidation. She just started talking softly so people would have to listen to hear what she had to say. Then, she slowly brought it up a few decibels. She had them hooked. She just kept talking to them. Most of the time we'd go into a place and the guy would see this woman with a gun and you didn't hear any more shit. Sometimes you go to a scene, a bar, where there's a bunch of jerks with their elbows on the bar, 'What's that broad doing here. What the hell is this police shit. What do you mean police, they ain't no more police than this glass of beer here.' But they kind of got the idea after a few minutes of the policewomen being there."

Howie watched Lucie at the crime scene. She really listened to witnesses. "She can make up her mind who's bullshitting and who ain't— she's got good judgment, very good judgment." He thought she was a good interrogator.

There was a lot to the job. New prints were checked against prints on file at Central Station. The examination was done with hand-held magnifiers, as the classifiers matched the suspect's loops, whorls, deltas, and arches with a fingerprint card on file. SIU classifiers were often the ones to take evidence to court and testify. Their desks were cluttered with fingerprint cards and coffee cups. They could be seen intently studying prints for hours at a time, looking through fingerprint lamps, magnifying glasses circled with fluorescent bulbs. Over the years it was a great strain on their eyes.

Lucie learned the routine from checking records and filing them to taking mug shots and showing them to victims. She fingerprinted prisoners and did the numerous hours of paperwork. Howie took the women to court when he testified.

Howie taught the women to be careful and precise. "You know a lot of people get pissed off at you when you take your time," Howie lectured. "I never liked to work with anybody like that. Processing a crime scene is an important piece of work. It is somebody's life you're playing with, and you want to do what you can for—or against—him. You don't fabricate it. You don't read anything into what you are seeing, or into what anybody says. But when it's there you'll know it."

The crime scene was investigated for evidence to be presented in court. Lucie had to keep that in mind. It was imperative that the crime scene not be disturbed; it could be the most important aspect of an investigation. She learned to take photos before and after the body was taken away by the coroner's office. If an item related to the crime, it was collected, preserved in an envelope, and tagged. Small items would be photographed with a ruler in the picture as a point of reference as to its size. But, first, she snapped a shot of the object exactly as it was found, as proof for court.

The pictures had to be without prejudice. They could not be taken from strange angles that might sway a potential jury one way or another. They could not misrepresent or distort the object. A distance shot of an object showed where it was in relation to the rest of the scene, a close-up showed its detail.

At a break-in scene she was trained to look for the point of entry and departure—a broken window or jimmied lock. If a door frame was covered with blood and fingerprints it would be photographed and then removed and brought into the lab in one piece. It was preferable to have the original frame than to just lift prints from an object for purposes in court.

Lucie carried an evidence kit with fingerprinting brushes, one for the lampblack powder and another for the white powder, made from chalk and talc. White powder was used to obtain prints from dark-colored surfaces, the black powder was used on light areas. A fluorescent powder was utilized on a multicolored background; ultraviolet light would illuminate the powder. Sometimes the runman took photographs of the prints, as well as lifting them.

Lucie only found one run as an evidence technician trainee disturbing. She was sent to process a car. She had already processed many stolen cars and vehicles used in the commission of a crime. But this car was different. It was a case of homicide. The woman murdered was Lucie's age, and she had been killed in the car. Lucie dusted the edge of the door and the trunk, the fingerprint brush swirling lightly, leaving its powder film on the windows. Lucie climbed into the car to dust for prints. The front seat was covered with dried blood.

She tried to follow her fingerprinting instructions. But as she sat on the seat the warmth of her body and hands softened the blood. The dark red flakes were sticking on her. There was so much blood. The woman had been pushed aside, shot several times, and left to die. The woman's glasses were lying on the seat surrounded by blood. It was the glasses that shook Lucie up, they were the same style as her own, large and oval with dark frames. I'm not even a policeman yet, she thought. I'm still impressionable. I'm a rookie, a policeman only in name.

* * *

Howie Filler snapped a photo of his evidence technicians, the first female rookies he had trained. The photo was crime scene size, eight by ten, of course. Phyllis, Sandra, Lucie, Karen Loy, and Karen Kilroy stood, pointing their guns in the air at shoulder height, their various smiles flashing toward their instructor. Lucie was in the center, the smallest of the five women.

Howie saved the photo as a keepsake, along with historical mementos of the famed criminal John Dillinger and noted syndicate figures. "I'll be a policeman 'til I die," Howie declared with pride, a pride he took in his SIU department with its historic contribution to solving crimes, a pride he took in the women rookies he trained, women who were too serious to be swayed, no matter how hard he tried to intimidate them.

Lucie and the other women were informed that they were being sent out to the districts as evidence technicians. The East Side districts. The highest crime districts. All the talk over the months, all the suspicions and denials, were vacant against the reality of the Fifth, Sixth, and Fourth districts. They talked together about the issue. They didn't even have their uniforms yet. Phyllis felt like a cowgirl when she put on pants and strapped a gun belt over them.

Their badges were based on a "his and hers style," which a *Plain Dealer* article from 1961 titled "Badge of a Policeman Shows His Authority." The picture under the caption showed a policewoman holding the badges. The men's badge extended to the tips of her fingers. The women's badge was swallowed up in the palm of her hand. Jane Picker said that in Philadelphia the policewomen were issued the same badges as the dog officers. The Cleveland badges were the same ones the department offered for sale to the policemen's wives and children.

The policewomen's badge numbers were different from the men's. The numbers were a 3,000 series. Several of the women bought the larger-size badges with their own money. But they still had the 3,000 series, which distinguished them from the men. All reports were identified by the officer's badge number. There was no difficulty in determining from the paperwork which officers were female.

The policemen were resentful because the new women were assigned to be evidence technicians. Normally, an officer with seniority would be in line for that type of job. It was considered easier than working a regular zone car. Evidence technicians in sedans wouldn't have to lift the heavy bodies or take people to hospitals.

Lucie did not consider herself a "women's libber." She was not out to prove she could do police work better than men. She didn't think the police had something particular against the women. It was just that they had a million reasons for not sending them on patrol. Some of them valid reasons. Lucie laughed—a man my size would never have gotten on.

Jane Picker wasn't sure either. When she went to Washington, D.C., she rode in a patrol car. She thought the senior officer must be quite nervous driving a civilian around; also his rookie partner was a female. She seemed very timid, Picker noticed. She had no presence. Picker couldn't imagine her being able to cope with an emergency. I would not have hired this woman and I would not have kept her on the job, Picker thought to herself. It must have been evident to them. Were they picking women to fail?

Members of Police Wives United were growing agitated. The group had formed after the 1968 Glenville shootout to aid families of wounded and dead officers. Now they were anxious about the women going out on patrol. Through letters, phone calls, and radio shows they expressed their concerns. One woman said, "Women tend to be more cowardly." Another wondered if the female officers could handle the weight of body armor while running up flights of stairs during a raid.

But one mother of a slain officer had a different perspective. Though her son had been killed, she knew he had enjoyed police work more than anything else. Now, she thought, women would be afforded the same positive experiences—experiences they would never get unless they worked in zone cars.

As the furor mounted, there were rumblings among veterans in the Women's Bureau. Jean Clayton had been trying for four years to get out of the Women's Bureau; she wanted to work in community relations. Now—with the knowledge that the fifteen new women were going out on patrol, other Women's Bureau officers put in their requests for transfers. Requests went in for the statement unit, the mounted unit, homicide, and vice. Some women requested a transfer to the districts.

"We wanted to integrate," said Kathryn T. Mengel, who had come into the Women's Bureau in 1969. "We wanted to see what other areas of the department were like."

Mengel's classmate Diane Parkinson became the test case for the rights of pregnant officers. Up until her suit, pregnant women were forced to take a leave of absence without pay; and they did not accrue seniority during that time, although men on temporary disability leaves did accrue seniority. A month after the Women's Law Fund filed the suit, the city's attorneys agreed to abolish the forced maternity leaves. Later, one of Lucie's classmates continued patrol work into her eighth month of pregnancy.

Jacqueline Christ, another member of the feisty 1969 class, heard that the fifteen new women would be patrolling in uniform—in pants. Jackie was enjoying police work—but the rules, they were really a joke.

The women had to dress in skirts. Pantyhose of a certain shade. Footwear with heels and backs. Policewomen were expected to be professionally feminine, instructed one roll call announcement. Jackie wanted to wear pantsuits. She asked the FOP and the CPPA for help, but neither union thought the issue was important. Jackie made a formal request to her superior, but Captain Violet E. Novak returned an emphatic no. Novak, an ex-Marine, had joined the force in 1950. In her day, Novak said, "We spoke no gutter language. We wore hats to court. We were ladies."

Jackie filed a suit with the Women's Law Fund. Clayton and Mengel filed affidavits in support. The policewomen were not permitted to use handcuffs, gun belts, ammunition holders, or gloves. They were strongly urged to carry guns in their purses rather than wear them in a shoulder holster, as the men did. "This is dangerous," Christ's deposition concluded.

Judge Thomas ruled on February 28, 1974, that women would be allowed to wear pantsuits. The discussion with attorney Rita Reuss of the Women's Law Fund on court costs read:

JUDGE THOMAS: When you talk about out-of-pocket expenses you are not talking about out of trouser pocket are you?

RITA REUSS: No, skirt pocket.

JUDGE THOMAS: I don't know what the proper designation is, female patrolman or patrolman female—

REUSS: Officers.

NOVAK: We are still policewomen in our Women's Bureau.

The Women's Bureau was disbanded January 25, 1975. In 1978, a settlement waiver was ruled in the Women's Law Fund case. Within ninety days of the decree, the chief was ordered to make any transfers necessary to ensure there were at least two female patrol officers in each of the units listed. For a five-year period, the department would be required to furnish the court with semiannual reports on the status of women. After two years the lawsuit was declared moot.

When the Women's Bureau was closed, its women officers were integrated into the department. Jackie Christ was transferred to the radio room, known as a "punishment tour." She felt that was a reprisal for her pants lawsuit. Jackie and Kathryn Mengel later became the first women from Ohio to attend the FBI National Academy. Initially, three of the women were sent on patrol duty in the districts; others followed and several became platoon supervisors.

In 1978, Captain Violet Novak was assigned to the Third District in charge of forty men, becoming the first woman in the 111-year history of the department to supervise a uniformed platoon of men. She wore the police department's uniform—pants.

Novak still did not think it was proper to put women in zone cars with the men. As supervisor over the men, she required shined shoes, neat clothes, and was not above checking mustaches by having the men "bite the ruler."

Jean Clayton never reaped the benefits of her pioneering efforts. She was not transferred to community relations, the move she had wanted so badly. She was sent to the juvenile unit and retired in 1977.

Kathryn Mengel, a small, blond woman of gentle dignity, reflected later that Jean Clayton had a positive effect on the department. The closing of the Women's Bureau motivated Mengel to achieve rank. Now, there were opportunities for advancement. Before the lawsuit, she said, women knew even if they scored a hundred there was nowhere for them to go unless a ranking officer in the Women's Bureau died or retired. Mengel studied hard; she was competing against all the other officers— male and female—taking the test. She scored number two on the lieutenant's exam. Then, in 1982, she made Cleveland police history when she scored number one on her test for the rank of captain, outscoring forty-one men. She later became the department's first female to hold the rank of commander.

The elder, retired policewomen observed the changes. Captain Wilma L. Neubecker had joined the force in 1931 and stayed for forty years. She had spent her night shifts going from one dance hall to another—the Rainbow Gardens, Shadyside, the Crystal Slipper—warning managers not to have the girls sit on high countertops. She gave a little smile remembering how she had to tell couples not to dance closely, "even despite Fred Astaire's 'Dancing Cheek to Cheek.'" All was not fun in the dance halls; girls were raped leaving them, and Neubecker was sent to investigate. She had other tough cases, a baby dead of malnutrition, children overworked in violation of labor laws. On the trail of doctors who "committed abortions" she rushed to hospitals to try to get a statement from a woman before she died of peritonitis.

One of the projects Lucie took on during her career was serving on the board and aiding in the creation of the new Cleveland police museum. When Neubecker was in her eighties, she donated all her records to the museum, a treasure trove of history. Neubecker had saved articles about policewomen from all over the country, as well as her own files.

In 1973 as Neubecker noted the unfolding changes, she did not relish the idea of going out in patrol cars. She felt her work a far cry from what women like Lucie would be doing. She was glad not to be there. It would be hard to be paired with men. Women could share "girl talk."

Despite her own feelings, Neubecker accurately predicted the forth-coming changes. Before retiring she gave a speech: "I believe the police-women's role will change in emphasis from prevention and protection to investigation and basic police work. She will be used more and more to do and to supplement some of the duties required now of men officers. This will be true whether she or her department particularly desires it. It will become a case of necessity. Society will require her to do her duties with emphasis on the police part of her title—*police*woman."

Sergeant Emma Schuller, who was one of the first four women to join the Women's Bureau in 1924, also did not envy the fifteen female rook-ies' horizons. She had her own prediction: "There will be more trouble in the police department than ever before."

An official memo from Chief Rademaker notified the fifteen new policewomen of their assignments. Six would go to the Sixth District. Six would go to the Fifth District. Mary McGee was sent to the narcotics unit.

The Third District was adjacent to Lake Erie. To the east of the Third were the Fifth and Sixth Districts. But the Fourth sprawled east and southward, below the Fifth and Sixth. It was the largest district and had the highest crime rate.

Lucie and Maryanne Kingzett were the only two going to the notori-ous Fourth District. "What did we do wrong," wondered Maryanne. "I guess we're the token offerings."

"What good are the benefits going to be," Lucie said, laughing, "if I don't live to collect them?"

5

PICK YOUR FELONY

Fourth District Captain Robert Feingold made the announcement at roll call. "We're going to have a lady present tomorrow," he told the rookies and old-timers. "I want you to be gentlemen. I want you to watch what you say."

The Fourth District readied itself for Lucie. The next day at roll call most of the officers said every foul word they could think of. But Lucie wasn't there. She missed her first roll call.

Lucie had heard all about the Fourth in the academy. It was a "punishment tour," the district where they sent officers who were drinkers, thieves, or troublemakers. It was a dumping ground, a world unto itself.

After she received the news, Lucie was upset and apprehensive. She went out with Sharon Caine to the Brown Derby at Hilltop Plaza and sought solace in a few glasses of wine. She went home, made Brad dinner, and called the Fourth District. She was told to start the next day on second shift—three in the afternoon to eleven at night. Carol could make Brad dinner, at least that wasn't a problem.

"How are you going to do this?" one of Lucie's girlfriends asked her. "You won't even take your trash out after seven at night."

Lucie wasn't sure what she was going to do. She said, "I'll just take it one day at a time. If I can't handle it I'll quit. It's as simple as that. I'm not going to get panicked."

It was a cloudy, wet May afternoon when Lucie prepared for her first tour of duty. There were still no uniforms for the women. The men

54

hadn't gotten theirs right away either, but they were able to piece together uniforms with hand-me-downs from other officers. A jacket from one
policeman, a shirt from another, pants from a third. Lucie put on chino
slacks, a blouse, and a lightweight, pale blue raincoat. She strapped her
gunbelt around her waist and hooked on her .38.

Now, if she could only find the place. Howie's zooming rides
through the city hadn't given her much of a chance to learn her way.
Cleveland was still a stranger to her.

There was no freeway access to the Fourth. Lucie negotiated a web of
side streets, driving through the warm rain. The address was 3600 East
131st, near Lambert. It wasn't even at an intersection. Cops said, "It was
on the street with Peppy's pizza."

When she found it, she was sorry she had. The condemned old station house looked like a prison. A sidewalk went up to the front door,
dividing the tiny yard into two patches of dead grass. The two-story, red
brick building was built around 1910, in the middle of farmland, when
paved roads didn't yet extend that far and police still patrolled on horse-
back.

When Lucie walked in, she was the only woman there. She saw some
familiar faces, men from her academy class. They said hello and began to
show her around.

A sergeant told her Captain Feingold wanted to see her in his office.
She didn't know that Captain Feingold had quite a reputation. He saved
quarters and dimes in fruitcake tins, and ran an extensive quarter-pitching
operation. Officers had to watch where they parked to avoid the quarters
that flew out the window. And he frequently entertained girlfriends in the
station parking lot.

When Lucie went into his cramped office, Captain Feingold informed
her, "Tuesday is normally your day off. We didn't want you to think we
don't want you here, so I thought it would be better to have you come in
today, even though the person you'll be working with today isn't your
regular partner." He schlurred and schlobbered as he spoke. "Your regular partner is off, because normally this would have been your day off."

"OK," Lucie said. None of it made much sense to her. She didn't
understand the department's system of days off. She was thinking that
she had never been in such a dreadful building in all her life. The ceilings
were falling down. Sparks were flying from the electrical outlets.

"We do have some problems with the officer you'll be working with
today," Feingold said, spit flying. "But you'll have to work with him only
for this one day."

Something doesn't sound right, Lucie thought. But she just said,
"Fine."

"Don't worry," Feingold added. "I'm sending a third man on the car with you. He was in your academy class. So *Jed Cranston* won't lay a hand on you."

With that encouraging comment, Captain Feingold took Lucie downstairs. Roll call was already over. We were worried about you, some of the guys told her later. What was Feingold doing to her up there? What a welcome to the police department.

Lucie's academy classmate Dale Neal walked her out to the car. "Don't worry," he assured Lucie, "I won't let Cranston bother you."

In the lot, Lucie saw the new chartreuse zone cars—nicknamed "greenies" by police reporters. Nauseating, idiotic, and putrid were the descriptive terms applied by police officers. The chief thought they'd be more visible. Sure, the citizens could see you, one cop commented, so could the suspects—from miles away.

Lucie, Dale Neal, and Cranston didn't ride in a "greenie." Lucie was supposed to ride in either car 4-1-0 or 4-2-0, the pale blue sedans, equipped for evidence collection. The women were going to handle processing of crime scenes and low-priority calls. Barking dogs, parking violators.

The first call that came over the air was about a man with a shotgun loose in an abandoned funeral home. Cranston sped off to provide backup. No one was taking chances with gun calls. The memories of the sixties riots were fresh in the minds of the experienced officers.

Policemen were piling out of their cars and running into the funeral home when they arrived. Lucie followed Cranston and Neal, thinking, I have no idea what I am doing. The academy had taught her what the laws were and how to make reports, and theoretically when she could shoot. But this was reality.

Scared, she concentrated on what the experienced officers were telling her: "There's a guy in here who may have a gun. Get your gun out and get ready. Keep it down at your side, but get it out!"

Lucie didn't like going into funeral homes under any circumstances. This one was dark inside. The electricity had been turned off. Paneled draperies covered the walls. Gun drawn, she and the other officers crept through the large dusky rooms.

And suddenly there he was—a young man standing in a dark room holding a shotgun. A neighborhood nut case. The officers swooped down, disarming and cuffing him before he had a chance to do anything. They dragged him outside and put him in a car.

Lucie's first call was over. She had been frightened. Later, she would say that any cop who tells you they are not scared is either: A. lying, or B. nuts. But at that moment she was just wondering what happened to the calls about barking dogs and parking tickets.

* * *

The idea of the women being solely evidence technicians fell by the wayside almost immediately. The districts were too busy. Lucie found herself bounced from partner to partner so no one would be stuck with the female. She was often given five or six assignments right at roll call, handling sometimes twenty-five calls a shift. Running all night long. A murder or a stabbing every day. Burglaries, shootings, car thefts, rapes. Zone car officers were report takers. Just take the information and pass it on to a specialized unit. One report after another. Only the name of the victim changed.

Lucie found out quickly that they never got far enough down the pile of tickets to hand out the barking dog type calls. "It was more like pick your felony."

Lucie was taught every step: search the zone car when you get in. Check the trunk, check the backseat, dig under the seat. Make sure nothing was dropped by a prisoner that the next prisoner could pick up. Like a weapon or drugs. Turn on the radio. Key the mike. Say, Car four-two-two to radio. When the dispatcher's voice answers, Go ahead, four-two-two, then say, We're on the air.

Half the calls were domestics. On one of Lucie's first calls, she walked in to see a huge man waving his gun, threatening his family. Without stopping to think, she just walked right up to him.

"I'll take that," she said firmly, as she reached up and took the gun from his hand. She put it in her pocket. "Now," she said, "what's the problem?"

The man was shocked. So was she—later, when she thought about it. She didn't know if she could do that again.

She was doing things she never thought she could do—taking guns out of people's hands. The work was interesting, exciting, and fun. For the first time, she had a job that really challenged her.

She answered a report about a missing child. He was eight years old and had been gone for four days. The mother explained that she hadn't reported him missing sooner because usually he came home after a couple of days. She told them what her son had been wearing.

Lucie was nonplused. She thought, If Brad were missing for twenty seconds, I would go berserk. Here was this mother letting a little elementary school kid disappear for four days.

Lucie found the child that evening. He wasn't crying or acting like a frightened, lost eight-year-old. He'd been sleeping in a car and making his way on the streets. He thought he was doing just fine. He did not like the police, and was not at all happy when Lucie brought him home.

There are people out there, Lucie realized, who are a lot different than I am.

*   *   *

When Fourth District officer Frank Krob went on his furlough in the spring of 1973 he knew a class of recruits was about to graduate from the academy. All the policewomen he'd known worked in the Women's Bureau. Krob thought that was a good deal. They didn't have to put uniforms on and deal with all the people on the streets—the trash.

On his first day back from furlough, he was changing clothes, standing on a little piece of carpet with his undershorts on, getting ready to put on his uniform pants, when he heard a high-pitched voice call out in a singsong, "I'm comming i-i-n."

What kind of sissies are they hiring these days, Krob thought, screwing his face into a scowl as he answered back, "Well—so what! Come on in."

He saw a woman with bright red hair take two steps into the doorway and stop. Krob froze. He had no idea what to do. Should he grab his civilian pants or his uniform pants? He was immobilized by embarrassment.

"It's all right," Lucie cracked. "I've been married. You don't have to hurry up."

Quite an introduction, Krob thought.

There were no locker facilities for women. When the women's uniforms finally came in after a few months, Lucie dressed at home. Brad thought Lucie looked kind of funny 'cause her hair was so short. The uniform was fourteen-ounce wool for winter, eleven-ounce for summer. An Eisenhower jacket. Dark blue pants, and a lighter blue shirt.

There wasn't even a women's rest room in the Fourth. There was a male washroom off the main room on the first floor, but Lucie thought it too awful to use. When she needed a bathroom, her partners drove her to St. Luke's Hospital.

Roll call was held on the first floor. About seventy cops jammed into the small, confining space, crowding—shoulder to shoulder in and around rows and rows of varnished wood lockers—and spilling out into the hallway. They had no place to sit or write. The OIC (officer in charge) stood behind a six-foot counter, pushed aside a banged-up manual typewriter, and shouted out names, car numbers and zones, and the litany of recent area crimes.

Officers from the preceding shift hauled in prisoners through the back door as civilians came in the front door to make complaints. They all converged on the same small window and counter area where the OIC was standing, barking out assignments. A citizen reporting a lost cat jostled next to a cop booking a murderer.

"Hey, Lucie," a voice called out as the platoon gathered for one of her first roll calls. "This is for you."

It was a large, sealed property envelope, marked with her name. Lucie opened it, and out fell a pair of falsies. Her blue eyes sparked behind her big glasses. The men were watching her reaction. Her classmate Fred Hafner noticed that she didn't get angry, she didn't even turn red. She started laughing, with the long-lasting, high-pitched laugh she became famous for. Lucie's ability to roll with the razzing gained her respect.

She was working with Bob Galaszewski when the call came in—domestic with shots fired. They pulled the zone car up front and heard the pop of a gun. "This is not going to be good," Lucie quipped as she called for a backup.

They went up to the apartment. There were bullet holes in the door. They drew their guns and stood to the side as they knocked. It was one of those situations Bob and Lucie would joke about later. About how after you hear shots fired, you tiptoe up to the door, tap on it lightly and whisper, police. Then look at each other—OK, no response—let's go.

A man opened the door. Whatever action had been going on behind closed doors stopped instantly as Lucie and Bob moved inside.

"There's no problem here, officer," the man said.

The wife was silent. Two small children stood quietly, eyes frightened.

Three backup cars spun into the street, sirens wailing. Car doors burst open, and six officers ran, heavy shoes stamping on the stairs, up to the apartment door.

"There were shots fired here," a cop said.

"Hey, I don't know what you're talking about," the man protested. "I don't have a gun."

The wife's not going to say anything, Lucie judged. She's too afraid. Lucie glanced down at the scared little boy next to her. He looked about three or four. He's seen everything. She took him aside. She put her gun back in her holster, pushed the nightstick back from her hip, and knelt down beside him.

"Does daddy have a gun?" she whispered gently.

The boy nodded his head.

"Where is it?" Lucie asked.

The child pointed to a laundry basket.

Lucie found the gun under a pile of clothing. This man was going to jail.

"You're under arrest. You have the right to remain silent ..." The officers patted him down, cuffed him, and escorted him out the door. The wife came running down the steps after them.

"I don't want him to go to jail," she screamed. "What are you doing! What are you doing!" she yelled again and again.

No way he's not going to jail, Lucie thought. We heard those shots fired. Hell, he could have shot us.

No one wanted to get booked at the Fourth, Lucie learned. Prisoners were abused. "Few people ever got booked at the Fourth that there was not some blood shed." It was called street justice. After prisoners were booked, they were dragged back into the jail. There were no toilets in the cells. There was one long pipe that looked like an old horse trough but was actually an old sewer pipe. Prisoners sat on open pipe elbows to relieve themselves; the constantly running water flushed the waste through the pipe. The building stunk.

Lucie watched the goings-on. She didn't judge. She hardly felt she was in a position to decide the best way to do law enforcement. She saw rapists get the shit beat out of them when they got to the station. She had seen the victims at the hospital and knew why the cops were beating up the guys. But certainly she didn't want to participate. She had the same attitude out on the street. She had no desire to fight her way through her tour of duty.

It was a hot night in late summer when it was Tom Guenther's turn to work with Lucie. Guenther had been a journeyman machinist, working for General Motors, on his way to becoming a tool and die maker when a friend took the civil service test and talked Guenther into taking it also, just to keep him company. While he was waiting for the test results, Guenther started watching "Adam 12," and his excitement grew. By the time he was appointed, a year after he'd taken the test, he was thrilled. Damn— One Adam Twelve—me, a cop, a hat, a gun, he chuckled to himself.

Guenther evaluated Lucie: she must weigh less than a hundred pounds, he estimated. She looks like the cartoon character Olive Oyl in a uniform. And what makes her look even more funny, he thought, is she always carries that big nightstick. He didn't like carrying his. You get in the car and you forget to take it off, and it damn near kills you. You sit down, and the big thing goes twang in your belt. None of the cops carried them. Except Lucie. A nightstick on me, Guenther chortled, looks like a nightstick. She looks like she's carrying a broom.

A complaint came in about a bunch of rowdies at a school on Miles Avenue. Guenther and Lucie found a group of teenagers clustered at the top of the steps near the door.

"Break it up," Guenther ordered. "We got a complaint, everybody out of the school yard."

Most of the kids got up and walked off. A few stayed, on the very top steps by the door. Lucie and Guenther started up the long flight.

Guenther raised his voice. "Everybody—let's go. I want you out of here. Now." He snapped his fingers.

They all left. Except one. He was the leader of the pack, Guenther surmised, a heavyset young man with black hair. This guy—he's cool, he's tough. He's the big man.

The man looked around, taking his time. He stood up to dust his pants. Slowly.

He was over six feet tall and weighed at least two hundred pounds. He was strutting. Guenther was halfway up the steps. He raised himself to his full five nine, 180-pound size, and said "Come on!"

The man continued his strut.

Lucie reached the top of the stairs. He towered a foot over her. He was drunk. Suddenly, he lurched toward her.

Her training drill flashed through her mind—keep him away. Her reaction was instantaneous. She slammed the end of her nightstick into his breastbone and pushed hard.

Guenther watched incredulous as the man who looked like he could cast a shadow for two blocks came hurtling past him down the steps, finally stopped rolling, and came to a halt. He stood up and stared at them, his face contorted with rage.

He's going to break us in half. Guenther began to sweat. The guy is Hercules compared to us. He felt responsible for Lucie. In the brief moment that the man stood up and started toward them, Guenther was the most frightened he had ever been and ever would be in his career. There was no way he could fight the guy off. If the man attacked, Guenther was going to have to shoot.

He yelled as loud as he could. "I told you to move it, I mean now or you're going to jail. GET!"

The man stopped. "Awright, awright," he said. "I'm going." And he left.

Sweat was raining down from Guenther's armpits to his elbows. The way he saw it, the guy was going to move, but wasn't moving fast enough, so Lucie hurried him along. Lucie wanted action. She was brand-new and was taught at the academy: when a policeman gives an order, you jump. You shit 'n git.

When they got back to the car, Lucie said, "Well—we took care of that, didn't we." She dusted her palms. Her voice was full of pride.

Guenther sighed. He looked at her sitting there, with her bright coppery hair falling across her forehead. He didn't tell her how afraid he had been.

"Yeah, Lucie we did," he said, "but we've got to get a plan together. If he had come back up, I would have had to shoot him. There's no way we could have fought him off."

Probably it had embarrassed the guy, Guenther thought. He knew he would be embarrassed if he was knocked down by someone a third of his height and weight.

Lucie was just glad the man hadn't hit her. Striking him seemed like the sensible thing to do. The guys always thought they had to protect her. Maybe I'm not as dumb as they think.

One of Lucie's first semiregular partners was *Sean Flynn,* a miserable old codger. Nobody wanted to work with him. But Flynn took a liking to Lucie. He had been on the force about thirty years. He was no longer impetuous. He was not about to play macho man, Lucie realized, and rush in on something and get her killed. And he wasn't on the make for her.

Most experienced officers did the driving when breaking in a rookie, but Flynn put Lucie in the driver's seat. She and Flynn got a call to a homicide.

The twelve-year-old boy was lying on the ground dead, shot in the chest with a .357. He had been shot accidentally by a friend while they were playing. He was one year older than Brad. Lucie knew her job was to protect the area and gather the evidence. The body is a part of the crime scene. If you're doing your job, she knew, you don't have time to react with horror or grief.

Each time she read in the newspaper about a child being killed with a handgun, the scene would come back to her, that twelve-year-old boy shot accidentally with the .357. "How would I react if something happened to Brad. Hysteria would put it mildly." It was the memory of the boy's mother, screaming and crying in her pain, that haunted Lucie.

Sean Flynn was a cadger, always out to get stuff for free. Cadging was a tradition in the police department, but Flynn, Lucie discovered, had elevated it to an art form. On third shift, eleven P.M. to seven in the morning, he took Lucie to his regular stops. The first stop was Franklin Ice Cream on Lee Road. Flynn scheduled his visit for the arrival of the delivery truck and took gallons and gallons of milk, ice cream, and any other dairy products available. Where in God's name is he going to keep all this stuff for the night? Lucie wondered. He stopped at the fire house to store the goodies in the fire house refrigerator.

Later in the shift, it was delivery time for Fazio's grocery store, also on Lee Road. Lucie watched as he took a tray full of loaves of bread and pastry. Not a half dozen ears of corn—the whole crate. Lucie's cheeks turned crimson as she grew more embarrassed.

"Here, take some," he told Lucie. We're protecting the truck driver while he's making his deliveries, Flynn explained to her. In return, we get some food. He became angry when Lucie refused the wares.

Alesci's was a chain of Italian grocery stores. Their food-processing plant and bakery were day shift stops. Sean was well known there. The people welcomed them in, made Lucie and Sean sandwiches with cold cuts and cheese, and gave them pounds of fresh Italian sausage, cheese, and gallons of spaghetti sauce. "Take the stuff, take it," they urged Lucie. She felt awkward, but they insisted. She didn't have to do much grocery shopping.

Lucie was a little surprised by the cops' behavior. At first, she sensed they tried to hide things from her because everyone was convinced the women were working for internal affairs, as they had thought in Elizabeth Metzger's day. But some things they just couldn't hide.

If a pop machine stole a cop's quarters—he shot the machine. There were bullet holes in the lockers. Word was Lieutenant *Curtis Marzden* was once an excellent officer. But now he was on the sauce so bad they couldn't let him out of the station. All he did was keep track of portable radios and car washes. He sipped his liquor out of a Pepsi bottle that a local bar filled for him free of charge. He was supposed to show up to work at six-thirty in the morning, sometimes he wandered in at six-thirty at night. "He would get confused," Lucie said. "He was that bad."

There were also swastikas in the Fourth—and in other districts. Police wore them on their gun belts and tie tacks. Mayor Perk ordered the graffiti washed from the walls. No officer was to wear a swastika armband.

Perk's orders didn't put an end to it. Bill Reese, one of Lucie's fellow rookies and future partners, was concerned about the racism. He immediately joined the Shield Club when he came on the job. He saw the Nazi belt buckles, and when he passed an open locker, he sometimes saw a swastika on the door. There were rumors that some of the cops celebrated Hitler's birthday every year. "No one ever actually approached me and said anything outright about what Nazis wanted to do to blacks and Jews," he remembered. "But police walking around with swastikas made me nervous," Reese said. "I thought it should make the whole country nervous."

The report room was in the basement. When it rained, it flooded. To use the telephone, Lucie had to wade across the floor, awash with six inches of water, toilet paper, and other sewage that had backed up through the pipes. Water poured out of the electrical sockets. The gas cans the cops used to fill up their cars leaked into the flood water, and the stench of the gas combined with the garbage. She sat on a wooden bench and wrote her reports on a picnic table, with a hundred-watt exposed light bulb dangling over her head.

There was no emergency medical service until October of 1975, when citron-colored ambulances started their runs. Meanwhile, the

police "greenies" were equipped with stretchers. Patrol officers with rudi-
mentary emergency medical training were often first at the scene, attending to injured accident victims. They hauled dead bodies to the morgue.
Lucie found the industrial accidents gruesome. Arriving on the scene of a
traffic accident, they found a boy whose arm had been tangled up with a
phone truck. "It ripped his arm off," Lucie said. "One of those bizarre
freak accidents. We just grabbed him, grabbed the arm, and drove like
hell to the hospital." The doctors were able to reattach the arm.

The Garden Valley Projects were a maze of low brick buildings.
There were no through streets; Lucie had to go in on foot. People there
hated the police. She would hear shouts of "motherfucker" and "pig."
They would spit at her. On routine calls—a missing child or stolen auto—
radio would send just one car. The numbers marking the buildings'
addresses had been torn off. When she got lost she beamed her long,
black flashlight into the pitch dark, looking for the right place. She had
no idea who could be watching her. Sometimes her portable radio didn't
work. She knew she could get trapped in a situation and not be able to
call for help. She could be killed and no one would know who did it.

But she told herself there was no point in worrying about it—if they
want to kill me, they've got me. Then her knees would shake so that she
felt that they were going to collapse underneath her.

Brad wasn't worried about his mother. He didn't think about the
possibility of her being hurt. He was becoming more self-sufficient as
Lucie rotated her shifts. He woke himself up in the morning, and if Lucie
wasn't there, got himself off to school. He prepared some of his own
meals. He was feeling good about it, knowing he had an unusual amount
of freedom for a fifth grader.

But Lucie was having a rough time. The shifts changed each month,
completely disrupting her eating and sleeping habits. On second shift,
she'd come home at midnight so revved up she'd be awake all night. On
third shift, her only chance for sleep was daytime, and she found that
impossible. She lost weight, her eyes looked sunken. After night shifts she
had to appear in municipal court at nine A.M. to testify about some misdemeanor charge. She would go home, change, and head right back
downtown, only to wait two hours and find out the case had been continued. It was so frustrating. She was totally frazzled. Dead tired. The swing
shifts combined with court appearances played havoc with Lucie's child-
care schedule. She worried about Brad. She was experiencing working
mother's guilt. Plus Brad was eleven, and Lucie felt he needed a father
figure. Terry had remarried and was teaching at a private school in Okla-

homa. If Brad lived with Terry, Lucie thought, he would receive a good education. Terry's family had always sent their kids to private schools, and education was a top priority for Lucie. She wanted Brad to have every possible opportunity.

She broached the idea to Brad, giving him the option to go or stay. He was interested in seeing more of his dad. He decided to go to Oklahoma. The move was a big adjustment. Brad went from the public school in Cleveland Heights to a private, Episcopalian Boys' School where a row of Mercedes and Porsches discharged the students daily. Brad didn't like some things about the school, but his love of reading stayed with him. He began to enjoy informative books, he would pick up the encyclopedia and page through it. There were also plenty of outdoors activities in Oklahoma. He rode his bike, played soccer and tennis. Terry's mother owned a condominium in Vail, Colorado, and Terry and Brad spent two weeks there each year. They also went duck hunting together and on camping trips into Colorado and Nevada. But he missed Lucie. She was the main thread through his life.

Lucie was sent over to the Seven Barn to work. The Fourth District sprawled out into a section called the Lower End. Cops who worked the Lower End of the Fourth were stationed at the Seven Barn. It was called the country club because cops working out of there had little supervision. They were supposed to report for roll call at the main building, but often they didn't.

Lucie's new field training officer was Arnie Hovan, a hot headed street cop who in 1973 made the *World Book Encyclopedia*'s synopsis of Cleveland's events of the year for charging Mayor Perk with assault after a meeting at city hall. Hovan claimed Perk pushed him as Perk passed through the crowd of officers gathered to protest Perk's stand against their hospitalization benefits. Perk was acquitted of the assault.

Hovan stood six five with a heavy upper body, a voice that boomed through hallways and around corners, deep-set light blue eyes, and a tattoo on his right forearm. He came on the job in 1965, was sent right to the Fourth, and stayed there for twenty years. He didn't take anybody's guff on the street. The other male officers at the Seven Barn were used to him, and he was used to them. Invariably, trouble would find them. They ended up in fights about three times a week, at different hot spots.

He didn't think females on the job was such a hot idea. He took one look at Lucie and thought that a good wind would blow her away. Third man on the car was *Joe Russell*. Hovan and Russell were both gregarious socializers and would leave her in the car while they went off on escapades. The lieutenant would come by and ask her where they were.

They're checking doors, she said, covering for them. Despite Hovan's antics and quick temper, Lucie learned to respect his knowledge of the city and its people.

The Seven Barn was a condemned building, with railroad tracks behind it. When the city eventually decided to tear it down, its walls were so thick that the contractor's wrecking ball couldn't break them. The old walls were three feet thick and full of stories. Stories the old-timers told. About the skeleton that was found out back when the horse barn was torn down. Probably some hobo off a train who crawled in there to die. About the captain who protected the bootleggers during Prohibition. About Shondor Birns, Cleveland's infamous Hungarian-born Jewish gangster, who in 1942 was arrested by United States Immigration officials as an enemy alien. They tried to deport him, but no country would take him. When he was ordered interned, he was jailed at the Seven Barn until the FBI secretly escorted him to Camp McAlester in Oklahoma.

Arnie Hovan was "100 percent" Hungarian. He had been raised on Buckeye Road, which ran through the upper end of the Fourth District. At one time there were more Hungarians in that area than anywhere else outside of Hungary. Hovan and Russell knew everyone on Buckeye Road, all the bar owners and business people. They were members of the Hungarian Businessmen and Tradesmen Club, which was frequented by politicians and judges. The manager was a personal friend. They took Lucie in and introduced her to "the Hungarian Hussars, the Wild Hungarians." She was a novelty, one of the first policewomen they had ever seen.

"Hey, Lucie," Hovan said on one shift. "We got to go in and say hi to someone."

"You guys are going to drag me in there again?" Lucie protested. "I don't feel like going."

"OK, stay in the car." Hovan got out.

"Do you mind if I ride around the block," she asked.

Hovan stared at her. "Are you crazy?" his voice blared. "If you ride around and get in an accident, the first thing the boss is going to say is where are your two partners. What are you going to do—tell him we're in a bar!" Hovan walked off to the club.

Lucie listened to the radio's constant sputter of car numbers, locations, calls, reports. Then the dispatcher checked for her car's location.

She didn't know where she was. Where had Hovan parked the car? She jumped out and ran to the corner. She looked up at the street sign, ran back, and answered the dispatcher. It was a typical rookie experience. Rookies easily lost their sense of direction. Remembering all the streets in their district took time. In Lucie's case it was even harder because the district was mapped out into zones, and each zone car covered an area.

When Lucie went from partner to partner she would have to learn the streets in yet another zone.

When Hovan came back, she told him what happened. "I had to get out and go to the corner and look at the pole ..."

Hovan's voice had the force of a wind blustering off Lake Erie. "Those things happen, Lucie. At least you had enough sense to get out and see where you were. Otherwise he would have thought something was up and sent somebody looking for us."

When it came to personal matters, Hovan didn't take any nonsense. There were no lockers for the women, not even a ladies room. Poor thing, he thought. She's going off work. She has places to go, and she wants to change clothes. He saw guys yank her chain. They would change right in front of her.

Hovan stood guard for her at the bathroom door. He never let anybody in. Lucie used the bathroom there, because she trusted him.

After he had worked with her for a while, he decided she was not a bad police officer. In fact, as the years went by, he decided Lucie was one of the best of the women. Lucie was sharp, he admitted. Lucie was slick. She had the moxie to carry her through. A lot of females came on the job and couldn't handle the pressure. She took the crap, handled the stress, and still performed the job. She hung with it. He had to give her credit for that.

Lucie was sent on details with the Fourth District vice unit about a year after she joined the force. She was part of a new team selected for their aggressiveness and integrity. There had been a shake-up. "A guy on my shift, Ralph McDuffie, decided to be the Serpico of the Fourth," Lucie said. She didn't know him personally, but she heard all about him. He blew the whistle on Feingold and other high ranking officers in the Fourth who were taking bribes from cheat spots (unlicensed liquor establishments) in exchange for letting them operate. McDuffie wrote a memo to Chief Rademaker outlining his charges. The memo was made public and the *Plain Dealer* ran a series on police misconduct. It was the first time a cop in Cleveland had gone on the record about corruption. McDuffie went before the grand jury, but no indictments were handed down. The city council praised McDuffie for his "courage and sense of duty in exposing police corruption." But on the job he was given a terrible time. There were threats and harassment. McDuffie finally resigned.

"The whole district damn near got indicted," Lucie said. She was still new on the job, but she was affected. McDuffie's charges had an impact. Feingold retired. Deputy Inspector Edwin A. Nagorski was put in charge of the district. Lucie liked Nagorski. "He was a real straight arrow. He came out there with the horrible job of trying to get this mess under control. There was absolutely no discipline. The Fourth was running amuck. It was F-troop. Feingold's platoon was the worst of the bunch."

When Frank Krob was asked to join the new vice unit, he laughed. He knew you had to know somebody or have political pull to get into specialized units. "Yah, sure," he said, with disbelief. He thought it was a joke, even though his sergeant told him it wasn't. They took him to Deputy Inspector Nagorski, who confirmed it. Krob's name was on the list for vice.

Krob's old zone car partner, Billy Riedthaler, was also in the new vice unit. Krob and Riedthaler had made enemies of their former bosses. They would park outside cheat spots conducting their own surveillance, and the supervisor would growl over the radio, "Car four-four-one, what's your location?" When they told him, he would say, "What the hell are you doing over there. Stay away from that place."

We were "bad" boys, Krob said with a smile. But after McDuffie's accusations hit the fan, he and Riedthaler wound up in vice, closing those same places tight as a drum. There is a God, Krob thought. We got ours.

After working vice for some time, Krob's partner was injured in a car accident. Sergeant Cannon, head of the new vice unit, came up to Krob and said, "You've got a new partner for a couple of months. I want you to teach her everything you know."

"Her?" Krob expostulated.

"Her name is Lucie," Cannon continued.

The girl that caught me with my pants down. Krob's mouth dropped.

Billy Riedthaler, an aggressive officer with a shock of blond hair and a red mustache, was legendary for his complete and detailed reports. He wanted people on the new vice unit who could write good reports—documentation is everything in vice cases. And he wanted cops who had been in the field and could take care of themselves. Cops who wouldn't run if the action got rough, who even if they got the crap beat out of them, they would try. Undercover vice work was dangerous. He had suggested Lucie.

Nagorski had then asked Lucie if she would like to work vice weekends. She said yes. She felt instinctively that refusing was not a good idea. Part of it was naïveté. She didn't think she could refuse. Part of it was her work ethic mentality. Whatever you want me to do, I will do it, that was her attitude. Later, she found out other women turned down some details. But that didn't seem smart to Lucie. Why would I refuse, she thought. She saw the men were not exactly antagonistic but hesitant about her. If I start acting like a prima donna, she thought, I'm only going to make things more difficult for myself. I might as well jump into this thing with both feet.

Lucie didn't realize it, but being chosen for undercover work a year after getting on the force was a sign she was on her way up.

On the vice team was fellow rookie Bill Reese, Charlie Rominski, and Jonathan McTier. McTier, who joined the department under the Stokes administration, wanted to make a difference in racial attitudes. He was featured in *Police Team,* a book for kids that was about a black officer and a white officer working together. In a department full of racists, Lucie stood out to him. She was all right with everyone.

But other officers felt differently about her. Krob was razzed, when word got out. Oh, you got to work with Lucie. You got to work with the female. But Krob found that Lucie learned fast and she wanted to learn everything. They busted a few places for serving minors liquor. Krob taught Lucie how to make reports. They wrote out two liquor citations, and by the third, she knew how to do them.

Lucie and Krob posed as a couple and went in checking for liquor violations. They went into all kinds of bars, looking for liquor sales to minors and illegal gambling—football or horse betting, shooting dice. People never suspected them. I guess we were blazing a new trail, working as a male/female team, Krob realized later.

Lucie also teamed with Billy Riedthaler. They responded to community complaints. Billy ran down the scenario: "Mr. Wonderful lost his paycheck shooting dice on the pool table, wife calls police and says my husband lost two hundred and fifty dollars at Sam's Bar and Grill. Two or three males come in, they're going to think it's a holdup or the men are cops. A man and a woman come in and take a corner booth—they're married, or they're messing around. Takes the heat off."

Riedthaler and Lucie checked out places like the Wooden Nickel, places where the Appalachians danced to country music. Appalachians migrated to Cleveland, escaping the poverty of the coal mines and farms. They had to face prejudice and were called "hilljacks," "stumpjumpers," and "ridgerunners." The bars they frequented were called shit-kicking bars and punch palaces.

Riedthaler and Lucie introduced themselves saying, We're new in the neighborhood. We saw you had a lot of cars out front and we figured you probably had good food. "We were just a cute little couple down there on the Lower End," Lucie laughed, "Like we had just come from West-by-Gawd-Virginia."

It was late on a Friday night when Lucie crouched down in the bushes behind a ramshackle building on Beaver Avenue. Above her head, through the window, she could hear a group of elderly black men enjoying their card game. Listen to every word, Lucie had been instructed. Supposedly, they were gambling. A ghetto dog was barking wildly. I hope it doesn't eat me, Lucie thought, peering through the bleak dark night. Or that someone doesn't see me and take a shot at me.

Earlier in the week Lucie had watched an episode of the new show "Police Woman," starring Angie Dickinson as Pepper. The *Plain Dealer*

TV guide described the exciting plot: "Pepper poses as a Las Vegas chorus girl in an effort to crack a kidnapping case in which a mobster's son is abducted by a rival gang leader."

As Lucie shifted uncomfortably in the dirt, she thought of the blond and beautiful "Police Woman" star, dressed in a slinky, sequined black dress, floating through glittering casinos. They both worked vice. But here I am, Lucie thought, in grungy clothes, squatting in rubble, just hoping the dogs don't get me—all so they can nail these old men on a misdemeanor gambling charge. Talk about small potatoes. Something is wrong with this picture.

The vice team went after numbers rackets. At policy houses, three balls, numbered from one to ninety-nine, were drawn out of a bag. The winning combinations could pay off in odds as high as four hundred to one, but the games were fixed. Before each drawing, bookies would mark all the numbers played on a large chart. They had two sets of balls, one convex, one concave. On heavily played numbers, they'd put in a concave ball. The puller knew not to draw that one.

Winning clearinghouse numbers, taken from daily stock exchange figures in the papers, paid off in even higher odds than policy. Any amount from a penny on up could be bet. Cleveland was one of three publishing centers for the midwestern edition of the *Wall Street Journal,* the paper of record for clearinghouse. The figures were found on the second page from the back, the last number in each column of the composite stock market diary's advances, declines, and unchanged. When the *Journal* and the *Plain Dealer* printed different figures by mistake, dozens of irate racketeers called in, barely trying to cover the cause of their concern.

Lucie and Krob drove around the ghetto in an unmarked vehicle observing the action. If they saw people on the street writing the policy numbers, they didn't bother them. They were after the whole operation. They'd drive down a street around ten and see only a few cars. Policy numbers were drawn at eleven P.M. Suddenly at ten-thirty, they saw 150 cars parked at a single location. A bunch of people had hit the number and knew where the numbers house was. Or, they might hear from an informant that this was the place. Inside there would be a dozen telephones, and all the paraphernalia for numbers and drawings.

Most of the violations were misdemeanors. Krob, Lucie, and the others were in court all the time. They worked Friday nights from eight till four in the morning making arrests, and then had to be in court Saturday morning to consult the prosecutor. It seemed as if they never went home. Just had breakfast and went back to work, working sixteen hours at a stretch. After court, they went home and tried to sleep—fast. They had to be back at work Saturday night, arriving late, at ten or eleven because they were so tired. Vice was night work. Weekend work.

Krob didn't tell his wife he had a female partner. It was only going to be for a couple of months. He reasoned that if he didn't say anything, twenty years from now, he and his wife could laugh about it.

But at a police get-together, an officer came up to Krob and his wife and said, "So—what does your wife think about your working with that sharp redhead?"

Krob's wife was not pleased. She claimed she was afraid for his safety working with a female cop. "But as we talked, the green monster popped out," Krob said. Cops spent eight, sometimes eleven hours a day with their partners. A cop's spouse had to have a lot of trust.

They went after cheat spots. One team drove around during the week, watching and taking notes. After the bars closed, they'd see people going in and out of houses and hear the jukeboxes inside. The unit sat down with the sergeant and made a plan for the weekend.

Three weekends in a row, they observed one place that was lively at four in the morning. They decided to go in. Krob, Lucie, and Joe McTier. They got out of the car and walked through backyards, with the wild dogs yapping. It was freezing cold. The bass sound from the jukebox was so loud, Krob could feel it through his feet as he walked toward the house. "They won't let white people in," McTier told them. Krob and Lucie stood to the side.

Tension was always thick going into cheat spots. They didn't draw their guns. But they clipped their badges on, or flipped them out as they walked in. McTier knocked on the door. Lucie and Krob followed him inside. There was a WHISKEY FOR SALE sign hanging on the wall. The beat-up house was set up just like a bar. They arrested everyone that night. The raid went without a hitch. Krob was relieved. He knew some cops were squeamish going into cheat spots. He'd seen people inside start jumping out of windows. Or they could swarm on you in a second. "There are three or four of you and thirty or forty of them, even guys start to get a little shy, but Lucie never showed any signs of intimidation." He didn't know how he'd feel working in uniform with Lucie, but he saw that she backed her partners to the hilt.

The most dangerous incident was a happenstance. Lucie was working with vice detective Charles Rominski. They were parked on the street, in their undercover car, when a man hit their car and took off at a high rate of speed. Lucie and Charlie chased him, calling for backup. Lucie sped along, whipping behind him into a driveway. They leaped out of the car. Charlie went to the right, Lucie went to the left. Lucie was coming around the driver's side when she saw him pointing a gun at her partner.

She drew her gun. She was ready to shoot but—what if his gun went off as he fell and he shot Charlie.

She pointed her gun at the back of his head and cocked the hammer. "Drop it," she ordered. He dropped his weapon and surrendered.

* * *

The media continued to follow the progress of policewomen. "There's a little lace and probably less cussing in Cleveland police cruisers," read one article, continuing, "'Adam 12' is now 'Adam and Eve 12.'"

The reality was not quite so cute. In the Fifth, Dana Garcia was taught by several of her senior partners about cooping—finding a spot to sleep. This is a good cooping spot, they told her, down by the museum or near Case Western. Sometimes on midnight shifts, when it was slow, five or six cars would be pulled up—not cooping then, but partying. Later on, when she was partnered with Diane Parkinson they wrote more parking citations than all three platoons put together. They were told: slow down, you're supposed to be somewhere cooping. You're making everyone else look bad.

In the Sixth District, Marilyn Mason overheard a cop say to one of the policewomen, "You can sit on my face anytime." Marilyn had never heard that expression. Then, she was called to a crime scene to process it. The place looked like a garbage dump. Where do you want me to do the prints, she asked the male officers. It's in the bedroom, they told her. In the bedroom she found a big candle shaped like a penis. She waited a few minutes and then went out. Did you finish, the guys ribbed her. Yes, I'm finished, she answered, laughing. Shrugging it off.

When Maryanne Kingzett arrived at the Fourth to report for her first tour of duty—a night shift—it was pouring rain. In her wildest dreams she could not have imagined such a building. She approached a couple of officers and asked them where to go. They wouldn't answer her. They don't want me here, she thought.

She stood outside in the dark and waited, the rain soaking her blond hair and clothes. When roll call began, she ventured inside and got her assignment. She was put in the backseat of a zone car, the two veterans rode up front. It was a quiet night. They rode around in silence, the rain spattering the windows. The men didn't talk. Maryanne didn't talk. They got no calls.

They pulled up to a restaurant. "Come in," they said to her.

She followed behind them, feeling like a little puppy. They ordered coffee and donuts.

"We don't want you here," one of the men said.

"I don't particularly want to be here myself," Maryanne responded.

That was all they needed to hear. From that point on, they treated her well. One of her coaches, she later found out, was one of the district drunks. But she grew to like him, and he was kind to her.

She shared a locker with two other officers. She took home most of her belongings after her shift, but she left her notebooks and other supplies at work. When she opened her locker the next day, condoms fell out of it. The guys were watching the ex-nun. How was she going to react? She was annoyed, but she tried to show no shock at all. One officer took her aside and whipped out pictures of his wife—nude. When she had to go to the bathroom while out on patrol they put on the red light to drive her to St. Luke's Hospital. "Talk about humiliation."

They called her Sister Mary. At least she didn't hear of any rumors about her sleeping around. She wasn't quite the saint they made her out to be, but she was close.

On one shift, when she was partnered with a captain, they got a call about a man threatening with a gun. "Go on inside, Maryanne," the captain told her. "I'll park the car."

Maryanne knew this is not the way things were supposed to be done. He wouldn't treat a man this way. But if they want to do this to me, fine. She walked inside.

There was a crowd of people in the tavern and a man waving a gun. Maryanne walked up to him and asked him to give her the gun. He did. Truly, the Lord is with me, she thought. What's the problem, she asked him. She kept him talking, trying to keep him calm. The backup cars arrived before the captain even bothered to come inside.

She was twenty-five years old and single. Her attitude was, If I get killed, I get killed. She never refused to do anything.

But when it was time for Maryanne to write up an evaluation of herself, her coach dictated her words: "I feel I am not as capable as my fellow police officers in certain physical activities." She didn't want to write that part, but what could she do? He was her senior officer.

In the Fifth and Sixth districts, the women were riding third on a car with two men. The Fourth was the only district where the women were allowed out with a single male partner. But after about six months, the women were partnered together in each of the three districts. It was another CPD tactic to keep the women separate from the men. It was unheard of to partner rookies. It was dangerous.

Lucie and Maryanne now rode together. One of their supervisors, Captain Nicholas Lusk, made sure they were trained well. He would call them over the radio and arrange for a meeting. Lucie and Maryanne would stand outside in wind, snow, and rain, shivering as Lusk gave them instructions. He expected them to do their work, and he wanted them to learn to do it right.

They both wore the women's badges—Maryanne described them as "a little girl's dream." Their uniform shirts were of heavier material than the men's, and their hats looked like a cross between a cowboy's and a WAVES hat. Maryanne and Lucie hated them, they blew off constantly. People came up, peering at the small badges and said—What are you?

Sometimes people laughed when they showed up on calls. Or they said, Good for you.

One winter night, near the end of second shift, Lucie pulled to the side of the road on Griffing Avenue so Maryanne could do their daily duty report. Maryanne turned on the dome light and began writing.

A shot exploded.

"My God, that sounds close," Maryanne said.

The shot had hit the quarter panel in the front of their car, on Maryanne's side. Two more shots skidded across the hood and a third hit the house across the street.

Lucie rolled out of the driver's side into the street. She grabbed the mike. "We're being shot at, send help," she yelled, giving their car number and location.

Maryanne unhooked the shotgun, loaded one shell in the chamber, and ducked out of the car.

It seemed to Lucie that the shots came from the house next to them, from higher up than they were, maybe from the porch. She drew her gun and crept around the car through the snow alongside the house to the back. She had begun to search when what seemed like a million zone cars came screaming—lights and siren—up the street. The officers found bullet holes in the home across the street. The trajectory indicated the shooter may have been aiming right at Maryanne and Lucie. The captain told Lucie and Maryanne it wasn't any big deal, as long there wasn't much damage to the car. It was the end of their shift. Lucie was glad to be going home.

When Lucie's friend Richard bought a house on Colonnade, he asked Lucie if she wanted to rent the second floor. Lucie moved in, and she introduced Richard to Judy Cooke. The two dated on and off, remaining friends throughout the years. For both of them, Lucie was their focal point. The house on Colonnade was an adventure. Judy thought of them as the three musketeers. They cooked meals together, shopped together, fixed their cars together, and went on a wine-making spree. They tie-dyed curtains, redecorated Judy's house, and put in carpet tiles. Lucie bought toddler swimming pools and planted tomatoes in them, making her own garden on her porch. She shared her funny police stories with Judy. But she learned quickly that she couldn't share most of what she experienced.

She didn't do much socializing with cops. She didn't go to platoon parties where they played cards and watched smoker films. She didn't want to become like so many of the policemen she knew whose entire lives became encircled by their job.

Brad liked coming back to Cleveland. He came for Christmas, Easter, and summer vacations. Each time Lucie met him at the airport, he seemed a lot taller, and a little more sophisticated. He thought the house on Colonnade was "cool." Lucie tried to schedule her vacations for his visits. Brad, Judy observed, was the most important person in the world to Lucie.

It was Good Friday when Maryanne and Lucie answered a call about a dead body. A woman in her midsixties let them in. On her dining room table, there were Easter baskets. She was in the middle of making them for her grandchildren. She led Maryanne and Lucie into the kitchen. Her common-law husband of many years was slouched in the corner, dead. She had stabbed him directly through the heart with a serrated bread knife and pulled it out. His blood had pumped out all over the floor. It looked like there wasn't a drop of blood left in him.

Oh, my God, Lucie thought. "Where's the knife?" she asked.

The elderly woman didn't try to conceal anything. She went upstairs and brought the knife to them. How weird, Lucie thought. A nice little old lady with a huge knife in her hand.

"Why did you kill him?" Lucie asked her.

"Albert didn't bring home the jelly beans for the grandchildren's Easter baskets," she explained clearly. "It was just one too many times."

Lucie knew it wasn't the jelly beans. "You're going to have to go downtown," they told her, gently.

She didn't want to go. The officers who came to take her away spoke to her kindly, and they didn't handcuff her when they led her to the car. She seemed confused.

Lucie and Maryanne interviewed her neighbors, who told them Albert was a mean old cuss when he drank. He had beaten her.

This time she fought back, Lucie thought. Something in her snapped and she killed him. Probably she had never done a violent thing in her life. How in God's name did this ever get so out of hand?

Lucie and Maryanne were about to go to lunch when radio gave them a call about a possible break-in. They drove to an attractive two-story wood frame house with brick facing on the lower level, topped with a scalloped overhang. There were pine trees and bushes in front, sprinkled with snow, and an old-fashioned streetlight on the sidewalk. It was a pleasant day for February, Lucie thought as they got out of the car.

Mrs. Waverly, the seventy-one-year-old black woman waiting for them, was visibly anxious. Her daughter, *Grace,* who lived in the house hadn't shown up for work that morning. That wasn't like her. She had called Grace the night before and gotten no answer. Her car was not in the driveway. Mrs. Waverly had keys, but she was too afraid to go in by herself. Something was wrong.

Lucie theorized that the daughter had probably stayed overnight at a friend's house. She and Maryanne began checking the outside of the house. The side door was intact. There were no signs of a forced entry. They got to the back door. A glass panel, twelve inches by thirty inches, had been broken out. The door was still locked with a deadbolt.

It does look suspicious, Lucie realized, but she also knew she couldn't just go barging into somebody's house because she hadn't shown up for work.

The mother was growing more agitated. "Something is wrong," she insisted. "I know it. You can force your way in, you have my permission. Do whatever you have to do."

She had a key to the inner side door, but not to the storm door, which was latched with a hook and eye. Lucie yanked on the door until the lock broke, opened the inner door, and went inside.

They didn't draw their guns. They were trying not to add to the elderly woman's agitation. With the car gone, they didn't think that a criminal was still in the house. Inside the door was a small landing with a few steps leading up to the kitchen. Grace's boots were on the stairs, one on each step. Her gloves lay next to one of the boots. On the top stair, they saw her purse, open.

That boosted their adrenaline. They put their hands on their guns as they walked upstairs. The mother hovered right behind them. They walked into Grace's bedroom. Plaid curtains hung closed across the windows. Cosmetics were arranged on the dresser top, which was polished to such a sheen that the bottles were reflected in it as if in a mirror. A few of the dresser drawers were partially open, there were curlers in one drawer. Nothing was strewn about. The bed was made. But there was an impression on it, as if someone had been sitting there. A pair of Grace's underwear had been taken out.

None of this looks particularly unusual, Lucie thought.

But Mrs. Waverly was becoming more and more upset. She's going to have a heart attack, Lucie worried. Maryanne took the woman downstairs into the living room. The broken glass from the door pane was scattered on the floor. Maryanne kept talking to the mother.

Good, Lucie thought. Maryanne is better than I am at calming people. Lucie continued to search. She went into the bathroom. On the white bathroom mat spread across the checkered tile floor, there were a few small stains of blood.

She could be menstruating—Lucie reasoned. It could be drops of something else.

The house seemed very quiet.

Lucie went back downstairs. There was only one more place to look—the basement. The mother's panic was increasing.

"Why don't you stay with her," Lucie suggested to Maryanne. "I'll go down to the basement."

The basement steps were off the kitchen. Lucie started down. Her heart was racing. She saw a knife on the step. A steak knife. The brown wooden handle was bent at the hilt, bent so badly that it was at a right angle to the four-and-a-half-inch blade. There was no blood on the knife.

Something was definitely wrong.

Lucie was frightened. Her breathing was heavy. It was dark. Her eyes adjusted as she descended, but not enough to see colors or objects in sharp focus. She reached the bottom of the steps, crossed the small throw rug, and turned left into the basement room.

Leaning against the concrete wall were window screens, a broken window pane, and cloth-ribbed summer deck chairs, farther down were several cartons packed with cement paint cans and turpentine, a roll of flowered wallpaper, a pile of old newspapers, and a stack of *Ebony* magazines. A Canada Dry soda bottle had rolled to a stop in the middle of the floor.

The screens were splattered with blood. The newspapers were spotted with blood. The linoleum floor was dark with blood.

But Lucie saw none of that then. When she turned the corner all she saw was a young woman, lying on her left side, her knees bent up slightly. She was fully dressed, wearing a heavy, imitation fur jacket.

Lucie shuddered. She moved toward her. Her eyes still adjusting to the dim room, she didn't see a lot of blood, but she noticed chunks of other matter. She wasn't sure what they were.

Lucie bent down and touched her. The woman's skin was cold. Her body was stiff. She's dead, Lucie realized. She ran outside to the car, called Lieutenant Lusk, and told him what happened. He would inform homicide and come to supervise the scene. She told the dispatcher they needed a wagon to take a body to the morgue. It was not a rush call, not a situation that required an ambulance rushing to an injured victim.

Lucie went back inside. She started worrying. What if the mother thought she hadn't done anything to help her daughter. Lucie knew the woman was dead, but what if Mrs. Waverly thinks she didn't do all that she could do.

She forced herself back downstairs. She walked over to the woman and kneeled down on the floor. I have to try to do something, she told herself. I'll try to get her pulse. She took the woman's hand in hers. Grace's hand was cold. Her body was rigid.

The woman moved.

Lucie gulped.

Grace's body was moving and she was making strange noises. No words. More like little moans.

"Maryanne!" Lucie shouted. She didn't feel her feet touch the stairs as she flew up them and out to the car. She called radio again. "Get that wagon over here right now!" she yelled, thinking, How am I ever going to explain this. Feeling stupid. Why didn't I realize she was alive.

Mrs. Waverly was in the kitchen, crying.

"Your daughter's alive," Maryanne told her.

Maryanne held Mrs. Waverly as she cried. "I want to see her," the mother pleaded.

"It's better if you stay upstairs," Lucie said. "You'll be able to see her at the hospital." Lucie didn't tell her how bad her condition appeared.

It seemed to Lucie that Mrs. Waverly grabbed onto the fact that her daughter was alive, and that was what got her through those moments.

I have to go back down, Lucie said to herself. Maybe she can tell me who did it.

She walked back down the steps into the basement. Her fear had left her. She knelt down on the floor, now she could see she was kneeling in dried and drying blood, chunks of brains and flesh. She knew she shouldn't try to move her. She took Grace's hand in hers again.

"Tell me who did this to you," she asked.

Grace moved a little and moaned.

"Can you tell me who did this to you," Lucie repeated.

Grace never said a word.

Lucie kept hold of her hand. She wondered if it was the warmth of her own hand that had caused Grace to respond.

The police arrived with the wagon and brought the stretcher downstairs. As they lifted Grace up, Lucie saw that the part of her head that had been against the basement floor was completely destroyed.

Under Grace was a broken piece of jewelry. Near where her body had lain were her two house keys, on a chain, stained with blood. In the corner, near where Grace's head had been, was a big, chrome claw hammer with a black rubber grip handle. It was completely covered with blood.

The officers rushed Grace to Suburban Hospital.

Mrs. Waverly told Maryanne and Lucie that two nights before, Grace had called her and said, I've just had the scare of my life. The *Cleveland Press* paperboy had shoveled the snow from Grace's yard. When he came inside to be paid, he blocked the doorway and said, Take your clothes off. Grace dodged away and told him to get out and never come back. But she was afraid. He was acting so strange and he was so big.

Lucie called the *Cleveland Press* and got the name of the delivery boy—*James Allen Redd*. He was fifteen years old. She called for a juvenile unit car, and after making more calls, she found out what school he attended.

Maryanne began photographing the scene. She took twenty photographs, of the blood-spattered bathroom rug, the opened dresser drawers in the bedroom, the broken window at the back door—the point of entry, the bent knife, the boots on the landing steps, the purse. She went down to the basement and took photographs from different angles, of the floor, thick with dried blood, the screens and newspapers smeared with blood. She lifted five latent fingerprints and gathered together the knife, hammer, and other evidence to take to SIU.

Lucie interviewed one of Grace's friends. Grace had eaten dinner with her the night before and left early because she wanted to get home before dark. She had told her friend about the paperboy, and called her mother before she left, dressed in the same imitation fur coat Lucie had found her in.

It was one-thirty in the afternoon when four homicide detectives and a sergeant arrived. They went down to the basement with Maryanne and Lucie, pointing out where Grace must have been when she was hit, explaining how blood spatters when blows are struck. It looked as if she might have dragged herself along the floor before she lost consciousness.

Homicide detectives Volk and Cummings began the meticulous recording of the scene, every aspect detailed by direction and size, color, and measurement. The side door facing east, the three steps leading up to the kitchen, the eleven steps leading down to the basement. They measured the blood patches on the basement, blood covered an area of twelve by twenty-four feet. They noted that the victim was found with her head pointing southeast and her feet pointing northwest.

The 220-pound Redd was arrested coming out of school. Maryanne and Lucie had gone with the juvenile unit detectives to John F. Kennedy High School. They saw Grace's white and gold Pontiac Catalina parked outside the school.

Redd was willing to tell his story. The detectives took him back to the Fourth District, brought him down to the report room, and asked Maryanne and Lucie if they wanted to hear him questioned.

He began talking. He told them he went to Grace's house at five forty-five P.M. He had broken the door window with a rock and crawled in. Grace wasn't home yet, so he went upstairs and watched television in her bedroom. When she came home, he met her at the side door and tried to stab her with the steak knife, but it didn't work because her coat was so heavy. He dropped the knife and picked up the chrome hammer from the ledge by the basement steps. He hit her and she fell down the basement steps. He followed her down and hit her three more times with the hammer on the back of her head. He walked back upstairs, took her car keys from her purse, and drove off in her car. He parked near his home overnight, picked up a friend in the morning, and drove to school.

His tone was matter-of-fact. Maryanne was amazed. He was telling the story in the same manner that a kid might tell what he did with his friends one day at school. Totally unemotional.

The doctor called and told the detectives that Grace was in critical condition with a fractured skull and paralysis on her right side. The right side, where Lucie had first touched her, was so cold because of the paralysis, caused by the brain damage on the left side of her head. The doctor gave Grace a fifty-fifty chance of living. It was one week before her fortieth birthday.

The two intensive care nurses were very upset. What a terrible thing had been done to this woman. One of the nurses was Maryanne's sister-in-law. The other was James Allen Redd's mother. She did not yet know it was her son who had left her patient in such horrible condition.

Grace's two children, both in their twenties, flew in to Cleveland from out of town.

Lucie wrote up three pages of reports, all the detectives involved wrote pages of reports, describing the victim in the code used at the time: 39/c/div—thirty-nine years old, colored, divorced.

By the time Lucie and Maryanne were finished, their shift was over. Their names appeared in the paper the next day, as having found the "hammer-beating victim." They heard that Grace survived, without regaining consciousness, and was eventually transferred to an extended care facility. Five months later, Lucie and Maryanne signed depositions about the case. Grace's mother was suing the Redds for two million dollars, to help with medical costs. Her daughter, said an article in the *Cleveland Press,* had been crippled for life.

Lucie and Maryanne never found out what happened to Redd. Uniformed personnel were not often called to testify on felonies, especially not with a juvenile suspect. He was probably turned over to the Ohio Youth Commission, Lucie surmised. He'd be out by the time he was twenty-one.

They discussed the case over and over again. Maryanne wondered whether the woman would have been in better shape if she had been found sooner. She had lain there for fifteen hours. Grace must have been a very strong woman to survive.

"Her whole life was destroyed," Maryanne said. She had made a career for herself. She lived in a lovely home. It was beautifully kept up, with beautiful furniture. Now she would never go back to that house.

Maybe it would have been better, Lucie thought, if she had died.

* * *

Lucie found herself unable to watch violent movies. The violence hadn't bothered her before becoming a cop. Now, it did. She didn't like to see human suffering. She saw enough of it at work. She learned not to take tomorrow for granted. It really hit her hardest later on when she arrived on the scene of a drive-by shooting. A young man gunned down on his way home from the corner store. How was his family going to cope with him not coming home? A completely unforeseen event. A life lost. A family stricken with grief. Lucie's whole perspective on life was altered by her police work.

As far as Bob Borsuk could tell, he was the first patrolman in the city to have a steady female partner. He wasn't upset when Lucie was assigned to him. He had heard the story about Lucie hitting the guy down the flight of stairs with her nightstick. When anything happened with a rookie—especially with a woman—it went through the gossip network. He'd worked with male partners who were cowards, men he couldn't count on at all. Lucie had a reputation for doing what had to be done.

Borsuk's hair had turned gray when he was a teenager and framed his face in sharp contrast to his thick black brows. His alert eyes were a deep sea-green. Along with Lucie, he was one of the few officers who didn't smoke, and he never drank on the job. He grew up in a poor family on the West Side of Cleveland, and ever since he'd been a kid he had wanted to be a cop. He was a veteran of the riots, both the Hough riot in 1966 and Glenville in 1968. He had been married a month when Lucie was assigned to him as his partner.

His wife was worried. "If you've got this girl partner, you're going to get a bullet-proof vest," she told him. He bought one but never wore it much. It was uncomfortable, too hot and heavy.

When Lucie first hopped in his zone car, Borsuk got nervous about her small size. There was something else that distinguished her from the men he had shared a zone car with. He caught a whiff of her delicate perfume.

Borsuk found out firsthand about Lucie's feistiness. There was a shooting on Broadway, and when Lucie and Borsuk approached the suspect, a man in a convertible, he reached for his gun. Lucie leapt over the car and bopped him on the head with her nightstick.

Then there was the time on third shift when they got called to a traffic accident. They put the driver of one of the cars in the backseat of the zone car while they ran a warrant check on him. He was wanted. He had a twenty-two-inch neck and was built like Cleveland Browns fullback Kevin Mack—about 260 pounds of solid muscle.

"Motherfucking bitch," he started screaming and cursing at Lucie.

There was no screen in the zone car, but that didn't stop Lucie. She turned around and yelled back at him.

"Lucie, shut up," Borsuk said. "This guy's going to kill both of us."

Backup arrived, and they all got the man out of the car. Lucie worried Borsuk that night. She had a temper and didn't take anything from anybody.

The two partners shared a wild sense of humor. Though Borsuk didn't take to his own bullet-proof vest, he offered to make Lucie something for her protection—an armored bra. He was going to make it out of tuna fish cans.

"But I'd have to put them inside out because your chest is sunken," he teased.

Lucie had a few tricks of her own. Surrounded in the locker room at the Seven Barn by nudie pictures, she brought in the pin up of Burt Reynolds that had appeared in *Cosmopolitan*. Borsuk snapped a photo of Lucie standing in her uniform, her locker door open, with the poster pasted on it. A grin lights up her face. Next to her is the Seven Barn mascot, a German shepherd called Queenie. Lucie's hat is perched over the dog's muzzle.

On a freezing cold Thanksgiving morning, one of the innumerable holidays Lucie had to work, she and Borsuk were riding around the Garden Valley Projects. They spotted a car with two people in the backseat.

Probably lovers on a rendezvous, they decided. They pulled up. There were two men in the car. Neither man was moving. They got out and took a closer look. Each of the men had been shot in the head. There was a mess of blood and brains over the backseat of the car.

An execution. Probably a drug deal gone wrong. Lucie got on the radio and called for a supervisor, for homicide detectives, and for a runman from SIU.

Lucie and Borsuk had to get the bodies out of the car. Not easy. The dead men were frozen rigid in a sitting position. Between rigor mortis and the cold, they were, Borsuk said, "stiff stiffs." They pulled the corpses out and tried to position them on stretchers. They yanked on one end of a body, and the other end would pop back up. The corpses' cold limbs cracked and crunched as Lucie and Bob tried to straighten them out. When they tried to cover the men, the sheets flapped in the bitter wind.

They drove the bodies to the morgue. Half their shift was over by the time they finished dealing with the blood-splattered corpses. Bob got on the air.

"We're on our way back from the morgue," he announced. "And now my partner would like to have lunch. She has a taste for chili."

* * *

On her furlough in 1975, Lucie took her mother to Ireland. Right after she came back, Judy's mother died, after a long struggle with cancer. Lucie helped Judy make the funeral arrangements. One of the pallbearers was a childhood friend of Judy's, *Eric Schmidt*—a dark-haired man with a solid build, gentle eyes, and a soft, deep voice.

On the way to the funeral, Lucie stopped and bought a ham and some loaves of bread to make sandwiches. It was all she could manage, but at least people would have something to eat.

Judy's mother had been almost a second mother to Eric. Lucie's behavior struck him—despite the occasion, she was outgoing, she laughed. She was different from everybody else. They talked there at the house, and he drove her to work afterward.

Eric's parents were of German and Austrian descent. His home life was stable, his parents got along well. His father was a letter carrier, who also had his own sign painting business and worked long hours. Eric started helping him when he was about twelve, learning to paint and earning some money. Showing an inclination toward hard work, he soon picked up a paper route and began mowing lawns.

Eric graduated from college in 1970 with a degree in accountancy, finance, and banking. When he joined a major corporation in 1971, he announced that he wanted to be a financial officer in two years. He was told not to be ridiculous. But in two years, at the age of twenty-three, he was promoted to financial officer, controlling a division where most of the hundred employees seemed old enough to be his grandparents.

Lucie called Judy a few days after the funeral and said, "I'm dating Eric."

"Eric who?" Judy asked.

"Eric Schmidt."

Judy was taken aback. Lucie was starry-eyed.

Judy's parents and Eric's parents had been best friends. Judy and her two sisters had grown up playing with Eric and his younger brother. The families went on vacations together. Judy felt her father looked on Eric as the son he never had.

As far as Judy was concerned, Eric was a nice kid who always had his hair parted neatly. She simply could not see him as a romantic leading man. But, she reflected, he was predictable, he was stable, and Lucie certainly hadn't had much stability in her life recently. There would not be a lot of surprises being with Eric Schmidt.

Lucie fell in love quickly. Eric called her all the time—he wasn't like some men, men that didn't call for three weeks after a date. They went out to dinner. They bowled and went ice skating. "Eric moved the relationship right along—he was pretty intense."

Eric had never been married. He was twenty-eight, four years younger than Lucie, and lived in an apartment when they met. Soon after they started dating, he decided to buy a house. Lucie helped him look for one. They searched for three or four months. He finally selected a ranch-style home in Strongsville. It was the kind of community he wanted to live in, upscale and suburban. Modern homes, with pools and patios, were set far back on winding quiet streets with names like Stag Thicket, Partridge Road, Raccoon Terrace, and Rabbit Run. Eric bought the house and then said to Lucie, "All we have to do now is get married."

They were married on May 1, 1976, after they had been dating for about a year. It was a small affair, held in the chapel of a church, with family and about forty of their closest friends. Then they celebrated at a reception in the Marriott. Lucie and Eric took off at the end of it all for a honeymoon in Aruba.

Judy was Lucie's maid of honor. She made it through the wedding and reception, and then when she went out to the car, she broke down. She sobbed the whole way home.

Lucie was her best friend. She was the person she knew she could count on if she needed somebody. No matter how busy Lucie was, Lucie cared about what was going on in her life. She listened, she commiserated, she never criticized. She did what a friend was supposed to do.

Now, the three musketeers were dissolved. Lucie was going off into another life—in suburban Strongsville. It was the end of an era.

A year later Judy moved to South Carolina and remarried. Their friendship had to be maintained long-distance. But it has endured. "I have the feeling," Judy said years later, "that if something bad happened and I called up and said, Lucie, you've got to come—she'd do it. She'd be there."

A year before Lucie married Eric, there had been a one-month police layoff. Afterward personnel were shuffled around, and Lucie ended up in the Sixth. She hated it there and stayed only about five months before asking to transfer back to the Fourth. She was allowed back, she observed drily, because no one ever wanted to go to the Fourth. But her brief tenure in the Sixth was to alter her career.

On May 12, 1975, she was dispatched to guard a bomb site. The home of Danny Greene, Cleveland's king of racketeers, had been blown up. Greene was a colorful underworld figure, and Lucie had read about him. He had worked for Shondor Birns as an enforcer in the numbers racket; he organized private trash haulers into the Cleveland Trade Solid Waste Guild—bombing, burning, and pouring acid on the equipment of those haulers who didn't want to sign up.

Greene was exceedingly proud of his Irish heritage. He wore green clothes, hung a green crucifix around his neck. He called his own business, which specialized in labor shakedowns, Emerald Industrial Relations. He handed out green pens and decorated his apartment in green. He gave his non-Irish lieutenants Irish names and taught them Irish history, giving them reading assignments and then quizzing them. And like the police, he drove green cars, except his were Cadillacs. He believed that he could triumph over the organized Italian faction and control Cleveland's rackets.

He had been sleeping on the second floor of his Waterloo Road apartment in Collinwood when the bomb came through the window of the storefront below. Greene walked away from the attack with a few broken ribs. It was one of a series of assassination attempts he had managed to survive—perhaps it was the luck of the Irish.

Called to the scene Lucie surveyed the rubble. It didn't look like anyone could have made it out alive. The space where the house had been was a one-and-a-half-story-high jumble of mangled roof, broken brick, and torn wood. Atop one pile was the upside-down remains of a couch. The two buildings adjacent to the mess were unharmed.

While she was waiting for the bomb squad, Lucie noticed that just about the only thing that was left intact was a Minnehaha water bottle. Maybe it had been on the back porch, she thought. She didn't know what possessed her but she did the one dishonest thing she ever did as a police officer. "Somehow the bottle ended up in the back of my zone car," she giggled. Later, she took it home, put dried flowers in it, and made a decorator item.

SIU runman Howie Filler spent a whole day at the site, digging it out from the basement up, taking what seemed like a thousand photographs, much to the annoyance of Greene. He and the other detectives were looking for contraband or automatic weapons, searching for evidence that would tie Greene to organized crime.

Captain Carl Delau, head of the central vice unit, was also at the site. His tangles with organized crime figures began in 1948, just two years after he joined the department. The distinguished-looking rookie with the slicked back dark hair caught Shondor Birns speeding, refused his bribe, took him in, and charged him. It was the beginning of a long relationship between the two. The *Plain Dealer* likened his pursuit of Birns to Sherlock Holmes's tracking of his nemesis, Professor Moriarty. Like Holmes, Delau outlived his arch enemy. About six weeks before Greene's house was destroyed, the seventy-year-old Birns was blown through the roof of his Lincoln Continental Mark IV. His upper torso was found beside the opened front passenger door. A priest rushing onto the scene performed last rites over a burnt piece of flesh identified as a pelvic bone and upper leg.

One of the suspects was Danny Greene, who supposedly owed Birns seventy-five thousand dollars. Birns had earlier tried to have Greene killed with a car bomb, which didn't explode—it rolled off the rear axle of the car. Greene was said to have promised to send the bomb back "to the old bastard who sent it." Meaning Shondor Birns.

Was the bombing of Greene's house yet another unsuccessful attempt by Birns's cohorts—carrying on the vendetta even after Birns's death?

Delau was a seasoned veteran of twenty-nine years, a legend and power in the department. He was crusty, opinionated, and outspoken. He had joined the force after serving in World War II—because he wanted action. He couldn't see himself working in an office the rest of his life. Now, he was seeing a lot of changes, such as consent decrees. He felt the police department was in great need of black officers, but good ones, not ones hired under quotas. He had worked with the Women's Bureau for years, utilizing policewomen in undercover details. Working with policewomen in that capacity had worked out well.

Put women on patrol and they'd go after lesser details like parking tickets. One in ten, he figured, was qualified to work in a zone car.

Delau watched Lucie as she patrolled the Danny Greene bomb site. She had nothing to do but watch—but she stood out. She was alert and attentive. She came up and talked to him, wanting to know if she could be of help.

This was a woman interested in police work. Delau took note.

6

TURNED OUT

It was three o'clock in the morning when Lucie arrived at a darkened building on Huron Road, near the Ohio Bell Company offices. She knocked on a door. A man unlocked it and let her in. People were sitting at the bar and tables, eating, drinking, and chitchatting.

Lucie sat down at the double-sided bar and ordered a drink, though it was half an hour past the legal serving time. *Nick*, the owner, was happy to see her. They made small talk about her job at Huron Road Hospital as he cooked her a Greek-style fish dinner.

"It's delicious," she said, her blue eyes radiant, as she dug in. Nick whipped up a Greek specialty for her every time she went to his place. She was hanging out there two or three times a week. The place had no name, and no liquor license.

Nick poured her another drink as she chatted with some of the customers. With a casual demeanor, she very carefully observed the activity at the back of the room.

There was a table set up, and the men sitting around it were playing cards. She watched them play, watched the money change hands. It was a high-stakes craps game, and she noted that sometimes the players stayed at it for days at a time.

A man sat down next to her at the bar and started talking to her. He bragged about how much money he spent gambling.

"I'm a cop," he announced.

Lucie nodded nonchalantly and continued conversing with him as she finished her drink. After a few hours she left.

Don't be surprised, she had been told, if you see police brass. They were either gambling in there or taking payoffs to allow Nick's place to run. That was one of the reasons she was picked for the undercover assignment. She was new on the force. She wouldn't be easily recognized.

Captain Carl Delau remembered Lucie when he decided to get someone inside Nick's operation. He called the deputy inspector in charge of the Fourth and asked for her.

She accepted. Again, it did not occur to her to say no. She figured that when a captain from central vice calls your deputy inspector and says he wants you—you go. Besides, she had had fun working with the Fourth District vice unit.

Delau explained her assignment. Go in and sit at the bar, he instructed her. Tell them a friend of yours has been in there and told you about it. Her job was to get known enough so that she could take someone else in, a vice man who would actually play the game.

Get them to trust you, he said, get them used to seeing you there. You're not a gambler, but you're a woman who likes to stay out late drinking. Move slowly.

He warned her to keep the assignment a secret. Nobody on the force knew, except for the deputy inspector. She still worked her regular zone car shifts. All the undercover work was done on overtime, which was not to be put on the books until the operation was completed.

Delau's initial plan was to put several layers of people between Lucie and a bust, so that no one would connect her with the raid. He did not want anyone on the force holding a grudge against her.

It didn't quite work out that way.

She decided to retain her own persona when she went undercover. If people asked, she said she worked at Huron Road Hospital. Most people didn't ask a lot of questions. Everyone in there was doing something illegal, so they didn't press one another for personal information. "It wasn't like twenty questions." She did her job well. Nick liked her, and no one seemed to suspect her true identity.

After a few months, she was able to bring in John Dalesandro, one of Delau's vice men. One night when they were in there, a group of policemen came in. Lucie didn't know them, but Dalesandro did. And they knew him.

"We got big problems," Dalesandro whispered to Lucie. "Get out of here. If I'm not right behind you, get to a phone and call for help."

She went out. Fortunately, Dalesandro followed shortly.

Soon after that night, Delau and his men closed down the place.

Lucie had been successful in her undercover role—a role that entailed developing a friendly relationship with the person she had under surveillance. She experienced the feelings familiar to many undercover officers—she felt bad when Nick's place was raided. He had been decent to her. He certainly had fed her well, and she was going to miss those wonderful Greek dishes. She knew he had run a big gambling operation, but she didn't think of him as a bad guy.

Some policemen were raking in quite a lot of money in payoffs. One of them was a lieutenant who was transferred to Fourth District basic patrol—usually a sign a cop had done something wrong.

"We finally figured out who you were," he told Lucie. "We kept telling Nick that you were a policewoman. He didn't believe us. But we knew who you were."

Before running his gambling operation, Nick had owned a legitimate and popular Greek restaurant. After the bust, he opened another one, and years later, Lucie stopped by.

"I just refused to believe you were a policewoman," he said to her. She thought he was very nice about it.

Delau was pleased with her work. He would use her again.

Marvin Carmichael held a good job as a computer data processor. When he left work on Tuesday, August 17, 1976, he did not head toward his home and wife in suburban North Ridgeville. He drove downtown to Prospect and Euclid avenues, Cleveland's sin strip, just blocks away from Public Square, where one month earlier a "One Nation Under God" worship was held, part of the city's bicentennial celebration.

It was rush hour. Women in miniskirts and high heels were strutting down the hot summer streets amidst adult bookstores, peep shows, and porno theaters, wiggling, waving, and whistling at the cruising cars. The *Call and Post* called them Pavement Princesses.

Carmichael slowed his Ford down. The woman at the corner of East Thirty-second and Euclid, just down from the Malibu Bar, was dressed like most of the hookers. She wore cream-colored hot pants, dark stockings, and a turtleneck top. Her hair was frosted curly blond. But she wasn't acting like the other "working girls." She wasn't wiggling, whistling, or waving. She slouched against a building, her blue eyes reflecting boredom.

Carmichael pulled to the curb. "Are you doing anything?" he asked her.

"Not really," she said, with a shrug.

"Do you want to go out?"

"What did you have in mind?" she asked, looking intently at him.

"I have fifteen dollars," the data processor began.

"For what?"

"A blow job," Carmichael answered. "Get in the car." She did, and they headed south.

Suddenly a car pulled him over. Two men jumped out, waving badges, and ordered the woman out of the car. Carmichael was told that a warrant might be issued for his arrest.

He had solicited policewoman Lucie Duvall.

It was the first time in the history of Cleveland that the "johns"—the prostitutes' male customers—were being arrested on the streets of the city.

The struggle for women's rights was hitting Cleveland on yet another front. It began when Captain Delau read an article entitled "Flatfoot Floozies" in the June 28, 1976, edition of *Newsweek*. Feminist organizations were protesting police departments' policies of arresting the hookers and letting the customers go free. The American Civil Liberties Union won several court battles to ensure that antiprostitution statutes were enforced equally against men and women.

Police departments responded. Washington started its Flatfoot Floozie Squad, with eighteen women decoys. Salt Lake City's vice squad recruited women from outside the police force for their decoy details, and officials said street prostitution decreased by 50 percent. In Oakland, California, in 1974, police arrested 663 prostitutes and 21 customers. That same year the California courts ruled on equal enforcement, and the following year the statistics showed a balance adjustment and an arrest rate almost double the year before—461 men arrested, and 651 women.

Cleveland's police department was under pressure to clean up the downtown area. Businesses were complaining. Cleveland's labor movement was always a powerful influence. The United Labor Agency met with city and police officials to encourage a crackdown on the growing number of prostitutes near many union headquarters.

City ordinances specify a mandatory three-day sentence for prostitution, but only about one in ten women arrested go to jail, Delau told reporters. "Picking up the prostitutes does not do the job of curbing prostitution because there is no cooperation from the courts. I'm disgusted with that," Delau said with his customary bluntness.

Councilwoman Mary Rose Oakar had suggested arresting the male customers.

Delau created a decoy squad. He had a difficult time finding policewomen he considered competent for the job. The women were too fat, too old, too slow, or unwilling to work as decoys.

Lucie was the girl to help us, Delau decided. She was aggressive, attractive, young. And willing. When he asked her about posing as a prostitute, she replied with her usual verve.

"I don't have any prior experience, but I'll give it a try," she said. Later, she would refer to Captain Delau as the "man who turned me out."

Lucie had been married to Eric just over three months when she got the assignment to work Cleveland's historic red light district in hot pants and high heels.

Delau picked two other women—Sandra Ramsey and Valerie Wilson. He explained the setup. Get dolled up, he told them, concerned that if they didn't dress like other hookers they wouldn't get the business. The crackdowns would take place at rush hour, the time that citizens were complaining about.

They could not entrap the men, Delau stressed. The customer must mention both a specific sex act and a price. Valerie, Lucie, and Sandra could not wave at the men, or make any first gesture.

Once they made a case—the man had offered money for sex—they were to get in the john's car and instruct him to drive to a prearranged location—a room at one of the trick hotels, Odell's, the Garfield, the Colonial, or the Sheraton. An unmarked police car would speed up and stop the action.

Delau knew, as did the street prostitutes, how dangerous it could be getting into a john's car. There were eight men in the unit. Two cars would watch the policewoman. Unmarked cars stood out to criminals as much as patrol cars, but they were equipped with radios, lights and siren, ready for a fast pursuit, able to call for backup. A team in an undercover car would also keep an eye on the women. They borrowed the undercover cars from Central Cadillac. Delau decided not to use body mikes or tape recorders. If the tape wasn't clear, the case could be thrown out of court. And he wasn't going to risk a john discovering a body mike on the women. The decoys would carry their guns in their purses, only to be used as a last resort.

Lucie went home to Strongsville and explained all this to Eric. Working undercover is a definite advantage, she told him. People don't know you're a police officer. It's different from being in uniform. If you want to kill a cop, you just make up a call, you have them come to your door, and you blow them away with a shotgun. It has happened plenty of times.

Eric had been experiencing the difficulties of being involved with a cop since he and Lucie started dating. He still didn't understand the shift rotation and days-off schedule. He just said, Well, tell me when you're not working and we'll do something. When he met Lucie, she was working in the Sixth and she told him stories about hauling three-hundred-pound bodies into the station wagon and carting them to the morgue. He worried about her, working a zone car in the ghetto. But what he worried about most was her habit of falling asleep at the wheel. She would get so exhausted working third shift that she would spend the other sixteen hours of the day trying to sleep. She just couldn't do it.

Delau gave Eric a call. "I don't want you to worry," Delau told him. "This is how we're handling it." He explained to Eric the safeguards.

Eric asked him questions and was reassured by Delau's answers. Delau was supportive. He didn't just say, she's going to do it and that's it. Eric felt that Delau really wanted him to be comfortable with it. They have things well thought-out, Eric decided.

When Sandra Ramsey had accepted the assignment, she called Michele Kratzer and asked her if she would be interested.

"I don't think that's for me," Michele said. "I really don't want to stand on a corner pretending to be a prostitute."

Neither Lucie nor Sandra thought the decoy detail was demeaning. Since graduating from the academy, Sandra's goal had been to get into the homicide unit. When Delau called her, she saw it as an opportunity to get into the detective bureau, a step toward homicide.

She had not been allowed to work with men in the Sixth. She heard the women in the Fourth District were allowed to ride with men. She went to the captain and told him she needed to work with men so she could gain experience. The men were rotated through different partners; they were learning different skills.

"I feel I should be afforded the same opportunities," she declared.

The captain looked at her and said, "Ramsey, I don't want you on the car because you'll be fucking my men."

"What the hell have I ever done to deserve that kind of remark from you," Sandra fumed.

"My former partner was Lebanese," the captain said. "I really like Lebanese people."

Just like Parkhurst, Sandra thought, remembering her new-recruit interview with the psychologist. Is that supposed to calm me down?

After the 1975 layoff, she was reassigned to the Fifth. Once again, she lobbied for the right to work with male partners. She was put on a car with a black officer who was a deeply religious soul. Many of the men didn't want to be his partner. He had a reputation for not having the ability to protect his partner if the going got rough. Sandra didn't care about his reputation. It was an inroad.

The president of the FOP complained to the Civil Service Commission about the policewomen's lack of physical competence. Sandra attended an FOP meeting with Michele Kratzer. Officers took the mike and griped about the women. One man turned livid as he hollered that the women were not strong enough to carry the bodies on stretchers. Michele thought, That's interesting, since he works in the Second District on the West Side, and there aren't any women assigned there.

Sandra asked to be recognized. She took the mike. "What do you know about working with females? I'll tell you what," she said, "I bet I can carry that stretcher to the car just as well as you can."

The men could be nasty; Valerie Wilson called their cursing the shock treatment. Valerie's form of swearing was to say "dag" or "shoot," but it certainly didn't faze her to hear stronger language. The male officers were just another bunch of dudes. "Whatever you do," she advised the other women officers, "never let them see you cry."

Valerie started in the Fifth, on B platoon. Her field-training officer, Robert Hassel, took her everywhere, even though she was only supposed to go to evidence calls. She was anxious to prove herself.

If she heard racist comments, she didn't let them bother her. If you're a jerk, you're a jerk, she decided. There is nothing I can do to change your mind. Her bosses called her Venus. They said she lived in her own world.

What did bother her was seeing that the black officers treated the black population worse than the white officers did. "We're supposed to be here to change all this ill treatment and you are worse than the white officers." She didn't hesitate to speak her mind to her fellow officers. They want to be accepted by the white officers, she thought. They want to show they are impartial—but in being impartial they lost sight of their objective.

After about a year and a half of zone car work, Valerie transferred to the jail. She worked straight days, weekends off. That was where she was assigned when she got the call from Delau about being a decoy.

She said yes, thinking, It'll be something different.

I look atrocious, Lucie decided, as she donned her hot pants and adjusted her wig. She had gone on a shopping expedition, buying hot pants in various colors, dark stockings, and two wigs—one frosted curly blond, one a brown page boy.

She applied just a little more makeup than she normally wore—a little heavier on the eye shadow. The shoes she had selected were not too high. She might have to run.

This is really embarrassing. What if I see someone I know? Of course, no one would recognize me anyway, she assured herself.

She slung her purse over her shoulder, gun and badge tucked inside, and left the ladies room. Heels clicking, scalp itching with sweat under her wig, she went back down the hall to the special investigations unit. The detail was ready to go.

One of the vice squad detectives was John Dalesandro, whom she had brought into Nick's gambling joint. He drove Lucie to her corner, Thirty-second and Euclid, and dropped her off.

It was evening rush hour, Tuesday, August 17, just four days after Delau sent his initial memo about the detail to the chief's office.

Attracting customers was easy. Any woman in the area was assumed to be a prostitute. At five forty-five P.M. a red Monte Carlo pulled up.

"What are you doing?" the forty-three-year-old married man asked Lucie. He was from suburban Parma.

"Nothing," Lucie said, remembering her instructions. The man had to be the solicitor.

"You want to have a good time," he said, his blue eyes running over her.

"What did you have in mind?" Lucie tossed back. It was a game of verbal Ping-Pong.

"How about a straight French for ten?"

"A straight French?" She wasn't yet sure of the lingo.

"You know, a blow job," he said. "Come on in."

She got in the car. Dalesandro and Jerry Boger whizzed up and pulled them over.

A few minutes later, Lucie was back on her corner. At 6:03 she nabbed the second man, six feet tall, thirty-nine, white, and married. He worked for an automotive company, but his business wasn't always legitimate. When the detectives ran a record check, they found out he'd been arrested for robbery.

Data processor Marvin Carmichael's pleasure stop was cut short at six seventeen P.M.

The evening was still young. A NASA employee from Brooklyn wanted "some loving."

"What did you have in mind?" Lucie asked. Always be fair. Give them the option to say dinner and dancing.

"How about a half and half for twenty?" he suggested.

Lucie pressed for details.

"C'mon baby," he said impatiently. "A blow job and some straight sex."

It was like shooting fish in a barrel. Every man in a car was a john. Car after car. The same cars driving around the block over and over again. They slowed up and looked her over, stopped and rolled down their windows, or drove on. It became apparent most of the men had done this before. They knew what they wanted, what terminology to use, and how much money to offer.

Lucie was getting the hang of it by the time *Casey Robertson*, an employee of a carpet company, spun to the corner in a red Cadillac.

"I'd like to get together with you," the forty-two-year-old married man said. He wanted a straight French.

"It's not free," Lucie said, walking over to him. Once the man made the first overture, she was allowed to go up to the car. He offered twenty bucks.

"That would be fine," Lucie said. She wasn't supposed to haggle over payment. Boger and Dalesandro stopped the action, put Lucie under arrest to maintain her cover, and advised the gentleman of his situation.

The first night was a success. The team worked thirteen days between August 17 and November 20, arresting seventy-two men for soliciting.

The three policewomen laughed, exchanging stories. There was the man who came up to Sandra, in her spiked heels and Afro wig, and wanted to pay to tickle her feet. They couldn't arrest him—that wasn't legally a sexual act.

Valerie was having fun, wearing a long crazy wig and a short skirt, strolling down the avenue. Another man pulled up along the curb. When she went to the corner she saw he didn't have any pants on. He was a flasher. She was angry but refused to blow her cover. He stayed there, shaking himself for a while, then pulled away.

They got all kinds—from sixteen-year-old boys to men in their sixties. One man Lucie arrested turned out to be an employee in Eric's company. Lucie waited to hear how the man would explain his absence from work. He was allowed to serve his jail time on weekends, so he didn't have to make up a story. Lucie was surprised at the number of middle-class professional men they picked up.

Sometimes Delau changed tactics. One night, the vice squad told the owner at the Colonial Motel to give them a room for the night, and they sent Lucie out to the street.

She hung out in front, along with the rangy crowd of regulars. A man made his request. She said, "Come on," and took him to her room. As soon as they got in, the vice men jumped out of the bathroom and arrested him. As she did this over and over again, it seemed to Lucie that the detectives were jumping through an awful lot of hoops. Surely this could be streamlined. But she wasn't planning it. The men were. And they liked playing cops and robbers, she decided. What the hell, they were having a good time.

After a while, Lucie began to question the tactics used on the street. The backup men arranged ahead of time where she would take the johns. Usually, her spot was behind the Sheraton at Thirty-sixth. If the john didn't want to go there, the backup cars would, theoretically, get to her in time—but that was difficult in rush hour.

The decoys tried to keep visual contact with one another as they worked from opposite street corners. It didn't take long for the pimps to figure out what was happening. All the street hookers had pimps, and the pimps were constantly watching their girls. A new girl had better pick her man within the first few days or—watch out.

One night, a pimp cruised the area in his custom-built Lincoln, warning the johns about the policewomen. When he saw Sandra Ramsey walking along Cedar Avenue, he jumped out of the car and waved his fist in her face. "I'm going to get you," he threatened. "I'm going to mess up that pretty face of yours."

It was early on a September evening when a man pulled up to Lucie in an Oldsmobile. He told her he'd pay twenty dollars to eat her pussy. Once she got in the car, he sped off.

"What are you doing out in the street?" he asked her. "You haven't been out here for very long. Who are you working for?" he fired the questions as he kept driving. They had started on Thirty-second street, they were now past Fortieth.

Shit, Lucie thought, her lips pursing. He's a pimp. How am I going to get out of here. She couldn't see her backup.

"I got some people I want you to meet," he told her. "You're going to do some work for us."

How far is he going? How am I going to get out of this car. Lucie's eyes scanned the area.

"Look," she said as they neared Forty-sixth Street. "Why don't you pull in here." She pointed to a parking lot.

She had her purse where she always kept it, beside her, near the car door. If worst comes to worst, I can shoot him.

He pulled over.

She had to get out of the car. She reached toward him and turned the ignition off.

"What are you doing?" he said.

She pulled her badge out of her purse. "Hey, pal, you're under arrest," she said, as she pushed open the door.

The backup car zoomed up behind her. "Sorry, we lost you in traffic," they told her. The pimp had driven her sixteen blocks. He had a record for assault and battery. Later, he shot and wounded a cop. She saw him around the streets for a while, then he ended up dead in "a pimp altercation."

John details made good copy. "For twenty-two men, it was a losing proposition," announced the front-page headline of the August 20 *Cleveland Press*. Both the *Plain Dealer* and the *Press* were printing the names, addresses, and occupations of the arrested would-be customers. The men complained they were being singled out.

Going to court was the hard part. The johns and some of the judges were as angry as the pimps at Cleveland's Flatfoot Floozies. Entrapment, lawyers accused.

The policewomen had to remember their conversations with the johns verbatim in court, as well as all the other details. Lucie learned to keep her conversations as short as possible. A case made in August might not come to court until November.

Being out on the street wasn't a fantasy role-playing game. She didn't stand there pretending to be a prostitute on Prospect. She was a police-woman, looking for the elements of a crime.

She kept a small notebook with her. As soon as the vice men made the arrest, she scribbled down what kind of car the john was driving, the color, the year, what he looked like, what kind of sex he wanted, how much money he offered, and which direction he drove her. That way, when they went back to Central Station at the end of the night to type up reports, they made sure to write up the right case for the right person.

The squad was pushing for arrest after arrest. If two or three of the women were working, they might make up to thirty arrests a night. Not only did Lucie see the men she arrested; she also saw the men the other decoys arrested. There was no way to remember one guy from another.

Most of the johns could afford their own attorneys. The men were charged with soliciting, and a court date was set. The attorneys would try to continue the case several times. Months would go by. The men did not want to be convicted. Many pled not guilty and demanded a trial by a judge.

Depending on the month, Lucie might have worked second or third shift the night before and then have to be in court first thing in the morning. By now, she shrugged that off. That's a policeman's life.

The defense lawyers continually argued entrapment. The decoy became the criminal. "What were you wearing?" The lawyers grilled Lucie as she sat in the witness box. "Do you engage in oral sex in your personal life?"

Lucie was outraged. She looked at the judge. "Objection," she responded, her chin tight, her eyes narrowing. She wasn't supposed to make objections, but she had to. The prosecutors were usually silent. Some of the judges were worse. Especially Judge Clarence Gaines.

Gaines had dismissed charges against a john Sandra had arrested, say-ing the police had entrapped him. "All those cases will go that way," Gaines declared.

"Is every woman who stands on a street corner in Cleveland solicit-ing?" Sandra asked.

Apparently so. On November 30, Lucie arrived in Judge Gaines's court to testify about her case against *Preston Mackintosh,* a nineteen-year-old she'd arrested in October.

He had driven up to her, she explained, in a gold Olds with a cream-colored vinyl top. He asked her, "Do you want to go out and have some fun?"

"I said 'maybe,'" Lucie testified. "He said, 'I have twenty bucks.' I asked, 'What do you want for your twenty bucks?' He replied, 'I want your body.'"

Ben Kozitko, the patrolman working with Lucie that night, took the stand and corroborated Lucie's statement. He hadn't been able to hear the conversation, but he had seen her actions and Mackintosh's actions.

Mackintosh had pled not guilty. He said he had let Lucie get into his car to give her a ride home. He did admit, however, that he had never met her before.

In closing arguments, the defense attorney argued that the police had confused the defendant with somebody else.

Not likely, Lucie thought. From the moment he was arrested, he was accompanied by the police to Central Station and booked. The jail officers took photos and so did the vice squad. They kept their own photos with the defendant's file, so there would be no mix-ups.

Judge Gaines said that since there was conflicting testimony, someone had perjured themselves.

"I believe every word the defendant has said," Gaines continued. He announced his verdict—not guilty.

They were challenging her integrity. Lucie was furious. If the elements for an arrest hadn't been present, there would have been no arrest. She had testified under oath. She was scrupulously careful about making cases. She would never lie, and the accusation that she had really bothered her.

She had problems with other cases in Gaines's courtroom. She wrote several memos to Captain Delau, accusing Judge Gaines of nonfeasance. "If the testimony of two police officers who had no reason to tell anything but the facts as they saw and/or heard them and who gain nothing from the verdict is not given more credibility than the testimony of one defendant who has a great deal to gain or lose by the verdict, then our Justice system has failed the People miserably," Lucie wrote.

Three years earlier Lucie had joined the police department on a lark. Now she was impassioned and knowledgeable about her role in law enforcement. She was committed to doing her job and she was damn sure she was doing it right.

Her memo concluded: "At that point, the police department becomes a sham and a scapegoat for Jurists who put their personal opinions before the collected opinions of the Public and thereby deny and ignore their responsibility to the citizens and to the society they represent."

One of the johns, whom Gaines found not guilty, sued Lucie, the two officers who arrested him, and the City of Cleveland for malicious prosecution. The case dragged on for two years, until, in October of 1978, it was dismissed.

Mayor Perk stood in sharp contrast to Judge Gaines and others who refused to address prostitution as a crime. Ridding Cleveland of smut and sin was one of Perk's favorite quests. As the primary campaigns heated up in the summer of 1977, Perk fought for his political future by making headlines with his newest battle cries.

Perk was already an object of derision—for accidentally setting his hair on fire during industrial ceremonies being filmed for the evening news. His actions in the summer of 1977 made him a national joke. He ordered a pornography poll distributed to 240,000 households. The questionnaire was delivered by the city's garbagemen. He banned *Oh! Calcutta* from Public Music Hall, and went on to pull *Playboy* and other skin magazines from the racks at Cleveland Hopkins International airport. The term "pornomania" was coined at the National Conference on the Blight of Obscenity he organized in July.

In August, with the primary looming in the fall, Perk had opened his second front to his war on sin. Moving from pornography to prostitution, he vowed that prostitutes had forty days to get out of Cleveland—or else. He announced that he would step up the arrest of customers, saying the "johns were as guilty as the girls."

Delau had already resumed the decoy operations in June of 1977. It would seem that Delau and Perk had the same goal. But the "or else" in Perk's message was directed at the captain's central vice unit. "If police were really doing their job, prostitution could not flourish as openly as it does. He [Delau] has another four or five weeks to clear the streets," Perk warned.

But Perk finished third in the nonpartisan primary, losing to Dennis J. Kucinich and Edward F. Feighan. Kucinich won the election. Delau survived the Perk administration, only to be felled by the next one. The Cleveland Police Department was historically a political football. Kucinich put in his own chief, Richard D. Hongisto. Hongisto dropped Delau as head of central vice. The man whom reporters said "lives a policeman twenty-four hours a day" was dispatched to the First District in February of 1978.

Delau was embittered. He said then, "I'm the most knowledgeable policeman in vice, rackets, and gambling, and I did more to curtail these than anyone else. Putting me back in uniform is like putting a football coach on parking lot duty."

On March 31, 1978, he resigned from the force. To this day he remains a legend.

The controversial decoy program had given the policewomen valuable experience. Lucie gained an understanding of how vice crackdowns and politics intermingle. She felt that more of the human element, more of the personal feelings of judges and lawyers, got mixed up in those cases than in other cases.

When she started the decoy work, she didn't have an opinion about arresting the johns. She didn't know anything about prostitution, and she wasn't one to form an opinion without knowledge. Later, she started seeing how prostitution fit in with the larger picture. She would formulate her own tactics for vice enforcement. And she would be given the chance to implement them.

By 1975, the old decrepit Fourth District station had finally been torn down and the *Cleveland Press* was on the scene to describe the spiffy new station that took its place.

The *Press* snapped a photo of Lucie, as she stood in her uniform, hand on her hip, smiling up at the sixteen television screens that monitored activity in the parking lot, garage, and jail cells of the modern building. No longer, the article said, would the Fourth District police have to dodge falling plaster or cart in drinking water from nearby restaurants. Nagorksi told the reporter, "The Fourth is dumping ground no more."

On October 1, 1977, after four and a half years in basic patrol, Lucie was transferred. She was going to work in SIU, as a runman. It was a step up, into a specialized unit. She would be out of uniform, doing the work Howie Filler had trained her for, fingerprinting bodies at the morgue and processing crime scenes all over the city. She had no idea how many high-ranking officers had seen her work in the Fourth and recognized her talents, her aggressiveness, her ability to deal with people—officers who, in the coming years, would launch her career.

Zone car work is the bottom line. It is the backbone of police work. Officers working in "soft clothes" as detectives, officers who have made rank and are supervisors, whether on the street or in offices, pay eloquent homage to the zone car cops. They are the front line, the first responders. They have the most dangerous job. Patrol work is how you learn to be a cop.

Lucie did her zone car time in the district with the roughest reputation in the city. Years later, when male officers would give her a hard time, she'd turn around and say with confidence, "I was in the Fourth. Where were you?"

7

HANDS DON'T LIE

Lucie strode through the wide beige door into the back entrance of the Cuyahoga County morgue. She walked past the scales and down the stairs. She pulled out a top drawer. Out came the remains of gangster Danny Greene. He's following me, Lucie thought. It was October 7, 1977—Lucie's first week as a runman for SIU.

Greene's foes had finally gotten to him. Leaving his dentist's office, Greene was blown up via the Trojan Horse method—a bomb was planted in a car next to his. The bomb was covered with a green blanket, his favorite color. Greene's left arm was blown one hundred feet away, the gold ring with five green stones still on his finger. His green Celtic cross was also torn off and embedded into asphalt.

Dr. Lester Adelson was the coroner on call when Greene's body was brought to 2121 Adelbert Road, or Adelson's "Club 21"—the Cuyahoga County morgue.

The bow-tied, bespectacled Adelson looked at what was left of Greene. "A man goes to have some tooth work, gets in his car afterward and—bang. This is a bad business. It is a very disturbing thing. If you are religious you say, thy will be done, and if you're not religious you say, that's the way it goes."

Adelson set to work, trying to recover foreign material that would establish how the bomb was made and who made it. He took X rays. The metallic particles embedded in Greene's body stood out on the X-ray plate. Color photographs were snapped of the fragmented set of remains.

Adelson shook his head. "God created man in his own image—look what somebody did to this."

It was the day after the autopsy when Lucie surveyed the notorious Irish mobster's corpse. Always looking for the positive, she concluded that considering what had happened to him, the front of Greene's body didn't look too bad. Not like Shondor Birns. There were only scattered pieces of him remaining, and the joke in the department was Shondor Birns's body could be viewed on Detroit Avenue between Twenty-fifth and Fifty-eighth streets. They found bits of him hanging in trees.

Greene's face was intact. He didn't have any back left, but Lucie didn't have to see the underside of him. His left arm had been completely severed. She had never printed a dismembered arm. The torn end of it was red. She inked the cold fingers and rolled them onto the fingerprint card. It was a little creepy, but not too bad. It wasn't as though the arm were dripping blood. Actually it was easier to place in position for rolling the prints.

SIU was no longer in the old Central Station. Lucie now worked on the seventh floor of the new Cleveland-Cuyahoga County Justice Center, a pink granite-and-glass, block-long structure on Lakeside Avenue, near the heart of Cleveland's downtown. Police headquarters was only one part of the huge Justice Center complex, a centralized location for the Cuyahoga County court system and related services. Witness/Victim Service Center advocates, city and county clerks of court, prosecutors, probation, and parole officers all were housed in the complex, which included twenty-four floors of municipal and county courtrooms, and eleven floors of jail cells.

October 30, a little over three weeks after Greene's murder, Lucie caught a run—an unidentified white male washed up on the shores of Lake Erie. She and her partner, Detective Roubal, drove to the scene. They had just finished collecting evidence from a B & E at an Arthur Treacher's Fish and Chips.

The body was wrapped in fifteen feet of chains, attached to a twenty-pound rock. His face was smashed. Lucie had been reading about the underworld wars in the newspapers. In her flush of new-detective pride, she quickly made her own deductions. "This reeked of a gangland killing." The man's head was so battered Lucie couldn't tell what had killed him, but she suspected he had been shot in the head. Noting his reddish hair, she concluded the victim was former Cleveland heavyweight Golden Gloves champion, Keith Ritson. Ritson was Danny Greene's red-headed enforcer. He had been missing for several weeks. Lucie and Roubal took nine photographs of the scene and followed the body to the morgue. They continued speculating—was this Keith Ritson? Clearly it was, Lucie insisted.

It wasn't. It was the body of a nineteen-year-old Case Western University student who had committed suicide. He left a suicide note for his girlfriend, wrapped himself in the chains, and drowned. When somebody reported him missing, the police put the pieces together.

Keith Ritson was found dead, eventually, in a quarry. Lucie later poked fun at herself for leaping to conclusions. But on that day, there was more work at the morgue. Two homicide victims to print.

Lucie loved her SIU work. She made up her own evidence kit, keeping it in a hard, oversized black briefcase. She kept her fingerprint powders and brushes in an El Producto cigar box. Gauze and tape she stored in a Dutch Masters box, other supplies in a King Edward Mild Tobacco box. She had a pearl-handled jackknife and a screwdriver. In the back flaps she put the manila sample envelopes of various sizes and identification tags.

Lucie was fascinated with the process of finding fingerprints. "To go through a place, to dust it thoroughly and come up with prints that could ultimately match up—to take your time, to work at it …" Lucie went on and on in her excitement. Not only did she like the work, but she also thought she was good at dusting for prints. The work was satisfying.

Lucie was one of twenty runmen. She was the only female. She had let her hair grow. Parted in the middle, her curls fell on her forehead. Her identification badge was clipped to her blouse collar. She wore a soft salmon-colored sweater and carried a multicolored patchwork bag.

Runmen were not assigned regular partners, but Lucie and her classmate Bill Reese developed a partner relationship. Reese had worked with Lucie in Fourth District vice. The top of Lucie's red head came to his biceps. "Lucie and I made detective at the same time," Reese remembered proudly, his rectangular face filled at the cheeks when he smiled.

They loved going to homicides. If one came in, even if it wasn't their turn, they would volunteer. Homicide scenes were more rewarding than burglaries. They were treated more importantly. They had to be solved. The crime scenes were a challenge.

There was a homicide at Fortieth and what is now Community College Avenue in the Third District—Lucie and Reese caught the run. They parked outside. Lucie grabbed her evidence kit and camera, and they hurried in. What would the scene be—a victim strangled, knifed, shot?

There was blood everywhere. A man had emptied his six-shot revolver into his wife. She had stumbled into the hall and fallen down the stairs. The hallway was covered with blood. She had been rushed to the hospital but had bled to death on the way. The husband was already in custody. Number one priority was to make sure no one contaminated the scene.

But the scene was already a mess. Zone car officers, neighbors, people from down the hall, and the lieutenant on the scene were all crowded inside, milling around and talking.

Lucie and Reese noticed right away that one shot had missed the woman or else passed through her body. There was a round stuck in the wall. There was blood everywhere; a lot of evidence to collect. He had thrown his gun out the window, breaking the glass. They went outside and found the space in the snow where the gun had landed. Someone had removed it. They were furious.

"This scene is being contaminated big time," Reese said, his large, dark eyes burning.

"Why is this lieutenant allowing all these people in here." Lucie was frustrated.

They tried to talk to the lieutenant, but he ignored them and continued walking around the apartment. The homicide detectives had not yet arrived. Lucie and Reese were the officers in charge. "Lucie, we have got to get him out of here," Reese said.

Lucie walked up to the lieutenant. "I want you, right now, to get yourself and everybody out of here," she said, looking directly into his eyes. "How in the hell do you expect us to do our job if you're walking around here. You are contaminating the crime scene."

She had gotten his attention. Angry, he began to argue. "Everybody out," Reese said, gesturing to the neighbors. They grumbled, but the lieutenant joined in, telling them all to leave. He's probably embarrassed, Reese thought.

Lucie and Reese knew they were right. They knew they would be backed all the way to the chief, but it was still nervewracking speaking up to a superior officer. Lucie hadn't been afraid to speak up to Howie Filler when she was barely out of the academy. And she wasn't afraid now. She wanted to do her job—and she wouldn't let anyone get in her way.

Finally, everybody was gone and they began their work. It took them about two hours. They collected blood samples on pieces of gauze. They located the gun and photographed it, and the imprint it had left in the snow. The suspect claimed that somebody from outside had shot into the window, hitting his wife.

A ridiculous story, Reese and Lucie concluded. There was only one hole in the window and it was a big hole—made by the gun when the husband tossed it out. There was no glass on the inside, so they knew nothing had come in from the outside. They recorded where the glass was found, and how much glass there was. They brushed the gun for prints. Contrary to popular belief and fiction, useful fingerprints were almost never found on guns. The guns are oily and the person holds on so tightly that the prints smear, or the jolt of the firing smudges the print. Lucie took a photograph of the round imbedded in the wall; Reese dug it out. Ballistics would compare the bullet to the gun.

When they returned to SIU, they told the old-timers about the lieutenant's behavior. Oh, they said, you meet him anywhere and he's got nothing for you because you're a detective. He always wanted to be a detective and didn't make it, and now he's a lieutenant and thinks he can boss us around. And he detests females.

I guess we had two strikes against us, Reese realized. Over the years, he worked with a number of women, and he never had a problem with it. He wasn't harassed for working with females, as Lucie's Fourth District vice partner Frank Krob had been. The white men were only too glad to let the black man take the women as partners. "It was two bad eggs, it got rid of her, it got rid of me," Reese said.

Sandra Ramsey had noticed that attitude too. She was partnered with a black man nobody wanted to work with. Marilyn Mason was given two black men as her field-training officers. "Instead of it working against me, all of us got along," she said. "They were very kind to me. I think they had been through what I was going through. They had a lot of compassion."

When Reese was in the Sixth working in uniform, he was assigned as field-training officer to a female rookie. They answered a domestic violence call. Reese tried to keep the husband calm, and he sent the rookie out to call for another car. Reese knew the guy was going to go off. He could feel it.

The man smacked his wife. Reese grabbed him, and he roundhoused Reese in the head. Reese fell. He heard a commotion as the backup officers ran in, subdued the man, and took him to jail. When the backup officers returned to the station they started the rumor that the rookie did not help Reese. That is how women get a bad rap, thought Reese, shaking his head. She did exactly what he had told her to. She was the best rookie he had ever worked with.

Reese was also frustrated by the racism of the cops. People used "nigger" around Reese, figuring he was different because he was a cop. "I was black long before I became a cop," Reese retorted.

Lucie and Reese treated each other as equals. They switched off tasks, Bill doing photography on one run, Lucie dusting for fingerprints and gathering trace evidence. Lucie learned the ins and outs of Cleveland, as she and Bill drove from crime scene to crime scene. Their unmarked detective car was equipped with two police radios; the high-band radio connected them directly to SIU. On the low-band radio, they monitored the zone car calls so they would not stumble into unexpected action. If they turned on the car radio, music played over the sputter of the dispatcher's voice, which perpetually announced the zone car runs, "Shots fired ... man with knife ... domestic ..."

Lucie and Reese became friends. They were both making enough money to take advantage of good dining, and they enjoyed eating out. Their favorite place was the New York Spaghetti House on East Ninth Street, downtown's oldest restaurant. Reese smiled. "I learned all the restaurants in this town with Lucie. We just had a ball." They called their meal lunch, whether they ate during third shift at 3 A.M. or on first shift at noon. Lucie took Bill home and introduced him to her family.

Lucie thought there might come a time she would get tired of working. Maybe she would fall into the suburban housewife thing. She had stopped using birth control; she was thinking about having another child. Family life was changing.

Brad had come home the first summer after they married and for Christmas vacation. He had grown taller. His hair was getting darker. But his eyes were the same, twinkling behind his glasses. Eric was under the impression his visits would be short—two weeks. But by the second summer sixteen-year-old Brad announced he wanted to leave Oklahoma City.

"I wanted out," Brad said. "But I didn't know what my options were going to be." Brad thought Eric was pretty open-minded. "I was not liking Oklahoma at all. It was too difficult for me to verbalize what the problem was."

Brad was sure he wanted to live with Lucie, but as he said, "At that point I was getting a little pressure from my dad—'Let's try it for one more year, for two more years.' I reached the end of my rope and went into devious mode and flunked every class—three quarters in a row. So once I got through to him with a little careful calculating of my grades, he saw the light."

But Eric and Lucie did not see it quite that way. Lucie told Brad, "We'll give it a try, but if you're failing school and you're causing us problems—so don't even think about that—you're going to be tutored all summer." Lucie thought, he needs tutoring like he needs a hole in his head. It was more a disciplinary plan than an educational problem; previously Brad had been getting A's and B's and was so far ahead of the Strongsville system it was ridiculous. But Lucie didn't want him to flounder, didn't want him to play one parent off the other and take advantage of the situation. She set strong limits, and the guidelines worked. Even if it rained and he couldn't ride his bike to the tutor, somehow she'd manage to give him a ride. She wanted him to understand: he's not calling the shots.

It's too bad to sacrifice the private school, Lucie thought. But if he's not doing well, then it just wasn't working out. She was a little apprehensive—how would this work out between Eric and Brad? Eric explained it wouldn't be like a vacation, there were chores to do. Brad agreed in advance. Lucie and Eric teamed up in their parenting values and Brad had a good summer. The tutor wrote Lucie a letter, the summer was a success, Brad was a delight.

"When Brad came home, Eric had a pal," Lucie said.

Lucie was greatly relieved. She had really missed Brad. She felt good that he had wanted to come back.

First shift usually caught the morgue runs, to fingerprint the dead. The job made detectives think about their own deaths. After seeing numerous autopsied bodies with the incisions and organs repacked in bags, one runman said, "I want to die naturally. They're not going to make a canoe out of me in the morgue."

Lucie didn't mind the morgue runs. But a suburban sergeant, *Alvin P. Mope,* who came to SIU for training, certainly did. Lucie was assigned as his partner. On the Tuesday after Memorial Day weekend, she arrived at the SIU office to learn that five homicide victims were waiting to be printed in the morgue. "A typical, bloody, big city holiday weekend," Lucie said, a shrug in her voice. She did a record check. If a victim had a record, only one fingerprint card was needed. But all the bodies were fresh—none of the victims had a record. Lucie was going to have to do three fingerprint cards on each one, a city card, a state card, and an FBI card. OK, fine, Lucie thought. Five at the morgue. She resigned herself. This is going to be half my tour of duty.

As she drove with Mope to the morgue, he said, "I've never seen a dead body."

"You're about to see plenty of them." Lucie minced no words.

"We've never had a homicide. I'll never have to—"

"You're a policeman," Lucie exclaimed. It would not occur to her to refuse to do a job.

"If we got a homicide, we would have the sheriff's department handle it. We would just have to watch the crime scene. I don't need to know how to do this."

"I'm going to be here all day if I have to do this all by myself. True— you're probably never actually going to have to fingerprint bodies, but right now you're my partner and you have to. You can't pick and choose your jobs."

Lucie pulled up to the morgue. Normally, she went in the back entrance past the scales where bodies were weighed, near the stinker and autopsy rooms. Lucie thought about Mope.

"We'll go in the front door," she told him. "You can just fill out the cards. I'll show you how, and the guy at the desk will help you. It will save me a lot of time. Just do that. It's just like an office. You won't have to see anything. I'm going to do the work." She sighed and added, "I'll never get done, you know."

Mope was unmoved. But he agreed to write out the cards.

They walked in the front entrance. Lucie demonstrated the work on the first fingerprint card. Then she took the card and walked inside.

It was awful. She had to push gurneys aside to get the door open. Autopsies were in progress. Blood was dribbling into the drains. Organs were being weighed. Bodies were wheeled in and out. Lucie printed the first homicide victim. She went back to the office to get the card for the second one. Mope was gone. There was the pile of blank fingerprint cards.

Where was he? She went outside. He was sitting in the police car. Lucie queried, her hand on her hip, "What is the matter?"

"I can't stay in there," the sergeant answered.

"There is nothing in there," Lucie said, exasperated.

"I just keep thinking of what's behind that door."

"All right," she sighed. What can I do, she thought. She gave up on him. She went back inside, pushed aside the gurneys and printed the four other bodies. They had died from gunshot wounds. It was a long job, printing each body three times for the three cards. On each card, she wrote the victim's name, address, date of birth, physical description, a two-line synopsis of how they died, the date and time she was there, and her name.

She was in the chill room with the bodies by herself. Stuck with the job. Nobody to talk to as she inked the stiff fingers and positioned them to roll the prints. The work was physically tiring and tedious. And gruesome. By the time she was done, she was definitely ready to leave. She was worn out.

Mope worked with her for a month. Whenever there was a body in the morgue she had to do it by herself. He wouldn't even go in the building.

Lucie's attitude was completely different. She seized every opportunity to learn more about police work. In February 1978, she attended a one-week fingerprint school given by the FBI. Her job as a runman was to collect prints, not classify them, but she still sought more expertise. She shared her learning experience with Brad as she had done in the academy, and he tried one of her tests. There were a hundred thumb prints, and Brad matched the pairs. He scored high, getting only two or three wrong. Lucie got five wrong. "Brad, you're excellent," Lucie said. "You have a much better eye than me."

Lucie enjoyed dusting for prints. "Some people say you can't get prints off certain surfaces," she said. "You can't just say you can't." Surfaces like concrete were too porous to print. Some plastics she could get prints from, some she couldn't. On the smooth side of a wooden board, she used the messy black powder, which got up her nose and made her sneeze. She learned not to swirl the black powder brush.

Lucie went out on a burglary in which a TV had been stolen. The antenna wire had been attached to the television with an alligator clip. Lucie removed her jar of powder and brush from their El Producto box. Burglary scenes were usually frustrating for runmen. Unless a suspect was caught in the act, the chances of getting evidence that really helped solve the case was minimal. Only about 5 percent of burglaries yielded significant latent prints. Collecting evidence became more of a public relations job, an effort to appease the victim.

But Lucie never let the odds deter her from methodically and patiently doing the work. She dipped her brush in the powder and carefully dusted the alligator clip. The powder adhered to the pattern of lines. New prints popped up right away. If the print had been old, the powder would have made a pattern of dots instead of lines, making a match difficult.

Lucie saw a partial print marked by the powder on the clip. If there were enough points in it, the fingerprint experts might be able to work with it. Television shows were misleading. Finding a print did not magically solve the case. There were about 150,000 prints on file at SIU. Unless a detective had a lead, fingerprint classifiers had the tedious task of matching, by eye, the crime-scene print to prints on file.

Lucie pressed a strip of the transparent lift tape over the powder and lifted it. The powder, in the pattern of the print, was transferred onto the tape. Steadying her hand, she took a strip of acetate and pressed the tape against it, careful not to get air bubbles trapped between the acetate and the lift tape. Now she had a fingerprint sandwich, the impression of the print protected by the acetate. She marked the acetate with the date, time, the address of the burglary, and her new badge number, 954. The 3,000 series of badge numbers for women had finally been abandoned in March 1978, another result of the sex discrimination lawsuit. The policewomen's badge numbers were now indistinguishable from the men's.

The partial print Lucie lifted from the alligator clip was good enough. It was matched to a suspect's, and a long string of burglaries was cleared up. When Lucie got word of it, she was thrilled.

"With prints, it's hard to deny that your little hands were there," she once joked with another runman.

"That's right," he said. "People lie, Social Security numbers lie, addresses lie, but hands don't lie."

8

STRIKE FORCE

The suspect entered the nearly one-hundred-year-old Arcade from the Prospect Avenue side, as Lucie and her new partner, Detective Bledsoe, approached from the Euclid Avenue entrance. Booker T. Bledsoe was often mistaken for the criminal when he pursued robbers. With his western hat set squarely atop his trim Afro, and his cowboy boots, nobody took him for a cop. Tall and lanky, he had a half-crooked smile that cocked one cheek into a dimple; his lips were framed by a black mustache that curled around into a rounded goatee.

The five-story Arcade was roofed with an arched web of iron and glass, ringed with four levels of balconies and decorated with gold leaf, brass railings, and lamps. The suspect Booker and Lucie followed through the Arcade fit the description of a man who had been robbing shoe stores, merchants, and haberdashers. This robber was brazen. He worked alone and he was armed. The original description included every facet of the robber's face, beard and all; the guy looked just like Teddy Pendergrass, the pop singer. Booker guessed the suspect was six two and 240 pounds. A big guy. They hadn't called for any backup because they weren't sure if he was the robber. Now, if this is the right guy, Booker thought, there's going to be a tussle.

Booker had a tendency to be a little protective when he worked with Lucie. She was the first woman he had ever worked with. Lucie would say, "Booker, I'm a policewoman."

"I forget sometimes," Booker admitted.

"Don't worry, I can take care of myself," she smiled. Her round chin set firm.

Booker started marching right up to the robbery suspect, but Lucie took right over.

"I'm Detective Duvall and this is Detective Bledsoe." She flipped open her badge.

We-el, I'll just back up a bit, Booker thought, his thin eyebrows lifted over the top of his sunglasses.

"We're from the downtown strike force," Lucie informed the suspect. She explained their business was to stop the robberies and assaults.

"We were wondering if we could question you. You happen to fit the description. That's why we stopped you," Lucie continued.

The man showed them his identification. He wasn't belligerent, and he didn't go into the "I ain't doing it" routine. Lucie and Booker asked him some questions and determined that his job schedule didn't fit the robbery times. He was just a regular working stiff. Detective work meant running down numerous leads that didn't pan out. Lucie and Booker kept digging.

Lucie was dispatched to the downtown strike force for the Christmas detail in December of 1978, watching for pickpockets and robbers around Public Square. The strike force picked up personnel from other units during the holiday season and flooded the area with plainclothes detectives to keep the street crime down.

Lucie's new job gave her the opportunity to employ her skills at dealing with people. She went into the shops to get to know the businessmen, let them know she was around. It was good PR. The proactive police presence encouraged people to come downtown to shop.

As they traveled on their rounds, Booker opened doors for her.

"Hey, wait a minute," Lucie said. "You don't have to do that." Her red hair was cut shorter, her long bangs parted to the right.

"I can't help it. That's the way I was brought up." He smiled. He was enjoying every minute working with her. He thought, She was just like a little fireball.

Booker was by far the more senior of the two officers. He had been a detective since 1959 and had worked robbery, central vice, and homicide. He walked a beat in the Fourth for a short time, when there were still rabbits there; at night they would be jumping all over the place.

Lucie and Booker finally got a tip on the Teddy Pendergrass look-alike from a private detective agency. Good PR paid off. The real robber was more slender than their Arcade suspect, but a dead ringer for the pop singer. About a dozen robberies were cleaned up when he was arrested.

The strike force was an elite, new unit run by Sergeant Roger Dennerll. It handled street crime, prostitution, bad check investigations,
investigations into fraud, dignitary protection, hostage negotiations, and
highly sensitive assignments from the chief's office.

Lucie's Christmas detail turned into a permanent assignment. Once
again, she was chosen for advancement because she stood out as a rookie.
Roger Dennerll had been one of Lucie's shift supervisors in the Fourth.
He was curious about her. How does a woman in a zone car do her job?
Especially in a hellhole like the Fourth. Just to have a woman out there,
willing to do her job, struck him as unique. To his knowledge, women in
zone cars tried to get out of the work as quickly as possible. But not
Lucie. Roger kept his eye on her, checking her reports. He watched her
running all night long, call after call, in and out of the office. She never
asked for any special treatment or benefits because she was a woman.

He found she had a different attitude toward police work, another
way of handling people. She didn't challenge a suspect the way men did;
she talked until she met resistance, then she would back off and go
around the suspect, calming the situation down.

Roger called Lucie in for an interview to see if she would join his
strike force team. He had also recruited Lucie's classmates Sandra Ramsey
and Marilyn Mason.

"I kind of watched you handle people, Lucie," Roger had begun. He
had big blue eyes and curly, somewhat unruly light brown hair, a heavy
nose, and etched full lips. At a glance, he looked like French movie star
Jean-Paul Belmondo. "I'm six two, I weigh two hundred and ten
pounds. I either intimidate people or else they feel challenged right away.
Here you are, five foot two, and you are able to deal with people a lot
easier than I can. It's not a challenge to them."

"You've got to understand, Roger, I've been a woman all my life,"
Lucie said. "I've learned how to deal with people. I know I'm not going
to beat them up, so I have to talk around it."

Roger laughed. This was a woman with credibility. This was the kind
of person he wanted for his specialized unit.

After his stint in the Fourth, Roger had been sent to the detective
bureau downtown as the duty officer. Citizen groups brought him their
concerns about crime. But the way the system was set up, Roger saw no
way to help them. Zone cars were tied to the radio. The detectives were
overloaded with investigations of crimes already committed. When the
New York City Police Department started a new anticrime unit, Roger
read about it in one of the police magazines. He was impressed with their
approach to handling neighborhood crimes, and he and other detectives
met with some people from New York. Why not create a team of specialists in Cleveland to go into the neighborhoods—free from radio calls,

without ties to the districts—free to attack a problem and then move on to the next one. The idea was approved. The central strike force was formed.

Roger took Lucie on as his partner. In the three years she worked for the strike force, Lucie gained departmentwide recognition.

Every Monday night Roger and Lucie ended up at city hall. City council meetings were a little wild. "Yelling and screaming, carrying on, people disrupting the meetings—so we had to have police at every meeting," Lucie remembered.

Dennis Kucinich had been elected mayor in November of 1977. "How would you describe Dennis?" Lucie paused. "God knows, he's been called everything, antibusiness, antiestablishment, rogue political activist."

With almost ten years of political experience behind him, Kucinich, at thirty-one, was the youngest mayor of a major U.S. city. His youth was only one factor generating national media attention. He called himself an urban populist. He was opposed to tax abatements and other special interest proposals of Cleveland big business. He had run a grassroots door-to-door campaign for mayor, catering to neighborhood interests and gathering the ethnic vote. His ethics and beliefs stemmed from a spiritual core. His early religious training was the foundation; later, Gandhi became one of his role models.

Dennis was small, with big ears, a wide, flat nose, and full, expressive lips. His brown eyes were wary, alert, watchful. He grew up in inner-city Cleveland, the eldest of seven in a poor Croatian-Slovak-Irish Catholic family, and he never forgot his roots. He told Robert Scheer in an interview for *Playboy:* "We wore poverty on our backs and on our faces and on our feet. And it became an identical twin that followed me and the members of my family wherever we went."

He was reminiscent of Charlie Chaplin—the endearing poor boy with humor and pathos. That was one side of him. Before his term in office was over, he would be called Napoleon, Hitler, Stalin, and Caesar—at best a political opportunist. To his supporters he was Robin Hood—dedicated to fighting the rich and helping the poor.

Controversy surrounded Dennis long before he became mayor. There were assassination attempts. In January of 1977, when Dennis was clerk of courts, he and his fiancée, Sandy McCarthy, were at home preparing their wedding invitations when the walls of the house shook. A shot from a high-powered rifle had burst through the front door of the house, exited the back of the house, and lodged in the awning. In 1978, when he was mayor, the mob planned a hit to take place at Tony's Diner, Dennis's favorite restaurant. The hit was called off when the mob became aware of police surveillance. After a 1984 probe by U.S. Senate investigators, Senate sources said they believed the motive was that Kucinich caused problems for dishonest businessmen and politicians, as well as for organized crime figures.

Lucie and Roger provided dignitary protection for Dennis and his wife, Sandy. "Because Dennis was very paranoid, but like they say—paranoid people do have real enemies—Dennis wouldn't go to a football game without ten or twelve cops with him," Lucie said.

As mayor, Dennis faced one conflict after another. He had inherited a city in financial crisis, forty million dollars in short-term debt. The city's books were in such horrendous condition that it took a year for him to determine the extent of the financial problems. Less than a month after he was in office, police walked out of wage negotiations and staged a "Blue Flu" sick-out that lasted two days. Kucinich hired a progressive and controversial police chief from San Francisco, Richard D. Hongisto, stirring anger among the police. Hongisto won the Cleveland cops over, but his relationship with Dennis disintegrated, and Dennis fired Hongisto—live on the six o'clock news, on Good Friday.

Lucie laughed. "Hongisto lasted only a few months. 'You're fired' right in the middle of the newscast, but hey, that's Dennis."

In July, Dennis had more problems with the police—another strike—this one lasting nineteen hours. It erupted over one-man cars being sent into the projects. Lucie wasn't involved in the strike, because specialized units were not affected. But Lucie thought it was right for the police to strike. Sending one-man cars into the housing projects was just too dangerous.

Next, Dennis faced a recall election, instigated by real estate, banking, and utility interests. Dennis won by a margin of 236 votes. T-shirts were printed, their slogan was I SURVIVED THE RECALL OF 1978. Sandy saved the T-shirts. She wanted to give them to their daughter.

"Only Dennis would have the nerve to win by a two-hundred-thirty-six vote margin and call it a mandate from the people," Lucie said, laughing. "Most people would go 'phew'—not Dennis." Lucie thought the whole Kucinich administration was just bizarre. "It was like being in a Fellini film half the time. We were always going through back stairways of city hall and down to the garages to get in and out of the building, because Dennis was always hounded. Dennis was a living, breathing media event."

What focused the national spotlight on Dennis was his stand on Cleveland Municipal Light Company, the city-owned electrical company. The issue was public power versus private power—Cleveland Electric Illuminating Company (CEI), the privately owned power company, fought for domination over its rival, the city owned Muny Light. The sale of Muny Light had been a legal and political firestorm in Cleveland since 1904, when it was established by Mayor Tom L. Johnson.

Muny Light became the symbol of Dennis's populist stance. Dennis believed that Muny Light's competition with CEI kept electric rates at a reasonable level. Pressure to sell the company built. In December, the city was unable to pay off fourteen million dollars in notes owed to the banks. Now the banks refused to roll over the notes. Cleveland Trust, Cleveland's dominant financial institution, with nearly four billion dollars in assets, was the leader of the banks involved. In previous administrations, the banks had routinely rolled over hundreds of millions of dollars in bonds. Dennis faced off against Cleveland's banks and charged that Cleveland Trust had innumerable links to CEI—CEI had a seventy-two-million-dollar credit line from Cleveland Trust. Dennis went on television, using charts to explain to people how interlocking directorships work. Renewal of the notes, Dennis contended, was predicated by Cleveland Trust on the sale of Muny Light.

On Thursday, December 14, Dennis met with the bank representatives. Five of the banks agreed to roll over the notes—but only if all six banks agreed. Cleveland Trust was the holdout. The president of Cleveland Trust, M. Brock Weir, did not like Dennis at all. In a *Boston Globe* article, he referred to him as "the little canker downtown."

In October, six councilmen, including City Council President George Forbes, and twelve others had been indicted for crimes related to carnival gambling. Despite the charges, the business community rallied behind Forbes. He supported the sale of Muny Light.

Forbes told the *Plain Dealer* that he had spoken with Brock Weir, chairman of Cleveland Trust, about a city bailout. "He indicated he [Weir] could go with the sale of Muny Light," Forbes said.

Dennis refused to sell. He appeared on the nationally televised show "Good Morning America" and repeated his pledge.

The showdown meeting was the night of December 15. At eight that morning, there was a meeting between Dennis, Forbes, Weir of Cleveland Trust, and Cleveland businessman Maurice Saltzman. According to Dennis, Weir said, If you sell Muny Light we'll roll over the notes. I can get you fifty million dollars' worth of help. (Weir later denied making the statement.)

Dennis responded by ending the meeting.

That night the city council convened. Cleveland Trust was staying open till midnight, just in case. Lucie and Roger were at city hall as Dennis and Forbes fought it out to the end. Various plans were offered. Dennis had offered income and property tax revenues, and city property as collateral. He had investors in the wings. Nothing worked. By eleven P.M. each side had determined that the other's plan was illegal.

At 12:06 A.M., Forbes gaveled the meeting to a close. Cleveland became the first American city since the Depression to go into default.

Roger and Lucie looked at each other. "What do you think happens now?" Lucie said.

"I don't know," Roger answered.

Lucie thought it was sad. She had grown to really care about Cleveland.

"I believed I was being given a choice," Dennis said later, "that was no choice at all. It was blackmail. That because I was mayor I was expected somehow to go along with this charade, this hoax against the people of the city and deprive them of the competitive electric system and force them into a situation where they were hostage to the utility monopoly. It wasn't just the fact that I gave my word that I was going to stand up for them—which means a lot to me. But it was a higher principle about whether the people of the city had a right to that facility, had any rights at all in a public setting."

Three days later, Dennis called a press conference on the steps of Cleveland's biggest bank. A chorus was singing Christmas tunes as Dennis accused Cleveland Trust of blackmail and intimidation and announced his withdrawal of his checking and saving accounts.

"Dennis draws out his ten-thousand-dollar savings. A statement for the little man," Lucie said, laughing. "He hated big business—I mean, it was the whole of his existence, he was for the little guy, get the fat cats kind of thing, a true Democrat. He was the most honest man and he just didn't have any money."

From his election in November of 1977 to the default in December of 1978, the Kucinich administration had ignited a whirlwind of controversy that finally gained worldwide media attention.

"Geez, what a disaster," Lucie said. "It was a hell of a way to get my political feet wet."

It was just the beginning.

On a May night in 1979, Brad was the only one home when the phone rang. "Hi, this is Dennis Kucinich calling," came the voice on the other end of the line. "Is Lucie there?"

Yeah, sure, and I'm Richard Nixon, Brad was tempted to say. Brad was sixteen and ready with a million quick comebacks. But something told him that this was really the mayor. Wow. What's he calling my mom for. Brad answered, "They're not home."

"If she returns home before midnight, have her call me at home," Dennis said.

Brad left a note for Lucie on the kitchen table. "Wake me up."

The famous note on the kitchen table always meant something was wrong. When Lucie and Eric returned from their dinner out, she woke Brad right away.

"We got this call from Dennis Kucinich, I don't know what he wants." As Brad followed Lucie out to the kitchen telephone he told her how he had almost made a smart comment to the mayor.

Lucie called Dennis.

"Just a minute—talk to Sandy." Dennis put his wife on the line.

The chief had mentioned something about Dennis calling the office, something about if Sandy wants to go out, maybe Lucie would drive her. She hadn't really thought anything of it. Lucie's impression was that she would be notified a week or so before a meeting would take place.

Sandy asked Lucie if she would pick her up at eight the following morning.

"Yeah, fine," Lucie agreed. She was used to quick schedule adjustments. Sandy filled Lucie in on the details of the plan. Lucie was going to be Sandy's driver, her bodyguard. This looks like it's going to be a full-time job, Lucie realized. She was about to go inside one of the most controversial administrations in Cleveland history.

Death threats had followed Dennis across the country. Barely a month after the city went into default, Dennis's life had again been threatened while he was in L.A., forcing the Los Angeles police to place extra guards around him. Back in Cleveland, Dennis had a metal detector installed at the front door of his office. Then a call came into city hall reporting that Sandy had been kidnapped when she was safely home gardening, a ploy to upset Dennis. Sandy was assigned a male bodyguard, and his constant presence irritated her. She couldn't even go out walking by herself. At a Browns game, she got up to leave, and the bodyguard came along.

"I'm going to the ladies room," Sandy said.

He just looked at her.

"You don't have to go into the ladies room. Let's be serious."

It dawned on them that a female bodyguard would not be as obtrusive to people. Sandy was relieved.

Dennis selected Lucie.

Brad thought that was kind of impressive—they select her out of the other possibilities. It was another novelty for him in his mother's career. "What's your mother doing today? 'Making pancakes.' My mother's taking the mayor's wife ..."

Eric absolutely hated Dennis and his antibusiness positions. Most businessmen despised Dennis. Eric would have to keep it pretty quiet at the office that his wife had anything at all to do with the administration. Lucie took Eric's reactions in stride: "He was, needless to say, just about doing flips. Here's Eric, the ultimate capitalist, and his wife is driving Dennis's wife."

Sandy McCarthy Kucinich was slender with shoulder-length blond hair, soft brown eyes, and creamy pink skin. Her glowing smile radiated in photos with a Jackie Kennedy kind of charisma. Sandy was the only mayor's wife Lucie had ever seen take an active part in city politics. Unlike Mayor Perk's wife, who could not pull herself away from her bowling league when invited to a White House dinner by President Nixon, Sandy was Cleveland's first lady full-time, and had her own office in city hall. Dennis described her as a magnetic, vivacious personality, a born performer.

Lucie "tooled around everywhere" with Sandy for the next seven months. "We virtually became twins," Lucie said. Sandy had had some exposure to the political life. Her father ran for president and business agent of Bricklayers Local Number Five. Talk at the union hall was Sandy's idea of an enjoyable conversation. Her father ended up with the top position in the state for the U.S. Labor Department.

Lucie thought Sandy was fun and down-to-earth. They shared similarities in their backgrounds. Both spoke about their fathers with a warmth of memory and admiration. Both were used to being out in public. Sandy had been a teacher before Dennis had become mayor, but her first career ambition had been singing. She sang on the "Gene Carrol Show," the longest running local television show in the country. Her father had taught her old favorites like "Suwannee River" and "Summertime." She learned her grandfather had been in vaudeville. She earned her Equity card right before her daughter, Jackie, was born. She was named Jacqueline Faith Kucinich, (her initials JFK); her godmother was actress Shirley MacLaine, a combination of the arts and politics.

Lucie's background also combined arts and politics. She had been in the limelight since she was four years old, performing in dance revues. She went to Binghamton, New York, and appeared on the "Ralph Carroll Show." "You have to have lived in a small town to understand this," Lucie explained. "They had a lot of parades and pageants. The flower mart had a big festival every year. They had Halloween parades. The bicentennial for the town—that was a big deal. I got to be on TV because my grandmother made all the prize-winning floats." For the Democratic parade, Lucie's grandmother made a life-size donkey. Jill remembered riding on the back of the float, "holding a dustpan under the donkey's tail as if to catch its poop."

Lucie accompanied Sandy as she worked on city beautification projects, the Year of the Child, youth programs, and with the Community Employment Training Act (CETA). Sandy took over the assignment of making sure all city events were brought off without a hitch. Lucie knew who to call for permits. Sandy worked with Women Together, an organization helping abused women. She was involved with the Displaced Homemakers Program at Tri-C (Cuyahoga Community College), which helped women become self-sufficient and financially independent. The term "displaced homemaker" was a new one. Programs that addressed women's needs were springing up across the country.

Sandy wondered whether there could have been two other women who could have done the job more easily. "If we encountered women who were competitive we would just blow them off. We dismissed them. Both of us have the same kind of focus and tunnel vision. A lot of the policewomen that I met would never have worked out." Sandy felt she could talk to Lucie. "We solved the problems of the world, the city, the feminist groups." Sandy's male bodyguard had gotten bored at the Women's City Club meetings. "Lucie could fold into things, make the necessary small talk."

Merchants tried to give Sandy gifts. The City Garden Center offered her some impatiens plants. Sandy loved gardening and wanted the plants, but there was a problem. "Dennis was dead set against any kind of taking anything from the city, even a handful of impatiens plants," Lucie said. She took Sandy in her personal car, taking her portable radio with her. "We put on our sunglasses and our babushkas and off we went to the garden center." Lucie thought, God, if anything happens, how am I going to explain how I've let this happen. I'm going to be in so much trouble.

Judy Cooke came to visit Lucie for a week. She was about eight months pregnant. "We just bipped into city hall," Judy said. She, Sandy, and Lucie went to lunch and then off to other events. Lucie traded her glasses for contact lenses; the three shopped for them together.

On some nights, Lucie continued with her strike force details, rounding up prostitutes or johns and raiding vice spots. Lucie entertained Sandy with the stories. They raided Winston Willis's place, Goldie's, a big plush cheat spot, which had been raided numerous times before. Every unit took a crack at it, but it just kept opening back up.

The place was secured with steel doors. But, this time Lucie, Roger, and other units were on the scene along with the fire department and its cherry picker. They went in with a battering ram, smashing through the cement walls. "It was the easiest way to get in," Lucie said. "Also the most dramatic. We made a lot of dust." She had a tongue-in-cheek attitude toward cops and robbers. Firemen scaled ropes, police burst inside the second-story gambling den. In the midst of the raid, someone had jumped on Roger's back. "The whole picture just totally blew my mind," Sandy said. "And then Lucie with all of her big build got on top of that person and was riding his back. I almost flooded my contacts I laughed so hard."

Lucie and the others carted out everything they could carry, par for the course in cheat spot raids—illegal booze, gambling paraphernalia. "What you couldn't carry out, you broke." The idea was to cost them money, make it harder to set up business again. Some craps tables they could carry out, some they couldn't. "That was the night I tried personally to take a fireman's axe to the pool table. It's a wonder I didn't chop my foot off," Lucie laughed remembering. "It was a big deal. It was a big night." But Goldie's reopened within a week. Such was vice work.

City hall controversy continued. Back in January, the sale of Muny Light and a tax increase had been placed on a citywide referendum. Voters said yes to a tax increase—and no to the sale of Muny Light. Yes to Dennis. In July, Dennis went to Washington. He charged that the banks' refusal to roll over the municipal notes was motivated by political rather than credit judgments. He took his case to the Committee on Banking, Finance and Urban Affairs, House of Representatives. The staff identified at least seventy officers and directors of the six commercial banks among the contributors to the recall effort. The study tracked the actions of Cleveland Trust and found it apparent that the bank "played a major role in scuttling any hopes for the mayor's plan by refusing to join the other five banks in accepting the plan, contingent on council approval."

Congressman Fernand J. St. Germain (Democrat, R.I.), in his opening statement on July 10, 1979, warned of the power of commercial banks. "The credit powers, alone, can be literally life or death for business enterprises and individuals and, as we have learned from New York and Cleveland, for large municipalities as well. When these credit functions are enhanced by trust investments, linked directorships and other ties, the potential for power and control is awesome."

The primary, a nonpartisan election, found Dennis up against a formidable opponent, Republican George V. Voinovich. Lucie sat in on political meetings and pounded the campaign trail alongside Sandy; they were always on the run. Sandy recalled: "Never ever dawdle over anything. It was always boom-boom-boom on the rubber chicken circuit. You go from one place to the other and eat chicken salad. Cold chicken salad was everywhere. Lucie would say, 'I think I'll pass.' I'd say, 'Fine. We'll go to lunch afterward.'"

Sometimes Lucie waved to one of her old partners, Joe Russell, who was now Voinovich's driver. That struck her as funny as the two cars would whip by each other on their way to campaign functions.

"It was interesting to see a big city mayoral campaign from that perspective because I saw how really dirty the politics get and how crazy it could be," Lucie said. "Dennis would keep files on what everybody had ever said, and he would go back through these and he'd say, 'George Voinovich, twenty-five years ago said ...' Dennis would throw it up to him during the campaign. There was all this behind-the-scenes maneuvering all the time. And Dennis, being paranoid anyway, was even crazier. 'Don't say anything to this guy, you can't trust him.' He would orchestrate things. And to see Dennis and George Forbes go at it—two masters of the media."

Lucie met the celebrities that were drawn to Dennis. Australian-born singer Helen Reddy, famous for her top chart hits "I Am Woman" and "Delta Dawn," held a benefit performance at the Palace Theater for Dennis's campaign on Friday, September 14.

But Voinovich raised almost three times the amount of money as Kucinich contributors. The polls predicted Voinovich would have a smash victory in the primary race. Voinovich did lead, Dennis was second.

City politics came to a sudden standstill on October 8. George Voinovich's nine-year-old daughter, Molly, was struck and killed by a van while crossing the street at lunchtime on her way back to school. On October 20, two weeks after the death of his daughter, Voinovich announced he would return to the campaign. Lucie's voice cracked twelve years later when she spoke of Molly's funeral. "It was awful. It was really sad."

Sandy thought Dennis had lost his gusto. "Dennis had people come up to him and say, 'I really believe in what you're doing, but I have to vote for George. He just lost his daughter.' It was heartbreaking for us."

On October 30, Ralph Nader came to Cleveland. He had been asked not to name candidates that he would support, but it was clear whom he favored. Dennis, an environmental advocate, had drawn Nader's attention in the past. Nader stood in the Amasa Stone Chapel at Case Western Reserve University, his eyes intent upon the audience as he described issues of the campaign. The *Plain Dealer* of October 31, 1979, quoted Nader: "In the last fifty years it is hard to see a more consequential battle than the one that's going on in Cleveland."

Former Mayor Carl Stokes arrived in Cleveland to lend Dennis his support. In his autobiography, *Promises of Power,* Stokes called the default "a disgraceful catastrophe" and Cleveland Trust's failure to roll over the notes "a political act of unprecedented meanness." Sandy, Dennis, and Carl Stokes, along with Lucie and another aide, began the day's campaign trail with a luncheon at the Colonnade Cafeteria down in the bottom of the Leader Building. "It's a typical kind of folksy office worker, secretary kind of place that probably would not have been Carl's first choice but was the type of place Dennis always went to," Lucie said. She was impressed with Stokes. "Carl was a very charismatic and attractive man." The *Plain Dealer*'s gossip columnist Mary Strassmeyer recorded the event, saying Dennis paid for three of the lunches. "It wasn't a gourmet feast, because the bill for the three top dogs came to less than nine dollars," Strassmeyer wrote.

Voinovich won the election by over twenty thousand votes. It was the first time in forty-eight years a mayor had had only a single term in office.

"We were at the Bond Court," Lucie remembered. "That was pretty bleak. Sandy took it real hard. I think she took it almost harder than Dennis. Because he is a politician, he has a better understanding that somebody has to lose. But because it was her husband, Sandy didn't have that touch of objectivity. I think Dennis thought he was going to lose." Though the death of Voinovich's daughter had altered the campaign, Lucie did not believe it was the deciding factor in the election. Lucie was upset from a more personal than political standpoint. "I think maybe the best thing happened." After Dennis lost the election, the term of office was extended from a two-year term to a four-year term, a long-needed change.

Lucie stuck by her friends. "I took a few days of my own time and helped them clean out the mayor's office. We carted stuff back to their house, put it away, stored stuff in the basement. 'Cause that was it. Dennis didn't have a job. Dennis literally had to get out immediately. Dennis had accumulated a lot of memorabilia, but that was the end of it. You couldn't help but feel bad."

Eric's perspective of the world expanded with Lucie. After Dennis lost the election Eric got to know him and felt he gained new insight into politics. They played golf together, and Eric read drafts of Dennis's autobiography. When Dennis ran for office again, Eric was asked to help out on the campaign. Lucie said, "I think you're making a big mistake."

"Well, I'm gonna launch right in," Eric said.

"The only reason I'm telling you this is I have seen Dennis the politician. Believe me, it is not what you have seen. When you see the cast of characters that lines up for these campaigns—they are going to drive you crazy," Lucie told Eric. She was right. Eric lasted about a month.

Lucie remained friends with Sandy and Dennis. She had the ability to see many sides of a person and still accept him. "Politicians have to be very egocentric. Dennis was probably one of the most sensitive men. But when it came to campaigning, you saw a different person who would get real short tempered and demanding of people. He did some real good things for the city. Probably the best thing he did was, he forced the city to keep Muny Light. But he was so antibusiness that he would not ever see that without these big businesses to create these jobs you're never going to help the little guy. He was just—the great idealist—but life doesn't work that way. I have to give him a lot of credit; he's a fighter, but I think he just maybe peaked too soon."

Lucie had developed political savvy. "The experience put me in a whole different arena from being a cop who never sees the rest of what's going on." Seeing the city's operation at the top levels, seeing the behind-the-scenes deal making and politicking, gave Lucie insight and knowledge which she utilized the rest of her career.

Later, as a sergeant, Lucie would do dignitary protection for President Reagan and then Vice President Bush. Paired with secret service agents she coordinated police protection as Vice President Bush threw out the first ball in the 1981 All-Star game. Lucie stood on the stadium roof peering through binoculars at the crowd, searching for potential assassins as Bush watched the game from behind a bullet-proof shield. But none of the dignitary protection would ever be as exciting or teach her as much as her stint with Sandy and Dennis.

9

A WOMAN'S NOTHING BUT A DOLLAR BILL

retty Matt was angry. His main woman, *Shandra,* said she had been mistakenly arrested for soliciting City Prosecutor José Feliciano when he was out with the strike force on a vice detail. She said she wasn't the one. *Matthew A. Corbett* had driven by and seen someone jump on Shandra. Shandra was pregnant and had fallen on her stomach. Matthew knew it was someone from the strike force. He found Roger Dennerll in the Justice Center the next day. They got into an argument. Finally, Matthew told Roger he was gonna kick his ass.

Later Roger got a call. "There's a contract out on you and Lucie." He recognized the voice. Matthew Corbett. Threatening them again.

Corbett had a reputation: "Slim in the waist, pretty in the face, whores all around, best pimp in town." That's the rhyme a detective said Corbett's women made up about him. His rap sheet began with a charge for carrying a concealed weapon in 1976. Matthew thought he was better than the other pimps because he didn't succumb to drugs like the rest of them. Like his brother shooting heroin or his sister smoking cocaine. Drugs had ruined his family. So he would never do drugs.

He believed he was born to be a pimp; he was groomed for the Life. There were other pimps in his family, not his immediate family, but in his bloodline. One in Tennessee, one in Akron. "I didn't have no education. I always had a dream of being rich. I wanted to be somebody." The Life was about flash. He bought cocky jewelry and wore his hair permed, the top locks streaked with blond. He tucked his silk shirt into tight jeans, his reptile shoes finished the image. He stood six three with a slim, broad-shouldered build at 165 pounds. He had a young, sweet look about him. Charming. Cocky. Devilish. His eyebrows were thin and he had a faint mustache.

What pushed him to threaten to kill two police officers? Where could it lead? Shoot a cop and the whole force would be on the street.

It wasn't overprotection of his prostitute, though she was pregnant. A story Corbett tells exemplifies his attitude toward his women. When someone was breaking into his home, Corbett grabbed for his gun under the mattress. He and his woman made their way down the stairs.

She said, "Well, Matthew, you can go down first—you the one's got the gun."

He pushed her down the steps. "You go first 'cause I can get another whore."

No. It wasn't for the defense of his whore, that he made the threat.

Things had changed on the stroll. That's what had Corbett mad. He hadn't been bothered much by the Third District vice men. He thought they didn't really care. They might take three or four girls in and then go get drunk. Then he saw someone come out with this group called the strike force. "And man—where did y'all come from? Shit."

Matthew pulled up behind a bar on the stroll, the track as some of his ho's called it, and he let his girls out of the car.

Roger and Lucie saw him and yelled, "Hey you, there's four girls here—c'mon, let's go."

"Took them all to jail," Matthew snapped. "Friday night. You ain't getting out 'til Monday. Goddamn ..." His eyes turned steely and his jawline tightened. "I'm mad. Shut me down for the whole weekend."

He had two kinds of women. One kind was a flatbacker, a woman that just turned dates. The other kind they called thieves. Thieves turned dates with the intention of pickpocketing. "Now, if I've got five thieves and one flatbacker—who do you think I'm going to value the most? I'm gonna value the thieves because the thieves gonna come in with ten thousand, a million dollars' worth. This flatbacker's only gonna cut me five hundred to one thousand. Big shit."

His ho's each brought in between two to three hundred a night, sometimes four. Sometimes they might bring in more, maybe hit a jackpot. They worked seven days a week, usually from nine at night to four in the morning. He let them keep the one-dollar bills. He might give them twenty dollars a day—spending money. Corbett was raking in anywhere from two hundred thousand to eight hundred seventy-five thousand dollars per year, depending on how many women were working for him. Usually he had five or six women working, and at one time he had eleven.

"Huh! They don't know that my first love is money. Money makes my day. Without money I'm just as grouchy and evil as can be."

No, to Pretty Matt, a woman wasn't a sex object. A woman's nothin' but a dollar bill.

And the strike force was costing him money.

The order had come to the strike force during Mayor Dennis Kucinich's term in office. Eliminate the problem of downtown prostitution, especially on Prospect and Euclid avenues. The Prospect Avenue Merchants Association had complained. Roger thought, How bad can it be? Tucked away inside the detective bureau, he had not observed—nor could he have ever imagined—what he saw the first night he drove down at three o'clock in the morning when he and Lucie went for a tour.

One hundred years earlier, Euclid Avenue was known as Millionaire's Row—home to magnates like John D. Rockefeller and Samuel Mather. The tree-lined avenue was replete with elegant mansions—gabled Victorians, Georgians, white-pillared Greek Revivals—set far back on spacious, manicured lawns. Euclid Avenue was said to be the most beautiful street in the world.

In another city, the beauty might have been preserved, the buildings utilized for other purposes, or turned into a tourist attraction, like Newport's mansions. But Rockefeller's house was torn down and the property was turned into a parking lot and gasoline station. Such was the fate of Millionaire's Row.

For the past fifty years the area had been the city's red light district. Among the warehouses and small cheap office buildings were peep show marquees, tacky bars, adult bookstores. Some described it as looking like a Las Vegas glitter strip. Others called it blight. When Lucie and Roger drove down the street they saw cars jammed bumper to bumper, rush hour traffic at three A.M. There were forty or fifty hard-core prostitutes working. Roger could not believe it. They were performing oral sex on guys, lifting a john's wallet, anything you could imagine—in the streets, in the cars, out in the open. He said, "I thought this was going to be easy." He shook his head. Pimps waited on the sidelines, jumping in and beating up someone if necessary. The next day Roger told the chief they might get a plane to come in low with napalm or something to eliminate them all at once. He had to have a sense of humor about it.

For three or four months, the strike force cracked down on downtown prostitution. Roger pulled two men from each of the district strike force units to add to his central strike force. Seventy hours a week, seven days a week, ten hours a day. Seven P.M. till five in the morning. You couldn't buy a day off.

Lucie was standing on the corner, posing as a prostitute. From across the street, Matthew Corbett watched her work.

His skin was caramel-colored and smooth, his eyes were large, chocolate brown. Corbett saw the johns—as the police called them—ride by and solicit her. He was shaking his head. Like, if they only knew. His lips quivered and curled when he spoke.

The younger group of pimps came by.

He was thinking, They don't know she's a police officer. Corbett could hear them. "So c'mon baby, be with me." He watched Lucie arrest them for promoting prostitution. He wanted her out: "Com-*mon!* Move! Hurry up—do what you gotta do." Corbett was losing money.

From inside the Holiday Inn lobby, Lieutenant William Vargo kept an eye on the strike force. He had thick dark hair and striking blue eyes. Vargo was the executive officer of the major offense bureau, or MOB, comprised of most of the investigative units: homicide, robbery, burglary, fraud, and the strike force. The crackdown was very effective. The pimps were actually trying to find out who Lucie and the other decoys were. He had information that they were going to do anything they could to get those girls off the street. He had personally been approached five or six times with offers—everything from trips to the Bahamas to a small fortune—if he would let the pimps and their women operate. When that didn't work, they made veiled threats.

Vargo's uneasiness increased when a male pulled up on a motorcycle and was talking to Sandra Ramsey. The next thing Vargo knew, Sandra was climbing on the back and away she went on the motorcycle. She directed the john around the building to the arresting officers. That clinched it, Vargo thought, they had to put the clamps down. Their tactics were dangerous for the decoys.

Roger called a meeting. "What do we have to do to provide safety for you?" he asked Lucie and Sandra. Lucie knew getting in the car with the john was dangerous. She was nervous doing it. For one thing the john could be a pimp. She and Sandra had both been threatened by pimps when they worked for Delau. It wasn't unusual to confiscate weapons—guns and knives—when they busted the johns.

Roger saw how the situation could deteriorate rapidly. "After a few seconds, the john realizes that he doesn't have a prostitute. He has a policewoman. He panics. The man's whole life flashes in front of him. He's probably a suburban white male with two point six kids or whatever, and he's down in the inner city looking for prostitutes. Now, he realizes his wife is going to find out. His job, his life are in ruins. So the gas pedal goes down to the floor and he's gone. Suburban male panic."

They all tossed around ideas and came up with a strategy. The decoy would lean into the car and have the conversation. As soon as she made the case, she would put her hand up on the hood of the car. That was the signal—the guys would swoop down.

Detective Bill Reiber suggested parking a van right across the street from the decoys, so the officers could watch their every move and radio to backup. "Lucie, talking to a white male in a gray Chevy." Step by step, the backup cars and the rest of the team would be informed of what was going on. The response would be immediate. Reiber understood the danger. He was often used on john details. With his mild-mannered and somewhat frumpy affect, hookers usually felt sorry for him. His gold-rimmed glasses framed what Matthew Corbett called his "papa eyes." One hooker called him "dorky."

Lucie changed the clothes that she wore. She purposely dressed conservatively. "I got a lot smarter about it—not just how it sounded in court, but I would go out to the community and lend validity to what the business people were saying: if you are in the area, people will assume you are a prostitute. Secretaries, clerical people were all being harassed by the johns. If I take a step out of the car and stand on the street, I get solicited. We got way past the idea of what a prostitute looks like."

They put their new system into play. No getting into the cars. Television crews followed them, from the strike force office where they made their plans, out onto the street.

Lucie stood on her corner as a car drove up. She leaned into the car, talking to a man. Booker Bledsoe was nearby, his trademark cowboy hat perched on his head, watching Lucie through his dark glasses. He couldn't hear the conversation. Casually, she put her hand up on the hood of the car.

"It's a go," Booker said into his portable radio. He jumped out from behind the bushes and ran, his long, thin legs racing across the street. He pulled the guy out of the car and placed him under arrest. A zone car screeched up. Lucie ran off, melting into the crowd, as if she were a hooker scared away by the police.

A television van moved in. As the john was handcuffed, bright lights flooded over him, a minicam aimed at his face.

"I was just offering her a ride," the men protested. "She's a friend of mine." Belligerent. Drunk. Some had drugs. Tow trucks hooked up their cars and took them away.

Lucie was back to her corner in a matter of minutes. Another car pulled right over. Booker laughed. It was so funny. Arrest one guy and another one pulls right up, unbelievable—with the zone car right there. What do these guys use for brains?

Roger liked being out there with the high-profile TV coverage, arguing with pimps, hauling prostitutes and johns in under the camera's eye. But it didn't endear him to the prostitutes. Most had children; they were embarrassed. The prostitutes had no respect for Roger's tactics. They had enough problems just trying to raise their kids. Roger was just this big ole macho man, said one prostitute.

Lucie preferred a low-key media approach. The media could be used to educate the public. She wanted serious treatment, not theatrics. But she was on television often, cameras panning over her as she walked the street. Lucie thought Eric was embarrassed by it. She always tried to warn him when she was going to be on. People said to him—saw your wife on TV. There was a lot of notoriety.

Lucie talked to the prostitutes in the street and at the station. She established information networks. They called her when they needed advice. She was good at listening. When a hooker told her a problem, she focused all her attention on her. Lucie's attitude was caring. Lucie was a stable person in an unstable world, one prostitute said.

Lucie saw the downward spiral of their lives. *Jenny* was a tall, white girl with long, straight brown hair parted down the middle. She had a relaxed comfortable look about her. She told Lucie she had been asked to go to dinner one night with a bunch of guys, acquaintances of hers. They needed women at dinner to accompany some businessmen. After she did that a couple of times, one of the guys said, "We'll pay you for sex." She just kind of fell into it.

"The bad thing was," Lucie observed, "a lot of the girls started out as call girls, a setup of sorts, an escort service, and then they'd keep lowering their standards. Pretty soon they were walking Prospect Avenue. Which is about as low as you can get in the hierarchy of prostitution," Lucie concluded. It was the classic case of low self-esteem.

The prostitutes encountered dangerous situations—johns who were violent. After several women had a problem with the same customer, they spread the word to the other hookers: watch it, he was back again last night. Lucie could keep tabs on the criminals through the prostitutes. One told her, "This guy had a gun and he wanted to put it in my vagina and threatened to pull the trigger."

Nikki looked like she was twelve years old. She got all the crazies. She was strung out on drugs for years. Her slender legs and fair-skinned face were gaunt from shooting. Her black hair hung against hollow cheeks. Her hands were swollen from the needles. "I was dying, I was seventy-five pounds. I was having seizures right and left. Couldn't take no more. I prayed to God and he helped me. A lot of hookers are very religious, I mean inside."

Nikki had trouble with cops. "Like the Third District vice that try to watch too much TV, talk too much shit. They're real sarcastic. They talk a

lot about sex and other stuff." She didn't bother to report it when she
was gang raped. What was the point?

It was a cop who gave Treetop trouble. He pulled her into his car,
"I'm a cop. You suck me." He locked her in with him and pulled behind
George's diner at Fortieth and Euclid. She grabbed the keys, threw them
out the window, and ran. Treetop was a white girl from South Carolina.
She was called Treetop because of her height, she was five foot eleven
with shoulder-length fluffy blond hair and green eyes.

Treetop had spunk and was adamant about her work. The tax payers
could have their money better spent than on the strike force arresting her.
"It's my body." She thought it was better than giving it away, like her
girlfriends did. But Lucie was all right. She was respectful. Lucie did
something for Sergeant Dennerll—an improvement, Treetop said. She
called them Mr. D. and Mrs. L.

Roger and Lucie were well aware of the hookers' problems with cops.
Roger sent detectives out in groups of men and women. "There was
never a question of what we were doing, the prostitutes would know
that—right away. They know you're doing your job. If you're legitimate,
they don't mind. They have a problem if you play games with them."
Everyone questioned a man and woman working together. Cops did.
Prostitutes did. At first. But Lucie and Roger were receiving excellent
information. Information other cops didn't get.

Word on the street through other hookers was that Pretty Matt had a
torture chamber in his basement. Nikki knew Pretty Matt's "family"—all
his women. "Girls wouldn't even take his bonds, 'cause they would be
afraid to come out of jail, 'cause if you went to jail you would get beat up.
He was crazy," Nikki said, "real crazy." Nikki had seen their bruises, beatings with coat hangers. "That was common for a lot of girls to get abused
like that."

Lucie thought if there was one thing pimps were good at it was how
to get to women. They just knew exactly what buttons to push, and they
seemed to know which women were most vulnerable: "This guy moves
in, he's gonna be the father, the boyfriend, the lover, the friend, anything
you want—here I am. I'm Mr. Slick. The pimp gets these vulnerable
women, and they're history. No doubt about it, they're real psychologists
when it comes to these women."

Lucie didn't get tangled up in the emotional aspects of it. She
thought about solving the overall problem, not one individual case. She
did whatever was necessary to allow these girls to feel they could come in
and talk. That's what could eventually get a conviction on their pimps.
Finally, they would realize, Somebody is gonna listen to me. They'd never
had the opportunity to get away from this guy. Every time they tried to

get away, he beat them up or threatened to keep their kids. They would die for him.

Lucie talked to all the prostitutes on a regular basis about turning in their pimps. She gave them the same message over and over again. This is a downhill road. You're just being used. You shouldn't live like this. You deserve a better life.

One conviction could lead to another, when the man that seemed so invincible was put into jail. Others would follow. Hookers might see something could be done, some cops were on their side.

But Lucie quickly realized that sporadic enforcement—hitting the streets when the politicians became concerned and then moving on to other jobs—was just not going to work. She wasn't satisfied with seeing how many women she could put in jail for the weekend. She wanted to effect change that would last, that had substance. She wanted to clean up the downtown area for good. No one had managed to do that in fifty years.

The laws made it difficult. Usually, the prostitutes were arrested on a felony, promoting prostitution. "Basically, they were bad arrests, false arrests, right from the getgo," Lucie said. "There was no question that you could not prove the elements of the crime. They were not there. Prostitution was engaging in sexual activity for hire. The cop would have to engage in the sexual activity with them to make the charge. The cops couldn't do that. With a felony, you're not eligible for bond until the detective does a follow-up investigation and makes a presentation of the facts to the prosecutor. These girls would be arrested on a Friday night, and the prosecutor consulted on Monday morning. But there was never sufficient evidence, and we knew it going in." The prosecutor threw the cases out. The hookers never got near a courtroom. They never even had a record of being charged with a crime. Arresting them on promoting was just a quick fix to get them off the streets for the weekend.

The system was fraught with corruption. There were defense lawyers who charged the hookers sex in lieu of a cash fee; there were cops in the Third District—the downtown district—who warned the hookers when Lucie and Roger were on the way. There were cops who had sex with the prostitutes; cops who demanded a cut of their money in exchange for not being arrested. There were councilmen who renewed bars' liquor licenses year after year—even though the bars were known to harbor gambling and prostitution. There were businessmen who made profits off the prostitution trade—trick hotels, restaurants where the hookers ate.

Corbett bragged that his girls got arrested three hundred times and never spent a day in jail. He knew international bondsmen. The best in the business. No matter where his girls were arrested, whether in Florida or Montreal, he could pick up the phone and the bondsman would have them back out. "Because I had a philosophy, if you in jail you can't make no money." If one of his girls jumped bond he turned her in, so he didn't have to pay the bondsman twenty thousand dollars. "She's in Akron," he told the bondsman, turning his own ho into the authorities. "If she got in a cross over that, so what, nine times out of ten she wouldn't show up to court to prosecute." Corbett had it all figured out. So what if they got his ho to turn on him. It never got to court anyway.

Corbett ate breakfast with public defenders who one day would be judges. His bondsmen knew the judge that sent one of his ho's to the workhouse for sixty days. Matthew wanted her out. The judge said to send two hundred food baskets to some church or other. Matthew didn't know about that. So, he gave the bondsman three hundred dollars to take care of it for him.

Corbett had a lot of women and a lot of money. He had people to help him keep an eye on them. And he had plenty of time to issue numerous complaints about the police. About Roger and Lucie.

Roger's idea was to do things by harassment. Lucie thought it was a good technique: high profile. Cause a lot of problems. Harass the hell out of people. Let's make it costly for them to do business. Hit and run. The two older women who managed the Capri, a stripper bar, complained vehemently about the strike force tactics. "Dennerll came in like a storm trooper, with his flashlights. He was a regular visitor. He'd flash his light all over, trying to find something. He started towing cars. Those customers never come back. Once you lose a customer, they don't want to hear, it's OK now." Lucie thought Roger's techniques were good, they worked, but she preferred to work behind the scenes.

It was early March when Lucie parked on the corner of East Thirty-sixth and Euclid in her undercover car. In the back, beneath a blanket, strike force Detective Mike Burger was hiding with his portable radio.

Burger was the strike force office man. His wide, round face and rugged hands gave him the appearance of quiet strength. He hated to go out on the street. They didn't take him unless they were absolutely pressed for people. Now here he was wrapped in a blanket on the floor of the car as Lucie toured the streets for johns.

A car rolled up next to Lucie's. The older man couldn't seem to commit himself to a request. She waited.

Finally, he got it out. "A golden shower."

Lucie and he arranged a meeting place. Under the army blanket, Burger didn't know what to do. He was supposed to put the call in on the radio. He'd been on the job about ten years. "But I had never in my life heard about nothing like this before," he declared.

"What do I say?" he asked Lucie.

She giggled and explained to him. "It's urination."

Burger turned a faint pink. He thought it was dirty. Well, that's part of the job, you learn something new every day.

Lucie thought she could arrest a hundred guys a night, it was just a question of having time to fill out the reports. You ran out of time, never out of customers. She was solicited by the whole spectrum, from professionals to guys that rode up and solicited on bicycles.

The male cops posed as johns, and when a hooker made an offer, she was arrested. The johns and hookers were charged with a misdemeanor—soliciting. Unlike the promoting, the cops did meet the elements of the crime. But the decoy details were labor intensive, requiring backup, zone cars, tow trucks. Because the soliciting charge was a misdemeanor, the prostitutes made bond immediately, and were right back out on the street—often before the cops had even completed doing the paperwork.

Lucie wanted to do more. Mike Burger nicknamed her the Little Corporal, because sometimes he wondered who was in charge—Roger or Lucie. Lucie knew the liquor laws. She formulated a long-term plan to remove the places that were catering to the prostitution and gambling. Pile up citations, and local councilmen could stop the yearly renewal of the liquor licenses. "There's millions of loopholes," she said. "They can get another license under another name, things like that, but the point is to give the councilmen enough justification to block renewal of the license. So we can, in good conscience, request that the license not be renewed." She wanted to try to do something that had a little more clout to it than throwing prostitutes in jail. "Let's put the councilmen on front street. Put it in their face and say, Hey, you want to get rid of the place? Here's everything you need—do it."

Going into the bars was traditionally the Third District vice unit's territory. No one was going to be happy in this turf war. Lucie didn't trust the Third District vice. She and Roger never shared any information with them.

The Biscayne Lounge was a bigger club than most, a rockin' and rollin' place, on the strip. The Biscayne was where the street people hung out. The bar rented prostitutes bar stools for the night. If you wanted to hang there, it was gonna be seven dollars to sit on the bar stool. That was their overhead, no drinks included. The Biscayne was causing a real problem for Roger and Lucie. Roger sent Detective Bob Kahl in undercover.

On the job only a few years, Kahl was a college graduate, and with his hair parted down the middle, wearing a Cleveland State fraternity sweatshirt, he looked young. His build was slight and his eyes a cool blue. His voice methodical and deep. He was detailed from the Second District strike force.

Kahl was sent out johning. He would walk by the lineup of pimps in front of the Biscayne, where they rocked back and forth, watching up and down the street, eyeing their territory. Kahl thought, This is a dirty little war, and there are tricks to play on those pimps: putting Super Glue in their Caddy car locks. Or towing the car and knocking out the taillights. Then the next day when they had them back on the street—pull them over and give them a ticket for no lights. But, he realized, the minute the cops walked—the pimps were back again. It was futile. "This isn't police work," he concluded.

Hanging out in the Biscayne, Kahl saw how you could get addicted to the street, addicted to the action. If he found it distasteful, he found it equally alluring. The city paid him to get drunk and pick up girls. Great job.

Kahl sat on his stool, his gun tucked under his pants near his hip, his shirt tucked in over the stock. The old-timers told him if the girl feels you up, checking for the gun, just reach over and grab her breast and let her know, Hey, I can't touch for free and you can't touch me for free. Kahl couldn't bring himself to do that. But then he never had much of a problem, he was a good actor. After a few months of the work he got cockier and cockier, sometimes haggling over the price with a hooker.

Kahl watched a pimp with his girl just three bar stools down from where he sat. The pimp just walked over and started to beat the hell out of her. That kind of did it for Kahl. A real policeman would have gotten up and knocked that guy down. I'd blow my cover, Kahl thought.

He had lost his stomach for it. He had seen some sad talented people turn funky, turn to waste.

The prostitute moved next to Kahl. "You want to party?" she said, recovering from her beating. She added, "My first night in from New York."

Kahl didn't know what to tell her at first, but what he finally said was, "Welcome to Cleveland—you're under arrest."

The Third District vice unit was very upset with Roger and Lucie going into the bars. Lucie saw it was more than territorial. Vice men were drinking in most of the bars.

A pimp and a madam were running the Biscayne Lounge. They were doing everything in there. Mike Burger had been solicited in the bar. Five women, known prostitutes, were arrested outside. The night manager told them, I didn't see anything. When Lucie and Roger drove by, prostitutes fled to the ladies room, to the office, and to the Biscayne kitchen to escape arrest. They went to *Beverly Brooks,* the Biscayne's day manager, who was happy to offer them protection, despite previous warnings from Roger and numerous arrests the strike force had made inside and outside the bar.

One night, Roger and Lucie entered the Biscayne determined to shut down the bar. They'd had it. The pimp stood six four and he carried a small bag. Roger thought it contained a gun. Beverly Brooks was an attractive woman about five ten and in good shape. She hated cops. She was belligerent and prone to attack, if swearing didn't get rid of them first. The fracas started very quickly. It was a free-for-all. Lucie ended up on the floor with the pimp.

Roger thought it was fortunate that he had taken on Beverly Brooks. He was having a hard enough time with her. Battling together with a woman—he didn't want to come out and hit her. But it was getting to the point where he would have to. She was all over him, her long nails scratching at him. How embarrassing, he thought. Hey, Lucie, when you're done with the big guy, come over here and help me. Finally, he got Beverly at arms' length, and he looked to see how Lucie was doing.

The pimp was on the ground and Lucie stood above him with her gun trained on him. He looked at Roger. "Help me, man. Don't let her do it."

"I'm so little and you're so big," Lucie told him, "you'll never know when this thing is going to go off. I'm so nervous." The pimp was not amused, he was terrified.

When it was over, Roger and Lucie laughed about it. But things were getting tense on the street.

In July 1980, Lucie was home on sick leave for a week after having her tubes tied. Following four years of trying to have a child, she and Eric had given up the idea. It just hadn't worked out. Lucie was thirty-six, and her doctor advised her that getting pregnant might not be a good idea at her age. Brad was already eighteen. Did they really want to have a baby at this point? Lucie and Eric decided they didn't. After the operation, Lucie's doctor only agreed to let her go back to work because she swore she would not go out on the street.

Then off she went to do her job.

Roger and Lucie circled the Biscayne. It was midafternoon. Prostitutes ran inside the bar, shouting, "Here come the rollers." That's what the hookers called the cops, the wheels rolling by. Beverly came to the doorway to watch them drive past. As soon as she thought they were gone, she returned to the bar, and the prostitutes came back onto the street.

Roger and Lucie parked in the rear of the Belmont Hotel and walked through the hotel to Euclid Avenue across from the Biscayne Lounge. They wanted to obtain enough evidence to request a citation from the State Liquor Board, and Roger planned to get another soliciting case. Lucie stayed in front of the hotel.

Carmen often worked the Belmont Hotel. "When I saw Lucie," Carmen said, "I got the fuck out of the way. Go home. Or go to jail. That was the warning." Carmen was a thief. A pickpocket. She could make two, three hundred a night. Maybe a thousand, if she knocked a guy out after jerking him off. She'd grab his wallet and run out of the Belmont. He'd be like all the rest—forget her face in a few days, few hours.

If she didn't bring a thousand dollars, she couldn't go home to her pimp. So she stole from Rosa's john. Rosa was jerking him off in the stairwell and Carmen slipped the wallet out from behind. Rosa was only a flatbacker, so what if the john thought she took the money. He'd hit Rosa. Carmen didn't care.

Lucie stood outside the Belmont waiting and watching the Biscayne across the street. The hookers ran into the bar again as soon as they saw Lucie and Roger. He pursued them to the doorway. Beverly threw herself in front of him. "You motherfuckers are not coming in."

He removed his badge from his belt and showed it to her.

"I know who you are, pig." Beverly dug her nails into his hand.

Roger walked her across the street to the front of the Belmont. Lucie took charge of her while Roger went back into the bar looking for the prostitutes.

"You motherfucking pig," she shouted at Lucie. She started to fight with Lucie, kicking her and elbowing her in the stomach, right on her barely healed incision. Lucie grabbed on to her, talking her down until she had her under control.

Roger came back out of the bar. He asked Beverly if she was in fact in charge of the bar.

Yes, she was, but it was none of his business. She began to walk back toward the Biscayne.

"I want to inspect the bar for a proper license," Roger said.

"If you want trouble, I'll give it to you," she retorted. "I'm sick and tired of you fucking pigs harassing the patrons of this bar."

Again, Roger tried to get through to her about hiding the prostitutes.

"Fuck you. I'll fix you once and for all." She grit her teeth. "I'll go to the prosecutor and the mayor and I'll get rid of you."

This form of intimidation will not stop me from performing my duty, Roger told her. He attempted to go into the bar to get the license number off the wall and to find where the prostitutes were concealed.

"You can't threaten me." She was getting more boisterous and obscene. She finally told them she would not let them in as long as she was in charge.

The liquor law allows police to inspect the premises, Roger said. He asked for her name. Beverly wrote her name out and handed it to Lucie.

A crowd had gathered around them. Lucie and Roger could feel the hostility. Roger went into the Biscayne and wrote down the bar's license number and they left. They didn't want the situation to get out of control.

Lucie and Roger consulted with the prosecutor, and he issued papers for Beverly's arrest. Obstructing official police business, two counts of assault on a law enforcement officer on duty, and obstructing hindering search of premises. Booker Bledsoe and another strike force detective took the warrant and arrested her.

Lucie had been hurt in the confrontation. Her abdomen was sore. The doctor at the medical unit was concerned about internal damage and bleeding. He told her to go home and stay flat on her back for four days, until he was sure she was not going to have any other symptoms.

Lucie recovered and went back to work. Frustrated. Progress was slow with bar citations. She wanted to attack the problem both inside the bars and on the streets. She needed the laws changed. Something to keep the prostitutes from getting back out so soon, or better yet, hit them in the pimps' pocketbook. Bigger fines. But how could anything be done if the prosecutors and judges didn't take things seriously? If they didn't see the magnitude of the problem?

She decided to get the city's Chief Prosecutor José C. Feliciano to pay attention.

José Feliciano was born in Yauco, Puerto Rico, and raised in Cleveland. He was tall, strikingly handsome, with a wide forehead and stiff black mustache. On the back of his office door, he hung his children's fingerpaintings.

Feliciano knew both sides of the trial table. He had been a public defender. He had lost the romantic notion he started with, of gaining an acquittal of an innocent person through his eloquence before the jury. Clients, he found, were not very truthful. Now, Feliciano looked at the entire city's problems. Homicide rates were among the highest in the country. He had been approached by other officers about pornography enforcement, and he couldn't see how the city would get "our bang for our buck" pursuing that issue. He didn't see prostitution in a much different light. "There's got to be a lot more important things to do than spend a lot of time on prostitution."

Lucie stood outside his office, with about a hundred cases she wanted to go over with him.

She and Roger were having problems on the streets, she explained. The pimps were retaliating against the strike force crackdown by making phony complaints about them. In one week, there were eight complaints of brutality, complaints that they were snatching people up for no reason at all, most of them from Matthew Corbett.

Feliciano finally agreed to pacify Lucie and Roger. He said, "I'll go out with you to get a feel for the problem." What they were describing to him just didn't make sense. They must be overstating their case. They didn't tell Feliciano he was going to be the john.

Lucie followed them in a car. Feliciano drove with Roger and another detective in the rear of the van.

"You drive. We'll be in the back," Roger said.

They were concealed by rug-covered windows. Down the marquee-lit street Feliciano drove. He thought Lucie and Roger were very creative to put him in this direct action position. He circled the block. It was as bad as they were saying. If not worse. He saw hookers everywhere.

One came up to the van. "Do you want to have a good time?"

"What do you mean a good time?" he answered, in good undercover cop style.

"Well, sucker, what do you think you're down here for?"

What was he going to do? He thought, I can't say, Would you perform the following sexual services. He went around the block again. The hookers knew exactly what to do, he realized, it was as if they had their lawyers next to them on the street. They came just short of the line that would put them in jail.

Another young woman approached him. "Do you want to have a good time?"

By now he was getting involved in the process. "Well, look. I've never really done this before." Why not try the truth? "I'm kind of nervous." He certainly was nervous.

"Oh, honey, I'll take care of you." She smiled.

He sunk as he felt his betrayal of her. The hooker spun off amounts and what she would do for him. Here she was, trying to help him out. But as quickly as the words were out of her mouth, the detectives sprung out of the van and arrested her.

Each time they stopped in an area, Feliciano saw a pocket of men, waiting to rob the johns. If they had been advertising, it couldn't have been more obvious. Prostitution was just the tip of the iceberg, he realized. Narcotics and robberies were entwined with it. This was not a crime in the abstract.

Roger and Lucie had convinced him. He now believed they needed to concentrate some effort on prostitution. Develop some initiatives to solve the problem.

"Sure enough, the next day, a brutality complaint comes in about this guy, and they describe José Feliciano to a T, right down to what he was wearing." Lucie laughed. The complaint said that the described undercover officer had beaten them up while arresting them.

"I can't believe this. This is ridiculous. This is me they are talking about." Feliciano was astounded.

He thought that, if anything, the officers had treated the suspects with kid gloves just because he was there. It certainly showed how egregious people were with complaints against police officers as a defense of the underlying crimes. He now could really appreciate the abuse of the system that was going on. Each time there was a complaint, the detective had to type out a long report.

Lucie was relieved. "So, naturally the police department just laughed off the complaints." She smirked. "And we just kept throwing whores in jail."

Corbett didn't laugh. That was the final harassment. His complaints weren't working. Nothing was getting the strike force off the street. On top of it all, his main woman, Shandra, had been arrested for soliciting Feliciano. Shandra said it was a mistake. Corbett challenged Roger at the Justice Center after the incident with Feliciano and Shandra. Then he called and told Roger a contract was out on him and Lucie.

Lucie didn't have time to get scared. She and Roger went downstairs to the first floor. There was Matthew Corbett—calling with threats to do bodily harm to them right from the courthouse pay phones. They placed him under arrest for aggravated menacing.

Corbett was convicted and sentenced to eighteen months. Euclid and Prospect were getting cleared of a few of their pimps.

On September 3, the liquor inspector advised the manager of the Biscayne of the violations that resulted from Lucie and Roger's investigation. Beverly Brooks was convicted of assaulting a police officer. Lucie had recovered from Brooks's assault, but five days after the liquor inspector visited the Biscayne, Lucie received another kind of blow—which upset her far more.

10

THE FIFTH

Lucie was mad. Mad as hops. Her cheeks flushed as she stared at her name on Departmental Order 80-247, which had just come down from Chief Hanton's office. Ninety-eight officers were reassigned, many shifted from specialized units to the districts. Lucie was dumped out to the Fifth District, back to basic patrol.

Chief Hanton would have a tremendous impact on Lucie's career. He would become her mentor and give her opportunities afforded no other woman in the history of the Cleveland Police Department. But on September 8, 1980, she was furious at him.

She didn't like this transfer one bit. She had done her zone car time. Since then, she had developed more skills—vice enforcement, dignitary protection, crisis negotiations. She wanted to continue gaining new knowledge, employing her expertise, meeting the challenge of the strike force. Her jaw tightened as the realization hit. She was being forced back to the job she did as a rookie.

On top of everything else, the Fifth District station was twenty-six miles from her home in Strongsville. She was bitter.

She was transferred because she and Roger had tried to close the Biscayne Lounge. She was sure of that. Rumor had it the bar owners were paying off a high-ranking officer. Other cops razzed Lucie when she got to the Fifth. Jesus. What the hell did you think, you closed down that place. Did you really think you were going to get away with that.

Thirty or forty years earlier, big city police departments ran on graft and corruption. It wasn't considered graft—it was the way law enforcement had functioned, until you got some of the Serpicos, then methods started to change. The transition period was the sixties and the seventies. But some of the old-timers were not about to give up those old ways. And she was taking the fall.

Lucie's former partner in Fourth District vice, Billy Riedthaler, was also sent to the Fifth. Rumors rampaged about his transfer. Riedthaler had been named the Cleveland Exchange Club Patrolman of the Year in 1979 for his work in a carnival kickback investigation in which George Forbes and city council members were indicted. The carnivals targeted poor black and Appalachian neighborhoods, bringing in illegal gambling and rigged games—where players blew their salaries and subsidy checks trying to win desperately needed cash. A ten-year-old was killed on a Ferris wheel because it was placed too close to another ride. Council members were accused of taking bribes to allow the carnivals to run in their wards; Forbes was also accused of threatening cops not to investigate citizen complaints. But the police did investigate, and the result was the largest number of public officials ever indicted in a single sweep in Ohio. It was another major crisis that hit the city during the Dennis Kucinich administration. The business community—virulently opposed to Dennis—rallied behind their ally, Forbes. A judge was brought in from Columbus to preside over the trial. The final outcome was a blow to Billy Riedthaler and the other investigators—Forbes was acquitted and the other council members were either acquitted, or the charges were dropped.

And in September of 1980, Billy, like Lucie, found himself back out in basic patrol. Was his reassignment connected to the carnival investigation—even though the transfer occurred about seven months after the trial was over? Lucie and other cops were certain of it.

There had been forewarning of the ninety-eight transfers. On January 9, 1980, the new mayor, George Voinovich, swore in the new chief of police. William T. Hanton was distinguished-looking, with wavy brown hair, and dark-rimmed glasses. During his tenure as chief, just about every workday at four-thirty, he slipped on shorts and a T-shirt, walked from his ninth floor command post down to the eighth floor, and ran several miles on the makeshift track. "If you can't walk away for five minutes, shame on you," was his philosophy. His body was taut, his demeanor stern and vigorous, his voice resonated with a rich timbred pitch. He exuded confidence, self-control, and power. He was fifty-one years old and had twenty-nine years on the force when he was appointed chief.

For almost a century—from 1866 through 1963—the department had just eleven chiefs. From then on, instability hit. There were ten chiefs between 1963 and 1980, as well as several acting chiefs. With each change, there was usually considerable internal reorganization and upheaval. Continuity was desperately needed.

Voinovich described Hanton as "the right cup of tea for the time." Naming Hanton was the first step toward ending the department's deterioration. "We have all seen the ragged cars and dirty stations," Voinovich said. "We know about the broken radios and inadequate equipment."

Hanton brought back the traditional black and white cars, eliminating the chartreuse ones. He enlarged the personnel complaint investigation unit, to ensure faster response to community complaints. The month after his appointment, Hanton reassigned eleven high-ranking officers, including the officer allegedly taking bribes from the Biscayne.

Public concern over the increasing incidence of street crime was heating up. Residents of the Cedar/Central area in the Fifth District threatened to withhold their city income tax unless there was a dramatic improvement in police protection. On September 4, the city council approved putting an income tax hike before the voters—only after Voinovich promised immediately to reassign fifty police from clerical work to basic patrol.

On September 8, Chief Hanton announced the ninety-eight transfers. Strike Force supervisor Lieutenant Vargo was transferred to the complaint investigation unit. Howie Filler, Lucie's SIU trainer, was moved to the First. Lucie's strike force colleague Bill Reiber was sent to the Fifth, as was her fellow Fourth District rookie, Marty Flask.

Marty Flask shook his head in disbelief when he got his transfer to the Fifth. He had worked his way from the Fourth District to the accident investigation unit. He was finally getting somewhere in his career—and now this. Going back to uniform. He was demoralized; he didn't want to go to work. Why was he the one they picked?

"We are robbing Peter to pay Paul," Hanton said.

"It was the purge of the eighties," Billy Riedthaler said.

"We did our time in purgatory." That was how Lucie put it.

Sergeant Bob Cermak of organized crime would later become a crucial support for Lucie. In 1980, he was one of Riedthaler's supervisors. His unit got the word that they had to get rid of six people. Hanton specifically said he didn't care who they were. A couple of people were transferred because they weren't performing. Riedthaler was transferred because they couldn't get him to concentrate on anything but the carnivals.

Cermak lived near the Riedthalers and drove to work with Billy. Don't give up on the carnivals, Cermak told him. Make it your number two job. But every time you turned around, Cermak said, Billy was working on the carnivals.

Roger had also been informed he had to give up some of his people.

He was told to put the newer officers on his list. Lucie was one of his choices because she had less seniority. He knew that after an election, officers got pushed back on the streets. The better ones returned.

"You'll be back," Roger told Lucie. "Just go out there and do it. Keep your mouth shut and don't bitch. Don't complain, don't start running your mouth. Just do your job."

Lucie took Roger's advice. She did her job to the *very* best of her ability. "They made a big mistake in the Fifth," Lucie said. "They put Billy and me in a zone car together. We didn't give a shit. We had nothing to lose. They had already flopped us back to basic patrol, so we were out there to cause trouble."

Lucie liked Billy. She enjoyed his gutsiness and sense of humor. He had a creative way of doing things. "We thought we were pret-ty slick," she said, with a devilish grin.

They rode around together night after night. Billy's narrow, blue eyes were intense. His thick, blond hair was brushed straight back from his broad forehead. His mustache was red and bushy. His humor crackled with a bitter edge.

"Next to eating jelly jars, I like this job the best," he kidded.

Vice enforcement was lax in the Fifth. Billy and Lucie took action on their own. One night, they drove past a storefront on Cedar Avenue. Inside was a cheat spot owned by William H. Seawright, an old-time numbers racketeer whom Booker called the Godfather of Cedar. While under indictment for gambling, Seawright had campaigned for Perk in his primary race against Dennis Kucinich. Seawright had clout.

"Let's hit the place," Billy said.

"All right." Lucie was ready.

They didn't call for backup. If a boss found out where they were, they'd get in trouble, and they wanted to know exactly what was going on.

They opened the door and faced a packed house; about seventy men drinking and gambling at a dice table and two skin tables. Patrons fled as Lucie and Billy moved in. Guns dropped to the floor with clunks and thuds.

"What gun? I don't have a gun. What's going on?" voices muttered, as Lucie and Billy frisked the remaining patrons.

The operator ran up to them. "You're not supposed to be in here," he told them. "Don't you know Captain Madison?"

Lucie could hardly keep a straight face. Everybody knew Madison was the one getting paid off in the Fifth.

"I was just transferred out here. I don't think I know the man," she said, a glint in her eye.

They searched the premises. There were holes in the walls for passing money. They found a gun in a garbage can. A .357 Smith and Wesson with a four-inch barrel, loaded with two live rounds. They ran a computer check and discovered it had been stolen in 1978 from the Santa Rosa police department in California and had been used in the shooting of a police officer.

By the time the intrepid duo returned to the station phones were ringing. "What the hell did you two do," a supervisor demanded.

"We saw a guy standing out in front of the place and we thought he was going in there to steal the copper plumbing," Lucie answered, her eyes wide and innocent.

Billy felt a kinship with Lucie. They certainly caused some consternation with their activities, and their superiors moved them around from zone to zone. They became attuned to each other's habits. If Billy got out of the car and went to the left, he knew Lucie would go to the right. He thought if it got down and dirty, she would get just as bloody as anybody else. That was the mettle test.

Six days after they hit Seawright's cheat spot it was January 15, Martin Luther King Day. Lucie had the day off. Billy was riding with *Charlene Lupich,* the rookie they were training. She had been on the force just fifteen days.

It was a cold cloudy day; there was snow on the ground. At five-forty-five P.M. they answered a complaint about somebody cutting phone wires at a pay phone. Phones were vandalized regularly. It was a routine call. What Billy didn't know was that phone lines throughout the area had been knocked out.

When they arrived, Billy saw a black man dressed as an Ohio Bell repairman, wearing a yellow hard hat with Ohio Bell Telephone Company decals, a utility belt, and a walkie-talkie. As Lupich talked to witnesses across the street, Billy questioned the repairman.

"What are you doing?"

"Repairing the telephone," he answered. He was heavyset, and about five nine.

"Where's your partner?"

"Somewhere in the area."

The man didn't have his ID on him. Something was wrong. Billy could feel it. He didn't have probable cause to arrest the man or handcuff him, but he had reasonable suspicion to detain him. Riedthaler patted him down, trying to feel through his thick, insulated vest and bulky layers of clothing. Billy put him in the backseat and called radio. "Five-one-four to radio, we've got a suspect on a wire cutting ..."

The man in the backseat had a gun secreted somewhere on his person. He drew it.

"He says he works for the phone company," Billy said. "Could we have some confirmation?"

The suspect pushed the gun through an opening in the Plexiglas divider, screwed it to Billy's ear, and pulled the trigger.

Jan Riedthaler was a broad-shouldered, big-boned woman with short, dark hair and a deep laugh. She was a nurse at St. Luke's Hospital in the Fourth District when she met Billy. St. Luke's was where veteran cops took Lucie and Maryanne to use the bathroom. The police stopped by often. The nurses gave the cops coffee and food, and treated them for scratches or bruises. They were grateful to the police for protecting them. When abusive people stormed into the ER and caused problems, the cops always rushed to help.

On Jan's first day on the job, her supervisor told her: don't ever get involved with a policeman. Jan didn't go out with Billy right away. He had to chase her. He called and called—exhibiting the persistence he showed on the job. Finally, Jan agreed to go out with him. She planned to show him a bad time so he would leave her alone. They were married nine months later.

Billy's safety on the job was an issue they discussed before their marriage. If you are going to be anxious, there's no sense getting into this relationship, he told her.

If you sit in the house worrying eight hours a day, you drive yourself to terrible things, Jan knew. But she worried anyway. Every time he went out the door.

On January 15, she was home watching cartoons with her daughters, who were two and four years old, when the doorbell rang. She opened it and saw two officers standing there.

"Billy's been shot," they told her. "He's still alive."

Jan went into a state of shock. She ran barefoot through seven inches of snow to the neighbor's house and asked them to watch her children.

Red light swirling and siren blaring, they raced Jan to the hospital. She begged and begged them for more information, but all they could tell her was: Billy is still alive. It seemed like hours until they arrived at the hospital.

Lucie was at home "being a Strongsville housewife" when she got the call. One of her other partners from the Fifth, Keith, called her and told her Billy had been shot in the head.

Shot in the head. Lucie's breath caught. Her voice cracked. "I'll come right to the hospital."

Keith advised against it. There are a million people here trying to get information about a suspect, he told her. It's chaos. You won't be able to see him.

Lucie hung up the phone. She was home alone. Eric was at a business meeting. She was distraught. She paced back and forth. What in God's name can I do at the hospital except be another body to add to the chaos? She got back on the phone, calling other cops. Trying to find out what was going on. How it had happened. Nobody knew anything. She was so frustrated. There was nothing she could do.

People that got shot in the head usually didn't survive. Billy was probably going to die.

She called Sandy and Dennis. She didn't really know why she was calling. Maybe Dennis could find out something.

"Sandy and I will come right out, so you're not alone," Dennis told her.

"No, that's all right," she said.

She paced.

The first bullet had burst into his ear and out his neck, breaking his neck. Billy fell forward. Angry, he reached down for his second gun. I've got to shoot back. He couldn't move. The assailant fired again. The second bullet tore into Billy's back and blew out his armpit.

He watched his blood pump over the front of the seat. He felt no pain. You are not gonna die. You are not gonna die. You are not gonna die in the front seat of a zone car.

Turning at the sound of gunfire, Lupich fired all six shots toward the suspect and ducked behind another car to reload. Billy's attacker kicked out the window of the back door of the cruiser, reached through the shattered window, unlocked the door, and escaped.

Lupich returned to the police car. Billy directed her as she drove. "Go down Central to St. Vincent's Charity Hospital." He told her where he thought his wounds were, so the doctors would immediately know where to look. Riedthaler got out of the car on his own, walked through the automatic doors into the emergency room, and collapsed.

The police chaplain, Reverend John J. Cregan, son of a police lieutenant, was called to the emergency room. Billy faded out, then faded in to see the priest giving him last rites. It was a terrible feeling.

"Why are you here," he asked Cregan.

"My son, you are seriously injured—" the chaplain began.

"We got two problems, Father," Billy said. "The first one is I'm Protestant."

"At a time like this, you shouldn't be concerned about that," Cregan said. "You should be concerned with making peace with your maker."

"The second thing is," Billy persisted, "I ain't gonna die."

Billy knew it wasn't a good sign—seeing his blood pumping out and not having any corks to plug the holes. But his belief was: You don't die 'til you say you're dead. It was gut determination.

Jan arrived and found Billy still in the emergency room. He will probably live, the doctors told her. But he might be paralyzed.

Lucie was on the phone, making call after call, trying to get information. The police were frantically trying to figure out what had happened. The pieces started to come together. Billy had called in for a check on someone he had put in the backseat of the car. Moments later, the dispatcher received calls reporting shots fired in the same location. Officers converged on the scene to gather evidence and information.

They found a .38 Smith and Wesson in the backseat of the cruiser. An Ohio Bell Company official examined the hat and utility belt and said they were not issued by the phone company. The walkie-talkie was stolen from an office at Conrail's Collinwood Yard a few months before. As more information came in, the police formed a theory. Billy inadvertently had interrupted plans for a robbery of a Wells Fargo Armored Service Corporation truck that stopped each day about five-thirty at the State Liquor Store at 7023 Central. Billy's assailant was one of the robbers, and he had panicked when Billy detained him.

There were other theories Jan heard. Was the shooting related to the carnival investigation? Had there been a plot to execute him? The officers talked among themselves. Maybe the gun was planted in the car and he had purposely been assigned to that car. A police guard was put on Billy. Why?

Lucie heard the officers go through every scenario imaginable. She didn't really see how it could have been a set up. You never know which cars are going to get which assignment. Billy just stumbled into this. It was a horrible coincidence. She wished to God she had been there.

Lucie's main concern was not who did it. Her main concern was for Billy. She was given time off to drive Jan to the hospital. She first saw Billy two days after he was shot.

They tied him down and placed sandbags around him to keep him from moving. The bullet had hit his spinal column. A fraction of an inch higher and it would have killed him. He had lost his hearing in his right ear, and he had no movement in his left arm.

"How are you feeling?" Lucie asked. He seemed chipper to her, glad to be alive.

Billy talked to Lucie with his usual sardonic humor. He told her about the shooting, told her that when he was down on the seat of the car he heard no sounds from the backseat and finally poked his head up to see what was going on. Why don't I hear the radio or sirens, he remembered thinking. I've been shot, there should be a million people coming to help me. Nobody was coming.

"You would have smoked the guy," Billy told Lucie. "No doubt about it."

Lucie felt so awful that she hadn't been there. She thought about what she would have done. What she hoped she would have done. There was somebody trapped inside the car—you don't have to shoot at the car. Wait—and then kill him.

The days blurred together for Jan. She described that period of time as "blanky" in her head. Once when she was driving to the hospital by herself she got totally lost. She waved down a police car, and they led her to the hospital.

Billy was overwhelmed with policemen visiting. They were dropping by twenty-four hours a day. The men that came on at eleven P.M. stopped in right before their shift. Or they came in after their shift. They came on their coffee breaks. They pumped him about what happened. He was getting no rest. Jan talked to the doctor and said something has got to give. The doctor put a stop to the visitors, and there was a directive issued at roll call not to visit.

The officers showed Jan car 5-1-4, where Billy had been shot. Lupich's shots had sprayed in an arc from the front driver side door across to the gas tank. How had she missed hitting Billy—or the gas tank? Jan was horrified. If Lucie had been there, Jan thought, it would have been different. Probably she would have caught the guy—and he wouldn't have lived to go on trial.

Billy was in the hospital about three weeks. He wasn't paralyzed, he was walking. But the doctors told him he would not regain use of his left hand, and they didn't think he could go back to work. He would definitely never shoot again. After coming home, he relapsed after a few days and went back for another week. He didn't want to stay at home. Some officers came and drove him in to work. He had to get his mind moving again. He was back on the job five weeks after he was shot, transferred out of the Fifth and back to organized crime.

He had seven surgeries on his arm, attempting to give him gross motor movement. Pieces of tendons from his leg were moved to his arm. "My arm looks like a baseball. I could qualify for a Spaulding." With his leg helping his arm work, he joked, "If I start walking on my hands, I am really walking right. I can't pick up anything small but I can choke the heck out of somebody. They only transfer body parts on the same side, otherwise they don't work as well. Scary."

He was in pain every day. But he practiced diligently at the range, and eventually was able to shoot perfect targets with his injured hand.

Lucie visited Billy while he was still at home. She brought McDonald's for the kids. When Billy felt up to it, Lucie and Eric and the Riedthalers went out for dinner a few times. Eric was disturbed by the shooting. This one certainly touched home.

Lucie went back to work in the Fifth District within a week after the shooting. She was without a partner, and worked odd man with different patrolmen.

She grappled with what had happened.

The bottom line of all police shootings, she realized, was that people are killing us because of our profession. It was a strange feeling. All of us have been in situations that could have gone bad. There but for the grace of God, it could be me.

SIU processed car 5-1-4 and returned it to the district.

"Your car is back," Lucie was told. She was assigned to work in it. She went outside and looked at the car. They had put autobody compound in the bullet holes. They hadn't even painted them over. Lucie opened the door and started to get in the front seat. She stopped and gasped. Billy's blood was all over it. They hadn't really cleaned up the car.

Lucie got back out. She went into the station and found some paper towels and supplies. She scrubbed the seat, cleaning up as best she could. She forced herself back in the car and sat behind the wheel. She waited. Then, she took a deep breath and keyed the mike.

"Car five-one-four," she said. "I'm on the air."

11

ONE OF OUR OWN

Lucie had taken the sergeant's exam while she was driving Sandy Kucinich. With her heavy schedule she didn't have much time to study, and she didn't do well. Between her low score and the consent decrees requiring minority promotions, Lucie wasn't sure she'd make it. Then the promotions were held up with lawsuits.

Finally Lucie got a call from Jackie Christ, who was working in personnel. You're scheduled to be promoted tomorrow, Jackie told her. There were vacancies in supervisory positions, and all of a sudden the department was filling them up.

Lucie was proud of herself. She was beginning her move up through the ranks, but after so many delays, the excitement was gone. Eric had a business event planned and didn't reschedule. Nobody else is very excited about this, Lucie thought. How excited can I get?

The ceremony was held at city hall on May 14, 1981, four months after Billy was shot. Sixty-six officers were promoted. Billy made sergeant with Lucie, as did her fellow rookies Sandra Ramsey and Marty Flask.

Roger and the strike force gang took Lucie out to lunch near Burke Lakefront Airport to celebrate. Roger gave her a pair of his socks, which had a badge with sergeant's stripes on them. There was an old joke in the military about soldiers who took their stripes so seriously they sewed them on their underwear. Right in the middle of the restaurant—with Lucie still in uniform from the ceremony, so everyone knew she was a cop—Roger gave her another present, a pair of underpants complete with sergeant's stripes.

150

Within a few months after her promotion, Lucie was finally sent back to the strike force. Standard procedure dictated that when officers made rank, they were transferred. It was considered too difficult for them to supervise those who had been their peers. But Roger wasn't about to give up Lucie. He spoke to Hanton. "I want to keep her." Hanton said OK.

Soon after she returned to the strike force as sergeant Lucie was beeped at seven-thirty on a Sunday morning. A call-up for the crisis negotiation team. It was a warm, sunny August day. Lucie threw on jeans, a shirt, and hooked up her bullet-proof vest. She grabbed her navy blue windbreaker and was off. CRISIS TEAM was emblazoned on the back of the jacket in red letters; SUPERVISOR on the front. Lucie drove quickly to the Justice Center, met Roger, and they raced to East Cleveland. "Here goes another one," she said.

Roger had formed the CNT—crisis negotiation team—over a year before, and Lucie had been his partner from its inception. They were called out at all hours of the night and day for situations where the patience and skill of Lucie and the other officers meant the difference between life and death.

Roger said that in the sixties and early seventies there was one approach to crisis situations: kick down the door, gas 'em, shoot 'em, and throw 'em in jail. Terrorism made frequent headlines. During the 1972 Munich Olympics, eleven Israeli athletes were killed by Arab commandos—nine of the hostages were killed when German police ambushed the terrorists. Traditional police methods were getting people hurt. Law enforcement agencies began developing negotiation tactics for hostage situations.

Roger loved negotiating. Under Chief Hanton, he went to Quantico, Virginia, and attended an FBI Hostage Negotiation School with people from all over the country and from Israel, Egypt, Ireland, and England. Roger formed a team of black, Hispanic, and white officers. Men and women. Cops who were not caught up in—I have a gun, I'm going to shoot you.

Roger felt himself to be an oddity in law enforcement. He had no children. He had been married about fifteen years. His life had been stable. He selected negotiators whose experiences complemented his. Lucie had gone through marriages and divorces. She was able to say to a desperate man barricaded in his apartment—I understand.

Lucie attended a local hostage negotiation school, and Roger conducted in-house training. Lucie thought women were good negotiators. "We have the patience necessary. We unconsciously become negotiators in our lives." Lucie was initially the only woman on the team.

She embodied the qualities crucial for a negotiator, among them, the ability to cope with uncertainty. She came to each and every scene no matter the time of day. She and Eric would be out to dinner, her pager would go off, and she'd rush to the car, where she kept a bag of clothes. She'd quickly change and speed off. The calls often came in the dead of night. The phone was on Eric's side of the bed; he got to know the dispatchers who woke him and asked for the sergeant. Jarred from sleep, she would throw on whatever was close by, a sweatshirt, a pair of jeans. "It wasn't a Rambo outfit," she joked. There was one man who kept threatening to jump off the top of a church. He threatened this every weekend; it went on for about eight weeks. Lucie was beeped in the middle of a pool party. Lucie told the jumper, "Come on down. I'm having a party, I gotta get home."

Lucie was Roger's counterpart. If he was negotiating, she was coordinating intelligence. If she was talking, he evaluated the information. Both Lucie and Roger selected additional negotiators and decided when to switch them.

Lucie thought the crisis team was one of the best-run parts of the police department. They trained regularly. They worked in tandem with SWAT, and she thought the SWAT unit the best in the country. They spent hours at the scenes. She went on a call where a woman was being held at gunpoint by her common-law husband. He had already taken some shots at her. She and Roger thought there was a good chance he might kill her. He had put furniture against the door, barricading them both in the bedroom. Lucie and Roger talked and talked to him. Finally, he agreed to release her onto the roof. Lucie thought he might shoot her as she came out—agree to let her go and then shoot her in the back. The SWAT men were ready to grab her as soon as she appeared. She started onto the roof, looked around, saw the SWAT and police, and turned around and went back in the window. She thinks we're going to kill him, Lucie realized. Jesus, lady, I'm tired of this, Lucie thought. But they kept talking. Eventually, they got both of them out and nobody was hurt.

They had never had to assault a position, fire on a suspect, or injure him. No officers or innocent people had been hurt.

On that clear August Sunday morning, Roger, Lucie, and their team sped out of Cleveland into East Cleveland. A man had holed himself up in his apartment and was shooting randomly into the street. The situation was unlike any they had handled before. The "barricaded male" was *Richard Palmer*—a Cleveland police officer.

Palmer was thirty-three years old and had been on the force about four years. He was a lean man, with a big smile. He was a member of the Shield Club and had at one point been detailed to the strike force. Lucie and the other team members knew him.

Something in Palmer had snapped. At a little after midnight, Palmer was walking outside Chin's Seafood Restaurant on St. Clair Avenue. Suddenly, he pulled his gun and fired into the night. People walking by dove frantically for cover. Palmer emptied six rounds, reloaded, turned, and fired two more shots in the direction of customers peeking out of the bar.

Two security guards, *James Johnson* and *Larry Banks,* acquaintances of Palmer's, were on the scene. Johnson thought Palmer was a nice guy. But as he looked in Palmer's eyes, he could see something was wrong. Palmer looked spaced out. He stared dead at Johnson.

Johnson called out to Palmer. Palmer fired. He hit Larry Banks in the side. As Johnson turned to run, Palmer hit him in the back. Palmer went on to the Shield Club and had a few drinks, never mentioning the shooting. When he returned to his apartment in East Cleveland, he saw his brother *Newton* in the parking lot. Newton lived next door. Palmer said nothing about having shot two men.

At three-thirty in the morning, Cleveland police dispatched homicide detectives to Palmer's house, the procedure followed when an officer was involved in a shooting. They knocked on the door but got no response. Newton came out and talked to his brother through the door. Palmer fired four shots through the door. Then he fired one more shot inside his apartment.

Newton thought his brother had killed himself. He kicked in the door and was confronted with Richard pointing a gun at him. The homicide detective pulled Newton out and slammed the door shut.

East Cleveland police and the homicide officers knocked on all the neighbors' doors and evacuated Palmer's building. SWAT was called up, and the twenty-man team arrived at four-thirty A.M. Dressed in black fatigues and military boots, they quickly went to the back door of the apartment house to the rear of Palmer's. They alerted the startled residents and positioned themselves outside the doorways, securing a safe exit. They escorted the people out of the line of fire and set up the house as a command post. They evacuated the building across the street and the homes on either side of Palmer's.

SWAT Commander John James organized the men. Sharpshooters—high ground cover—took position in an upstairs apartment across the street, each man armed with a 30-06. They had a view into Palmer's home. An eight-man entry team lined the stairway leading up to Palmer's apartment.

James's family had come from the hills of Western Maryland years before, up Route 21 to Cleveland's steel mills. When James took over SWAT, he went to hostage negotiation school at the FBI academy and dignitary protection school at the Secret Service academy in Washington.

He learned from each crisis situation. He learned that you can never predict what is going to happen. His pale blue eyes surveyed the scene.

He was physically fit, cool, and pleasant in personality. He had an in-charge attitude.

Lucie and Roger arrived at five after eight in the morning. Palmer's block was a sloping, tree-lined street with small apartment buildings. There were neat, bright green patches of grass bordering the sidewalks. The sky was cerulean, it was a warm, sunny summer day. But Lucie and the others were walking into a nightmare.

Lucie and Roger made their way into Palmer's building. SWAT had secured their operation post, the apartment downstairs from Palmer's. Chief Hanton was within the secured perimeter.

The tension was palpable. This was an extratough situation. It was a fellow officer behind that door.

Mike Burger went to find out any information he could from family, friends, and neighbors. The team had to check their identities carefully. People would come off the street and say, Let me talk to him. He's my brother. I'll get him to come out. Then the team would discover that person was a total stranger and just wanted to get on television. With a tight face and grim lips, Detective Ed Kelly crossed the phone wires so no incoming calls could come into Palmer's line, except from the phone the crisis team was using.

Bill Reiber thought Palmer was a super policeman; a quiet kid, well educated. Burger relayed information to Lucie. Palmer had worked Third District vice, been detailed to the strike force, but then was put back in uniform. He was working in the minority recruitment office and had been recently reprimanded by his supervisor for coming in late. He was facing another possible transfer.

Lucie knew from her experience that a transfer out of a specialized unit was a blow. A blow to the ego, and more—a whole change of life-style. Another job to do, new people to deal with. Palmer was going to school, a transfer would disrupt his schedule. He's bitten off more than he can chew, Lucie surmised.

There were personal problems. He had been depressed recently. He had gone through two divorces, the last divorce had just been finalized a few months before. Another police officer and friend of Palmer's said that Palmer couldn't hold his liquor anymore. He became reckless after drinking more than five drinks. Palmer was working part-time jobs to make more money and on top of the liquor was taking sleeping pills.

He had his service revolver with him, an off-duty .38, a 9mm automatic, .25 automatic, a rifle, and three hundred rounds of ammunition.

He shot into the street. The rule was, when a suspect started firing, negotiations were to break off and SWAT was to move in. This time the rules changed. Orders were not to fire.

The SWAT men held their positions, rifles raised. In a crisis situation, they had to maintain that peak of readiness for hours and hours—and yet they were successful only if they never fired a shot. Tension mounted. They waited. They watched.

Bill Reese was working in the Sixth District, back in uniform. He got off night shift and had just climbed into bed when a friend called. She lived across the street from Richard Palmer. "Palmer is going crazy," she told him. "He's over here shooting."

Reese jumped up and went right over. Roger and Lucie had just arrived.

"Do you know him?" Roger asked Reese.

Reese knew Palmer from the Shield Club. He liked him. Everybody liked Palmer. He was a hard worker and friendly. A go-getter. Busy, busy, busy. He was tall, and his movements were quick. He was so thin that Reese used to wonder how he could be a cop—"he seemed so tiny." His face was kind of sunken, his bone structure visible through his skin.

Reese took the phone. Palmer sounded confused, but he recognized Reese's voice. He called him by name.

"Why don't you come out," Reese suggested.

"Don't worry about it," Palmer said. "Everything will be all right. I'll take care of it. Is the man I shot OK?"

"Yeah, he is," Reese said.

"Everything will be all right," Palmer repeated. That was all he said. The conversation ended. He hung up the phone. Reese went to the command post to wait out the siege.

Lucie called Palmer on the phone. "Richard, can you hear me?"

He was chanting biblical phrases. "The Lord is my Shepherd, I shall not want." He threw down the phone.

Lucie concentrated. She could hear him walking around.

He hung up the phone. Lucie dialed again. He picked up the receiver. He does want contact, she thought.

"Richard," Lucie tried. "What's wrong? Let's talk about it."

He hung up. Lucie dialed again. Again, he picked up.

"He leadeth me beside still waters; he restoreth my soul," Palmer chanted Psalm Twenty-three.

"Is there anything we can do for you, Richard?" Lucie asked him gently. She was hoping he would make some response. Some rational comment. Nothing came back but chanting.

"Yea, though I walk through the valley of the shadow of death—" He threw down the phone. In the background, Lucie heard the sound of a religious program on the television.

"Richard, can you hear me? Come to the phone and talk to me," Lucie urged. She tried to pick up on what he was babbling. Maybe there is something I can say that just for a flash will bring him back long enough to talk some sense into him, to get him out.

The chanting continued. "The Lord is my light and my salvation ..."

Roger attempted to break through. "I'm here to help." Palmer had been at crisis situations. He knows exactly what I'm doing, Roger thought. He's seen it. That is the most difficult person to deal with, somebody who knows what you're doing and what you are going to do next.

For over an hour, Lucie and Roger tried to establish some sort of contact. Chief Hanton tried talking to him. One of the tenets of crisis negotiation was the chief was never supposed to negotiate. When a suspect made a demand, the negotiator should be able to say, I'll see what my supervisor says. But this situation was breaking all the rules.

Hanton told Palmer who he was, and Palmer recognized him enough to call him chief.

"We can solve this," Hanton said.

No response. Hanton kept trying. Over and over again. "We can solve this."

Palmer didn't answer. "I can't talk him down," Hanton said finally. His brow was furrowed, his expression somber.

Lucie and Roger kept on. Dialing the phone. Talking. Palmer hanging up. Dialing again. Talking.

Palmer threw down the phone. Lucie heard his footsteps.

The counter snipers could see into Palmer's apartment. "He's at the window." Lucie heard their voices over their hand-held transceivers. She couldn't see anything that was going on outside.

"Shots fired," SWAT men announced tersely. Palmer was an "active shooter," and every shot he fired added to their stress. There was no way to predict how far a bullet would go, where it would wind up, if it would ricochet off something and hit someone.

Chief Hanton believed in the crisis team. As long as the negotiators think they have a chance, we're going to keep talking. He was not one to jump the gun.

Lucie dialed once more. Palmer picked up the phone. "The Lord is the stronghold of my life," he chanted. Then, he asked for his priest, Reverend Paul Marshall. "I need to pray," he said.

Paul Marshall had a kind voice and gentle manner. He was short and plump, his face round and youthful. He had been called to Dayton on Saturday and had arrived home five o'clock Sunday morning. Early in the morning he had visited a nursing home. He had had practically no sleep. On the way back, another priest met him outside. "You better hurry," the priest told him. "The police are at the house and they want to talk to you."

"The police, what for?" Marshall hurried into the large house behind the church.

Detective DelRegno showed his badge. "Richard Palmer is in trouble. We need you. Can you come immediately."

Marshall had known Richard Palmer in Cathedral Latin School, where Palmer had been a year behind him. Palmer came from a devout Catholic family. He was Marshall's parishioner and had come to the church several times to talk about recruitment of minorities into the police department.

Marshall knew the situation must be bad when Detective DelRegno did a wheely—backed out on the street so fast the car went up on two wheels. As they sped toward the scene, DelRegno filled Marshall in.

Richard Palmer's mother and sister arrived on the scene and were kept in a nearby apartment house. Dana Garcia, Lucie's classmate, came. She had known Richard Palmer since he was eight years old. He was like her brother. Her family and his had lived together for years. She was put on the phone, but he didn't hear her at all. He was chanting biblical verses. She waited with the family.

Two miles away, the Murray Hill neighborhood was celebrating the Feast of the Assumption. Thousands thronged the street to honor the Virgin Mary. Children squealed as they spun on amusement rides. There was gambling, fun, and lots of food.

DelRegno parked a few blocks away from Palmer's apartment.

"Follow me," he told Marshall.

Crowds had gathered at the edge of the area. East Cleveland zone cars blocked off the street as residents tried to see what was happening. Teenagers with boom boxes strolled by. People peeked out from doorways. Patrol officers crouched behind their cars. The sounds of police radios echoed through the street.

Marshall ran behind DelRegno, ducking down until they got to the building next to Palmer's, where Palmer's mother was inside. She was a parishioner. Marshall talked with her for a minute.

"Do you mind running?" the detective asked. They exited the back of the building and ran across the backyard. DelRegno pushed Marshall past the hallway that was filled with cops. Marshall saw Lucie, Roger, and the other team members in a small apartment.

"We have telephone contact," Marshall was informed. "We're going to put you on right away—but we are trying to negotiate with him to come out."

More information had come in. Palmer's girlfriend was in the hospital, ill. His father was in the hospital, following a car accident. Palmer had visited him; he had asked his father to forgive him and gave his father a religious article.

"We're trying to get him to put down his gun," the team members told Marshall. "We don't know how he is going to respond to you."

"He may try to bargain with you to get the police to leave," Roger said. "Don't compromise our position. Don't make any agreements with him."

Marshall got on the phone. "Richard, why don't you put down the gun," he encouraged him.

"The Lord is my shepherd, I shall not want."

"Let's talk about what God is saying to you," Marshall said, concern evident in his dark eyes. "Let's find out what the Lord is doing." If he was hallucinating, let's try to find out what, Marshall reasoned.

Palmer didn't respond. He just listened.

"It's going to be all right," Marshall assured him. "The man you shot is going to be all right."

No response.

"I talked to your mother and she just wants you to put the gun down," Marshall said.

Palmer didn't answer.

"Keep talking," Roger told Marshall.

"Rick, why don't you put down the gun and come out of the apartment. Nobody is going to hurt you."

Marshall could hear Palmer breathing. He talked to him for twenty minutes. Palmer never said a word. Marshall stayed with the team. Lucie felt his support, and she was very glad to have him there.

At 10:35 A.M., Detective DelRegno and a patrol officer turned off Palmer's electricity. Fifteen minutes later, Palmer threw down the phone. He refused to come back to it.

Lucie and Roger decided to try a bullhorn. They went into the hallway and positioned themselves at the bottom of the stairs. The SWAT entry team lined up in front of them. Lucie looked up at the door, took the bullhorn, and spoke. Her voice echoed through the hall. "Richard, what can we do for you?"

A shot exploded through the door.

The SWAT men tensed. Everyone stared up. Lucie held the bullhorn up to her lips again. She talked. Roger talked.

Another shot burst against the door.

They tried for an hour. Palmer's only response was to shoot.

A gray armored tank moved to the front of the building. The SWAT men called it Mother because it protected them. The windows had flaps.

SWAT men were inside. At the bottom of Mother was a hatch; if someone was wounded SWAT would pick them up through it.

Palmer fired at Mother when he saw her outside. Lucie and Roger stayed in the hall, speaking through the bullhorn.

"You have to talk to us," Roger said.

"That won't help. You're a policeman, you know you can't harm that vehicle. You are only going to endanger the civilians. Talk to us," Lucie coaxed.

They were getting nowhere. Roger sent for the consulting police psychologist, Ross Santamaria.

Santamaria was a burly man with dark brown hair and a bushy mustache. His eyes were bright behind wire-rimmed glasses. He had been working with police for over ten years. He was having a cup of coffee, preparing to go to church, when he got the call about Richard Palmer. He arrived at the command post. He could smell chickens barbecuing, the neighbors preparing Sunday dinners. Officers took him down the street, creeping alongside the apartment buildings.

Lucie and Roger continued talking to Palmer. He was singing and yelling. Outside, glass shattered and fell into the street. Palmer was breaking out windows. Smoke filtered out.

"Suspect setting small fires inside apartment." The information came over the radio.

"Richard, put the fire out," Lucie called through the bullhorn. It was 1:10 in the afternoon. They had been trying to talk to him for almost five hours.

Palmer's brothers watched from outside. Santamaria talked to the family members about Palmer's problems. It's been one thing after another, Santamaria thought. Piling, piling. Normally, when he practiced psychology he knew he would be seeing his client week after week. He ran tests, he talked to the person. In crisis situations, he was flying by the seat of his pants. Interviewing people. Is this one reliable—OK, we'll use her to negotiate if we really need to. This one is too upset. He did a quick analysis of the family and took stock of the situation. A building next door where fires are being set, a guy shooting out the windows. Normally he thought in terms of treatment. In this situation he was thinking, Can I get this guy out?

Santamaria started making calls. He had practiced in the community many years. His colleagues knew he did police work. If he asked them, Are you seeing so-and-so? they would break confidentiality because the information was critical. Sometimes they had situations where a person was a walk away from a state hospital. But no one had information on Palmer.

Dana Garcia was upset that the crisis team wouldn't let Palmer's mother talk to her son. Maybe, possibly, a mother can talk to her child. They had taken over. The family kept begging, please, just let my mother try to talk to him.

Usually, family members were not allowed to negotiate. Santamaria and all the team members knew the danger involved. Lucie was firm: you don't put family or other people in a situation where they would bear the failure. One time, a woman barricaded herself inside with her children and asked for her brother. When the brother arrived, a neighbor warned the team: She hates her brother. As soon as the detectives told her he was on the scene, she shot herself. That's what she wanted, Reiber realized. To let him live with that for the rest of his life.

Dana was furious. The crisis team seemed cold and callous. She tried to talk to Lucie, but Lucie yelled at her to get back and told her she was getting too emotional. Dana would never forgive them. Never.

Chief Hanton was worried about the SWAT entry team positioned on the stairs. He talked to Santamaria. If Palmer came out and was firing at them, Hanton was afraid they would not be able to shoot back. "I want to know," he told Santamaria. "I don't want to lose any more men. If we have to, we'll take Palmer out. I don't want anyone else hurt."

Santamaria watched as Hanton asked each of the men, "Can you shoot if you have to."

"Yes," they replied, one by one.

Santamaria told the chief he felt they could shoot.

Channel 5 and other television reporters were out in the street. Sirens and police radios echoed up and down the block.

"What caused this entire mess?" the Channel 5 newscaster asked. "The best information we have is that it is something of a personal nature ..." The commentator talked as neighborhood kids converged behind him.

"Palmer is totally incoherent. That is the best we have," the reporter continued.

The kids behind him grinned and pressed forward as he spoke of the unfolding tragedy. "Hi, Ma!" one boy shouted. The young faces turned somber when the cameras were not focused on them.

Television newscasts of the scene aired at intervals throughout the day. Early on, someone came into the hospital room where Palmer's father was recuperating and pulled the plug on his TV set.

The detectives turned off the gas to Palmer's apartment. The fire chief was ready to alert SWAT when the fires got out of control. Palmer fired into the street. One of the bullets whizzed right near the head of a counter sniper in the opposite building. It almost hit him. Still, they held their fire.

East Ohio Gas turned off the gas to all the apartments in the building. The fires were getting larger.

Palmer paced from window to window, his weapon in his hand. He screamed out, "I'll kill you motherfuckers," and fired through the apartment door.

Marshall picked up the bullhorn. "Please come out, please put the gun down," Marshall begged. Palmer shot at the door. Police grabbed Marshall and threw him into the utility room. "Stay in there," they ordered. "We don't want anybody hurt."

Palmer started another fire and put it out. Smoke was pouring out the windows. Palmer tore out a window frame. It crashed to the sidewalk. A white sheet came out next, hung on the window ledge, then fell to the ground. Palmer tied a rag around his face to protect himself from the smoke. The fire subsided.

Two minutes later he was back at the window, with a hammer in his hand.

Roger and Lucie kept trying anything that might work. Booker Bledsoe knew Palmer. "Book, talk to him," Roger said. Booker tried, but Palmer didn't seem to recognize his voice.

Marshall watched Roger and Lucie with admiration. Lucie kept talking about what might be bothering Palmer. The SWAT team said they had him in their sights, but they did not get authorization to shoot. "I'm losing a good officer," Hanton kept saying. "What is going on?"

They were waging a losing battle, Lucie thought. Is this ever going to end? We're not getting anywhere. I don't know how to resolve this.

The report came from SWAT over their portable radios. "Standing in the window. He's got his uniform on."

"That's it," Lucie said. "He's coming out." He had snapped back to the reality of being a police officer. He was going to come out as a policeman. He's ready to put this behind him and go on to something else.

He disappeared. Lucie waited. He's coming out, Lucie hoped. It was two o'clock. She had been there for six hours. Thinking they were getting nowhere. Exhausted. Frustrated. Now—he was coming out.

The next report came. Another fire had started. Palmer came to the window, held his uniform shirt out on a broom handle and set it on fire. He showed up at another window. Naked, except for the scarf around his neck and a gun in his hand.

"He was real proud to be a police officer. To burn that uniform is an indication that he is probably going to take his own life," Santamaria said.

He's going to kill himself, Lucie acknowledged. He's given up. He's not going to come out with no clothes on. "We're not going to get this guy out, are we," she sighed. Tension tightened her face.

SWAT reported the sound of a shotgun being loaded, locked.

Roger resigned himself—this is going to end with the death of Richard Palmer.

Roger and Lucie talked into the bullhorn. "Richard, don't kill yourself, don't Richard. Don't do this. Come out."

Palmer shot beer bottles and threw them outside. He tossed shoes and boots out one window. He stalked to the bathroom window and hurled out toilet paper, shampoo, and towels. "Walking to window one," SWAT reported. "Throwing objects from window two. Went back to window three."

Finally, he threw the phone out into the street.

The smoke billowed out the windows, charring the brick. His curtains had caught on fire. The flames were out of control. The wide metal flashing on the flat roof was black, it began to curl and melt above one window.

"The roof's gone," somebody in the crowd hollered.

Hanton ran in. "You've got to get out of here," he yelled at Lucie and the others. They rushed out as the roof was swallowed in flames. Fire burst from the windows. Acrid, white smoke smothered the street. Black tufts of smoke shot up in the sky.

A fire truck pulled up behind the building, on the safe side, and sprayed water from a distance. Lucie felt the drops.

The building next to Palmer's was close to catching on fire. The fire department could not move in safely. Hanton talked to James. Hanton made the decision. If Palmer appeared again with a weapon, SWAT was to fire. The code was green light. Palmer had shot at the fire department, at police officers. I can't allow him to kill somebody, Hanton said. It was not an easy decision. It was only one of a few times that he had to make it.

Lucie appreciated Hanton's taking the responsibility upon himself. He was the kind of person who would not expect anybody to make a decision like that. It was the only situation she was ever in where the decision to shoot had to be made.

Palmer, at a window, seemed to be gagging from the smoke. Five minutes later, at 4:20, SWAT fired three tear gas grenades into the apartment. Palmer appeared at the next window, throwing things out.

"He's going into the closet."

"Let's hold for two minutes," James ordered.

Six more grenades were fired in. They were trying to get him out. SWAT members saw the closet door open, but they couldn't see Palmer. The smoke was thick. James ordered one more grenade into the bathroom window. Flames reared up and came through the roof. SWAT could not see anything through the smoke. Visibility zero. They heard glass breaking from one window.

The order "green light on visual" was given as the fire department came down the street. The whole apartment was engulfed in flames. Debris floated in the air. The firemen made their way inside. They saw a big hole in the living room floor, the fire still roaring in the rear room. No one was found yet.

A doctor stated that Palmer must be dead. The order came: green light is off, repeat, green light is off. Red light on suspect.

Fire trucks and ambulances sped down the street. SWAT team covered the firefighters as they made their way inside. It was five thirty.

Marshall went to offer comfort to *Mrs. Palmer*. She was crying. The family asked him to anoint his body and pray over it.

"I've lost a damn good officer," Hanton told a reporter. "And I don't know why yet." Hanton's brow was creased.

"The ultimate answer to that question," the commentator said, "died in the flames."

Marshall followed the firemen and SWAT team upstairs. The smoke was thick, the search slow and tedious. They found Palmer curled in the fetal position in the closet. Charred. Dead. Marshall prayed over him. The body was wrapped in a sheet and strapped onto a stretcher. Television cameras moved in as EMTs lifted the body into an orange and white ambulance and drove off.

Reese watched as the body was brought out. Palmer must have felt as though he had lost it all, Reese thought sadly. He figured he had shot somebody, so he was going to prison. The negotiators had tried to get him to understand that wouldn't happen. But he would have lost his job. And the job was everything to him. Losing it would have been almost like dying.

Lucie and all the crisis team members drove back to the Justice Center. They put away their radios and other equipment. Nobody said much. They were supposed to fill out reports right after an incident. This time they didn't.

Burger just wanted to get out of there. He didn't want to talk about it. He was beat. He went home and fell asleep. When something bad happened, he just wanted to forget it.

What a helluva way to have to go, Reiber thought.

Lucie went home. She drank a glass of wine. And another. And another. She was drained. Worn out. The details of the day played back in her mind. She couldn't think anymore. She couldn't concentrate on anything. She didn't want to have to. She didn't have a sense of guilt. It wasn't as if Palmer had been in touch with reality and the whole thing fell apart because she did something stupid or said the wrong thing. This situation was impossible at best. They had been hoping for a miracle. It never came.

Eric watched Lucie. He knew it was very important for her to be in control professionally. That was part of survival on the force—the ability to make nonemotional decisions. When she came home, she could release some of her feelings. Lucie always seemed to be on a great high or a great low after the crisis situations, depending on their outcome.

Lucie was very upset that she hadn't been able to talk Palmer out. No matter what she had said or done, she just didn't have any impact on him. Eric thought she looked like somebody had just wrung her out. She was emotionally drained. For days and days.

Marshall said the funeral Mass. The church was packed with police and neighborhood people. It was hard for him to preach. He pondered, How do I create a sense of hope?

Booker was at the funeral. He had been through other deaths in the department. One of his partners had been killed. His brother-in-law had been a cop, and he had been killed. It was so strange to have Palmer gone. He was such a quiet, laid-back person. He wasn't aggressive. He was unassuming. Booker was surprised by his behavior, it just wasn't like him. He could hardly believe it. Maybe that's why—maybe he kept everything bottled up and it exploded. What a loss.

Policewoman Jean Clayton, now retired, was there. She realized when she arrived that she knew Mrs. Palmer. They had gone to Catholic school together. Clayton knew Richard Palmer from the Shield Club. She had seen him at their last meeting. He was on the building committee. They had been looking for an office, and he came in with some suggestions and reports on available locations. The next thing she heard, he was dead.

A few days later, Santamaria took Lucie out for lunch at Pier W, a restaurant overlooking the city. He always tried to have lunch or coffee with the negotiators after an incident. He knew the department put more pressure on females. If a female was involved in a shooting, she was open to more criticism. If a female negotiated, she was scrutinized more closely.

Palmer's death bothered the crisis team more than any other incident they had handled. One of their own had died. He wondered how Lucie was dealing with it. He asked her how she was feeling.

"Fine," she said. Her normally warm voice was clipped.

"I just want you to know you did everything right," he assured her. "You did everything you could."

"I know that," she said.

"I don't want you to feel responsible," he proceeded.

"I don't," she answered.

"If somebody wants to commit suicide, you can't stop them."

"I know that."

Lucie did feel terrible. What she also felt was anger. As they tried to put all the pieces together afterward, she found out some members of the stress unit had talked to Palmer and had refused to share that information.

Lucie was outraged. "They hid under their everything-that-is-said-to-us-is-confidential cloak. They had been on the scene. They had been out there and talked to Palmer. And they never told us. They never even took his guns away. They practically could have predicted what happened. You got to be kidding me. These guys were out here—they talked to him—saw what state he was in and they didn't take his gun away—nothing?! Jesus. We're all out there and they knew. They had information about his problems, but they wouldn't say anything. We didn't know about all his financial problems. He was working three extra jobs, working sixteen to twenty hours a day. They had all that. They just left us there blind."

Santamaria's reaction was the same: "Why the hell didn't somebody tell me these things." The information he was gathering was already known by some people in the department. That's that closed society of police, he thought. Members of the stress unit were sitting right next to him while he made all his calls.

Lieutenant James tried to find out more about Palmer. He wanted to know what would make an officer go off the deep end. It made him reflect. Is it going to happen tomorrow or the next week? Is it going to happen to another fellow officer down the line?

Kelly was supposed to be the hardhearted one on the crisis team, but he kept thinking about it. What could they have done better? What could they have tried? But he knew it wasn't helpful to second-guess himself. You never survive that way.

Reiber knew that the family was angry; he could deal with that. That's the way it is. He had hardened himself to those reactions. He would have felt worse if a family member had gone to the door and gotten shot. How would he explain that? He didn't want anyone hurt.

Roger felt that it was a situation where you don't win no matter what you do. If he hurts somebody, a civilian or another officer, you're wrong. If he kills himself, you're wrong. Some of Richard's friends came by and said to Roger: He was a friend, thank you for trying.

The FBI considered a hostage or barricaded situation successful if no officer or citizen was hurt. If the suspect was hurt or killed himself, the situation was still considered a success. You're going to lose some. It was a reality Lucie and the other team members lived with.

Palmer's death hurt. When asked about it ten years later, all the officers involved said the same thing: he was one of our own.

A year after Palmer's death, Lucie received a commendation from Chief Hanton for her handling of another crisis situation. A man barricaded himself inside his home with several other people and was shooting into the street. He shot to death one man. When Lucie arrived, the victim was lying dead in the street. The district commander was there. But once the crisis team arrived, they were in charge. Other high-ranking officers had to back off. The commander didn't like that. He became territorial, he wanted his people in charge. Lucie and Roger talked to the commander as politely as possible. "Either we are going to resolve this peaceably, or we'll call the chief at home."

District personnel would panic. They would see the media and want to get the damn thing over with. The crisis team's philosophy was time. The district could not afford to dispatch personnel to the area and keep them there. There were other calls to answer.

Lucie and Roger took control and talked the suspect out. Nobody else was hurt. Hanton's commendation cited Lucie's dedication, patience, and professionalism.

Lucie shrugs off the commendation. She doesn't remember much about the incident. When she talks about her work with the crisis team, it is Richard Palmer's death she brings up. She, like the others involved, remembers it in intense detail. The rest of the situations have faded from her mind; that one is deeply imbedded in her consciousness.

12

POLICEMEN DON'T DANCE

Out on Prospect Avenue, Lucie was running a john detail. Hauling them in. She heard a guy mouthing off to the detectives, "I'm calling my attorney."

Quiet Mike Burger had been dragged out again. He came over to the car. "Lucie, this guy wants to talk to the boss."

"OK, fine," Lucie said. She didn't want to start any big problems. Of course, she knew he was expecting a man. Someone he could talk to—man to man.

He took one look at Lucie and demanded, "I said I want to talk to the boss."

"Well, I am the boss." She smiled. "Here's what we're going to do. You're going to jail. Unless you get somebody to tow your car, your car will be towed." She paused and let it sink in. Sometimes these johns just didn't comprehend the finality of the situation right away. There was a period of belligerence, then denial. Finally acceptance.

"I'm going to call my attorney. He'll be here in five minutes." The man was testy. He was a Prospect Avenue businessman.

"Fine, call him," Lucie said calmly. Surprisingly, the attorney appeared in a few minutes.

The lawyer asked Lucie, "What's going to happen?"

"If he gives you the car, fine. I couldn't care less if I tow it. Take the car. He'll be charged in the morning, he'll go to court. It's as simple as that."

The businessman started again with her.

"Right now, this is a misdemeanor," she warned him. "Not a big deal. Don't start a conversation on anything else, because you're going to get yourself in a lot more trouble."

Most of the johns who were first offenders were getting SIP—selective intervention program. They didn't have to do the whole ten days in jail. Lucie thought, He's a nice guy, he'll probably get that.

A few months later, she was out to dinner with Eric in Westlake. She saw the same man sitting across the room at another table. "That's a guy I arrested a few months ago," she mentioned to Eric.

She didn't think that much of it. She certainly would never talk to him. Or embarrass him. "I don't hold it against him. He did a stupid thing. He went to jail." So what, she thought, who cares. She continued eating her dinner.

But the gentleman spotted her. He insisted that she and Eric come over to the table and join him. He was sitting with two other couples. Six of them altogether.

"C'mon, I'll buy you a drink," he said. He proceeded to tell the whole group how he happened to meet Lucie. How he was down on Prospect Avenue soliciting whores. Comments flew. "I'll be darned." Laughter around the table.

Isn't this a stitch, Lucie thought. He meets Eric, just as though it were under totally different circumstances. This guy is a little odd.

For Eric, it was another one of those occasions when his view of the world was turned inside out because of Lucie.

She later got a call to the guy's business when it was vandalized. She always thought he was a little strange. He just wasn't embarrassed about it at all.

As supervisor of the unit, Lucie organized the decoy operations. She took charge when Roger was on furlough and on days off. To Mike Burger it seemed as though she had been running things all along. It's very difficult to supervise people who you've worked with, Lucie realized. Many of the officers had more years on the job than she did. Things would be a lot tougher for her now.

Thin-lipped Detective Ed Kelly was described as the guy that never smiled. He would chew Roger out. He was probably the officer most opposed to women. If he set down his paper and said, in his raspy voice, Oh, all right, she did a nice job—that was the ultimate compliment. His eyes were an ice blue. He was grouchy, tough skinned.

He called Lucie the Cobra after she made sergeant. "Let's put it this way. You either did it her way or it wasn't going to get done," he said. "If

Howie Filler's photo of his first female SIU trainees, May 1973. (*Left to right*) Phyllis Trappenberg, Sandra Ramsey, Lucie Duvall, Karen Loy, and Karen Kilroy. (*Howard G. Filler, Jr.*)

(*Left*) Lucie and her partner Bob Borsuk in the notorius Fourth District Station. (*Robert Borsuk collection*)

(*Below*) Rookie Lucie Duvall on patrol. (*Robert Borsuk collection*)

Lucie at her Seven Barn locker—with *Playgirl* poster. (*Robert Borsuk collection*)

Lucie at her desk in SIU, third shift, about 1977. (*Lucie J. Duvall collection*)

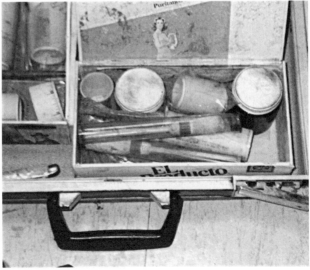

(*Above*) May 12, 1975. The bomb site of gangster Danny Greene's Waterloo Road home. Detectives search the rubble. (*Bernie Noble. Courtesy of the Cleveland Press Collection/ Cleveland State University Archives*)

(*Right*) Lucie's fingerprint brushes and powder. (*Authors' collection*)

(*Above*) May 14, 1981. The strike force celebrates Lucie's promotion to sergeant. (*Left to right*) Bill Reiber, Booker Bledsoe, Roger Dennerll, Lucie, Harlan Worthington. (*Roger J. Dennerll collection*)

(*Left*) Lucie with Channel Eight reporter Bill McKay at her sergeant's promotion. (*Roger J. Dennerll collection*)

Roger Dennerll pins on Lucie's new gold shield. (*Roger J. Dennerll collection*)

1984. The Third District vice office. (*Left to right*) Lucie, Paul Scott, Jimmy Davidson, Mark Hastings, Tim Bright. (*Chris Stevens*)

1984. Lucie and Bigfoot George Deli. Note padlocked file cabinet on the left. (*Chris Stevens*)

1984. Lucie working vice on Prospect Avenue with her detectives. (*Left to right*) Alan Strange, Clarence Ware, Lucie. (*Chris Stevens*)

CRIME STOPPER ALERT

I AM OFFERING A REWARD FOR INFORMATION LEADING TO THE RETURN UNHARMED OF BELOW PICTURED BEAR.

LAST SEEN WEARING BLUE SLICKER, YELLOW HAT, RED/WHT. F.B.I SHIRT, BLUE NECKTIE.

ANSWERS TO NAME OF PADDINGTON.

ALL REPLIES WILL BE KEPT STRICTLY CONFIDENTIAL. She has been known to lie

CALL X-3678

(*Left*) 1984. Lucie's Crime Stopper Alert for Paddington Bear at the FBI National Academy (*Lucie J. Duvall collection*)

(*Below*) Lucie receives her diploma from the FBI Director, William H. Webster. (*FBI*)

1990. Lucie, in her sex crimes office, prepares to go to the range for annual firearms training. (*Authors' collection*)

Lucie loads her snubnosed .38 Smith and Wesson. (*Authors' collection*)

Lucie straps on the laser gun at the FATS machine. (*Authors' collection*)

I didn't like what she was doing, maybe she didn't like what I was doing."

She had her quirks after she became boss. No breaks for anybody. Kelly thought you ought to use discretion. Not Lucie. Everybody went to jail.

He and his partner, Reiber, could not have seemed more different, yet talking about Reiber brought a smile to Kelly's taut face. They had gone to high school together, had come on the job together, and were partners for eighteen years. They planned to retire together.

There was only one time when Bill Reiber really had a disagreement with Lucie. One of the decoys was solicited by a guy who was getting married the next day. "We had a policy where we put these guys in on a pink or an investigation card, where we kept them overnight. This could really cause them a little more grief at home. It's a little tough to explain." Reiber thought the guy should be given a break.

Lucie said, "No way. He's staying." Lucie stuck by their policy, everybody else was going in on a pink that day, and so was the groom-to-be.

"Usually they say they'd been picked up on a DWI," Lucie said. "They think up something to tell their wives."

Roger felt he was learning from Lucie. He felt more macho, stronger with a gun. He relied on it. He talked differently when he wore the gun. But he had been watching Lucie's technique of calming suspects, and he learned a better way of negotiating from her method.

One day, he rushed out on a call for crisis negotiation, and in the midst of talking to the suspect, he realized he didn't have his gun. After that, it just became a lot easier not to carry one. Now he would talk forever.

Roger and Lucie had a lot to talk about. She had enrolled at Dyke College to complete her credits. Roger was also going to college. Lucie didn't like rehashing the same old cop stories on a tour of duty and neither did Roger. They talked about a movie they had seen or a book they had read. They both liked to travel. It was just a lot more interesting for Roger than, I just got this new gun and it shoots.

Wherever they went, they would try to blend in by doing what everyone else was doing. They made the job of dealing with the street life fun. When they went into a bar to watch for violations, they would dance together. People would relax, forget they were around. As far as other people were concerned, policemen don't dance.

Lucie loved to dance. "I made Eric go to Arthur Murray. He said it was the low point of our relationship. Eric just hated it. But I talked him into going, God bless him. It really was the pits. We did finish the course, needless to say, but it just didn't work out. He still couldn't dance."

Roger did like to dance. For Lucie's birthday, they decided to go to the State Theater. The State was running a show called "Stompin' at the State" with audience participation. The show was a huge success. The big band played forties tunes. There were "dime-a-dance" girls, a conga line, and a ragtime pianist in the outer lobby. Lucie and Roger entered the jitterbug contest and won—a seventy-five-dollar gift certificate at Rinaldi Jewelry. They split the gift money and Lucie bought a pair of earrings.

One night, Roger and Lucie "got the gift of the gab" over a bottle of wine.

"Lucie, there's got to be a better approach." Roger shook his head. "I just experienced this real B.S. situation. You're an outsider, what do you think."

Roger was a licensed real estate broker, and he had been doing real estate as a business and hobby, his getaway from police work.

Ohio had passed a law requiring all agents and real estate brokers to have thirty hours of continuing education every three years. Roger took a course right away, and he really resented it. He told Lucie it was one of those seminars with six hundred of the biggest names in real estate, and this evangelist of real estate telling them for close to three hours how they could make a million dollars if they only bought his tapes and followed his program. Roger felt it was a waste of time and money.

Lucie sipped her wine and listened. She was always up for new endeavors. They started brainstorming.

Roger said, "Captive audience. Money to be made."

Over that bottle of wine, they started the RJD School of Real Estate. Their school would provide the required continuing education and actually help the salesmen. It would give an outsider's view to real estate people, improve the image. They figured out what they thought was really important for people to know to sell real estate.

Roger went to Columbus and got the forms. Lucie sat down with him and they developed a curriculum. The state approved it. Teaching was a way for both of them to escape from the stress of working vice-related crimes and crisis negotiations.

Roger taught the classes that were more technical. They had an attorney come in to teach the required segment on racial discrimination. Lucie became director of continuing education. She taught advertising, negotiating, handling objection to sales. The principles were a lot like the hostage negotiation techniques, at least that was how Lucie translated her material. She studied and did quite a bit of homework, reading in her spare time. She had developed the habit of educating herself.

The RJD School of Realty was the only school in the State of Ohio under the auspices of a real estate company. The rest were run by colleges. They did advertising and sent out fliers. "The good part was when people started sending checks and signing up for the school," Lucie laughed. "We were scared to death."

They ran the school out of a building Roger owned. One side he used for his realty business and the other side he usually rented out. But it happened to be vacant, and Roger decided not to rent it again.

They had one course on Monday nights, three hours a night for ten weeks. The other course was on Saturday and Sunday mornings for five hours; perfect for people who wanted to get it over in three weekends.

Lucie was a person from outside. She told the students, Here's what we think of real estate people: you have no ethics. She was her usual forthright self. Despite her nervousness, she was confident, and she held their interest. Later, she would take her teaching skills to the police academy.

Eric could not believe Lucie was doing this. "This is great except for one major flaw," he told her. "You don't know anything about selling real estate."

Eric dropped by for one class on advertising.

Behind the classroom was a hallway that divided either side of the building. Eric, standing in the hallway, could hear Lucie but not see her.

He was astounded. Here was this voice, talking about things he never knew she knew anything about. And here she was, teaching it to other people. And they're paying her. Really bizarre. Eric had underestimated Lucie's abilities.

Lucie had matured over the five years they'd been married. Police work had taught her how tenuous life is. She was a person with high energy and many interests—she had learned to wear life lightly. In her work she pushed forward, had made rank in a tough male world. She was mentored. Respected. Her future looked as though it could really take off.

The lieutenant's exam was coming up.

"I've only been a sergeant a short time," Lucie protested.

"We'll study here," Roger decided. They put up work tables where they could leave their books out. There was a blackboard and anything else they needed. Promotionals required a lot of studying. Roger encouraged Lucie to go after it.

Lucie studied hard and she was really excited when she passed high on the lieutenant's list. She was number eleven. Roger didn't score high enough to get promoted. The guys on the strike force teased, "Lucie's got the bars, Roger wears the stripes."

The actual promotion wouldn't come through for quite a while. It was held up in court again, due to the Shield Club case and a lot of countersuits. They were told that when the promotion did come through, they would get back pay covering the delay time. But this was a significant move in her career. Where would she go when the promotion finally came through?

The strike force was really rolling. Decoy details at night. Touring for robbers and street crime during the day. Lucie supervised a compelling prostitution case of Booker's. A john had tipped them off because he felt sorry for the underage prostitute who told him her story. The pimp, who was thirty-one, had kidnapped two teenagers and forced them to work on the street, picking them up one day after school. Booker started the investigation in July. By November, the grand jury indicted the pimp on rape, compelling prostitution, promoting, and drug charges.

Tips from the street were bringing in other leads on call girl services and escort businesses. Some services they busted from ads in the paper. That was in late summer. The street prostitutes thought it wasn't fair that they were busted all the time and the call girls weren't bothered. Sometimes they gave the strike force leads.

Lucie and Roger got a call on a shooting. A prostitute was involved. They knew she frequented the Garfield Hotel. They went right over. It was the middle of the afternoon, but it was pitch black inside the hotel bar and packed with people Lucie and Roger recognized from the street. Lucie saw the prostitute they were looking for standing next to her pimp at the bar.

Lucie eyed the pimp. He was carrying a small square leather bag, the kind that a lot of the pimps carried. She thought he had a gun inside of it. Roger and Lucie looked at each other. A split second of: was he going to shoot at them? Working vice was dangerous. They were in plainclothes, without portable radios. Someone could shoot and then say, I didn't know they were cops.

Lucie wedged herself between the pimp and the prostitute. She put her hand down on his leather bag and could feel the gun. She told him, "Why don't we step outside. We want to talk to you about this."

She took his bag, and they went outside. The whole bar emptied out and followed them. Lucie looked around. It's just me and Roger. We're talking serious street people, she thought, scanning the crowd.

"What about the gun?" Lucie asked the pimp.

He turned and asked Roger, "Who are you?"

Lucie knew Roger didn't have his badge with him. Or his gun. This was not unusual. Once, chasing and cornering an armed robber, Roger realized he didn't have his gun. Lucie had tossed hers over the fence to him. The robber broke out laughing.

Now, Lucie took charge. "Say, look," she said. "I'm the police. I don't know what's going on here, but he's with me."

Roger was busily searching his pockets for identification. The crowd was tightening around them. He managed to find his realtor's license.

Oh, please, give me a break, Lucie thought. "He's with me. Don't worry about that," she asserted.

Usually Roger and Lucie tried to talk and use humor to mollify suspects. But this crowd was too aggressive. Hostile. Lucie already had her gun, so Roger took the pimp's gun from her.

"Don't anybody move," Roger yelled.

The one thing that was always nice about being on the strip, Lucie thought, there were always enough guns to go around. You just had to get them off the people and redistribute them.

But the pimp didn't find anything funny. Roger and Lucie would never back away. The crowd could see that. They ended up in a knock-down, drag-out fight. A strike force car rolled up to help. They took a lot of people to jail. The pimp was charged with carrying a concealed weapon and the others with disorderly conduct.

Lucie walked into work the night of September 24, 1982, with Roger. Two of the guys were already in the office. They yelled out, "Hey, Lucie, guess what? You don't work here anymore."

"What?" Another transfer? She looked at Roger. He didn't know what was going on. They handed her a departmental notice. She thought they must have written this up themselves. This has got to be a joke. She just couldn't believe the chief had done this without telling her. Or Roger. She was stunned.

The notice was effective the next day, Saturday. Lucie was off to Third District vice. As its chief.

13

TOUGH AND GRIND

There was a cold silence as Lucie walked past the patrol officers, down the hall of old Central Station. They know I am here to cause problems, she thought, steeling herself. She reported to one of her supervisors, Captain *Edwards*. His welcome was succinct.

"Lucie, I want you to know you were rammed down my throat and I don't want you here."

"Captain Edwards, I'm just here to do my job," she answered. Her chin tightened. Her eyes hardened.

She was taken aback. She hadn't expected to be welcomed with open arms, but this was worse than she thought it would be. There were problems in the Third District vice unit. She was sent in to clean them up. If Captain Edwards hates me now, she thought, he ain't seen nothing yet.

Chief Hanton had shaken up the vice squads, placing all his own people in as supervisors. He had worked vice for years. "I had a good handle on the doggone thing. Vice is a very strong problem area, and you have to take control. I wanted new people, with new ideas." He knew the commanders would be angry. The districts were their little fiefdoms. "But I was the chief and I was responsible and I was going to do it my way. If I was wrong, prove me wrong."

In every district but the Third, the new vice supervisors were lieutenants. Lucie was at a double disadvantage. Although awaiting promotion, she was still a sergeant. And she was a woman. There had never been a woman as head of vice in Cleveland. No one had ever heard of a woman commanding vice anywhere.

* * *

Lucie and Roger were at the tail end of a covert operation when Lucie was transferred. They had worked all summer piling up citations against five bars that posed the worst problems in the downtown area. All five would be hit at once, with state liquor agents, media, SWAT, and lots of other cops. A high-profile crackdown.

Hanton gave Lucie advice. If there are any vice men you trust, take them with you. If not, just work with the strike force. Don't say anything about it. Notify Captain Edwards when you are walking into the first bar.

Lucie tried to call Edwards but couldn't get hold of him. She called radio to page him. He didn't answer his page.

They started at the Prospect Lounge, where a customer could sit at a barstool, and a broomstick with a slit across it popped up through a hole in the floor. Put money in the slit, the broomstick disappeared and then reappeared, drugs replacing the customer's money. Prostitutes sold their services. The winning numbers in illegal numbers games were wrapped around liquor bottles with rubber bands.

The entourage arrived—Lucie, Roger, and a total of about thirty police officers, SWAT men in their black fatigues, carrying their high-powered rifles, a *Plain Dealer* reporter, TV crews with bright lights and cameras. Police relieved patrons inside of one shotgun and five revolvers.

And one vice man lost his job with Lucie. *Dave Phillips* was supposed to be on duty. Instead Lucie spotted him in the Prospect Lounge—drying beer glasses with one hand, his other hand fondling a barmaid. I bet you are one surprised little patrolman, Lucie thought. You know you are history. He was the first vice man she transferred out of her unit.

With residents and businessmen crowding them, cheering, and applauding, Lucie, Roger and the group hit the Wine & Roses on Euclid. At the Sir Charles Lounge, they seized a .38 caliber revolver, listed as stolen from the Massachusetts state police.

Lucie and Roger gave press interviews on the street and walked under a bold blue and white billboard to bust Stage Door Johnnie's, a champagne hustle bar where prostitutes took customers into round booths, closed the red velvet curtains, and performed sex acts—after the customer had bought a bottle of cheap champagne for a hundred twenty-five dollars, plus ordered three drinks at the bar at ten dollars a pop. The sex was an extra fee.

Next door was the New Era Burlesque. The marquee was red. White and red glittering words flashed: LIVE BURLESQUE, FRESH AND EXCITING NEW LOVE ACT. Inside, dancers performed live sex shows.

Bar number five was the Malibu Lounge on Euclid near the corner where Lucie did her decoy details. According to citations, the Malibu featured dancers exposing breasts, vaginas, buttocks, pubic areas, simulating masturbation, and performing "lewd and suggestive dances."

When they finished, she and Roger reported to the chief's office. As Lucie waited to see Hanton, she called Captain Edwards one more time. This time, she got him.

"Captain Edwards, I tried to notify you earlier in the day and I wasn't able to reach you."

"Where are you?" he demanded. "Are you going to see Hanton?"

"Yeah, I'm waiting to go see him right now."

"You tell him to call me." It sounded to Lucie as though he spoke through gritted teeth.

"Fine," she said.

She and Roger went into Hanton's spacious office. "How'd it go," the chief asked them. "It looked like it went well. Everything's fine, everybody's happy, good job," he commended them, his tenor voice resonating.

"We-el," Lucie said, "I just talked to Captain Edwards. He's not happy. He wants you to call him."

Hanton called the captain. Lucie could only hear one end of the conversation.

"I know she didn't tell you," Hanton said. "She did exactly what I told her to do. Be glad there is someone over there who can solve some of your problems. Just let her do it."

Hanton had considered different people to head downtown vice. He asked for recommendations from people he trusted. Lucie stood out. Hanton had first noticed Lucie in the Fourth. When he was a captain there, Lucie and her then-partner, Diane Parkinson, told him they weren't being utilized to their utmost capacities. Hanton realized that the laws had changed, women had the right to all the work, but they were being overprotected. He did what he could for them, but he was transferred out soon afterward. Lucie and Parkinson's attitudes were a welcome change. Somebody asking to do more.

The Third District was unique because of all the prostitutes there. He thought Lucie might handle that problem well. A female can't fool a female, he figured. She knew what the hookers were doing and how to stop them. They wouldn't be able to con her. Plus, Lucie had a good relationship with community groups. Some guys—if they couldn't get it done in five minutes, it's over with. It could take forever to get the simplest things done. If you don't have the patience, intelligence, and ability, it won't get done. Lucie took the time.

"Here's how we are going to run this," Lucie told her remaining vice men. Her red head bobbed as she stressed her words. "We can get along, but we're going to do it my way or you're going the way Dave Phillips went."

The vice men were not happy.

Kenny Kirchner was a salty veteran, strong shouldered with a wide face, thick neck, and large ears. His hands were powerful, his fingers broad. Kenny was called the Blade. He carried a small pocketknife. When they went into cheat spots he would check to see if the felt was nice on the pool tables. With his knife under his palm, he cut across the bank, from one pocket to the other, and told the owners, How do you play pool on this table, it's all sliced up.

"That's operating outside," Kirchner said. "Whether anybody would condone that, I'm actually damaging their property, but it's done to keep other damage from being done. People lose money, they get violent, they come back with a shotgun."

On the job since 1965, Kenny had gone into vice after fourteen years. Vice was different; it was a tough and grind type of job.

"I thought Lucie didn't know the techniques for busting cheat spots. You have to operate on the gray side," Kirchner said. "Where we would go through the back door, she wanted to go through the front door." Kirchner didn't know Lucie had been busting cheat spots since she was a rookie.

He knew of Lucie—she was the one called Roger Dennerll's wife. Kenny resented her being a female. He thought his previous boss was fantastic. What was going to happen now?

Jimmy Davidson, one of Kenny's partners, was born in Scotland. He had come to the States in 1967 and had worked hard to lose his accent. He came on the job in 1977 and had been in the vice unit about six months. A part-time model, he cut a handsome figure, his dark hair contrasting with his fair skin. Davidson did not like Roger's high-profile act. He preferred to run silent, run deep. Lucie worked for Roger—one strike against her. And Davidson made no bones about his feelings about women cops. He informed the whole country about them on a "20/20" Geraldo Rivera segment. Policewomen could give out parking tickets and moving violations. That was about it. Davidson figured Lucie might cramp their style. They were going into strip joints and country bars, shit-kicking bars. Those bars were tough, there was always fighting. If the shit hits the fan, what's she gonna do?

Davidson didn't know how Lucie was going to change the unit workings, and quite honestly, he didn't want to find out.

Lucie called her old Fourth District vice buddy Frank Krob, for support. "I don't want to put my foot in it," she told Krob.

"You've got to be the boss," Krob encouraged her. "I could work for you because I like you, and I know you're capable and your being a woman doesn't make any difference to me. But some guys can't stand it. You've got to let them know where you stand right off. Don't worry, they'll come 'round eventually. You've got to put your foot down." She has a rough way to go, Krob thought. It seemed to him that things had become tougher for her since she had been promoted to sergeant.

Lucie knew that to run a vice unit effectively, she had to have people she could trust implicitly. They had to be her people. She took a different tack from most new supervisors, who move out all the old crew. She made a conscious plan to pick the brains of the vice men already in the unit and then move them out one by one, and choose her own men. She couldn't be fast in getting rid of them. She needed to know what they knew.

From her work with the strike force, she knew which cops were a heartbeat away from causing problems. Those were not the people she would pick for her unit.

Hanton set up a support system for Lucie. Call Bob Cermak in organized crime or Ron Kosits in professional conduct/internal review (PCIR), he told her, if she needed information on cops. Hanton chose well. Both men would become her professional allies and good friends. Lieutenant Kosits had smooth, thin black hair, slicked down close to his head and parted way over on the left side. His face was narrow, his eyes deep brown, his mustache full and thick. His heavy dark eyebrows angled down, giving him the look of the Wise potato chip owl.

Kosits knew Lucie was having a hard time. He knew Lucie wanted to run a clean outfit. Information was supposed to flow into internal affairs, not out, but he ran checks on people whom she wanted to bring in, and on people she wanted to move out.

She started with eight vice men. Jimmy Davidson was new in vice, she kept him on. Kirchner was an expert in liquor violations, he stayed until he was promoted to sergeant. One vice man she got rid of because she suspected he was leaking information. Another man had a drinking problem and a problem with women. Lucie liked him, but he was an accident waiting to happen. He didn't need a job where he barhopped for a living. One man found the stress of constant on-the-job socializing too much. Her office man, Bob Singleton, she thought was wonderful.

Kirchner resented Lucie bouncing these guys out, one at a time. What did she have in mind? Putting her own people in like pawns in a chess game?

Lucie put out an anticipated assignment, but almost no one wanted to come work for "the red-headed bitch." She couldn't pick just anybody. Her selection pool was limited to Third District officers who applied for the job and who met union requirements.

She chose Mark Hastings, who had a good reputation and wasn't tied in with any of the old vice crew. His hair was shaggy brown; his eyes blue-gray and full of light, his fair Irish skin blushed easily. He was close-mouthed and matter-of-fact. Like Lucie, he was an only child and friends were important to him.

He had joined the Olmstead Township police force in 1970 and worked there for nine years, becoming a sergeant in charge of the juvenile unit and the gang task force. In July of 1979 he joined the Cleveland force and worked a zone car until he joined Lucie's vice unit.

Hastings was glad to have a boss who had a reputation for integrity. One of his patrol partners downed three-fifths of alcohol a day. Hastings spent most of his tour of duty in bars, especially Stage Door Johnnie's. "A place where they ripped off people, there were whores running around and dancers and drugs," Hastings said later, his full cheeks turning purple. "My partner was at the bar, I'd be sitting there drinking a cup of coffee, calling in the police reports. That's where he wanted to go. What are you going to do?"

Hastings replaced Phillips. Kirchner introduced Mark to Dave Phillips. "Why don't you give Mark the keys?" Kenny said.

Phillips threw them at Mark.

The problems escalated. Ready to go home after a long night, Mark took the rickety, small elevator, divided in half by a moving gate—for transporting prisoners, down to the basement garage. Ages ago, the garage had been used for roll call. It smelled musty. The cinder block walls, covered with peeling white and black paint, the orange doors, orange pipes crisscrossing the ceiling, and black and white pillars created an eerie atmosphere. Hastings's steps echoed on the cement floor as he walked toward his car—more than ready to go home. It was four o'clock in the morning. He spotted his car. He sighed. The air had been let out of one of his tires.

Tires were slashed on the other vice men's cars. The garage was locked. No one but cops had access to it.

The cops harassed the vice men. Lucie's Angels. Lucie's Punk Boys. Lucie's Dancing Bears. Ten years later, Mark was still being called a dancing bear by a lieutenant. "What are you doing hanging onto her skirts," they taunted. "You're selling out working for that red-headed bitch." Bitch was the nicest name applied to Lucie.

Davidson resented the razzing he got. He'd been on the streets, and he had done a good job. Now he found himself in a unit headed by a woman, and all of sudden he was one of Lucie's Angels.

The zone car men resented Lucie. Another problem, Kirchner sighed. "The patrol cops are the eyes and ears. They used to give us information, there was a camaraderie. Now they didn't want to tell Lucie nothing. The grunts—the officers in the black and whites—they were the backbone. Without those people you cannot operate."

Lucie knew her men were going through hell working for her; she knew it was hard when peers turned against you.

Captain Edwards called Lucie into his office. "We've got a terrible problem," he started.

"OK. What is it?"

"After-hours dancing."

"I beg your pardon," Lucie said.

"You know, dancing isn't allowed in the city of Cleveland after midnight. We've got some bars downtown that stop serving liquor at two-thirty, but they continue to sell soft drinks and juice and permit dancing."

"Yah, I know," Lucie said.

"They are in violation of the After Hours Dancing law. They've got to stop."

Lucie just looked at him. She ducked her head slightly sideways, her eyes narrowing. She was thinking, I'm sure there are laws on the books about not spitting on the sidewalk, too. This law must have been on the books since the 1930s.

She was right. It was the same law Wilma Neubecker had enforced when she toured dance halls, warning couples not to dance cheek to cheek.

"What's the problem?" Lucie asked him.

"All these people are going out into the street, and we don't have a lot of zone car coverage. There could be problems."

Lucie had never heard of any problems.

"I want you to work on this," Edwards finished.

"You're right," Lucie said. "I'll take care of it."

Another diversionary tactic. Lucie smoldered, her cheeks scarlet, her eyes blue fire. Divert her into garbage, that's his idea. She'll get tired. That's the name of his game.

Lucie chose her tactics with care. She didn't want to be in out-and-out opposition to her superior officer. She didn't want to embarrass him. She had the chief's backing, but she didn't want to just throw things in the captain's face. By the same token, I have my job to do, she reasoned. She had to walk a fine line.

That Saturday night she took two of her men with her and hit Rumors, a downtown club. It was four in the morning and hundreds of dancing patrons were living it up.

Lucie went to the owner. "You're closed," she informed him.

"For what?" he asked.

"After-hours dancing," she said.

"After-hours dancing?" he repeated, incredulous.

"That's right. You're in violation of municipal code six ninety."

"We're not serving any liquor," he protested.

"I know that," Lucie said. "I had a drink at the bar and I know you're not serving alcohol. No problem with that. It's the dancing. Everybody out."

The startled owner told everyone to leave and closed his establishment.

As Lucie left, she threw her parting shot. "Quite frankly, I'm only operating on complaints. Right now, I have to do this, you are in violation, but I think this is very bad legislation. What I suggest is that you contact the captain and contact your councilman and have them take a look at this piece of legislation, because I think it should be taken off the books."

They hit four clubs. By the time they reached the third one, the owners were calling ahead, warning one another.

Monday morning, Lucie went to the chief prosecutor's office in the Justice Center and spoke to Patrick Roche, first assistant prosecutor. She asked him to take a look at the legislation.

"I don't think this should be enforced anymore," she told him.

He agreed with her and wrote a memo to Captain Edwards: "My opinion has been solicited by members of the Third District vice unit on the subject of the constitutionality of M. C. Chapter 690 as it is applied to after-hours dancing.... It is my opinion that dancing after hours is not presently illegal." He cited two municipal court cases in which the statute was found unconstitutional.

Memo in hand, Lucie's next stop was Captain Edwards's office. His phone had already been ringing with complaints.

"You know, I got to thinking about that, Captain," Lucie said, "and I just don't think this is good legislation. So—we don't have to worry about after-hours dancing anymore, because the prosecutor's office won't enforce it."

"No," was patrolman Tim Bright's definite response when Lucie asked him if he wanted to join her unit. Working vice was like working in a sewer eight hours a day as far as he was concerned. You get burned out and your productivity goes right in the dumper.

Tall, with thick dark hair, a bushy mustache, ruddy skin, and a craggy outdoors look, Bright had been a fireman for four years but joined the police force because he wanted more action.

"Would you please give it a try," Lucie persisted. "You don't have to make the decision right away. If it doesn't work out, I will see to it that you are put back on your old car in your old platoon."

Lucie's assurance gave Bright a sense of security. He turned the idea over in his mind. Working vice would broaden his experience of police work.

Vice units are kick-ass-and-take-names units. There were old-timers in vice, and Bright agreed with Lucie: a vice unit needed guys that were full of piss and vinegar, who were going to run around and give her 200 percent every minute they were there.

Bright was prone to spouting unusual phrases; he was open, funny, and a little crazy, Lucie discovered. She wanted people with a sense of humor. Vice work was almost all misdemeanors. "You have to take it seriously while having a good time." "Barney Miller" was what police work was really like.

Lucie took Tim Bright and two others to raid Wash's, a notorious cheat spot at Forty-sixth and Cedar. It was down in the basement of a dilapidated building. Dressed in civilian clothes, they knocked on the back door.

Bright was carrying his long, black flashlight, wrapped as usual with three or four sets of handcuffs around it. The extra cuffs were handy for nights they made arrests in bulk. "Plus it makes a nice weight if you have to do any persuasion."

The doorman said, "Yeah, can I help you."

"We'd like to come in for a drink," Bright said.

"Yeah, sure, come on in," he answered.

That was easy. Bright looked at Lucie, and Lucie looked at him. They all went inside. The bar was at the far end of the basement. The four undercover cops walked through the pool table area, and past the pinball machines. If we don't look like four bumps on a pickle, Bright thought. But no one questioned their presence.

He put his flashlight lined with handcuffs on the bar.

"Can I help you?" the bartender asked.

"Yeah," Bright told her. "Give me two Millers."

"OK," she said, giving him the beers. You could have knocked me down with a feather, he said later. I couldn't believe it.

He paid for the drinks. They had their case.

"Police. This is a raid." Lucie took charge, directing the operation.

The proprietor, Hiawatha Carlton, came over to her. He was in his seventies, paralyzed on his left side from a stab wound inflicted in 1938—when, a half hour after he was married, his "outside woman" knifed him in the chest.

"This is just an old folks' home," he told Lucie in his raspy voice.

"Mr. Carlton," Lucie said, "we're gonna have to close you down."

The vice men placed the employees and patrons under arrest. Lucie kept an eye on the crowd, watching for any trouble. They took inventory, writing down everything they found, and confiscated the evidence. Bright was impressed with Lucie. She went in "like one of the boys," but she didn't start screaming orders at the half-drunk, doped-up crowd.

She was beginning to make her own team. Beginning to gain their respect.

"Dahlin'," Mr. Carlton said to Lucie as they left, "I knew you'd be coming. I was waitin' for you. You're just as charming as I've been told you were."

Lucie just couldn't fathom the vice tradition of drinking the evidence. After raiding a cheat spot, vice men returned to the office to inventory any items confiscated—liquor, cash registers, jukebox, gambling devices. Sometimes they broke open a six-pack of beer to drink while doing the tedious paperwork and took home unopened bottles of liquor. Lucie put her foot down.

All items confiscated went into the property room. She didn't allow her vice men to drink any evidence—not even a bottle of pop. They were not allowed to accept free drinks from bars either. No free food—not even a glass of juice.

"We are going to play by the rules," she told her crew. "You may laugh and not like the way I do things, but you'll never get indicted while you are working for me."

She was just as upset if her vice men were wrongly accused. One of the other vice lieutenants told her he thought some of her men were hanging out in a cheat spot. It wasn't true, and she stood up for them.

She believed in keeping control. She had watched other supervisors operate. She was determined to do things differently. She wasn't going to place any of her vice men in a position where they had to lie or cheat to get out of something. And if one of them wanted to operate on his own agenda, God help him if she found out.

She changed the expense system. Vice men spent money—drinking at bars, looking for prostitution, gambling, and liquor violations. At the end of each month, they turned in their expense reports and received reimbursement. When the first check came, office man Bob Singleton offered to cash it and distribute the money. Lucie said, OK. He disbursed the money and gave some to her.

"I didn't spend any money," she told him. "I wasn't there."

"We all split it equally," he explained to her. They had been doing it that way for years. Even he got a cut because he did all the paperwork.

Lucie wasn't comfortable with that system. Something wasn't right. The feeling nagged at her.

"From now on," she announced, "everybody will be paid for exactly what they spent."

What a hardass, she heard the vice men muttering. Right down to the penny.

The vice office was on the first floor. The door wasn't locked. It didn't take her long to learn there were leaks. Anybody could go in there. She found reports rifled and files stolen.

Lucie prowled through Central Station, the oldest left in the city, looking for a place to move. She went up to the second floor. Walking through the dreary, beige marble halls, she found a courtroom, left over from the days when the municipal court was in the Central Station. Next to the courtroom, Lucie discovered an old judge's chambers tucked behind a wooden door. The room she entered was narrow, so narrow that two people sitting behind desks, back to back, would bump their chairs against each other. A doorway led into the second room, slightly wider, but also very small. Off the second room was a half-bathroom, a sink, and a toilet. My own bathroom, Lucie thought. Finally. The ceilings were falling down, and the paint was coming off the walls. The old judge's chambers was ugly as sin. But it would serve her purpose. It was out of the way.

She faced Captain Edwards again. "I can't ever know where the leaks are if I start from an insecure atmosphere. I'm moving upstairs."

"There is no room up there," he told her.

She informed him of her plan to take over the old judge's chambers.

"It's a mess," the captain said.

"I'll clean it up," Lucie responded.

She relocated, she and the vice men lugging file cabinets and paper-work upstairs. She turned the inner room into her office, hanging posters of the Terminal Tower and other attractive Cleveland sites on the peeling old walls. She changed the locks on the door and ordered a telephone. None came. Every time she checked, she was given excuses about it. She brought in her own phone from home and hooked it up herself.

"We're operating," she informed Captain Edwards.

"You don't have a phone," he said.

"Yes, I do," she declared.

Once her phone was plugged in, it started ringing off the hook. Citizens complaining: "There's six whores on the corner of Thirty-sixth and Prospect. Put them in jail, now." Furious businessmen. "The hookers are stopping traffic. What are you going to do about this?"

Lucie threw her hands up. The whores have been there for fifty years and they want me to get rid of them overnight. The frustration was horrible. She felt like she was operating from an armed camp, fighting on all flanks. Her own vice men didn't want her there. She didn't have enough men to do the job, and some of those she had she didn't trust.

Roger was in a snit because she no longer worked for him and she was getting promoted to lieutenant and he wasn't. He saw her as the person who worked for him; it seemed to her he didn't like seeing her on an equal level.

She felt as though everyone wanted her to fail. She had to prove herself. She was hanging by her fingernails. There were days she came home totally exhausted.

Eric had developed a theory about his life-style, which he called the garage door philosophy. Leave business at work and leave the personal stuff at home. He didn't relate day-to-day stories socially about his work. A lot of people didn't even know what he did, all they knew was that he worked for a big company. Eric worked long hours under the enormous pressure of the corporate environment. But he found Lucie's vice job to be very stressful. It started to put a strain on the marriage. "She just seemed to be overwhelmed with this enforcement issue between the prostitutes and the liquor violations and all those kinds of things, I mean there's a zillion bars downtown. Somehow she should erase every prostitute, every liquor violation, every illegal drinking thing."

Kirchner heard that Lucie wanted to shut down every downtown cheat spot. "That's like saying it won't rain tomorrow." His laugh was clipped.

Lucie called Chief Hanton. "Are you sure I'm not in over my head?" she asked him.

"You're not," he assured her. "Just do what has to be done over there. If it ever gets real bad, come and see me. You can hide out in my office. I'm here to help you—but I'm not worried. You're going to go through hell. You'll probably have a very bad six months at least, but once you get it running the way you want, you'll be having a ball. Trust me. You know what you're doing. And remember, nothing is sacred. I don't care whose toes you step on. I'll take the flak. Just tough it out."

14

MIXING THE P'S

Brad was in and out of Lucie and Eric's life while she ran vice. He was off to Ohio University and would come home some weekends. He thought his mom liked running vice better than any of her other jobs. She had her own office and set her own hours. He met most of the vice officers, Tim Bright, Jim Davidson, Mark Hastings.

Eric had not expected to marry a police officer. Lucie thought he married her because "I scrubbed up well. Except for my job—which Eric thought I would quit." Lucie knew all the social graces. "That's what I was raised to do, was to give cocktail parties. I was wonderful at it. So from that standpoint, it was perfect for Eric. When he reached that point in his career where he felt he needed to get married, because there weren't single executives, I happened to fall right into his lap," Lucie said later, irony in her tone.

But being married to a police officer could sometimes be socially inhibiting, Eric felt. Days off didn't always fall right for business combined with personal socializing. Plus, no matter where they went, some city person or street person would know Lucie.

Lucie laughed describing the two times Eric's ultimate pin-striped-suit image was shattered, while they shopped at Saks in Beachwood. The first time was in early summer. A man had come up to Lucie in the store.

"Hi, Lucie, how are you?" He and Lucie had a conversation. Eric turned to Lucie when he left and wondered, "Was that a pimp?"

He was dressed like a pimp, Lucie acknowledged. But, no, he wasn't. "He's a policeman in organized crime, Eric."

186

Lucie and Eric were back shopping at Saks at Christmastime. A woman came up to Lucie and started talking to her. The woman was Shandra, with her baby. *Jewelle* had been born on January 15, 1981—the same day Billy Riedthaler had been shot.

"Oh, Shandra, how are ya?" Lucie asked. "What are you doing?"

"Christmas shopping."

Lucie and Shandra chatted. Behind her came Matthew Corbett. Lucie thought, If Eric has an image of what a pimp looks like, Matthew is it. If you asked Eric what a pimp would wear shopping, he'd probably say, some kind of white fur. Matthew was wearing a long white mink coat and a matching white mink hat. With his white mink high-heeled boots he seemed almost seven feet tall. Lucie looked at Eric. It seemed to her he was turning pale and just about ready to back into a rack of clothing, a "get me out of here" expression on his face. He's probably thinking, Why is it always when we're in a nice place the worst-looking outfit in the whole place knows *my* wife?

After they left, Eric said, "Let me guess. That was a policeman?"

"No, that was a pimp." Lucie's eyes twinkled.

Matthew Corbett had learned a lot from the police. "Like stay out the way. Back up. Even though I was what I was, we began to look at each other differently. She's a police and I'm a pimp and we kind of grew up together. I learnt a lot about my own self. Plus, I don't know how to sell pussy, so what am I down there for. Hunh." His voice dropped lower and he smiled. His eyes didn't sparkle, they had a dulled look.

He was having a problem. There were a few cops that were trying to take Corbett's women away from him. One tried to crack on *Cynthia* for sex. She said no. So the cop put her in jail. The next day Cynthia told Corbett about it, and he saw the cop at the Justice Center.

Outside the courtroom with a friend, in front of a crowd, Corbett started in: "Yeah, Officer, why don't you take some pussy now or is you scared too many people watching." Then Corbett saw another cop. "Here comes this fool, *Parker*." Parker was shaking down hookers on the street. Arresting girls if they wouldn't give him a cut of their money.

Officer Parker ran up and started to draw his gun.

"Oh, punk, you ain't gonna shoot me. Hah." Corbett was talking crazy in front of judges, bailiffs, and other officers. "You not gonna pull that trigger, you coward."

A veteran officer grabbed Parker. "C'mon man. What you doing." The older officer walked Parker out of the Justice Center.

Parker's buddy was Officer *Alex Hull*. Pretty Matt had had a physical confrontation with Hull at the Justice Center earlier in the year when he caught Shandra with Hull. While Matthew pointed his finger at Shandra and talked to her, Hull grabbed him. Corbett slammed him to the floor. Hull was not in uniform; he reached in his pocket for his badge, flashing it to the people in the hallway.

"Better get out of here before they kick our ass," Matthew's friend warned.

Shandra came back to Matthew at the time, but now Hull was together with Shandra again. They had gotten married. "But her plan was to hook up with this police," Corbett explained. "And once they got their thing established, here she comes three days later wanting the baby that me and her had."

Hull came to the house with another officer and Shandra. Corbett gave him Jewelle. But he didn't like Hull's look.

"Hand me my gun," Matthew said to one of his girls. He pointed it at Hull. "Bring my baby back here, because I don't like the way you look. In fact, I don't even like the way you come out to my house with your uniform on and your gun on."

Hull gave Corbett the baby, but Hull's fellow officer ordered Corbett to give the baby back. Matthew gave Shandra the baby but told them: "I'm going to prove to you you've got your P's mixed up. Police and prostitutes don't go together. Pimps and prostitutes go together."

Corbett set out to make it his business to get Shandra and Jewelle back. He did it on spite. It would turn out to be his biggest mistake.

Lucie had been in charge of vice only a short time when Corbett came to her. He bumped into her at the Justice Center. He thought Lucie was a decent person. Lucie was cool. He could talk to her if he had a problem.

"I don't know what to do," he said to her. "I don't know who to talk to." He looked directly into Lucie's eyes. His gaze was flat but intense.

"What's the problem?" Lucie asked.

"I got a problem with a Cleveland policeman."

"What do you mean?" Lucie asked, her hand on her hip, waiting for the story.

"Well." His jaw tightened, he was angry. "He's got Shandra and the baby. I don't know what to do about it."

Lucie listened. No doubt about it, Matthew was a bad guy. But Corbett and Lucie had come to a peaceful coexistence since she and Roger had put him away for aggravated menacing. That did get respect. He didn't give Lucie any trouble after that. Lucie thought Matthew was a violent guy, but he wasn't a criminal in every aspect of his life. If a pimp or prostitute comes to you with a legitimate complaint, you look at it as a legitimate complaint. If they come to you because they've done some crime, you put them in jail for it. You just stay objective.

Pretty Matt wouldn't give out the name of the cop, but Lucie figured out he meant one of two cops. Parker or Hull. She told him she'd look into it.

Within days of their conversation Parker was found shot to death in his apartment. A .357 Magnum lay next to his body. The bullet had gone through his head. Lucie knew Parker and Hull were pals. She wasn't sure which one Matthew was talking about. But she had heard they shared an apartment in a building where some of the more successful pimps lived. We have police who go bad, she thought. It would not be beyond the normal possibility that we have a policeman that's a part-time pimp. Sure as hell won't be the first time.

Lucie was thinking, wondering if this is the cop Matthew was talking about. Did Matthew kill this guy? Corbett could kill a man, no question about it. I mean, he put out a contract on me. She wanted homicide to know, just in case there was any question about the death at all. Homicide said Parker shot himself. "Let me know if anything comes up," Lucie told the detectives, "because Matthew Corbett says this officer took his best whore. That could lead to trouble." She found out later Corbett had been talking about Hull, not Parker.

Corbett's problems with police were not over.

Cynthia Stone was Matthew Corbett's regular "whipping post"—scars over 90 percent of her body. Scars from braided coat hangers and belts.

Cynthia stood on the corner of East Thirty-sixth and Prospect with two other women in the snowy night—working. It was past midnight when they saw a light blue car approach with two men inside. Cynthia recognized the driver. He was a cop, Patrolman *Raymond Derkach*.

She ran into an alley, the car chasing after her. Derkach jumped out, threw her into the backseat, and took off.

Over two hours later, at three in the morning, the two men dumped her in an alley on East Nineteenth and Prospect. Her lip was swollen, her face cut and bruised. She told Matthew the cop and the other man had raped her at gunpoint.

Matthew's main concern was to find out if she had contracted VD. He didn't want to take any chances of getting a disease from her. He took her to St. Vincent's Charity Hospital.

Later he told Lucie to let Derkach go. "It ain't no big deal. You know, basically I took the girl to the hospital just to check for venereal disease. I didn't take her to the hospital for her to tell."

But Cynthia did tell. She was interviewed at the hospital.

Lucie talked to Cynthia. Then Lucie talked to Matthew. "Derkach has to be dealt with, and the police will do it," she insisted. She convinced them it was all right to cooperate. Lucie had developed a relationship with Cynthia, and Cynthia had called her on a number of occasions. She wanted Cynthia to be able to trust her advice and call when she needed help. That was the goal in working with pimps and prostitutes. Get their cooperation. Get the pimps off the streets. Lucie knew Pretty Matt didn't consider sex with a cop a big deal, but Derkach had slugged Cynthia, and she thought Matthew was pissed off enough to go along with prosecuting the cop. Cynthia was scared. But Lucie told her, "You have to prosecute."

Now Cynthia would go through the ordeal of a PCIR investigation. The case went to Lucie's friend Ron Kosits in professional conduct/internal review (PCIR). During his six years in PCIR, he put thirty cops in the penitentiary, for crimes ranging from burglary to murder. He estimated 20 percent of the city's officers were dirty—but based on data gathered and conversations he had had with other departments, he still rated Cleveland one of the cleanest departments in the country.

Kosits told Cynthia he would listen to her story, and then they would talk. They would talk about a lie detector test.

He had a rule with prostitutes and drug dealers. They had to take the lie box. It wasn't something he was supposed to do. He was supposed to take everybody's word for everything. "I realize a whore can be raped. I realize a drug dealer can be robbed or burglarized or victimized." But he considered both groups lowlife. He also realized the problems going into court and putting these people on the stand, having their pasts attacked. He always insisted from the getgo—you will take a lie box test. "If you pass, you've gotten by me. Now I will defend you and your reputation, good or bad, as far as I can." He made sure the prosecuting attorney was aware of the test, even though the results wouldn't be used in court.

Kosits felt the prosecutor would fight as hard for Cynthia as he could, because Cynthia passed with flying colors. Kosits knew the box was not unbeatable, but it was a tool that he had faith in to an extent. Now it was a matter of evidence. "Let's go and get it."

Kosits and his sergeant took her out the day after the rape. "Where did the rape occur?" he asked her.

"Over off of Orange in the factory area." It had snowed that night. They drove up and down the streets. As they approached a warehouse, near East Thirty-first and Croton, Cynthia said, "Stop the car. It happened back there, behind this building."

"What are we going to find back there?" Kosits asked her.

Cynthia explained: he drove in. He drove around. Then he parked behind the building. He slapped me around. I was laying on all kinds of clipboards and papers and I'm reading these reports.

Cynthia remembered pieces of the reports that surrounded her as

Derkach and the other man beat her. At gunpoint, she was forced to have oral sex with both men. Derkach had gotten out of the car and gone to the trunk. When he came back from the trunk, he had rubbers. Both men raped her, using the rubbers, then threw them out the car window.

Kosits said, "OK, you sit here." He and his sergeant took a walk behind the building. There were the tire tracks, circling, parking, footprints getting out of the driver's side going around toward the trunk area and then back into the rear of the car. Kosits saw packages from the prophylactics on the ground, scraps of paper. He drove back to the Justice Center and called SIU. He had them photograph the scene and collect all the evidence.

He took a detailed statement from Cynthia. What was Derkach wearing? She described everything she could remember in the car as well as the car itself.

With a search warrant issued, Kosits went to Derkach's house. There he found everything Cynthia described still in the car, including the clipboard and reports. He found three used condoms, one empty red box of condoms, and two empty blue packages. Cynthia said strands of hair from her wig were torn while she was attacked. Kosits found hair fibers in the car.

When they entered the house, Derkach was still wearing the clothes he had had on the night before, and the same boots. SIU had made casts of the footprints at the scene. Kosits gathered everything up, including Derkach, and took them in. Derkach came up with alibis about being with different women, about bowling, or being at a show. Kosits went around and picked up all of his different girlfriends. "He had a lot of them, including his ex-wife. We shot holes in their stories. They all tried to give him an alibi. The trouble was he tried to set up so many alibis he was in six different places at the time the rape was supposed to have happened, and all these gals swore to it because they loved him." Kosits's mustache turned down, his cheeks drooped with disgust.

Later, the owner of the Prospect Lounge said that Derkach had been in there most of the evening. At the bar, Derkach met an electrician, *Steve Nesterenko,* for the first time. The two spent hours drinking. Cynthia picked out Nesterenko's picture from a photo spread. That was the man with Derkach, the other man who raped her, she said.

Kosits ran the case by Lucie. "People like Matthew and Cynthia didn't trust people like Kosits," Lucie said. They didn't know him. Anytime Kosits had a problem talking to a prostitute, he asked Lucie to talk to her, to tell her, Hey, this guy's OK. You can talk to him.

Kosits thought Matthew was despicable. "He was scum. He was weird. I never had any use for him. I don't have any use for pimps. He's a blow hard. 'I'm not a pimp. These women just love me, that's all. I don't really put them to work in the street. They want to do this for me.'" Kosits mimicked with disdain.

He knew he would have trouble with "these gals in court, simply because of their reputations." Corbett had a lousy reputation, and he could get in a mood sometimes; then Kosits wouldn't be able to talk to the girl. Matthew wouldn't let him near her. Kosits asked Lucie to intercede.

Lucie listened to Matthew's ranting and raving about what a great stud he was. How much he loved his children. How he wanted them all to have diamond rings before they were five years old.

"For chrissake," Lucie told Matthew, "let Cynthia go and let her talk." Finally Matthew agreed.

Through the years, Kosits tapped the expertise of Lucie and a few other officers with specialized knowledge. "When you work internal affairs, you're ostracized from the rest of the department. Nobody ever knew I used them."

Usually, reports of alleged rapes became public record shortly after the report was made. Cynthia's wasn't. But her "brother" called the *Plain Dealer* with the story, and they ran it, after the police confirmed an investigation was under way and the suspect was an officer. Another city council-police controversy ensued. The timing was perfect. It was the opening session of a week of proposed budget hearings, including the budget for the safety forces. George Forbes commented in the *Plain Dealer,* "There's a code for them and a code for everyone else." Later, he said that police conduct in Cleveland was becoming worse than in Birmingham, Alabama. Mayor Voinovich ordered the department to make all crime reports public, even when they involved police.

Janice Rench, executive director of the Cleveland Rape Crisis Center, hadn't had very good experiences with police attitudes toward any rape victims. And this was a black prostitute accusing a white cop. Janice didn't know Lucie. Later, they would work closely together to bridge communications between police and sexual assault victims. At this point, Janice was curt in her comment to the *Plain Dealer.* "She doesn't have a snowball's chance in hell of getting a conviction."

Captain Edwards told the paper that prostitutes often file rape charges when customers refuse to pay.

Lucie was clear: "Police who say a prostitute can't be raped do not know the law." She thought the case looked solid. Kosits did, too. He didn't know if there had ever been a rape conviction with a prostitute, but he decided to take the case to the grand jury.

Cynthia testified, and the other corroborating evidence was presented to the jurors. The grand jury indicted Derkach and Nesterenko on eight counts each of rape and one count each of kidnapping. Derkach was suspended pending the trial outcome. He and Nesterenko pled guilty to gross sexual imposition and attempted gross sexual imposition. Both men were sentenced to six months in jail. Derkach lost his job.

For years afterward, some officers referred to Cynthia as the "whore who lost a cop his job."

15

THE COP IN THE FUCHSIA BERET

D on't go out there and do something foolish," Lucie told the street crime team as they readied for a drug bust. "Don't get hurt. If we don't catch them this time, we can catch them later. Nine times out of ten they are not going anywhere."

Two months after she was transferred into vice, Lucie was handed more responsibility. She was given two other units to supervise—the spyglass unit, and the Third District street crime unit. Plus, she was supervising two officers who worked the warrant car. She was now in charge of twenty-one men.

Lucie mapped out the night's game plan, the signals they would use, and their positioning. She took out a twenty-dollar bill to make the buys, making a mark on the face of Andrew Jackson. She photocopied the bill to record the serial number.

They drove into the projects, driving where there were no sidewalks. Beige brick, squat buildings. Broken, boarded-up windows. Swing sets with no swings, just metal bars standing up in the brown used-to-be lawns.

Greg Gamble was one of the street crime detectives. He had sideburns and a fuzzy mustache, watery brown eyes, small ears, and black thin hair he wore shoulder length for the undercover details. He dressed in jeans and sneakers.

"The projects is a jungle. You in their territory." He had heard talk. What did Lucie know about the street. What did a lily white lady know about working the projects.

She knew a lot, he found out. She knew how to position the men so if the pusher broke one way, they could get him. She knew how to circle the area. She understood the geography of the projects, the nooks and crannies. Drugs were sold out of the pool hall. Gamble bought marijuana and barbiturates. T's and B's—Talwin and Pyrobenzamine, or tops and bottoms—produced a heroinlike high when mixed and injected. Gamble drove by. A man quickly flashed his hands, forming a *T,* then a *B.* He noticed the gesture out of his side view mirror and pulled over.

"Hey, man, what you want?" the salesman said.

"What you got for me?" responded Gamble.

"T's and B's," the man said and gave his price.

Gamble made the purchase with the marked bill. He drove off and got on the mike, hidden under his seat, stating the man's description and location.

Lucie and the other officers in undercover cars, working with zone cars, converged on the pusher and made the arrest, confiscating drugs and cash, including Gamble's marked bill.

They went out again. Gamble made a buy.

"Ten minutes later, another guy in jail." Lucie laughed. Gregory Gamble, she said with pride, made that twenty-dollar bill last a whole tour of duty. They made the reports while the incidents were fresh in their minds.

They confiscated everything from guns to needles. All evidence was marked and tagged. The money went to the property room after being initialed. Drugs were taken to the seventh floor of the Justice Center, to the forensic lab for inspection. "Money and drugs had a tendency to disappear, and you never want to be caught for that," Gamble said.

He worked with Lucie, raiding after-hours joints in the projects, stopping the dice games played on the pool tables. They confiscated pop machines, jukeboxes, and stereo systems and checked the serial numbers, to see if the property had been stolen, so they could notify the owner. They seized liquor and beer. With Lucie, Gamble smiled, no taste testers. No, no, no.

Gamble was born in Alabama but grew up in Cleveland. He went to Glenville High School, along with a quiet young man who later became Squirrel—one of the pimps. Gamble never would have thought Squirrel would turn out to be a pimp. I guess it's true, he thought, it's the quiet ones you have to watch out for.

Working for a woman was an adjustment for Gamble. But he got used to it. Later, Gamble worked for Lucie's classmate Michele Kratzer, and he reflected, "Have to wake up to the nineties. Women are in—no doubt about it."

A couple of times he saw Lucie get mad. Her cheeks turned rosy red.

She wouldn't say too much, she kept to herself until she had something to say, then she would say it one on one.

Bad arrests angered Lucie. Not following the ground rules. Missing items, missing money. She wouldn't get upset over petty stuff. She was the supervisor, if something was missing it fell right in her lap.

"When you saw those rosy red cheeks and she wasn't smiling, you get out of the way, unless she points her finger and says, 'I want to see you in the office.'"

But most of the time the tiny, cramped vice office had a comfortable atmosphere. It was like a family.

Bigfoot George Deli was also part of the street crime unit. He came on the job in 1977 and worked the Third District projects. He was a hulking six foot seven and one-half inches tall and weighed about 270 pounds. He wore a navy ski cap, his beard was rough, his eyes had a wild gleam. He set down his own laws, he married and divorced people. "Put this hand on the badge. By the powers invested in me by the City of Cleveland...." All over the city he was known as Bigfoot. The name originated when he chased down a gang of rapists and robbers who were terrorizing the projects. He threw them against the wall.

"How can you step on us like this," one gang member complained.

"'Cause he's got a big foot," another one said.

The name spread. At first, Deli was insulted. Then he grew to like it. Even the *Plain Dealer* called him Bigfoot. One of his partners made up business cards for Deli to hand out to people he arrested—YOU HAVE BEEN STEPPED ON BY BIGFOOT.

Within the department, Deli was known as a black cat. Someone that things happen to. Meow. Meow. Bigfoot had five contracts taken out on his life. He shot expert with a pistol and boxed. In 1979 and 1981, he won medals in the Law Enforcement Olympics. He fought as he did police work—as a heavyweight.

Bigfoot was partners with Jimmy Davidson out on patrol. He dubbed them the boxer and the model. They'd get into something and Bigfoot would say, "Jimmy, watch your face."

When Lucie inherited the street crime unit, Bigfoot went upstairs to meet his new boss. The top of her head came somewhere between his solid abdomen and thick long chest. This is going to be my boss out there in the ghetto busting pushers and murderers? This is going to be a trip.

Lucie stood next to him, looking way up into his eyes, and told him what to do.

"Whatever you say, Boss," Bigfoot responded. It was kind of funny. He grinned.

Bigfoot had formed his own opinions about women on the job.

When he was a field-training officer, an FTO, his supervisor took him aside and told him, "I don't want you to teach the women nothing."

"What is that supposed to mean," Deli said.

"They're taking our jobs away," his supervisor said.

"Look, pal," Deli said, "if you think these women aren't here to stay, you're out of your mind. You're an ostrich with your head in the ground. They are here, they are here to stay, and you better teach them everything you know about this police work because they might be the only backup coming in on you."

Lucie had worked the streets, she had worked the car. That was good enough for Bigfoot.

People called her motherfucker. He heard the word *bitch* a lot in reference to Lucie. He didn't know why. If it was a man doing the same job she was doing, they wouldn't make all this fuss and crap about it.

Bigfoot had his own creative way of doing things. He found out about a pornographic film ring. Instead of telling Lucie about it, he decided to bust them on his own. He kicked in the door and marched in with his shotgun. Naked women grabbed blankets and sheets and ran, screaming. Chaos ensued.

Bigfoot ended up back at the station with one of the men's lawyers hollering about how Deli pointed a shotgun at him. Everybody he arrested was released.

"You did OK, George," Lucie said, with a smile, "but there is no law against making pornographic movies."

"There's not?!" Bigfoot was dumfounded. "What kind of country do we live in?" Lucie was respectful, he thought, in how she explained the legalities to him.

Lucie was pulled into the investigations that ultimately led to the downfall of Cleveland's Organized Crime family, once the most influential in the country after Chicago's and New York's. The killing of Danny Greene, which involved most of the city's made members, led to a rare outcome—most of the conspirators landed in jail or turned into FBI informants. Carmen Zagaria, called Jingle Bells by his friends, picked up the pieces of what was left of Greene's organization and emerged as the West Side overlord, with a drug business revenue estimated at fifteen million dollars in one year alone. Mob gambling operations financed the narcotics trade—and a task force including the organized crime unit and county narcotics were hitting those games. Lucie worked with them and supervised the raids in her district.

Assistant County Prosecutor Tom Buford, who would later be a good friend of Lucie's, had been pulled out of the major trials division where he had prosecuted rapes and homicides to work full-time on the Zagaria hits. "I had already tried and convicted a mob hit man, so I was kind of hot material in that mob world." For the next two and a half years Buford practically lived in the OC office, sleeping on their couch and accompanying the detectives on every search, carrying his "deadly briefcase." His fingers were yellowing from cigarette smoke, his hands rough, like a worker. He had a lot of style, and he fit well in the theater of the courtroom.

They had to be extraordinarily cautious. There were death threats. Two FBI agents working on the cases moved their families out of town. Buford was named as the third most likely target. "I always felt I should be first, I was a little affronted by that." Security precautions were remarkable. A secretary typing an affidavit had to put everything away when she went to the bathroom. Big-time mob figures with national import were involved. Money was no object to them, and they had sources within law enforcement.

Buford and Lucie shared a quick-flash sense of humor. Lucie called him flypaper brain, because he accumulated and retained hundreds of odd facts and minute details.

The Prime Provision Wholesale Meats Company on East Fourth Street provided catering for restaurants. The brick building also housed the Market House Social Club, an organized crime gambling operation running barbute, a Greek dice game, and rumico. The money was going into drugs. Zagaria later told Buford the barbute was raking in ten thousand dollars a month.

Lucie supervised the raid. Under Prime Provision's green awning, near the main door, was another door marked Members Only. She, Jimmy Davidson, Cermak, and Buford, with his deadly briefcase, charged up the stairs at four-thirty on a January afternoon. She had exchanged her warm weather trademark, sunglasses on her head, for a fuchsia beret, and she marched into the shabby gambling den like a streak of bright light.

The old men looked up, astonished. Score sheets and Bee playing cards, boxes of cookies, and baskets of red and yellow apples shared the round, felt-covered tables. The kitchen had a homey look, tiles with a design of roses on a trellis framed the window. The officers snapped pictures, Lucie looked for evidence of gambling records. The disgruntled Italians stood against the wall to have their photos taken. Davidson laughed as he later remembered the raid. "All the wiseguys going, What are youse messing with us for. This is a social club."

Buford went on many raids with Lucie, but his most vivid image of her was from that day. He later teased her, with his own version of the gamblers' shocked reactions: "What is the world coming to? Busted by a woman in a fuchsia beret."

* * *

Lucie had her hands full. Just the administrative duties were overwhelming. Supervising all the cases: reading the reports from the vice men, the spyglass and street crime units, and the warrant car officers.

Bruce Zuchowski, warrant car officer, and his partner did not require much supervision. They had been doing their job for years. Nevertheless, Lucie wanted to learn as much as possible. She looked over their format critically, Zuchowski noticed, and then said that what they were doing was good and just to continue.

She gave them her beeper number. "Any time you need me, just call," she told them. "Any hour, day or night."

Zuchowski had never before been afforded the opportunity to get a hold of a supervisor twenty-four hours a day.

It was an icy, snowy night when spyglass detectives Robert Beck and Bill Plank came upon an auto theft in progress in a lot at Fourteenth and Superior. There were two thieves. As they drove in, one thief was getting out of the car he was stealing. He didn't have the usual screwdriver in his hand—he had a gun. He fired one round at Plank and Beck. They both hit the hard slick ground and shot back, missing. They leapt back in their car and took chase on the slippery street, but the suspects escaped.

Beck called Lucie on her pager and asked if she would handle the investigation. "Absolutely," Lucie responded. She called the street supervisor and asked him if it was all right. Technically, the street boss was in charge. He said, fine. Lucie drove out to the scene.

"Just keep doing your job," she had told the spyglass men. All she asked was that they show her the ropes. Cuyahoga County was the stolen car capital of Ohio and trendsetter for the nation. Cleveland was where the dent-puller and one-screwdriver methods of car stealing were pioneered. Downtown had a big problem because of all the parking lots, the number of cars that parked there daily. Lucie dug right in, riding with the team and learning the operation.

The perches, stationed on top of tall buildings, acted as spotters. Lucie went up with the perch men to the top of the Erieview Tower and Cleveland State University and peered through their binoculars. Sometimes they perched on top of the Justice Center, the Terminal Tower, where they were out on a catwalk, and the Ohio Bell building. The outdoor perches were tough; the men went up in all kinds of weather, using spotter scopes mounted on tripods. They wanted a clear sighting of the suspect's face. Lucie rode in the ground cars.

They moved in when the thief made an overt act on the car. They shouted and hollered as they leapt from the undercover car, badges out, guns in their hands. "I become the Tasmanian devil," the gruff and bear-ish Beck said, a smile appearing in the midst of his sandy, thick beard. "It is controlled rage."

They treated the thief as if he were armed until they found out he wasn't. Then they lowered their voices and relaxed—a little bit—but not until he was controlled, searched, and secured.

Lucie checked the operation from every angle. Most other spyglass supervisors did that, Beck said, but Lucie was different. She kept her hand in. She enjoyed it, and that endeared her to the men. She respected their opinions, backgrounds, and expertise, and that, Beck recalled, allowed them to be effective. The spyglass unit was a close-knit group. There was a chemistry among them. Lucie did not make any changes in their personnel. "She was intelligent enough to know that if it's not broke, don't fix it," Beck said.

"They were great, but crazy bananas." Lucie laughed. "Getting into car chases, pulling thieves out of car windows."

She would not cover up for dishonesty or the abuse of a suspect. She knew from her own experience on the street how things went down. She knew there were times when the only way to get a situation under control was physically. But once the situation was under control—that was the end of the physical part of it. Or it should be. Police officers who carried it beyond that needed to be disciplined. "But to say all police work could be done without violence was ludicrous. It doesn't work that way. Police are the thin blue line between order and chaos. All the people who say you should never lay a hand on anybody—they wouldn't want to live with what was left," Lucie asserted.

Lucie knew the spyglass men were good cops, but she was their supervisor and she had to explain their aggressive actions. The detectives teased her, saying they were going to get her a T-shirt that said I TYPED FOR THE SPYGLASS DETAIL. She read between the lines of their form one's and left them little notes about their tactics.

When Lucie arrived the shooting team was also on the scene, called whenever a police officer fired a gun.

Lucie heard the facts. "What is the problem?" she asked.

Beck had fired his 9mm—an unauthorized gun. Officers were allowed to carry them off duty, but not on duty.

"Oops," Lucie said. George Forbes was against police officers carry-ing 9mms. That was the first thought that crossed her mind.

"Where's the gun?" Lucie asked Beck.

"We gave it to the shooting team," he told her. Plank and Beck told her they would never switch guns.

They had told her the truth, and Lucie backed them. She typed up an explanation. If her men deserved to be protected, she protected them. If not, she nailed them.

On December 17, 1982, just three months after she was transferred to the vice unit, Lucie was promoted to lieutenant.

At the city hall ceremony, Lucie sat in the front row, in her uniform, her bright coppery hair curled into a pageboy. Three others were promoted to lieutenant. Her face was animated. She chatted with the officers on either side of her and smiled. Eric came to the ceremony this time. One by one the officers rose to receive their appointment from Mayor Voinovich as television crews taped the event. Afterward, Eric took the whole vice unit out to Fagan's for lunch. When he left to go back to work the partying continued.

Of the 195 recruits who had come on the job with Lucie in 1973, she was one out of only three to have made the rank of lieutenant.

16

SHOW BARS AND CHAMPAGNE HUSTLES

H i, Lucie. Carl Monday."

"Hi, Carl, how are you?" Lucie's voice was cheery as she spoke into the phone. Carl Monday, one of Cleveland's top investigative reporters, was with Channel 8's I-Team. She had developed a good working relationship with him. Her attitude was, If the media was going to do a story, they are going to do it with you or without you, so you might as well do it with them, or you're going to end up being the story.

"Listen to this," Carl said. A man had called up the station with an outrageous story. "He says he's a salesman. He cut out of work one day and went down to Stage Door Johnnie's. He drank at the bar and went into a booth with a woman and had sex. He stayed a couple of hours and drank too much."

Lucie rolled her eyes. It was the usual story. So far.

"When he got up the next day, he looked at his Visa receipt and found it was for four hundred dollars. He was outraged. He went back to complain about the bill—and ended up spending another five thousand two hundred and seven dollars."

"WHAT?" Lucie roared with laughter. "Five thousand ..."

The story wasn't over yet. "This guy wants something done. He doesn't want to have to pay his credit card. Isn't that fraud?" Carl asked.

Lucie raided Stage Door Johnnie's periodically. When she went through the receipts she found American Express and Visa receipts for seven, eight hundred dollars.

"No." Lucie caught her breath from laughing. "There's nothing illegal about taking the credit card. The sex for hire is illegal, how you pay for it isn't."

The bar had called in for authorization numbers on the credit card. But, she added, "I'd be happy to raid them again. Hell, any nail in the coffin."

Stage Door Johnnie's was just one of the many bars she was determined to shut down. Right after making lieutenant, Lucie was given the task of formulating a plan for ridding the city of obscenity. "The mayor said, I want to get rid of obscenity in this city. Get somebody to figure out how to do this. It always ends up what they mean is, find a lieutenant to do it. The chief's not going to do it. Somehow I ended up being the person who was going to do the plan. The grand plan."

Mayor Voinovich wanted to close the adult bookstores. Lucie had her own ideas. "If you want to clean up the city why would we start with a magazine and disregard a live sex act going on next door. That to me was stupid. You start with the most blatant and you work down." With the more overt problems, Lucie felt, you're not going to run into First Amendment violations so readily. "After we attack the blatant, then get down to the magazines and books and videos and things like that. I thought that made a lot more sense."

Lucie wrote up a three-page plan. She suggested that vice officers first observe violations without making arrests, then take their reports to the prosecutor for a ruling. On-the-scene arrests had weakened cases in the past and left more room for civil suits against the officers. Making arrests at the time of the performance also necessitated more manpower than might be available and could jeopardize the officers' safety.

She suggested that vice officers could be accompanied into performances by a community representative who was willing to testify in court. That would strengthen the case, affording the city a surprise witness and, Lucie emphasized, "the support of the community will be of obvious benefit to the overall long-range objective of cleaning up this type of activity."

Lucie submitted her proposal. They not only adopted her plan but also put her in charge of its implementation. She coordinated all the city's pandering obscenity investigations. Every month, each vice commander sent her a report, and she compiled the paperwork into one report for the prosecutor's office. The amount of paperwork was huge. Reports had to be very detailed. Blow by blow. A vice officer who went into the Follies Burlesque described his experience with the dancer: "She said, My, you look serious, she then rubbed her breasts into my face, she then reached down and placed her hand over my private parts and briefly groped me … squatted down on my right leg, rubbing her bare vagina back and forth in a humping motion."

The prosecutor's office updated Lucie's report, adding information on the status of prosecutions, and sent a copy to the mayor.

At first, Lucie controlled the obscenity funds for all the districts. She didn't like that. She thought it unwieldy. "I didn't have the money in my hip pocket, so to speak." The vice commander had to write a request to Lucie, and she had to go down to the Justice Center, get the money, and give it to the vice unit that requested it. That system fell by the wayside, but Lucie remained in charge of the overall plan.

After talking to Carl Monday, Lucie tried to obtain a phony credit card so she could send a vice man in, to try to charge sex at Stage Door Johnnie's. She was refused. Somebody would have to use his own credit card and foot the bill. There was only one card Lucie had with a man's name on it. Eric's. He said she could use it. She talked to Carl Monday, and he assured her they would cover Eric's name when they showed the card on television.

The vice men were in hysterics. "That piece of ass cost him five thousand dollars." Bienvenido Santiago was astounded. Santiago was a new addition to Lucie's vice team. He didn't know much about vice when he came into her unit. Lucie taught him how to cite for liquor violations.

The TV crew set up at Sixteenth and Prospect outside Stage Door Johnnie's. It was just two blocks from Playhouse Square, which was in the midst of renovation. It was "one of the jewels of the city," Monday said. Later, Lucie would frequently enjoy ballet and theater performed there. It was a cluster of historic theaters with expansive lobbies, curving staircases, chandeliers hanging from lavender and pale blue ceilings, inlaid with gilt flowers and angels.

Quite a different mood permeated Stage Door Johnnie's. Monday explained the situation to his viewing audience.

Paul Fields went on camera. Full face. His own voice. He explained that for one hundred and fifty bucks he bought a bottle of champagne and a girl—who "performed oral sex and that and so forth and we had a good time."

Asked by Monday about the total tally of his dalliance, he replied, "I could have bought the place for that."

The camera switched to Lucie. Her eyes crinkled. "It's a staggering amount of money," was her comment.

She and Roger did the raid together. Bill Reiber, "Papa Eyes," wearing an I-Team hidden microphone and carrying Eric's credit card, went inside.

The microphone picked up the ensuing conversation from the dark bar. A woman asked, "Do you want to have a good time?"

"Yeah," Reiber replied. "Can I put it on my credit card."

"Yeah," the woman answered.

Lucie, Roger, and the vice men quickly moved in. Lucie carried a camera for photographing any evidence. They arrested the woman for prostitution.

Lucie and Monday had a laugh over Fields, but later Monday did a serious investigative piece. Why were the police unable to close the place? What was going on?

He looked into the bar's history. "Since 1976, Stage Door Johnnie's has been cited twenty-eight times for prostitution and other related charges," he told viewers. Monday noted that despite fines of thirty thousand dollars the bar remained open for business.

Lucie worked hard piling up citations presenting them to the city council when bar licenses came up for renewal—only to be frustrated by the council's continued approval of those establishments. Sometimes the liquor commission yanked the license. "It's a lot easier if the councilman just puts his foot down—some are real good, but in other wards you had to wonder: if you've got a license to have a business, what's it worth to you to keep that license."

Marilyn Chambers, former Ivory Snow model, had stopped by Cleveland to perform at the New Era, under the same management as Stage Door Johnnie's. The New Era's shows were live sex acts. One woman had been cited for allowing the patrons to perform cunnilingus on her.

Lucie sent James Kennelly into the New Era. He was brand-new in the unit and eager to prove himself. Kennelly grew up in the suburbs and it showed, there was a certain naïveté about his looks. He was fair skinned, with brown hair and soft blue eyes. He knew Lucie expected action because Marilyn Chambers was there. "I go there and sit down in the middle of all these guys, and she did absolutely nothing wrong. Somebody had to know I was in there. There was an off-duty policeman that worked there. He didn't know me and I didn't know him, so I don't know how he knew." Kennelly felt badly. But the police kept at it and in Christmas of 1985 the porn queen got her very first conviction, arrested at the New Era by Roger Dennerll.

Carl Monday did a record check and discovered that no councilman had opposed the bar's permit over the past six years. There was no record of Council President George Forbes ever opposing the liquor permit renewal.

"But then again, his law partner Clarence Rogers represents Marilyn Chambers, the porn queen arrested over the weekend," Monday pointed out.

Lucie heard about someone whom cops called That Fireman. Tim Spencer was a city firefighter who had unusual extracurricular business ventures. He had owned a dancer bar in another district, and a vice cop there put him out of business. There were rumors Tim was connected. Where did Tim's money come from? Kevin McTaggert, Danny Greene's nephew, and drug kingpin Carmen Zagaria had been seen in Tim Spencer's West Side bar.

Lucie got a call. Tim Spencer is going to open a stripper bar in the Flats. He may try to compromise you, Lucie was told. He'll probably try to bribe you. Be real careful.

Oh, no, you've got to be kidding, Lucie thought. On top of everything else, the dreaded Tim Spencer, That Fireman, was moving into her downtown territory. It was just a few months after her transfer. She still didn't feel as though she knew what she was doing. Oh, well, she thought, I'll deal with it when it happens.

Lucie didn't know it, but her path had already crossed with Spencer's. He had taken the civil service exam on the same day she did, in July 1972. He scored ninety-six and joined the fire department. He had been in the army. The things he learned there he thought he would never use, even if he lived till he was ten thousand years old. But in their Leadership Preparation School he gained skills he applied to business. All the principles worked.

When Tim's brother Al wanted to open a topless bar in Cleveland, Tim said he would help. They opened the Crazy Horse Saloon. After a while the partnership fell apart. Tim and his brother had never gotten along, and they didn't get along running a bar together. He left the Crazy Horse to Al and opened a bar on the West Side.

Tim hated bars. He had never been in a topless bar before he owned one. He could count on one hand the times he had been in any kind of bar. He almost never drank, he preferred tea. He wanted to be in the field of construction design, but he needed money. And he had some ideas of his own about dancer bars, discos, and restaurants.

He got the word via the bar grapevine about Lucie's transfer. "You get the transfer list before most of the police," he chuckled. His experiences with the police had been less than positive. When he owned the Crazy Horse, they arrested him for ridiculous things. A high-level municipal official had been put down by one of the girls, and he took it out on the bar by refusing to renew Tim's music permit and then having the police arrest him for playing music without a permit—that was like being arrested for picking his nose in the street, Tim thought. They never got him. He got a tip-off and bailed out the back door. He had dealt with nothing but trash as far as police were concerned. I better call the new lieutenant, he decided. Lay everything out on the table.

Lucie was taping her phone calls because she expected someone to bribe her. Cermak told her, be ready—it's hot in the Third District.

"Hello, my name is Tim Spencer." His voice had a deep Johnny Cash twang.

"Could you hold just a moment, please," Lucie said. She switched on her tape machine. "What can I do for you?" she asked him.

"You might know, I'm opening a place up in the Third District."

"Yes, I had heard that," she said.

"I'd like to talk to you," Spencer said. "I'd like to have you come down."

Here he goes, Lucie thought. But what she said was, "Fine." They set up a time to meet the next day.

She called Bob Cermak. "Tim Spencer wants me to meet him down at his new bar at two in the afternoon. What do you think we should do?"

"Come on over tomorrow," he advised her.

She stopped at the organized crime office. They detailed five cars to watch the area. She was going to wear a wire; they tried taping it across her waist. She was sweating from nervousness. I'm going to electrocute myself, she laughed.

They decided Lucie could carry the wire; they pinned a pen-size microphone close to the zipper on her purse.

"Leave the zipper cracked," Cermak instructed.

An external antenna on the police car would pick up the transmissions. They generally assigned two people to record the conversations because none of the equipment worked that well, no matter how new or sophisticated.

Lucie drove down to the Flats and walked to the site where the new bar was going to be, on the banks of the twisting Cuyahoga River. Conical piles of ore and salt speckled the shore, like a child's sand castles in large form. Bridges crossed overhead, a network of steel over the old, wooden buildings. Large ships slowly edged by, carefully maneuvering the river's crazy curves. The Flats was slated for redevelopment; it was to become a harborside tourist area, with weekend visitors strolling the narrow winding streets. Abandoned warehouses would be converted into bars, shops, restaurants, clubs. Jazz, reggae, and disco beats would enliven the crowds. Yuppies would sip on imported beers, nibbling from raw bars after work. And there would be a few stripper bars to entertain the visiting businessmen. But that was in the future. When Lucie ventured forth to meet That Fireman, the Flats was a ragged waterfront, and Spencer's future dancer bar was a noisy construction site.

Lucie picked her way through the shell of the building. Workmen were hammering and sawing. The organized crime men are not going to hear anything through this wire, she worried. The devices were attracted to mechanical sounds before they were attracted to human voices.

She walked up to a man wielding an electric saw. He was broad shouldered and strong-muscled, dark haired, and six foot five. A diamond glinted in one ear.

"I'm looking for Mr. Spencer," she announced, drawing herself up to almost five foot three.

"I'm Tim Spencer," he said in his husky voice. He had an old thin scar on his upper lip. His smile was slightly crooked, but his face lit up at the sight of Lucie. He didn't know what to expect when he called her, but he certainly didn't expect a midget with red hair and sunglasses on top of her head. "You must be Lieutenant Duvall," he said.

No, she thought. I'm history. Everyone had warned her what an awful man he was. Corrupt. Connected to the mob. He's going to drag me off and chop me up and the guys won't hear a thing.

"Why don't we walk over to Fagan's and sit down where it's quiet," he suggested over the screech of the saws and the whine of the drills.

"Fine," Lucie said, inwardly relieved. Fagan's was a riverside beer bar. Tim ordered tea. Lucie sipped her coffee. She was afraid to say anything. She played it cautious.

"I'm going to open this bar," he told her. "I want to tell you what happened to me."

"Fine," Lucie said.

His face was rugged and intense one moment, thoughtful the next. His nose was chiseled, his eyes blue.

"The story goes like this," he began. A vice cop, *Harlow,* had railroaded him. Lucie knew the cop to be something of a maniac. She paid attention to Spencer's version.

I do know some people, Tim said, but I'm not criminally connected. Every day he met people. He couldn't prequalify them. One night a customer had introduced him to some people, Carmen Zagaria, the Cleveland capo, Kevin McTaggert and Hans Graewe. Spencer later found out they were under indictment or surveillance for drugs and murder. Harlow told Spencer he must be a front for the Mafia. He brought Tim into the station and showed him pictures of the mob.

"The upshot was Harlow just kept citing me and told me he was going to put me out of business," Tim said. "You can do that." He looked at Lucie.

"Yeah, I know," she said.

Spencer told her they were citing him on a part of the municipal code about prohibitive conduct on a permit premise that was no longer used.

That was true, Lucie knew. That law had been taken off the books.

"I tried to sue for malicious prosecution, but the liquor license was in my mother's name and Harlow threatened to arrest my mother and bring her into court. I dropped the lawsuit. I told him—fine, put me out of business. You got me." Tim was angry. "I did let the place run wide open at that point," he admitted to Lucie. "I did it so I could recoup, and make as much money as possible, 'cause I knew he was going to put me out of business. I let the dancers wear nothing if they wanted to. But I never allowed any prostitution and I never allowed any drugs."

It did sound as though he had been railroaded, Lucie thought. "I really don't care what happened to you with Harlow," Lucie told him. "I only care what you do down here now that you're my responsibility. I won't hold it against you."

"I'm not going to cause you a problem." Tim paused. "You're going to have to set the standard down here. You're going to have to draw the lines. I'm going to run a tits and ass bar. I intend to make money. Then, I'm going to open another place. I've already designed it. It's going to be a legitimate disco with a cocktail lounge." He planned the design to please women. Feminine decor, flowers, lightened areas, feminine colors. That was good business, as far as he was concerned. If women liked a dance club and came there, men would follow and spend the money.

"You're going to love it," he told Lucie.

He laid out his goals: "The dancer bar business in Cleveland prior to the Crazy Horse was a real trash business. I want to bring it up out of the gutter, get rid of the prostitution, the gambling, the champagne hustles, the drugs, anything shady. I want to cater to businessmen, because businessmen have nowhere to go in the city. If they want to look at girls dance, there is nowhere safe for them. My bar is going to be just like the Crazy Horse.

"All I'm asking from the police is to be afforded the same considerations that anyone else in the same business is given. I want absolutely fair treatment across the board."

Tim knew his brother had established contacts with the old Third District vice unit. They were siding with Al. They didn't want him to have Tim as competition. If Lucie was going to put both of them out of business, that was fine. That was fair.

"I don't prejudge anybody," Lucie said. "As long as you're not a problem to me, I really don't care. I can only tell you that I will treat you like everybody else. You don't give me a problem, I won't give you a problem. That's all I can promise."

Lucie went back to the Justice Center. What do you think? she asked the organized crime men. We'll just have to wait and see, they told her. We think he's up to something.

The Circus opened. At first it was a narrow bar with one stage. Later, it expanded. The white façade was decorated with long legs in high heels painted on either side of the door in two shades of pink. Inside, the walls were paneled in wood and flowered wallpaper. Topless dancers, dressed in silver spangled black bikinis and other colorful costumes, slid up and down the brass poles that circled the three stages, spinning into splits and somersaults.

"Cra—zy Chris," the announcer chanted the next performer's name. There was a smattering of applause from the businessmen sitting around the small tables. Crazy Chris swung around the poles at high speed, hanging upside down, and hurtling into a backward roll.

Small chandeliers with crystal drops softly lit the room, pink track lights illuminated the performers. On each table, there was a sign. PAY $5–$10 TO HAVE A DANCER COME TO YOUR TABLE. The "private dancers" performed for the customer right in front of him, moving between his legs, arching and swaying. Dancers were not supposed to touch the patrons—Lucie and the vice men cited Tim if they saw them do it.

Some of the dancer bars hired girls through agents. Bar owners asked for mixers—soft or hard mixers. Girls that mingled with the customers and sold champagne, or girls that turned tricks. Tim abandoned that system and hired local women. They were cheaper and much better.

The dancers made from two hundred to seven hundred dollars a night, the waitresses one to two hundred. Some were going to college, or working on master's degrees. When they graduated from college, some came back because they couldn't make that kind of money anywhere else. Others quit dancing, got married, and came back to pay off their homes. Tim said he offered Lucie a job several times, but, he smiled, she refused.

Tim gave the employees a sheet of rules. They must smile continuously. They must wear makeup. No dating the customers. Waitresses must touch each patron on the shoulder when taking his order. They must act like ladies at all times.

He cut a deal on prices with the Cleveland Clinic for dancers who had breast augmentations, lipos, and rhinoplasties. "It's a silicone city. Guys come in here to see something they can't see anywhere else, particularly at home. I can't sell fat and ugly."

Tim was proud of his showbar.

"Businessmen come in from all over the country and they know where the Circus is. Their first stop is the hotel, the next stop is the Circus."

Soon after her first meeting with Tim, Lucie dropped by with her vice men. A policeman hanging out inside fronted her. In response, she cited the bar. She wasn't going to tolerate police warning bars she was there. She had to establish her power base.

Though she believed Spencer's account of what happened with Harlow, she was still cautious of him. She started getting calls complaining about his place. Calls about underage dancers and prostitution. She went there with her men and watched and never saw anything. She finally found out the calls were coming from a competing bar owner. It was a game that bar owners played when new competition opened, she discovered. They were trying to get her to react and close their competition.

Lucie nosed around for information. A friend of hers, Don Hart, was Tim's financial manager. Spencer lived on his fireman's pay, Hart told Lucie, and he put his money back into the businesses.

Lucie saw her job in vice as not just arresting people but also keeping the bar trade up. Spencer's places were part of the Flats development. The Third District was the downtown district, and her philosophy was: downtown, let's get it up and moving with a minimal amount of crime. That was why she didn't unduly harass the upscale stripper bars, the Crazy Horse and the Circus. Well, they're downtown, she reasoned, they are not in the neighborhoods, and we are trying to bring back downtown. How in hell are you going to do that if your main goal in life is to close every place down. That made no sense to her.

She began setting standards of what she would cite for, and what she wouldn't bother with. She wasn't going to hipshoot. She was going to be evenhanded, set certain limits, and stick with them.

Tim and Lucie were wary of each other. Neither had any idea that they would later be close friends. She continued monitoring the Circus.

Tim's distrust of law enforcement was not diminished by the liquor agents who came in early in the evening, stayed until closing, and then showed their badges. They took him in the back and said, We got to write you up for this, but it was a great show. All they had to do, Spencer griped, was walk in the door, get a violation, and be out of there in ten minutes. But no, they stayed, had a great time, the best time of their lives, and then they busted us. They apologized for it. Very comforting. They called it improper conduct and they could make up anything after that.

Next thing he knew, Lucie and her entourage would come around. Lucie and the huge guys following behind her. The front door had a high window in it, and he could see Lucie jumping up and down trying to peer through it. Dead giveaway—Tim laughed huskily—if somebody with sunglasses on her head was jumping up and down, it was Lucie. With her monsters, trailing her like little puppy dogs.

He was prepared. He mounted a theatrical light called a pinspot on the far wall. There was a switch by the door. When she showed up, the doorman flipped the switch and the spotlight shot across the room and aimed right into the cash register, alerting the bartender: Lucie is here. The bartender passed the word to the manager, and they changed the show a little bit, cleaned up whatever they thought they might get busted for that time.

He started to appreciate her. She wasn't badge heavy. A lot of cops came in badge first, gun first, I'm a cop, look at me, you have to do whatever I say even though my IQ is slightly above room temperature.

He noticed who she moved out of her unit. She had a remarkable ability to weed out the scum. Not that some of them weren't good people—but they were in jobs they shouldn't have had. He wouldn't wish that job on anybody. The temptation to make money was too easy, and the drinking was almost mandatory.

Those guys that worked for her were tough, crusty, salty individuals—and they did what she said. He never heard anybody that worked for her say one bad thing about her, and he found that remarkable. His respect grew.

Tim knew a lot of bar owners besides himself were shocked—even the bad guys got breaks—when Lucie started running things fairly. Nobody ever expected that.

Prior to Lucie, if a dancer exposed one breast, the police would bust you—or else, take something from you. Lucie took no bribes. She set guidelines. You can expose two breasts, but not the butt. For nothing.

"I'm not going to bust you and I'm not going to take anything away from you. I'm not going to take your money. That's how it is," she told them.

She cited Spencer, but never more than she cited anybody else. Tim never argued with her. Lucie's trust in him built. Everything Tim told her turned out to be true. Lucie found him smart and energetic. Tim opened several places in the burgeoning Flats. He bought and redesigned Fagan's, turning it from a fishermen's bar into a spacious airy restaurant and bar, colored in mauves and pastels with plants hanging from the ceilings. Lucie went to the grand opening of the PLAYDIUM, the disco he had told her about. Tim's parents attended and thanked her for being fair and giving Tim a chance. Lucie was touched by their gratitude. It was important to her to be a fair person.

Lucie felt the same way about gay bars as she did about the Circus. They were part of downtown, and she was all for revitalizing the area. Gay people had been treated rottenly by police, Lucie knew. Vice men were repulsed. They called gay men fags, peepee touchers, weenie puffers. Lucie didn't share the prejudice and fear some of the men had. With Lucie, we were taken everywhere, said one of her crew. "Black joints, white, hillbilly, bikers, fags—it didn't matter."

She looked at what was realistic to enforce. She didn't harass the gay bar owners, and eventually she overcame their suspicion and distrust. She became a liaison to the gay community.

She checked the gay bars for liquor and gambling violations, but she was also there for them if they had any problems. Mark Hastings was matter-of-fact about them and backed her in her policy. "At least they knew they could call us and we would help them if they had a problem with straights coming in and beating people up. They got to know us and trust us. We weren't there to hurt or harass them," Hastings said.

Anti-gay violence was gaining public attention. In September 1982, just as Lucie took over vice, the *Plain Dealer* reported that in the past nine months three men and one woman had been murdered in crimes that the police said "appeared homosexually related." Frank Spisak, a man with ties to Nazi organizations, shot and killed a pastor in a rest room on the Cleveland State University campus. The bathroom was known as a gay hangout. Spisak targeted gay men and blacks, killing three people and wounding one before being arrested. In June, a forty-two-year-old schoolteacher, Mary Ann Finnegan, and her companion were abducted by a gunman when they left Isis, a downtown lesbian bar. Finnegan was shot to death. Her companion survived, after being raped, shot, and left for dead. The killer was never caught.

One afternoon, Lucie received an anonymous call. There was going to be a homicide attempt in Man's World, a leather bar that was even less palatable to her men than the classier gay bars. She took Mark Hastings and they went over there. She asked to speak to the owner.

"I've gotten a call," she informed them. "There is going to be a problem in here. I don't understand why. Maybe you know of a problem in the gay community. My concern is that you will not get immediate police response. If you have a problem, here's a number to call the police radio. Tell them I was here. Tell them to send a car now. I'll also call police radio and advise them of the call I received and that if they get a similar call, it's probably legitimate." Fortunately there was no murder attempt that evening.

When the Ritz, a new gay bar, opened downtown, Lucie got word that it had a lot of fire violations. She arrived for the grand opening. Everyone was dressed in tuxedos, excited about the event. She went in with the fire department and did an inspection. Lucie saw the manager was nervous. The opening was their big moment.

Lucie thought about what to do. She couldn't ignore the violations. There were hundreds of people in the place—if it caught on fire, Cleveland wouldn't have any more gay community.

She compromised. She let them stay open, if they posted fire marshals at the doors. The fire department was going to come back the next day and do another inspection and monitor them until they cleaned up their act. She wasn't out to close them down or embarrass them. Complaints about the gay bars were rare; they didn't run them after-hours, and there weren't calls because of fights.

Lucie developed friendships with some of the bar owners that lasted for years. Word spread that she had contacts in the gay community. Lakewood was a suburb with a large gay population. Lakewood police called her when they had problems, because they couldn't get anyone to talk to them.

When Cleveland's first AIDS benefit was held, Lucie was invited. It was held for a man who had lived in Cleveland most of his life. He had AIDS and was going back to Texas to die. The organizers were afraid something would happen. They were worried the uniformed patrol officers would start hassling people in the parking lot. Lucie told them she would bring some of her men, to eliminate any problems. As she watched the tribute to the young man who was dying, tears filled her eyes.

17

PERMANENT RED

Her throat was slashed. A two-inch army knife was imbedded in her chest. Her feet were tied with hotel sheets, her mouth covered with electrical tape. White cream was smeared over her nude body.

Homicide and SIU detectives were on the scene when Lucie arrived. She had received the call while out on the air and had driven right over to the Dallas Hotel. The victim's name was Stella. She was twenty-two years old, a dancer who worked the circuit. She had come to Cleveland to perform at Mickey Finn's, a topless bar in the Flats. She never made it to work.

The Dallas Hotel was where traveling dancers often stayed. The building was owned by an appellate court judge.

It wasn't Lucie's investigation, but she was there because she kept tabs on vice-related crimes in her district. The case was solved within a few weeks. Stella was murdered by another resident in the hotel. He had strangled and robbed her—then mutilated her to make the crime look like a sexual homicide. The purse he stole from her contained only a few dollars in change.

How awful, Lucie thought as she looked at the young woman's body.

She heard complaints constantly from the public: why are you wasting your time? Sex-for-hire was a matter of morals. Not something to waste police time enforcing. Obscenity violations, prostitution—they were victimless crimes. Weren't they?

* * *

From her office on the fourth floor in a white terra cotta building on East Forty-sixth and Prospect, urban planner Margaret L. Murphy could hear women being beaten. From her window, she could see mothers drive up and push their young daughters out of cars to go work the street. She saw drug-addicted prostitutes staggering around. She saw women pregnant time after time, still out there. She watched hookers use attention-getting methods that were so ingenious that she, as an Irish Catholic girl, thought they didn't need to be described in a book. It was just too graphic.

Murphy's phone, like Lucie's, was ringing constantly. Residents were calling: "Hell, the goddamn hookers are out there again." Residents were getting wind of the fact that something was beginning to happen in the area.

Political and economic forces converged, creating the environment for Lucie to implement her plan. The concept of urban renewal was taking hold in downtown Cleveland. The five-bar raid was the beginning— Lucie saw that the area's businesses were actively concerned about the prostitution problem.

Margaret Murphy was hired by a group called Midtown Corridor to help them implement a plan of revitalization. It was a private initiative, a plan for development, and it covered a fifty-five-block area that was backed by new and established businesses, labor unions, and social service agencies.

Amidst the pimps, prostitutes, and sex shows, and despite the drugs, robberies, rapes, and murders, long-established businesses were trying to survive. Midtown Corridor was conceived by Morton L. Mandel, chairman of Premiere Industrial Corporation, a multimillion-dollar distribution company that had been in the area for forty years, and Thomas H. Roulston, founder and president of Roulston & Company, the only American brokerage house to own a Swiss bank. Roulston had worked on the state's criminal justice coordinating council overseeing the federal anticrime monies and was described by *Cleveland Magazine* as a "law and order stockbroker."

The number one problem was the need to eliminate prostitution. Female workers at the wholesale, retail, and light-manufacturing firms were propositioned from passing cars. Some quit rather than put up with the constant badgering. Customers, clients, and salesmen were harassed. People were afraid of crime. Some businesses were forced to close their doors.

Lawrence D. Altschul was vice president of Midtown and president of Blonder Companies, on Prospect near East Fortieth. Blonder was one of the nation's largest distributors of wall coverings. But the neighborhood gave him headaches. Bringing in out-of-town visitors was an embarrassment, Altschul said.

Business clients were brought by way of Martin Luther King Boulevard down and around the lakefront. This long circuitous route was all to avoid what Murphy and Lucie saw every day.

"You can't do business very well if there is a girl standing in front of the place with her skirt lifted above her head," Lucie said. "I mean, that's tacky."

Once you start talking to people about money, you get their attention, Lucie knew. This is not about morals, Lucie said to anybody who would listen. This is not about who is sleeping with whom. Who is in charge here? Is it going to be the street people or the positive element?

Lucie broke through the blue wall of police isolationism to work with Midtown Corridor: "We don't talk to anybody. We don't tell anybody what we are doing, and we function autonomously. Well, on some things you can't do that—and prostitution is one of those. It isn't just a law enforcement problem. I mean, I can arrest whores 'til I'm dead, but unless something comes in to replace it, something that is positive—nothing is going to change. Here's my part, and I'm going to make a plan to help fit in with the other parts."

She and Murphy joined forces. "We both liked an unrealistic challenge." Murphy smiled. Her energy and excitement for her own work were like morning coffee percolating to a frenzied brew. Her short brown hair suited her small features. Her face had a softness that the fierceness of her green eyes betrayed. She approached the problem from her urban planning background, thinking of new zoning and financial incentives. "All those things you think of with economic development programs." But that wasn't going to work at all. "It was the environment. How do you make it a place to do business?" Murphy asked.

Lucie served on Midtown's security committee, attending meetings. Larry Altschul was committee president. Lucie went out and talked to businessmen, telling them how to fence off the parking lots and put in lighting.

"Just make it inconvenient for the street prostitution to flourish," she told them. "All we can do is clear a path and give it time to let the positive element get a foothold in the area." Altschul wrote a letter to Lucie's captain. He commended her work but also let the captain know he wanted continued support.

Murphy kept bugging city hall. She was trying to get a trash receptacle. It took forever. She sputtered with anger: "People throwing wine bottles and you walk over these goddamn condoms. They are everywhere."

* * *

Lucie cooperated with Roger and the strike force—a major change from the past for the two units. They coordinated investigations, shared information. Lucie kept the lower profile she preferred and "just kept dogging along." But she valued Roger's tactics and realized neither of them had enough people in their units to effect change alone. Success was her priority—not competition.

Just two months after her transfer, in November of 1982, the difference was noted by James E. Young, director of law, in a memo to Mayor Voinovich. Young explained that until recently Third District vice was responsible for patrolling inside bars, and the strike force handled street prostitution. "This dual system was not without its conflicts," Young wrote. "A former sergeant in the strike force is now officer in charge of Third District vice. The results are already apparent."

Arrests for gambling, liquor law violations, and prostitution were the results of the combined efforts of the strike force, Lucie's vice unit, and the Ohio Department of Liquor Control, Young continued. He concluded that the investigations "made it evident that prostitution and obscenity are related." A woman arrested one week for an obscene performance was arrested the next week for prostitution.

Lucie's efforts at long-range planning and cooperation were working to raise awareness as to the scope of the problem.

She changed the face of prostitution enforcement. Instead of arresting prostitutes for the felony charge of promoting prostitution—which meant the women were held over the weekend and then released because the charge could not be proved—Lucie booked them on a misdemeanor, aggravated disorderly conduct. It was called "being booked on a white"—in a misdemeanor, the booking card was white. The arrest and charging were the same process. The hookers made bond as soon as someone arrived with their bond money, and they were right back out on the street. That was the down side of arresting on a misdemeanor charge. But Lucie could make more arrests—she wasn't limited by jail cell availability. And there were other reasons.

Police complained about the judges' indifference to prostitution. Though Lucie had her own judge problems back in 1976 when she worked as a decoy under Captain Delau, she understood the judges' perspective. "The judges don't ever get to see the prostitutes because they're never charged and never get to court."

Booked on misdemeanors, the prostitutes had to appear in court—because every single time Lucie made an arrest she had met the elements of the crime. The judges would have to see what was going on, even if they only charged the hookers minimum fines. Lucie flooded the courtrooms.

The disorderly conduct law said that no person should make unreasonable noise or offensively coarse utterance, gesture, or display, or hinder movement on a public street or road. Doing so was a minor misdemeanor, the violator was given a ticket, not arrested. But if the person persisted after a warning then it became a fourth-degree misdemeanor, an arrestable offense. Lucie and her vice men warned the hookers, and when they didn't stop, they made their arrests.

"Who wants to buy some HOT! HOT! Pusssssssaaay?!" Cynthia Stone yelled at the passing cars. *Cynthia Rodgers,* another of Matthew Corbett's women, strutted up the street dressed in a black and white striped bikini and red jacket.

The hookers didn't care about the zone cars. They walked right in front of them, soliciting guys in the next car. Any time of day or night, any season, at least a hundred girls were out on the street.

Lucie and the vice men cruised the area, jumped out of their cars, flashed their badges, and made their arrests. A tall prostitute towered over Lucie, tussling, shouting, and cursing.

Lucie spun her around. "Get your hands up on the car, sweetheart, and leave them there." Lucie's voice left no room for doubt: do what I say.

It took Lucie about nine months to pull her vice unit together. Over time, a tight, cohesive team emerged. Lucie was finally free to concentrate on vice full-time, no longer hampered by other investigations, as she was in the strike force, and no longer held back by other people's methods.

"We are going to do things the right way," Lucie told her vice crew. "I don't care how hard it is. We are going to get things straightened out. We are going to make a difference."

She put together three two-man teams, and they covered the Third District twenty-four hours a day. Week after week, month after month, hammering and hammering, sweep after sweep. Lucie worked split shifts. Days, she dressed in a skirt and suit jacket and string of pearls and made her rounds of the local businesses. At night—"You can't run a vice unit from behind a desk," Lucie said as she donned jeans and a khaki fatigue jacket to join the men for the night shift.

Bigfoot grinned as she gave the orders. She was like a general with soldiers. But, he said, she was a woman general: "Here's your fingers and here is your thumb. She was the thumb."

She drove into the projects for drug busts. Cruised along Prospect, arresting hookers. Strolled into stripper bars to make sure her rules were followed. Raided cheat spots.

"There's *Pat Houghton.*" Santiago pointed. Houghton was wearing a mesh football jersey with nothing underneath. He arrested her for public indecency.

Cheryl Powell, aka *Gloria Clifton,* was strolling in a white jacket with a white miniskirt and red top. They pulled her in. The vice men knew all the women. As they drove, they reeled off their names, aka's, Social Security numbers, age, height, color of eyes and hair.

They picked up Donna, a regular arrest. "If you break my legs, I'll crawl back here to work," she once told Bigfoot.

They arrested a hooker who was a grandmother and almost forty when she hit the streets, broke and needing money.

They picked up *Tandy,* who had the worst disposition of any hooker. She wore lipstick for eye shadow. It turned out she was a juvenile. And a junkie.

The back of the car was packed when the detectives saw *Candy.* The vice men started to pull over. "No, no, please don't! Just take us to jail," the women screamed, waving their cuffed hands frantically. Candy smelled bad and all the girls knew it.

"Awright," the detectives agreed. They passed Candy by.

They picked up one girl who had been out since she was twelve, and another who started at fourteen. When they asked one hooker where she lived, she said, on the roof. She lived in a refrigerator box on top of a building.

"Let me see your purse," the detective asked one prostitute he had just arrested. It was a routine check, for weapons or drugs. He found a credit card machine. He was amazed.

Santiago and Kennelly checked out the alleys between the main streets where the hookers worked. "You could retread tires with all the rubbers lying here," one joked as he swung onto the dark side street.

They pulled out of the alley. Two girls ran when they saw the car. Santiago and Kennelly chased them. The women ran right out of their shoes; the cops stopped, picked up the shoes, and put them in the trunk of their car. They had twenty-five pairs of shoes in the trunk. The hookers came back. This time they didn't try to run, and they were arrested. The men opened up the trunk. "Pick out your shoes," they said. If the girls gave them a hard time, they wouldn't get their shoes back.

They arrested hookers with college degrees; a police captain's daughter from Parma; a prostitute who had her pimp's name written across her chest: PRIVATE PROPERTY OF——. They arrested "he-shes"—transvestites. They were more violent than the women, the detectives said. The he-shes repulsed them.

Kennelly checked the Blue Bayou where *Julia Jordan* and her gang of robbers worked the parking lot, robbing johns. He found *Linda Ewing* and one of the *McCray* sisters working a guy over. The john had his pants off. His wallet was four feet away from him. The woman had a knife. The john insisted the wallet had fallen out of his pocket. "He took a bus from Lakewood for this." Kennelly shook his head.

What do you say to a prostitute, Shirley Aley Campbell wondered. How's tricks? She got out of Lucie's detective car. Lucie was ahead of her, bouncing up to a group of hookers.

"Hi, Lucie," the prostitutes called out, a high-pitched cacophony.

"Hi," Lucie greeted them. "This is Shirley. She wants to paint you."

Shirley was amazed. Lucie had arrested these women so many times, and yet they were friendly to her. Shirley had never met anybody in law enforcement with Lucie's attitude. She was sympathetic, yet she didn't really let the women know that. She just treated them like equals.

Campbell was a renowned artist whose work had traveled the world. She saw herself as a social painter. She had visited Scotland Yard in London and painted abused children. She had finished a series on civil rights. Now, she was working on a project for an automobile dealer; he titled it *Sordid and Seamy*. She rode with vice detectives in Los Angeles and San Francisco. In Cleveland, she was told to call Lucie. Shirley was just bowled over when she met her. Here was this woman, feminine and giggly, who reminded her of Sally Field in *The Flying Nun*, with a gun in her hand—and in charge of all these cops. Lucie showed her the underside of Cleveland's downtown. Shirley never knew places like these existed. They were places she certainly would not want a drink in. Lucie walked in as though she were going in for a cup of coffee in a respected establishment. Another series Shirley worked on was called *Women in American Life*. Lucie later went to Shirley's studio, and she posed for her, pointing a gun.

Back in the cramped office, the men typed their reports. "Who wants to buy some HOT! HOT! Pusssssssy?!" the detective laboriously typed Cynthia Stone's report on the battered Royal typewriter. She was causing a traffic hazard, he noted.

The pimps circled the station, looking for the police cars. The phone rang. Santiago answered. Click. "They know we're here," he said, fingering his curly, black beard. They had arrested prostitutes with calendars on them. The women marked down the times and dates of their arrests, to see when the vice men were on and when they were off. Pimps used binoculars and CB radios to track the vice cops.

Report after report. Bored, the detectives looked through the thesaurus to find new ways of wording what they saw—"the use of lewd body gestures" Davidson typed on one report. Occupation: hooker. Or call girl. Or sex therapist.

They let Donna type out her own booking card. She knew the routine.

Lucie kept the arrest book meticulously. Before Lucie, the arrest book was hardly kept up, one vice detective noted. Davidson developed a grudging respect for Lucie. He saw she was efficient, intolerant of ineptitude. It seemed like prostitution arrests had doubled since she took over.

Lucie's drawer was unlocked. "Guys," Lucie said, "right in this drawer is two, three hundred dollars. If you take money out, leave a note."

"Any other boss," Santiago said, "you had to go through Fort Knox to get money." The most important thing about Lucie, Kennelly thought, was trust.

Only the vice men had keys to the office, only they were allowed inside. Nobody was allowed in the files without her permission. They had files on the liquor establishments, prostitutes, pimps, and female impersonators.

Tim Bright worked on his reports carefully. Every fact had to be correct, had to stand, from the arrest until the guilty verdict, with no deviations. "You really have to have all your ducks in a row. You have to be thinking all the time."

Bright kept a crib sheet, as Lucie had done when she first did decoy work. A folded piece of paper, a running log of the information. He and his partner booked their own prisoners, called for their own warrant checks. They had to write duty reports, recording the time of the arrests, then prepare affidavits so they were ready for the court docket in the morning. Sitting for hours behind a typewriter that barely worked, his eyelids felt propped open.

Lucie had to go over all the reports—plus write her own. A lot of bosses didn't write their own reports, but Lucie did. She worked at a hectic pace, returning home for a short break between day and night shift, surviving on just a few hours of sleep.

"For the past three mornings, there have been prostitutes walking down the center strip of Prospect Avenue at eight-thirty in the morning, hailing traffic in front of the Garfield Hotel. That's right ... the center line of the road! If you have not traveled down Prospect Avenue recently, I would suggest a trip; you won't believe your eyes!"

The indignant letter arrived on Mayor Voinovich's desk from Frank H. Porter, Jr. VP, general sales manager of Central Cadillac, a downtown firm. Letters poured in to the mayor's office, to Chief Hanton, to Lucie's captain. They were all forwarded to Lucie. Third District vice was her headache.

Mayor Voinovich's approach was the opposite of Dennis Kucinich's. Voinovich was probusiness. He formed an operations improvement task force, utilizing ninety executives from the business community to study city government and make improvements. He made a plan to get the city out of default.

Voinovich held regular early morning breakfast meetings for business leaders. At one meeting, he invited the business owners from the red light district. Mayor, they said, if you are so interested in helping business, do something about the prostitution problem.

Voinovich looked over at Safety Director Reginald Turner and Andi Udris, assistant director for economic development, city hall's business liaison. I want Prospect Avenue cleaned up in three months, the mayor told them.

Are you kidding? Udris thought. Mayor Perk had lost his office trying to clean up Prospect. Udris saw his political career going down the toilet.

After the meeting, Voinovich said, I'm serious, I want it cleaned up in one month. I want two months of clean streets.

Safety Director Turner was tied up with union negotiations. Udris was told: it's your job, and you better work on it full-time. Call Lucie and Roger, they'll teach you everything you need to know about prostitution.

Lucie took Udris out for a tour, much as she and Roger had done with Feliciano, only Udris didn't have to play a john. He sat in the front seat of Lucie's detective car as she piled hookers into the backseat, until they were nine deep and lapped on top of each other.

All Udris saw was women—then he heard a man's voice. The last hooker Lucie had arrested was a he-she. He looked at Lucie.

"Hey." she shrugged, her eyes teasing. "It takes all kinds."

"If you say so," Udris laughed. It was certainly an eye-opening evening for him. He finally fell into bed at four in the morning. He had to be in court by eight-thirty. He was following the process from beginning to end.

I can pick up prostitutes all night long, Lucie told him. But they're going to be right back out, and they're only going to get slapped with a minimum fine. About twenty-five dollars.

What's a twenty-five-dollar fine, Udris thought. Half a trick? A quarter of a trick? Just the cost of doing business. The police are doing a real fine job, he told the mayor. The problem is the judges.

Lucie was criticized for arresting the prostitutes on aggravated disorderly conduct. It was unconstitutional, some lawyers argued. Defense lawyer Pat Blackmon was stern: it was unconscionable what Lucie was doing.

Pat had heard of Lucie back in 1977, when she was assistant municipal prosecutor. She knew of Lucie's reputation because there were so few women police officers. Then Lucie became sergeant. "Her career sort of zoomed off." Pat called her Sergeant Lucie.

Lucie and Pat Blackmon later became best friends. But now they were on opposite sides of the courtroom. Pat is a serious woman. Her broad face is a medium brown, her voice bass. She was born in Mississippi, one of eleven children. She wanted to become a lawyer to right the wrongs perpetrated against her people.

Pat tried to get the pimps to band together, pool their money, and sue the city for illegal abuse. Corbett interviewed Pat but never hired her. She represented Donna and her pimp Tweedie Bird. "It was boasted that Donna made—on the street—almost a hundred thousand dollars a year because she was constantly out there," Pat said. "And she wasn't out there because she enjoyed it. She was out there because she was forced out there—I mean I'm real clear about that issue. A lot of violence put her out on the street, a lot of violence from her pimp. But I asked her one time—making the mistake of asking her—how in God's name could you make all this money and give it away to this guy. And she said, I hired you to be my lawyer, not to be my priest."

Pat didn't hold Lucie's actions against her personally. She knew the prostitutes respected Lucie, and that Lucie had integrity. Both Pat and Lucie handled the prostitutes differently than some other cops and lawyers. "Most of the men attorneys that represented prostitutes also received favors," Pat said. "I was a clean lawyer; I was in it for the money—you pay me the money, I will represent your client. And so there was an ethical code between us."

José Feliciano upheld Lucie's arrests: "If you look at the statute of aggravated disorderly conduct—it fit. It wasn't what you primarily think of as aggravated disorderly conduct, but the language of it was broad enough to cover the conduct observed there."

Lucie was well aware that she was skating on thin ice. But there was no law that specifically addressed street prostitution. She did research and embarked on a campaign for such a law, one that would give vice units a permanent way to handle the problem. Akron had a law against loitering for the purpose of prostitution. The law was ruled constitutional in a 1981 case. The ruling cited ordinances in Seattle, upheld in a 1971 case. Lucie lobbied for a similar law for Cleveland. She testified at "zillions" of city council meetings. The councilmen thought it was a joke. The oldest business in the world. Ha-ha. As long as it wasn't in their part of town.

Voinovich held a breakfast meeting with the municipal judges and talked to them about prostitution. What's the problem? he asked.

You're discriminating, they said, arresting prostitutes, not johns.

We made a deal, Udris recalled. Pick up eight guys, pick up eight prostitutes. For every john arrested they'd give the max to a prostitute, smack her with a full fine and jail term.

Lucie coordinated with Roger. Strike force policewomen were already trained to do decoy details; he handled most of the john arrests. Lucie and her unit hauled in the prostitutes.

The vice unit checked bars for liquor violations, the OK Corral, Silky Sullivan's, the Wild Goose. They went into biker joints and burlesque shows. Madam's Place was an old-style burlesque house where women in long gowns sashayed down a long runway. They hit T & A bars in the afternoons and evenings, looking for liquor violations. The vice men called the black stripper bars bush palaces, because the dancers didn't shave their pubic hair or underarms. Exposing pubic hair was one of the many violations they looked for.

The vice men rolled past Odell's "No Tell" Hotel on East Fortieth Street, opposite Central Junior High School. It was so crowded, Mr. Odell was in the lot, directing traffic, handing out ten-minute parking stubs with one hand. In the other hand he held a 12-gauge shotgun "to keep it down."

Twenty prostitutes lined up outside. There was one white guy in each car, circling the block. The vice team stopped and watched. They counted one guy circle sixty times. He never picked up a girl.

Odell's was in its heyday, averaging over a thousand rentals per week; he admitted to raking in a hundred fifty to a hundred ninety thousand dollars per year.

The wood-framed building with the large porch used to be somebody's mansion. The rich wood on the ceiling curved into the walls still paneled in walnut. Red curtains shaded the windows of the once-elegant rooms. Handwritten signs advised customers to PUT ALL RUBBERS IN THE WASTEBASKET OR FLUSH DOWN TOILET. The rooms were bare except for bed and wastebasket. They looked old and worn out.

Customers were waiting five and six in a row, as the maids hurriedly changed the sheets. Near the registration counter was a candy machine with popcorn, Reese's, Fig Newtons, Mr. Goodbars—and two types of condoms.

Odell was a small man of sixty with a short, round Afro under his black beret. He had merry eyes behind his glasses and a wise look; he smiled easily. His family had come from Chicago in the twenties; his father was a tool and die maker. Over the years, Odell had accumulated eight families that bore his name and four that did not. He ran his business for the money—fourteen of his children finished college. One daughter became an engineer. His philosophy was: the world is here for us. We are supposed to enjoy it.

Lucie used the place for sting operations, and sometimes went in and made arrests. Mr. Odell thought Lucie was kind of rough. Lucie and her Angels were out there all the time.

But Lucie told her detectives, "This job isn't everything." Vice work was a quick burnout assignment. The only way to keep up the relentless enforcement was to keep morale high. Traditionally, vice men worked every Friday and Saturday night from eight in the evening till four in the morning, which played hell with their home lives. Lucie made sure that one team had a weekend off about every month. That was unheard of. She gave them a three-day bagger every so often, so "we could enjoy life with our family," Santiago said, pleased.

He heard all the comments: Oh, you're working for Lucie. You got to be out of your mind. Santiago just laughed. "I tell you what—they didn't know what they were missing."

Mark Hastings made rules for himself: he never dated a dancer, a prostitute, or a barmaid. He didn't care what they looked like. He thought it was dangerous. A dancer working at the Body Shop who was a part-time whore and probably taking drugs was not the type of person he wanted to have a relationship with, anyway. Next thing you know, she'll be going to the chief or the mayor or Lucie or somebody, or she'll want something done for her. It's just not a smart idea.

Kennelly found a sixteen-year-old from Lakewood who had run away. She had been picked up by a pimp, raped, and turned out. Lucie took her out to lunch and called her mother. The pimp was arrested.

"There are kids out there," Lucie sighed. "One girl from West Virginia, we tried desperately to get her on track. We tried to let them see. We tried to give them a chance to get home, see the light—but it was an uphill battle."

"It has been clear to me for some years," Lucie later wrote, "that jail alone will not break the cycle of recidivism nor decrease the erosion of lives of these women." The letter was in support of funding for a program, Project Second Chance.

The project was initiated in 1984 by Dr. Leonard Soldt, the pastor of the First Methodist Church, and Dr. Andrew Edwards from the Department of Social Services at Cleveland State.

The pastor had had problems with prostitutes congregating in his church parking lot. He got to know them by face and name and talked with Lucie about them. How could he help? What could the police do to intercede? They were performing tricks in the cars on Sunday mornings; they propositioned church members. One prostitute had come to him crying. Later, she committed suicide. Project Second Chance had been an outgrowth of these concerns. They proposed a three-pronged solution to the prostitution problem: the law and its effective enforcement through police prosecutors and judges; media coverage of the arrest and prosecution of johns and prostitutes; and the rehabilitative program that would help get the women off the streets. Lucie referred prostitutes to the program.

Lucie's schedule was nonstop. One day, at eleven in the morning she met with Judge Adrine, Udris, and Safety Director Turner about Project Second Chance and the loitering law. At eight that night she dealt with a juvenile runaway from Canton. She educated the public at every opportunity, speaking at the Brooklyn-Cleveland Exchange Club and Baldwin-Wallace College.

At ten one morning, she went up to the chief's office to discuss child pornography investigations with Hanton, then met with Larry Altschul about the installation of a police ministation in the Third District. She was in the prosecutor's office, then over at court. Another day, she drove to Columbus for liquor hearings. Then, back to the Third for a meeting with a representative from the Growth Association. Margaret Murphy called with a narcotics complaint; Lucie went over to investigate. She was scheduled for shooting practice at the department's indoor range. At the police academy, she taught recruits how to treat crime victims with sensitivity, and she compiled statistics on child prostitution for a councilman.

Early on some evenings, she left Central Station and went to Playhouse Square. She donned pink tights, a black leotard, and black slippers and entered another kind of world. She was taking ballet lessons. She always needed some activities outside police work. She hated formal exercise, but she thought it would be fun to take dance again. Pirouettes and pliés were a reprieve from champagne hustle bars and condom-strewn streets. But she soon found she couldn't keep up with the lessons. Her schedule was too heavy and kept conflicting with the classes.

The article on Lucie in the October 6, 1983, issue of *USA Today* began, "Cleveland's top vice cop is used to being asked, 'What's a nice girl like you doing in a place like this?'" Lucie responded: "Sometimes I'm not so sure myself."

Lucie and Murphy passed a swarm of prostitutes and walked into an elegant, old-fashioned building. Elderly men were discussing a literary find—something about a publisher from Philadelphia ... 1802 ... 1778 ... Lucie and Murphy heard the murmuring. The change of environment from the street was jolting.

They were inside the Rowfant Club, an association formed in 1892 and housed in the Prospect Avenue location since 1895. The club was as eccentric in its own way as the Diogenes Club, the favored spot of Sherlock Holmes's reclusive brother, Mycroft. Rowfant Club members were collectors and lovers of books; the club's name came from a book collectors' association in England. They abhorred publicity. Their mascot was the groundhog. Lining a bookcase in the library were candlesticks, each one hooded as a remembrance of a deceased member.

The outside world was encroaching upon the nineteenth-century atmosphere. Next door, the Hotel Sterling housed a four-million-dollar numbers racket, gamblers picked up bets at the bar. Sex trade flourished. Murphy had complained to Lucie, "You know, last night I came by the Sterling Hotel and there's seventeen hookers."

Some of the club members were involved with Midtown Corridor, and Lucie and Murphy had been invited to attend a ladies luncheon. Then Lucie was invited for a Saturday luncheon. No woman had ever spoken at a Saturday luncheon. No women were allowed as members.

The gentleman who introduced Lucie that Saturday explained that a long-held tradition was about to be broken. Lucie looked down the table. A candle was lit at each place. She gave her talk, explaining what the police were doing to combat the prostitution.

The Rowfant Club made efforts to stop prostitution, but some local businesses catered to it. Lucie, Murphy, and Midtown staff members discoursed over lunches in such establishments. They dropped into Hatton's, where four or five hookers were having lunch. Murphy talked to the owner, Duane Hatton. "Duane, you can't keep doing this," Murphy said. "Duane, we're going to get you, Duane." They invited him to join the security committee. They convinced him to donate deli trays. They nagged him with phone calls. "The hookers are out there again." The idea was to get him involved. "He allowed it to happen," Murphy said. "I learned real quick that it won't go on if you don't want it."

Lucie worked with Midtown to set up a police ministation in the area. It wasn't easy. They finally succeeded in opening one at Fortieth and Prospect. Businesses donated carpets and air conditioning. Murphy's colleague, Connie Perotti, raised money and organized volunteers from what Murphy called the "godforsaken hotels. People with the world's worst life stories and health problems—they came, and it made them feel a part of their community. It was hometown America solving hometown problems. Taking control."

Lucie tackled the crime in the derelict buildings. Murphy fought for acquisition, frustrated with a slow ineffective system. Owners of buildings could be delinquent on taxes for up to three years before any action could be taken by the city; buildings might be left derelict for up to five years. Midtown targeted buildings and establishments for their privately funded land bank: buildings that should be demolished, businesses that were contributing to the area's crime problem and were fire and health hazards. Code enforcement on a building with an out-of-town tax-delinquent owner did not usually work. Murphy tried to convince the city council to use eminent domain and back the Midtown group.

Parcel by parcel, piece by piece. Murphy kept a map for Midtown Corridor, showing which buildings were vacant, marking when new businesses moved into the area. Forty businesses expanded, and sixty-five new ones moved in by 1985. There was an overall reinvestment in the area of two hundred million dollars.

Lucie was pleased with their efforts. Midtown was instrumental in revitalizing the community. It was a citizens' group that she could count on her side. She was as thankful for the help she got from the community as they were for her efforts.

Safety Director Reginald M. Turner sent her a letter of commendation for her outstanding performance and professionalism only a year after her transfer. He wrote, "My office is constantly being reminded by the business community of downtown Cleveland of your fine efforts in controlling vice within the District."

Lucie knew the admininstration was a key factor in downtown vice enforcement. "Voinovich was very pro big business," Lucie said. "He went actively out and solicited businesses to come to Cleveland, to get the city back on the map. George just went very quietly behind the scenes and gathered people together. A lot of people say George never did anything for the neighborhoods, and maybe in some respects that's true, but prior to that, not only did we not have neighborhoods—we didn't have a downtown either."

Supported by some, she was slammed by others. Not all her press experiences were serious or positive, and her gender continually affected the way she was treated. In May of 1983, less than a year after Lucie became "top vice cop," the Associated Press ran a story on their wire service saying that "prostitutes who once flocked to a one-mile stretch of inner-city Cleveland's Prospect Avenue no longer find it a haven." The article seemed to have struck a raw nerve in *Plain Dealer* reporter Jim Parker. His Focal Point column of July 19, 1983, was a vicious attack on Lucie.

Parker began the column with his own version of the AP article— Lucie had "… almost singlehandedly driven the pimp and his merchandise from their familiar haunt." But the AP article never actually said that. He wrote, "… two intrepid, if disbelieving *Plain Dealer* types went prowling Prospect Avenue." They found that "the girls were gone." Their reaction: "Beaten in their own backyard. A female Baretta had managed what years of male police work had failed to do…." They went inside for some beer. They found prostitutes. The reporters decided they had scored a victory over the truth they said that Lucie had proclaimed.

"Now, while [Duvall] and company had technically cleaned up the street, the stuff of which TV movies are made, they hadn't done much to end prostitution on Prospect Ave."

Parker found prostitutes inside the bars and some prostitutes still on the street, but he had to conclude they were no longer so brazen. One has to wonder if Lucie were a "male Baretta" whether Parker would have been inspired to write such a column.

Other cities had tried and failed to clean up street prostitution. Lucie was succeeding. And the national press was paying attention.

As Lucie combined her political savvy and talent for working with businesses and community groups with her tough policing, the prostitution problem diminished. The collaborative efforts were effective. Margaret Murphy named the time "the Lucie Years."

The judges, seeing how severe the prostitution problem really was, were handing down stiff fines and jail sentences. The hooker—or the pimp—had to pay the fines. If she didn't appear in court, a warrant was issued for contempt of court. The fees began to snowball; it nickeled and dimed them to death.

Lucie had the prostitutes running scared. The arrest book showed the results. In June of 1983 there were 159 arrests. In July, 184. The stats stayed high even in the winter—126 arrests in January of 1984. In May of 1984, 271 arrests. Her vice unit was averaging 142 arrests per month in 1983. The arrest rate increased in 1984, and was up to 177 per month in 1985. There were over 3,500 arrests in twenty-three months. Constant, unrelenting enforcement was crushing the prostitution business.

The prostitutes felt the heat. One autumn evening, a group of them broke into a traffic control box and solicited every motorist stuck at the intersection—stuck because the prostitutes had switched the lights to permanent red.

18

THE SILENCE OF THE TEDDY BEAR AT THE FBI NATIONAL ACADEMY

Y ou have been selected by the department to be a candidate for atten-
dance at the FBI National Academy, Quantico, Virginia." It was
Lucie's formal notification from Sergeant White, training coordinator.

The National Academy is an elite school for law enforcement officers
who are in supervisory and leadership positions. One thousand officers
from all over the world are chosen each year to attend. Officers are nominated by the head of their agency, in Lucie's case, by Chief Hanton.

Hanton thought that anybody who was going up in the department
should have the National Academy training. Making lieutenant in the
department was quite an accomplishment. Officers who made it—he
tried to give them a push. Lucie filled out the pages of required forms,
attached the requisite photograph, and sent in the materials. She now had
to pass the FBI selection process.

FBI requirements were strict. Only promising career officers were
accepted. One out of every eight graduates is head of a department, many
hold top command positions. Candidates must possess "outstanding
character and reputation and must have demonstrated unimpeachable
moral conduct and integrity, must show an aptitude and interest in aca-
demic achievement"—because the course was rigorous. The FBI con-

231

ducted an investigation into the background of every officer nominated.

Lucie not only was committed to increasing her own knowledge of police work, but she was also dedicated to teaching other officers and improving the professional and educational level of the department. She was already certified by the Ohio Peace Officers Training Council and was teaching courses at the police academy in crisis intervention, defusing hostile situations, and problem identification. She was the kind of dedicated officer the FBI looked for.

Lucie was accepted.

She was attending the session running January through March. For their Christmas celebration, she and the vice officers went out for dinner. Over wine and food and with much hilarity, the men gave her a teddy bear, Paddington Bear, to take with her to the academy. A photo snapped at the restaurant shows the vice men grouped around her as she sat in Jimmy Davidson's lap, grinning and holding her bear.

At home in Strongsville, she packed for the three-month stay. Eric and she drove down in her car, and Eric flew back. Lucie drove through the peaceful surrounding woodlands into the modern training complex situated on the United States Marine Corps Base at Quantico, Virginia, about forty miles south of Washington, D.C. Enclosed walkways linked the facilities. There was a library with a dial access system, classrooms with closed-circuit television, an automated informational storage and retrieval system, and a forensic science research and training center. Hogan's Alley provided the practical side of training. Students enacted crime scenarios in mock settings: a bank, post office, drugstore, and a pawnshop that was really a front for a clandestine casino. The equipment available at the National Academy was far more upscale than anything in the Cleveland Police Department.

Lucie had already been to Quantico, for a one-week Gambling School, one of the Academy's toughest courses, in January 1983, just a few months after she took over vice.

At the National Academy certain classes were required—constitutional law, firearms, and physical education. There was an optional fitness course for the "real super athletes." Lucie did not sign up. "Are you crazy?"

On the outdoor and indoor ranges, they trained with .38 revolvers. In Cleveland, she was taught the point-shoot method. At the FBI, she was trained in the Webber method—standing sideways. It made sense, she thought, the shooter became a smaller target.

Lucie chose applied criminal psychology, taught by Supervising Special Agent Robert K. Ressler, as one of her electives, because she had heard that the FBI profiling classes were interesting.

With Ressler, Lucie would find, as she had with Bob Cermak and Ron Kosits, a long-lasting professional and personal friendship.

Bob Ressler grew up in Chicago and became interested in criminal issues early in his life. In 1946, a man named William Heirens slaughtered a six-year-old girl, cut her body in pieces, and put the fragments in the neighborhood sewers. As a boy, Ressler was fascinated. How could somebody do something that awful? Later, as an FBI agent, he almost passed out when he learned that John Wayne Gacy had lived four blocks from where he grew up.

Ressler's interest in bizarre crime led him into prisons, where he interviewed serial murderers, gaining insight into their personalities. John Wayne Gacy called and sent a card every now and then. Though Ressler had no intention of inviting them to his home as guests when they got out of jail, he had a genuine interest in the killers he studied. His philosophy was similar to Lucie's—people are people. You have to give them credit for whatever good there is in them. If you look down on them, you won't get anything out of them.

When Lucie arrived at the National Academy, Ressler was working on VICAP (Violent Criminal Apprehension Program). Pierce Brooks, the investigator in Joseph Wambaugh's *The Onion Field*, had developed the original idea of VICAP, a system for tracking serial killers. Ressler teamed up with Brooks in 1982, and with funding from the Department of Justice, the idea was further developed. The program kicked off in June of 1985, with Ressler as its first program manager.

Thomas Harris, author of *The Silence of the Lambs*, consulted Ressler when researching his book. Ressler thought Harris was a good writer but was disappointed in the film. In the case of a serial killer, the FBI had no power to investigate or pursue. They did consultation. "The movie had the FBI do everything, and that flies in the face of the reality of cooperation between agencies." Like Lucie, Ressler believed in interagency cooperation.

Ressler's aim in teaching the police officers was to explain the profiling process, to help them understand abnormal criminal behavior. But on the first day of class, before he plunged his students into the world of the psychopathic personality, he began by introducing himself and explaining his background.

Lucie was late. Everybody was sitting down already when she ran up the stairs and roared into the classroom, clutching her books. Ressler looked at her, startled. Oh, no, what is this? he thought. Gosh. What a small policewoman. She looked like a lost kid, disheveled and confused, as if she had just come from the gym.

Ressler continued with his introduction. He had started his FBI career in 1970 working interstate prostitution—in Cleveland. Lucie sat there quietly as Ressler went into a long dissertation about how the worst years of his life were spent there. How he and his partner hated the city, and figured out how they could plant land mines and drive all the residents to Canada. Cleveland was the city where the river caught on fire and Mayor Perk set his hair ablaze. It was a joke.

"I hope nobody here is from Cleveland," he said.

The disheveled, petite policewoman raised her hand.

Thus, their friendship began.

Lucie enjoyed Ressler's course very much, even though she had to endure three months of Cleveland jabs. Ressler not only joked about Cleveland, he tried to sprinkle humor into his teaching, and he liked Lucie because she appreciated his wit. She shrieked with laughter, banged the desk, and just about fell off her chair.

Ressler had never heard of a woman commander of a vice squad. He had conducted trainings in every state of the country. Vice was traditionally a door-kicking and cigar-smoking operation.

And she turned out to be one of the sharp cookies in his class. They had to do a term paper, a case study of a murderer. Ressler asked Lucie if she would do her paper on Cleveland serial murderer Frank Spisak. Ressler was especially interested in what he called paranoid personalities, and Spisak was a superparanoid-type psychopath. Spisak, who had targeted gay men and blacks for his murders, had ties to Nazi organizations. He was someone Ressler wanted data on.

Lucie called Lieutenant Howard E. Rudolph, who was in charge of the homicide unit, and told him she was doing a paper on Spisak, whose case had recently come to trial. He had the court transcript printed for Lucie, and gathered together the files and crime scene photographs for her. Lucie drove home one weekend to pick up the reams of material. She pared it down to about forty pages for her paper. Ressler was pleased she was able to dig up the information. The FBI had no jurisdiction over most homicide cases, and relied on police departments for data. Lucie's work helped Ressler build his research base. She had done a real fine job. He was impressed, and he gave her an A.

Lucie had developed strong feelings about Cleveland during her tenure as a police officer. She tried to convince Ressler that while there may not have been much of a downtown when he was stationed there, things were different now. "When you're in Cleveland, you better visit me. I'm going to take you out. Cleveland has changed," Lucie promised him.

Lucie benefited greatly from Supervisory Special Agent Kenneth V. Lanning's course on child sexual abuse, another elective. The field of child pornography investigations was new; and it captured and sustained Lucie's interest from that moment on. Practically everything she learned about it, she learned from Lanning. Over the years, she would phone him many times for advice. She later called him her "child pornography mentor."

At the beginning of his course, leadership, problem solving and decision making, Supervisory Special Agent and instructor Robert F. McCarthy, of the management science unit, told his students that he was going to change the way they made decisions.

He did, Lucie said.

McCarthy brought management techniques alive. He utilized the theories of transactional analysis; course material included concepts and exercises from Dr. Eric Berne's best-seller *Games People Play,* and Thomas Harris's *I'm O.K., You're O.K.* He adapted the concepts for police officers. He discussed Abraham Maslow's hierarchy of needs, Frederick Herzberg's two-factor hygiene-motivator theory of management, and the motivational theories of Harvard psychologist David McClelland.

Lucie worked on exercises that defined her management beliefs and practices. Working on grids, she learned to look at the pros and cons of each decision and how to prepare for what could go wrong. In law enforcement, she knew she could make the best decision in the world, but something might come along and change it. She gained clarity, the ability to sit back and ask what are the ramifications of this decision. Maybe she had done that before, she thought, but not to the extent she did after the course. Over time, the process McCarthy taught became second nature for her. Eight years later, she said, "I use it all the time."

Supervisory Special Agent Daniel L. Schofield taught constitutional law. Lucie liked him as a teacher, he kept the subject interesting. They learned about violation of First Amendment rights, search and seizure, arrests, evidence, confessions, entrapment, civil liability, the juvenile justice system. Schofield went over specific cases, which made the dry legal information engrossing.

The academy was like college. Classes all day, working on papers at night. The 250 people in the session were divided into five groups of fifty. Lucie was the only woman in her group. Each group of fifty was divided into sections. In Lucie's group of eight was an officer from the Texas Department of Public Service, who had worked statewide narcotics; the youngest captain in the history of the Washington Metropolitan Police; a fire marshal from New York; and officers from Chattanooga, Tennessee, from Racine, Wisconsin, and Elmira, New York. Lucie's roommate was Sergeant Karen Green, from the Los Angeles County Sheriffs' Department.

As the weeks went by, the students let loose their tension through antics. They stayed in dorms, Jefferson, Madison and Washington, and visited back and forth. The doors could only be locked from the inside.

Once Lucie left her room, anybody could get in. And she could get into anybody else's room. She was accused of illegal search and seizure—stealing some beds and leaving them outside the rooms. In retaliation, someone came into her room and kidnapped Paddington Bear.

It was totally unwarranted. Even if she had stolen some furniture, a crime of which she was accused—but not convicted—there could be no comparison between that and stealing her teddy bear. He was being held hostage.

Lucie opened her door one day and found a pile of stuffing and a note that said "We mean business." Lucie designed a wanted poster with a picture of her bear and offered a reward. "Crimestopper Alert. I am offering a reward for information leading to the return—unharmed—of this bear. Last seen wearing a blue slicker, yellow hat, red and white FBI shirt, blue necktie. Answers to the name Paddington. All replies will be kept strictly confidential."

One of the posters was sent back to Lucie with "known to lie" written across "all replies will be kept confidential." Vicious. Lucie laughed. This was big-time crime.

She suspected the kidnappers were among her cluster of eight. She finally bought some beers for the guys as ransom, and Paddington was safely returned.

Networking was a major thrust at the National Academy. Everyone kicked in money, and they went to Washington to eat at a restaurant, or they partied right in Quantico. One officer was with the sheriff's department in Golden, Colorado, where Coors beer was manufactured; he had Coors shipped in for the lively group. They took pictures, and Lucie made a photo album. They partied at the Boardroom, Quantico's local bar.

Lucie's group put out a newsletter—"Raul's Raiders Rag." Raul Salinas was their group counselor.

Lucie went home once during the three months, for the three-day Presidents' Day weekend. She wasn't really homesick; she had been too busy. And on Valentine's Day, her classmates made her feel right at home. During a morning administrative meeting, a Valentine's Day card was passed around and everybody, including Lucie, signed it. She didn't know who it was for. The meeting stopped and the officer who was head of Lucie's section stood up.

"Since we are all away from home, you are our Valentine this year," he said to Lucie. The guys presented her with the card and a big box of candy.

"I was spoiled rotten," she laughed, her eyes sparkled. On their social outings, she was the only woman. "I really got wined and dined and pampered."

The three months passed, and graduation day arrived. Eric and Brad, now twenty-two years old, drove down for the ceremony. They were taken on a tour of the Academy. Brad thought it was neat to be at the FBI facility and see what was going on. Lucie finagled getting Brad a small arms training hat by making a deal with the shooting instructor— one of his hats for one of her police hats. It was blue with FBI embroidered on it. "The kind guys wear on the range at Quantico," Brad said. He liked it, he had a collection of hats. "You can't buy them at the souvenir shop. It's one of those editions that you don't see sitting around everywhere."

The graduation ceremony was "full of pomp and circumstance," and Lucie wore a business suit for the occasion. Her graduation photograph shows her amidst a sea of men in suits and ties. "I'm the one in the skirt." Lucie laughed when she showed the picture.

Back in the Third District, things were not at all as she left them. There were serious problems with *Dick Walker,* a ranking officer in her district. Lucie had never been comfortable with him. He drank in cheat spots and spent altogether too much time with prostitutes, as far as Lucie was concerned. While she was gone, he allowed a friend of his, *Tyrone Morrison,* to open a cheat spot in the Third District.

She was upset. It was the kind of upset that made her cheeks turn rosy red. She confronted Walker.

"I'm going to give you a chance to close this guy down yourself," she told him.

He was scheduled to hit the place one night soon after that. It's taken care of, he told her when he returned. The place was closed down, although he couldn't arrest the owner, Morrison, because Morrison had been standing outside.

In the meantime, Lucie's unit had been cut. Two of her men had been sent back to basic patrol. A few nights later, she was working alone with Mark Hastings.

"We're going to make this a real short night," Lucie said. "We'll get out of here early, because there's just two of us, there's not that much we can do." Lucie hadn't been out at night in a while. "We'll just cruise around a little bit, throw a couple of whores in jail, and go home."

"Sounds good to me," Hastings said. He was tired. It had been a heavy week.

The first thing they did was drive over to Cedar Avenue. Some guy was running a half-assed cheat spot operation out of a truck.

"Gee. What the hell is going on here," Lucie exclaimed.

They had turned a tractor trailer truck into a bar. A light bulb was plugged into an apartment building via a hundred-foot extension cord.

Lucie moved in and showed her badge. "That's it," she told them.

"You're out of business." She turned to Hastings. "Start putting the stuff in the car." Lucie and Mark loaded all the beer and booze into the car and carted it back to the station.

The short night wasn't over. "Let's take one quick pass," Lucie suggested. "I want to make sure there is nobody over at Fourth and High. I'm sure it's taken care of, but I want to be certain."

They drove down to Fourth and High streets. There were about sixty cars out front. In fact, Walker had not closed Morrison's place down.

Lucie flushed with fury. "That's it. I'm pissed now," she told Mark. "We're getting that place. We're closing it down. That goddamn Dick Walker," she ranted. "You want to play hard ball—batter up!"

They drove back to the station and Lucie went up to the OIC. She asked him to call in Tim Bright, who was working uniform.

"Go upstairs and put your clothes on," she said. "You're going out." She turned to Bright's partner. "You stay in uniform," she ordered. "We're hitting the cheat spot."

"Oh, no," Bright groaned.

Lucie and the men marched up to the doorman. "Police," Lucie announced. "You get in the back of the police car. Move."

Lucie positioned Bright's uniformed partner at the door and relayed her plan to Bright and Hastings. "Get rid of the customers. I just want the stuff. And I want Morrison, if he is in there. We're going to arrest that asshole, 'cause Walker wouldn't arrest him. The rest of them, I don't care about. Get everybody out of here. I'm going to watch them come out of the door." She stood at the bottom of the steps.

Bright and Hastings stalked up the stairs, Bright carrying his hand-cuff-ringed flashlight. "Police," they shouted. "This is a raid."

For several hundred intrepid partyers, the party was over. Bright and Hastings saw vice men—they were from the district where Walker used to work. They were living it up at the cheat spot in Lucie's territory. Bright and Hastings chuckled to themselves. The wayward vice men had no idea Lucie was waiting downstairs.

"We're hitting the place, just get out of here," Bright told the officers.

The cops filed out with the rest of the customers. Lucie was standing at the foot of the stairs. They had to walk right past her.

"You're a little out of your district, aren't you guys?" Lucie said.

"Well, we heard he was operating again," they began their excuses.

"Get the hell out of here, I'll deal with you later," Lucie responded sharply.

She and her officers closed the place down. There were cases and cases of liquor to confiscate. Lucie had to call in zone cars to help bring in the booze. By now it was five in the morning. They still had to inventory everything they seized; Mark must be ready to strangle me, Lucie figured. This was the night I told him we would work a few hours and go home early. The quick tour of duty had stretched to over twelve hours.

She called the man who owned the building. He was an administrator at Dyke College, where she had taken classes several years before. "I don't know if you know what is going on over there," she informed him.

"I'll padlock, I'll throw him out," the owner said. "I had no idea."

"Who is the place rented to?" Lucie queried.

"Tyrone Morrison," he said.

Lucie called the utility company. The utilities were in Morrison's name. Armed with that information, Lucie had enough to get a warrant to bring him in on charges of operating a cheat spot, even though he hadn't been on the premises the night of their raid. She went down to the prosecutor and apprised him of the situation. She got the warrant.

She called Walker into her office. "I've got something I want you to do today." She handed him the warrant. "I want *you* to put him in jail," she said. "Today. You got it?"

Later she faced Walker. "You had a chance. You let this get out of hand."

She had given him the opportunity to clean things up, and he wouldn't do it.

Eventually Walker was transferred.

Lucie did not feel so much betrayed by Walker as ticked off that he took advantage of her absence. How could he, in any good conscience, allow this to happen? To let Morrison come down and open his cheat spot. Lucie didn't think policemen should drink in cheat spots off duty. Not only because it was in violation of the law, but you just get too close to the people that you are policing. There was no way to walk that line.

19

STING

Spring 1991. A classroom in the Mandel School of Social Sciences, at Case Western Reserve University. The class is social work with child abuse; the instructor, Gerald A. Strom, takes a seat in the back. Graduate students sit, their seats forming a U, notebooks open, pens poised. As the guest speaker begins, the students put down their pens and just listen—rapt in her story.

Lucie's voice is soft and melodic. "Child pornography is different from adult obscenity." She writes on the board: "Child pornography is NOT protected by the First Amendment." She underlines the word *not* three times. "We are not talking about free speech," she continues. She makes eye contact with the women students. "I don't know if you've seen adult obscenity." Her eyes twinkle. "You don't have to raise your hand."

The women laugh. They don't raise their hands.

In 1977, the first federal child pornography legislation was passed. Before the law, there were 264 different commercial "over the counter" magazines showing children nude or engaged in sexual conduct. One producer-distributor made a profit of between five and seven million dollars. The strict new law quashed most of the commercial production in the United States.

"*Playboy,* etc., is a multimillion-dollar market," Lucie explains. "Child pornography is at best a cottage industry. The materials are traded or sold for small amounts of money by people who are sexually gratified by children.

"The last one commercially produced here is literally a collector's item." Lucie passes around the book, *Moppets,* a collection of photographs of nude children playing at the beach.

"The majority of child pornography is very subtle. It is not particularly sexually explicit. It is not *Penthouse* with small people.

"The market is different from that of adult obscenity. An adult is looking for an age mate. A child pornographer is sexually aroused by children."

Lucie picks up her piece of chalk. "If I spell this wrong, I'm not a school teacher. I'm not good at writing on boards."

She writes: Preferential. Situational.

"The preferential molester's sexual preference is for children. It doesn't mean he is actually molesting children. He may be married, he may appear to have an age-appropriate relationship—but his sexual fantasies are always about children.

"Everyone has sexual fantasies. You don't have to admit it ..." she says as the students giggle. "You may, like I do, have sexual fantasies about Kevin Costner." Lucie's blue eyes sparkle beneath her red bangs.

"Someone unattainable," one student teases her.

"We-ell, I don't know ..." Lucie feigns insult.

"Then comes the reality," the student continues. "Sometimes that isn't as good."

Lucie resumes the lesson. "At times of stress, the preferential molester may act on his fantasies. The situational molester is socially, morally, and sexually indiscriminate. If a child is available, he'll molest a child. If a woman is around—he'll molest a woman, an elderly woman, anyone. There are child molesters working in senior citizen homes. They are abusive, indiscriminate people.

"But most people don't fit nicely into either category. The preferential molester is strange, interesting, predictable—but I don't want you to think that every time you come into contact with a sexually abused child, that there has been a picture taken. Probably there hasn't been. When you hear word of an abused child, don't assume child pornography. But I want you to be aware, if you see it, or if a child describes it.

"There is also child erotica—a term coined by Ken Lanning of the FBI to describe what is found when pedophiles can't get hold of child pornography. They settle for child erotica. They make photo albums of cutouts from Sears or JC Penney's children's underwear ads. If you come across someone who has ten, twenty, or thirty albums—something is not right.

"Child erotica is not against the law. He can have ten albums of Sears cutouts, you can't arrest him for that—but it tells you he wants to molest, or is molesting, but he hasn't been able to get child pornography.

"What turns them on is the innocence of the child, the lack of sexual identity. Normally, their preference is for a child, the sex of the child is secondary. Some only want girls, some only boys, but you can't think of it as homosexuality or heterosexuality. It's the child they want.

"With the preferential child molester, repetitive behavior is the key. It makes them stick out like a sore thumb. God built in a flaw—so we can catch them," she smiles.

"They protect their collections with their life. They will never throw them away. Which is very nice for us. If we get a tip today, he'll still have it next week—next month.

"When you look at your high school yearbook," Lucie's eyes shimmer, "the pages of mine are yellowed," she adds. Her forty-six years have not aged her voice. "You like to look at them to relive what you did. Homecoming, senior prom. A family album. It's fun. Why did I go out with that jerk ..."

The women join in Lucie's levity. The tension breaks for a moment.

"Child pornographers like to do that, too. They take a trip down memory lane. They look at pictures of the children they molested and fantasized about. Was it a Kodak ad that said 'A child is a child forever in a picture.'"

A student raises her hand. "Is the fantasy against the law?"

"A fantasy is not against the law," Lucie clarifies. "The photograph is the sexual exploitation. The child unclothed is used for sexual gratification even in just the taking of the picture. It can turn up twenty years later. Think of yourself as a child—you don't know where the negatives are, the videos are out there—that is the reality. That child is defenseless in this process.

"Child pornography helps the molester lower the resistance of potential victims. They don't start with taking the child's clothes off. They relate well to children, they like children. Children like them. They spend time with children, play games, and gain their trust. They show them other pictures.

"When you meet someone," she says, "you tell friends, 'I met this guy in the Flats.' It's normal to enjoy talking about meeting someone. Pedophiles like the same thing. They like to talk about their sexual experiences, fantasies, people they find attractive. Except if the person is four years old, you can't go to Fagan's or the bowling alley and talk about it. Now, they communicate through computer bulletin boards. They have quasi-underground publications, organizations. Pedophiles can join these organizations and get the names of other members.

"There is the Lewis Carroll Collectors' Guild, which used to put out a newsletter called *Wonderland*. Allegedly, Lewis Carroll was a child molester and collector of child pornography. If you think about it, Alice got smaller and smaller every time you wanted her to. NAMBLA,

National Man-Boy Love Association. There is the Rene Guyon society, whose motto is 'sex before eight or else it's too late.'"

Lucie passes around *Wonderland*. "Did you see this," a student whispers, shaking her head, and passing it to the next student. There are drawings of nude children. A review of the children's movie *Black Stallion* notes that the boy star is a twelve-year-old beauty.

"None of this is illegal," Lucie says. "Drawings are not illegal. These people are not stupid. They are very bright. They have information about the laws. They are articulate, well written. They have money behind them. They lobby for lowering the age of consent. Don't sell these people short," she cautions. "They are not a bunch of goofs.

"The age of consent in Ohio is now sixteen. Pedophiles would like the age of consent to be from the minute someone is born."

Initially the child pornography laws addressed the problem as a business. Put the business out of business. That didn't work. On May 21, 1984, President Reagan signed the Child Protection Act. Law enforcement officers no longer had to prove child pornography was commercially produced, making it possible to prosecute those who exchanged and traded child pornography. Ohio passed a similar law, which additionally made possession of child pornography a misdemeanor offense.

The laws reflected rising awareness. State representative Francine M. Panehal, who sponsored the Ohio bill, said that when it was first introduced, "Most people in the Statehouse and around the state were not aware that kiddie porn is a major factor in the overall mosaic of child abuse."

With the new legislation, for the first time law enforcement officers had a shot at catching child pornographers. But it wasn't going to be easy. Lucie was there from the start.

Her soft voice rises as she tells them what was done: "We had to develop an extremely creative, intricate sting operation."

The students' eyes rivet on the policewoman.

Early in 1984, before the new legislation, Lucie began learning everything she could about child pornography. She attended a seminar in Columbus, and she took Ken Lanning's course at the FBI National Academy. At a workshop in Middleburg Heights, U.S. Postal Inspector Paul Hartman made a presentation. Lucie had known Paul while she was in the strike force but had never worked with him.

"I've got the vice unit now," she told Paul. "I'm gonna start doing kiddie porn."

"Great," Hartman said. Hartman was an English major turned cop. He worked eighty to a hundred hours a week, and it showed. He had a tired, worn-out, raw-eyed look. One day a stubble covered his face, the next a scruffy, sandy blond beard. The press likened him to Columbo and to Don Johnson on "Miami Vice." Lucie described him as one of the "most creative and dedicated cops—an absolutely total banana policeman." He had stumbled into the child pornography assignment; once in it, he was obsessed.

Hartman of the Postal Service, Bob Cortesi of customs, and Lucie—local law enforcement—formed a team to attack the problem of child pornography. Cortesi had been a postal inspector before he became a Customs agent and had been Hartman's partner. Now, their partnership continued across agency lines.

The sting began with Customs. Child pornography was produced legally in Sweden, Denmark, and Holland. Men in the United States ordered the books and magazines, and Customs agents seized them as contraband at the port of entry, usually New York. Agents were seizing fifty to sixty packages a day. Much of the pornography was made in the United States, sent overseas, commercially packaged, and sent back. Customs agents developed lists with the names and addresses of people who ordered child pornography and turned the lists over to Postal.

Hartman jumped in, forming Research Facts, his cover organization, and sent letters to the people on the Customs lists: "We are an old Cleveland firm that does surveys. Your name was given to us, and we'd like to send you a questionnaire to fill out." The letters included buzz words to catch the interest of child molesters: "If you are interested in the youth of your community ... please write to us at this address, and we will send you this questionnaire."

The response was tremendous.

The questionnaire was lengthy and carefully thought out. Police had to show the respondent had a predisposition to commit the crime of trafficking—so that entrapment charges would be avoided. Hartman and Lucie were also interested in gathering data on the people.

The questionnaire asked the respondent his age, sex (virtually all were male), educational background, profession, and hobbies (many answered photography and collecting). Respondents checked off their answers: In your opinion, your community attitudes toward sex and sexual materials are too liberal, too conservative, about right.

Did they have any dependents? (If they had children in the home, they might be abusing them.) Question nineteen asked: At what age did you have your first sexual experience? Hartman and Lucie were trying to ascertain if they had been sexually abused as children. Many were.

What do you think is the best age for a first sexual encounter? Many checked off "five to eight." Some felt the best age was the same age that they themselves had their first sexual "encounter."

The questionnaires came back to Research Facts' post office box, and Hartman and Lucie went over them.

The next step in the sting began. The eager respondents received a letter thanking them for filling out the questionnaire and telling them "We have computer-matched your response with other responses, and to thank you for going along with the survey, here is a list of some other people who share your interest." Included was a computer list of five names with post office box addresses all over Ohio.

All the names on the list were, in fact, cover names for Lucie and Paul. They began corresponding back and forth with the pedophiles.

Child pornographers wrote letter after letter to dozens of pen pals, describing explicit activity with children, their fantasies about children, their observations of children. One letter read in part: "Saw a girl about eight pee her pants real good down at the beach last weekend. Her mother was mad as hell. The girl was a cute blond and really wet herself good. Also, saw a group of four boys about twelve to thirteen on bikes that were all good-looking. They stopped at a red light, were standing waiting for the light to turn green. One cute blond had a great boner showing in his tight jeans. He adjusted it so it won't stick out so much ..."

In their letters, Paul and Lucie could not describe sexual actions. It was similar to the techniques Lucie had learned doing decoy work. "You become the master of the double entendre—saying absolutely nothing but leading these people on," Lucie explained. There could be no direct sexual references. "We didn't ever want to be in court and have the policeman describing sex with a four-year-old as graphically as the alleged suspect, because then the jurors are going to get real confused and think, Wait a minute, what the hell is going on here."

The material Paul and Lucie sent through the mail was borderline pornographic, and they never sent original pictures. They would send photocopies. "These guys will take anything," Lucie exclaimed. The operation was a long, drawn-out process, but Lucie was having fun thinking up ideas. Their procedure had to be checked with the U.S. attorney. "You can't break the law to enforce it," Lucie said.

They created another organization, Ohio Valley Action League. OVAL, they explained in their letters, was the company that had contracted with Research Facts to do the questionnaire.

"This was so believable we were believing it ourselves," Lucie enthused.

"Thanks very much," the letter read. "We want no money, we only want your support. We want a voice in the community."

The post office boxes were stuffed with letters. They spent hours writing to seven or eight people at a time. "We were losing track of our identities. Who am I tonight?" Lucie laughed.

Hartman was glad for Lucie's humor. "When you're doing people who are doing kids, it can get the best of you. It was depressing stuff. Lucie made some of those tense situations not quite so tense."

They sent the test letters to about four hundred suspects. The goal was to get the correspondent to send child pornography through the mail. Ten eventually did.

One of the first people they caught in the intricate sting was a Cleveland police officer.

Paul received the photocopy of a photograph from a man named *Phil Ritter.* "Geez," Lucie said. "We've got an officer by that name. That's a coincidence." It never occurred to her that Phil Ritter, child pornographer, and Phil Ritter, Cleveland cop, were one and the same.

United States Customs agents at a New York airport had intercepted pornographic materials from Scandinavia addressed to a Phil Ritter. The materials included an illustrated ad for child pornography. Hartman sent test letters, and a correspondence began. He sent Ritter a photocopy of a photograph. Then, he got a photocopy in return.

Hartman looked at the photocopy. It showed the bottom half of a black female. She was dressed in bobby socks, so she looked young, but he couldn't tell how young. Paul was used to identifying the age of robbers and burglars. By their faces. There was no face in this picture.

He called Dr. Trina Anglin, head of the Division of Adolescent Medicine, Department of Pediatrics, at Metro General and made an appointment. He showed her the photocopy. She gave him a lesson on how to determine the age of a person by their body. This female, she told him, is under fourteen.

There were some oddities about the case. For one thing, the man used his real address, not a post office box. Hartman did some checking. Another oddity. Ritter was black. Virtually all child pornographers were white.

"I think this is your Phil Ritter," Paul told Lucie.

"Holy shit," she exclaimed. She thought she was prepared. Intellectually, she knew child pornographers cut across all lines, any profession. But to be in operation just a few months and get a detective—she rolled her eyes. "I've got to call internal affairs and tell them we're about to arrest this guy on a felony."

She called Ron Kosits. "There's a problem," she told him.

At one time, Ritter had worked for Kosits as a detective. Kosits liked him. Ritter was a good, conscientious worker. He had sixteen years on the job. Part of that time he had worked in the juvenile unit.

Lucie told Kosits she was working with Hartman. Officially, I can't tell you anything, she said, because it is Postal's investigation. Unofficially, I'm going to tell you everything. After Lucie briefed Kosits, he began feeding her documentation on Ritter to give to Hartman. Hartman needed information that Kosits could get faster. After a while, Lucie said, "This is silly. Why don't I introduce you to Paul and tell him that you know what is going on and then we'll all work together."

Hartman was chagrined about Ritter. "The one thing you hate to do in this business is arrest a policeman." He was worried. He had worked in Cleveland for about ten years. He had friends in the Cleveland Police Department. Would they think of him as a headhunter? But Ritter had committed a felony. Hartman was not prepared to give the man a pass just because he was a policeman.

He obtained a search warrant and went to Ritter's house with two internal affairs officers to make the arrest. Kosits had procedures to follow in PCIR: how to get such arrests handled quietly, get the cop in and out of the system in a hurry, and off the job, in compliance with all the union requirements.

Hartman recovered the original photographs. "Who is this girl?" he asked Ritter.

She used to live down the block. I took these years ago, Ritter said.

The child was now about thirty years old. Hartman had to show her the picture and talk to her. She had never told anybody about the abuse.

On July 29, 1985, Phil Ritter became the first person in the country to face a federal grand jury under the Child Protection Act. He was charged with three counts of trafficking. He admitted sending the pictures but claimed entrapment. The jury found him not guilty on the first count and guilty on the second two. He was the first person in the area, and among the first in the country, to be convicted by a jury under the new law.

When the Ritter case made the front page of the *Plain Dealer*, Lucie's name was mentioned nowhere in the article. She was never given any credit. In fact, hardly anyone knew about her part in the investigation.

Lucie threw herself into child pornography investigations whole-heartedly. The cases were not hers. Postal had jurisdiction. Many of the cases were from outside Cleveland.

Chief Hanton had given her the go-ahead to work with Postal. He didn't know how Lucie became involved in the pornography, but it was great that she had. She was doing a helluva job. Hanton encouraged initiative. That was how he got where he was.

The Department of Justice created the Law Enforcement Coordinating Committee (LECC), which targeted five crime areas, including child pornography, and encouraged interagency cooperation. Lucie joined the child pornography committee. She and Hartman traveled across the state, training police and prosecutors on child pornography investigations. "Anybody that wanted to know about child pornography—we'd go out." They told them how to recognize child pornography, how to do the investigations, how to prosecute.

Lucie urged the police department to tackle the crime of child pornography. She made her case in a memo: "Because of the peculiarities of the pedophile and the fact that these situations are rarely brought to the attention of law enforcement, it is necessary to conduct investigations of a proactive rather than the usual reactive nature. At the moment, over two hundred pedophiles have been identified in the Northeastern Ohio area, with forty of them living inside Cleveland. Given the large number of children each pedophile can and does victimize, we cannot dispute nor hide the severity of this problem."

In her memo, Lucie requested an additional five hundred dollars per year be added to the fund to Control Obscene Performances to cover seminars, the purchase of pornographic test material, and other expenses.

Her three-page memo ended with a powerful plea: "Because we are the largest law enforcement agency in the area ... I feel it is appropriate if not imperative that we assume the responsibility for conducting these investigations and display a progressive, knowledgeable, and organized approach to this reprehensible crime which is devastating the lives of so many of our society's children."

On November 7, 1984, she addressed a district commanders' meeting and outlined how the districts would be involved.

She also shared her expertise with her vice unit. She took Jimmy Davidson to a seminar. She brought Hartman in to show them how to look for child pornography. Then, to Tim Bright's surprise, Lucie suggested he give a presentation to the city council about child pornography and prostitution.

His first reaction was: Holy Cow. He was scared to death.

Lucie was giving him the opportunity. Instead of carrying the ball, she said, "Here, you go do it."

It was a good experience for him. He ended up going back several times.

The vice men went into the adult bookstores, looking for films of minors. If one looked suspect, they bought it, and Lucie would look it over, and call in Paul Hartman. They bought men's and swingers' magazines, searching the ads for pedophile code words: family fun, youth training, European material. They watched for johns who always wanted a young-looking prostitute.

Officers across the country were investigating child pornography and coordinating their leads. An Indiana state officer answered an ad in a swingers' magazine and received a sexually explicit picture of a little girl. The photograph came from her parents, *John* and *Sue Bates*. He passed the lead to Paul, who began corresponding with the Bateses. They also sent him pictures of their daughter, displaying the girl's vaginal area. Hartman contacted the local police. The local officer's wife was a teacher in the town's school, and she identified the child as the Bateses' little girl.

John and Sue Bates lived in a split-level home in an upscale small town in northern Ohio. He was an accountant with a large corporation. They had three children, two boys and a girl.

Hartman obtained a search warrant. Postal had jurisdiction over the trafficking of child pornography. The local police would take action on the sexual abuse of the children. Lucie went along on the search warrant, even though it was not only outside of Cleveland but also outside of Cuyahoga County.

Hartman, Lucie, and the local police drove up to the attractive home and went inside. They began searching the rooms. Lucie opened a drawer. It was filled with pornography. In room after room, in every drawer and cabinet, all the officers found was pornography. The officers began carting carload after carload of pornography away as evidence. Lucie saw a video camera mounted at the foot of their bed. They found another copy of the picture of the daughter. They found the bed sheets that were visible in the picture and confiscated them as corroborating evidence.

In the refrigerator, there was only beer and a couple of old pork chops. "There is practically no food in the home. This is nuts," Lucie said. "They're spending all their money on pornography, on writing to people, taking pictures. Their photo developing costs alone must be outrageous."

The Bateses were into group sex with adults, swingers' groups, engaging in these activities while their children were present.

The children's playroom was in the basement. Their games were stacked in a pile—Aggravation, Stratego, Monopoly. But off the playroom was a half-bath. "The pornography in that bathroom was unreal," Lucie expostulated. "This was the bathroom that the kids used when they were playing." In the cabinet under the sink, there were magazines piled next to Comet cleanser. *Young Love, Incest.* Lucie threw her hands up. "This is hard-core—not *Playboy* or *Penthouse*—hard-core stuff. The children were exposed almost exclusively to pornography."

Lucie and the officers suspected the Bateses were sexually abusing their children. But none of the children would talk.

The case went before a local judge. The Bateses pled guilty. Sue Bates was sentenced to four years probation. John Bates was sentenced to three to fifteen years—on each of four second-degree felony counts and to one year on a fourth-degree felony.

The judge said John Bates was an outstanding citizen but had "certainly let this get out of hand." He recommended John Bates receive shock probation. The children were initially taken from their parents, then returned.

Shock probation was usually used for first-time offenders. Perpetrators spent three months in jail and then were released, on the premise that they would be so traumatized by the incarceration that they would have learned their lesson.

Hartman had his own definition. "Shock probation is when the court decides to shock the shit out of the police. Someone does ninety days and gets out. It shocks us invariably—every time."

Lucie thought, This judge sees Bates as a classic executive; he wasn't going to send him to jail. In Cuyahoga County, we could have been a little more aggressive.

Hartman seized the Bateses' post office box. He became John and Sue Bates. "All the dumb shits who corresponded with them don't know they are in jail and I am them."

Wonderland published one of their reader alerts, announcing that Research Facts was probably a sting. Too many people who responded to the questionnaire ended up in jail. Paul and Lucie started another company, Euroarts, which transmitted film instead of pictures. Videos were increasing in popularity.

The Indiana state police officer sent them another lead. It was about a man named *George Devlin*. "I think he is molesting kids right now," the officer advised them. "There are children he has access to." Lucie and Paul began corresponding with Devlin. They wrote a few letters back and forth.

In 1976, when Devlin was forty-three years old, he was living with his common-law wife and her three daughters, ages twelve, fourteen, and fifteen. He was accused of forcing the girls to place their mouths on his penis, putting his mouth on their private parts, and of taking nude photos of them. He served two years in jail, and, because Ohio was operating under the Ascherman Act, which stated that sex offenders were mentally disturbed, Devlin was sent to Western Reserve Hospital in Northfield, Ohio, a facility for the mentally ill. He stayed seventeen months, was released, and placed on five years probation.

The five years was up on May 31, 1984—ten days after President Reagan signed into law the Child Protection Act. Devlin scrawled "Probation Ended" across the top of the June sheet of his calendar. Devlin kept his 1984 St. Joseph's calendar hanging on the wall. On the front was a picture of Santa Claus with two children, a horse and sleigh next to them. A cheerful holiday scene. Each month was printed on a separate page, along with recipes, famous quotes, and historical notes.

There was a small box for each day. In the boxes, Devlin crammed a record of his activities in a tiny handwriting. Some of the entries were in all capitals, the words underlined. On June 29, he noted that his girlfriend, *Susie,* was moody and that he had chest pains. He wrote down when he got a haircut and one day—SUSIE ME HOT SEX.

There were other entries. He was babysitting for several infants: Susie's nephew and the daughter of a friend.

On April 7, Devlin wrote in the calendar: *Amy,* aged six months, sucked and licked me. On June 2, underneath his announcement "Probation Ended" and near a recipe for strawberry meringue torte and a Coppertone ad, Devlin wrote: Licked Amy, ass and pussy.

Lucie and Paul knew none of this when they got the tip from the Indiana policeman. They only suspected that Devlin might be a child molester. All they knew was that he was sending child pornography through the mail.

Lucie tells the Mandel School class how they obtained the lead and started corresponding with Devlin. One of the students is literally on the edge of her seat, her back stiff and arched.

"Then Devlin stopped writing to us," Lucie continues. "His mail was returned nondeliverable. He left no forwarding address. We couldn't find out anything." Lucie pauses, her voice low. "George Devlin had disappeared."

20

STRAWBERRIES AND SHOELEATHER PIMPS

Hanton called Lucie in July of 1985. "You're being transferred," he told her.

"What for? What did I do?" Lucie enjoyed running vice.

"I'm starting a sex crimes unit. Remember, I told you?"

"Yah—but—" Lucie began, startled.

"I'm gonna transfer you. Take a couple of sergeants so you can start the unit. Then, when you're ready, we'll transfer your people and the operation will begin." He told her she had about six weeks lead time. Lucie was stunned, but excited.

She took the vice team out to the PLAYDIUM and broke the news to them. She was leaving. They were upset. Anxious. They didn't know who would be their new boss and what would happen to them. Mark Hastings decided to go to sex crimes with Lucie.

Downtown had been changed dramatically under Lucie's leadership. "It was hard on the streets, and the prostitutes all left town," Defense Attorney Pat Blackmon commented in her deep voice. "Lucie put me out of business."

Hotels were torn down. "Bars?" One hooker grimaced. "They don't exist anymore. There used to be an invisible wall around all of us. A way of bonding. Now—nothing is left. No girls with designer clothes, these girls were not poor, honey, these girls were classy." But Lucie had kept after them, making arrests every day. "Now everything is gone."

For Tim Bright the Third District had been a cesspool with shit hole bars that just really disappeared. He felt a sense of accomplishment. Lucie's hard work laid a foundation that effected change after she left.

Eventually, the Rowfant Club bought the Hotel Sterling next door and demolished it. Margaret Murphy commented, "Now there's a lovely parking lot with a wrought iron gate. There was controversy about tearing it down, because it had historic significance. We had a lot of review, a lot of discussion, and finally said good-bye."

Derelict buildings were demolished, one between the Star Express and the Sara Benedict House. The derelict building had once been filled with mattresses on filthy floors for prostitution, and people lived in rooms without furniture. It was now a vacant paved lot.

The bars with the most prostitution, the Malibu and the Biscayne Lounge, were closed down. The Prospect Lounge and the Wine and Roses had both been defused, though still in existence under different names. Handling Stage Door Johnnie's took longer than most, but eventually all the work paid off—it was closed too. The Garfield Hotel was shut down and boarded with plywood. Lucie didn't take all the credit for sealing up vice in the Third District; there were many contributing factors—some places had fires, others were closed due to liquor violations. "All these things piling on these people, and eventually they fade off," Lucie said. "But they were a haven for every type of criminal activity you can imagine." Odell's stayed open, but Mr. Odell no longer needs to direct traffic in the parking lot. Most of the live sex acts and the bookstores are gone. The Colonial Motor Inn—gone. Bought up for urban renewal and bulldozed.

Midtown Corridor's work continued. Reinvestment in the area did not show on a grand scale. It would take time, just as the deterioration of the area had taken time. Morton Mandel, cofounder of Midtown Corridor, won the national George S. Dively Award for corporate leadership in urban development.

Even after leaving vice, Lucie continued to testify for the passage of the loitering for the purpose of prostitution legislation. She wrote several reports predicting what was going to happen: "We'll get rid of prostitutes downtown and they're going to go someplace else." There was a long history of prostitution moving from one area to another. In the late eighties, prostitution increased in Ohio City, a West Side residential area. "Once prostitution impacted on enough people they started to realize the problem. When it became an economic issue in Midtown, when it became a social issue in Ohio City, then we started seeing some changes." Lucie was patient. She kept on fighting.

She enlisted the aid of Pat Blackmon, who was now chief city prosecutor. Pat supported the law. "The loitering statute was designed to make arrests more legitimate," Pat said. "Police officers actually had to prove and show evidence of the prostitution. Some cops' approach was, you bang 'em, you hit them hard, and you do it illegally. Lucie's position was, you bang 'em, you hit them hard, but you do it right. I think that's why she fought so hard for the loitering statute. She knew that what they were doing with the disorderly conduct was unconstitutional, but it was the only thing that they had available to them. I used to go to city council and say to the general assembly, 'If you want these people to do their job, give them the proper tools to do it.'" Pat spoke to her friend George Forbes about the law, and he changed his long-standing position and backed it. The city council finally adopted the loitering legislation on March 17, 1987.

Pat and Lucie became friends through their collaboration on the law. "Most people thought it was the most bizarre event of the century that we could actually become friends, because to me she's so typical small-town-Irish-exposed-to-the-big-world person. And I'm so southern and distrustful of white people. I'm very clear about talking about that issue. The fact that she and I could be friends, people thought that it had to be some underhanded devilish thing that was being plotted." Pat's laugh rumbled.

On the West Side prostitution dramatically increased with the influx of crack cocaine. It was a neighborhood—the residents didn't have the money that Midtown Corridor businessmen had—but they followed Lucie's approach to the problem and demanded arrests. Now they had a new law to work with, and they wanted more. Residents suggested a change in the court's treatment of first offenders—no shock probation for johns. Ann Marie Wieland, who belonged to the Ohio City Redevelopment Association and was the crime watch coordinator for the area, and Ward 14 Councilwoman Helen K. Smith called for the elimination of the Selective Intervention Program (SIP) provision for anyone arrested for soliciting a prostitute.

Crack cocaine also changed the prostitution business. Nikki had stopped using drugs in 1986. A veteran of the streets for thirteen years, she found it really hard to make her money. "Girls are going cheaper for the narcotics. Hundred-dollar dates turned into twenty-dollar blow jobs." Before, Nikki had not always used rubbers, but now with AIDS she used them all the time. "Even if somebody offers you a hundred dollars extra, you know he's up to give you something." Nikki wasn't happy with the new law. "They really didn't charge us with anything. Now, for not doing anything you get charged for that—loitering. In reality, the City of Cleveland got greedy, they figured they could get some money—it's the truth."

There weren't really any of the pimps left, except for Treetop's man,

T, and two others, but they weren't around much either. "The days of the flashy Cadillacs are gone. The girls are all strawberries," Kennelly said, women who sold sex for drugs. "The pimps got holes in the bottom of their shoes, shoeleather pimps we call them, the ones that walk."

It wasn't drugs that finally got Matthew Corbett off the streets—it was his women.

Lucie's constant crackdown on prostitution had taken its toll on Matthew Corbett's business. Too many fines and too many warrants drove him to pimp in other states. By 1985, he returned to Cleveland primarily for the holidays.

Matthew called Lucie from all over. He called her from Florida, when he took the girls down there for the winter. He called from Atlantic City. He called her from Montreal and told her how great the action was, and he ought to stay up there where the police didn't bother him.

That is one of the few good ideas you have ever had, Lucie thought.

Shandra was Corbett's number one woman. Beautiful. Stunning. Lucie and every other detective commented on it. When Matthew met Shandra, he told her he was a self-employed carpenter. She was eighteen. She had graduated from high school and was working at a modeling agency. She had never worked as a prostitute. When Corbett told her who he was and what he wanted her to do, she said no and refused to see him. But he kept calling her.

She finally worked the streets—first in Canton, then in Akron. When that got bad, she started in Cleveland. Her father chased them on the Freeway one day. Her family was trying to get her away from Corbett. After a couple of weeks of that, she decided that she wanted to leave.

Matthew went after her. He gave her the first of several severe beatings. He dumped her at her mother's house. Then, she went back to him.

In 1983, Shandra's husband, Officer Hull, shot a man during an argument. He was convicted of felonious assault a year later, and given a sentence of two to fifteen years. Though Shandra had married Hull and had a child by him, she continued to work and live with Corbett.

In the spring of 1985, after returning from a trip to Atlantic City, Matthew caught Shandra talking to another pimp on Prospect. He drove up and forced her into the car. When he was through with her, her jaw was broken. In three places. The doctor had to wait a few days before operating because her face was so swollen. Welfare paid the two-week hospital bill. When she pressed charges, he threatened her. She believed he would kill her or have her killed.

Lucie liked Shandra and found her pleasant and intelligent. But Shandra was too afraid of Matthew Corbett to be talked into testifying against him.

He had used Shandra to make an indoctrination film to train other women into the Life. He used her and his other women to actually do his work for him. To bring the women to him.

Star had been pulled into Corbett's "stable" in 1986. When Corbett jumped up out of bed and hit her hard—her love turned to hatred. She tried to take her four-year-old son and escape several times. But Matthew caught her and beat her. He cracked her ribs. He beat her in front of her son. Star turned on Matthew. Mayfield Heights police arrested him, and he was charged with compelling prostitution, kidnapping, felonious assault, and rape.

When Corbett was arrested on Star's complaint, Shandra still loved him. As his trial date approached, she struggled against his pattern of harassment. She had a new full-time job—supervisor in the kitchen of a fast-food restaurant. But she had a daughter from their relationship, and her attachment to Matthew was very strong. He found out where she worked. He called and cussed out her boss. Shandra thought her job was lost. Her boss told her to take the call. Corbett threatened to have Shandra put in jail so he could take their daughter, Jewelle. He was successful—Shandra was arrested on a false complaint, but she managed to straighten out the mix-up and keep Jewelle.

When Corbett's case went to trial, Shandra testified against him and described her own beatings. The two women's testimony substantially corroborated each other.

But Matthew was contemptuous. "Fourth day of the trial Shandra starts crying up on the stand and the juror starts to vomit." He was convicted and sentenced to a term of ten to twenty-five years. After five years in prison Corbett reflected: "You slap her. So what. You slap her three times, so what. Don't take that three times and turn it over to a beating. I know what a beating is." He had watched the video of the L.A. police with suspect Rodney King on television. "That's a beating. If you call mine a beating, what do you call that? Huh … I considered that a beating. Brutal beating. Now you telling me that's what I did to them? Hah. No, sir. No, ma'am."

Lucie was unequivocal. "Matthew is just where he belongs." He called her from prison, trying to get "shock" parole. Lucie thought, How long will it take him to get right back into business when he gets out. He could walk out the door and Shandra could fall right back in love with him. But she has a legitimate job, now. If she is completely out of the prostitution, Lucie thought, she might do OK. Shandra had really gone to the wall to testify.

Project Second Chance, after the death of Pastor Soldt, had lost its office space. The program's future looked bleak. Ann Marie Wieland wanted the prostitutes to have a place to seek help if they wanted to get off the streets. She wanted Project Second Chance operational. She talked with Lucie and Cleveland State Professor Andrew Edwards about using the program's name. Edwards didn't mind. The Gund Foundation gave fifty-eight thousand dollars to Project Second Chance, to reestablish it in October 1990. Its billboards appeared around town: DEAR JOHN, I QUIT. PROJECT SECOND CHANCE. Strike force detectives now hand out the program brochure to prostitutes they arrest. Nikki was one of the first prostitutes to try out the program.

Lieutenant Marty Flask replaced Lucie as head of Third District vice. "I had to take her place. I had big shoes to fill. About a size five." He laughed, his green eyes narrowing. Seriously, he felt challenged. "She had a reputation for having done a good job. It was good for me. It gave me a goal." He didn't replace any of her men. "Lucie picked them. I made an assumption they had to be great people." Lucie's vice men liked him. He continued her policies. The high arrest rates guaranteed no setbacks.

Lucie had been unhappy at home for some time. Her marriage was falling apart. The stress of vice work and the amount of time she devoted to her job were part of the problem that had unfolded over the previous two years. But her career was not the only factor. Eric also worked very long hours, and his job had a high stress level. It was hard for Lucie to pin down what had gone wrong.

Finally, they separated in 1985. Tim Bright and some of the other vice men helped her move into an apartment on Lake Avenue. She wanted to live in the city.

Judy Cooke, who had known both Eric and Lucie for years, wasn't surprised. "Eric always had a hard time with her job. He kept waiting for the day when she was going to quit and join the Junior League. She didn't fit the role of Mrs. Corporate America. Lucie is Lucie. She can be a decoy and that's part of the job, but I don't think that she wants to live a life trying to be something she's not."

Eric thought the quest for professional recognition and Lucie's career took a more important place than the family environment.

Later, Eric reflected, "I think we did well in managing all those crazy different hours. Would I marry another policeman? I think not."

Lucie said, "My preference would have been: we just lived happily ever after. I don't think we can blame it all on the police department, probably it had something to do with it. But it seemed—a change in values." She felt very bad that the marriage did not work out.

Their personality differences had weathered the years well. Lucie had matured through the marriage's stability. She capitalized on the positive aspects of their relationship, their deep affection for each other, and remained close friends with Eric even after their divorce was finalized. They continued to share their parenting and love of Brad.

Brad was six feet four inches and well built, his blond hair had turned pepper and salt. Like Lucie, it took him a while to find a career that satisfied him. Then, he saw an ad in the paper for air traffic controller and thought, This will be cool. Toward the end of college, he had majored in aviation and obtained his private flying license. He earned about a hundred hours toward his commercial license and then ran out of money. Lucie had taken flying lessons before joining the police department, and Brad had always had an interest in aviation, "plastic model airplanes, radio control, the whole nine yards."

He was accepted and was back off, coincidentally, to Oklahoma, where he attended the FAA Academy in Oklahoma City. The training was so stressful that by the time of his final exam his skin was flaking off the palms of his hands, and one eye was twitching. He called Lucie at one in the morning. "I can't sleep," he told her. "It's not looking real good. I need a major miracle out here to get through." Lucie talked to him for a while. Poor kid, she thought. She felt so bad for him.

He made it. Fifty-two people had entered the three-month training, only nineteen had passed. Brad was hired at an airport in Muskegon, Michigan. He loved his work and bought his own home. Lucie and Brad made the transition to an adult-to-adult relationship with ease. He asked Lucie for advice about problems with girlfriends. "You got to go to your mother with those," he felt. Lucie was comfortable asking Brad for advice, too, which surprised one of her friends who said he couldn't imagine listening to advice from one of his kids. But Lucie felt, "There's a lot of things Brad knows more about than I do. I usually listen to him— he's right." Brad called Lucie "Toots." Their relationship was relaxed and affectionate.

Lucie went to see Chief Hanton. "I want to keep child pornography," she told him. She was dedicated to the issue and concerned that others might not push so hard.

"OK. Have you given any thought as to sergeants?" Hanton asked her.

Jacqueline Christ was working in his office. Lucie and Jackie had partnered briefly in the Fourth District, and Lucie had seen her work over the years. Jackie was very good at organizing. She knew a lot of people in the system and in the police department. Lucie was starting a unit from the ground up, and she needed someone who really understood the clerical workings. Besides, Jackie had told Lucie she was tired of working in the chief's office.

"How about Jackie?"

Hanton laughed. "I've given you your own unit. Now, you're coming in here and asking for my sergeant."

"Yeah," Lucie admitted. "Basically, yes."

Hanton transferred Jackie Christ to the new unit along with Sergeant Ruth Lanier. Lanier had also worked in the Women's Bureau and later had supervised a downtown beat patrol in the Third District. Lucie did not want all female supervisors; she didn't think that was a good idea. But that was the way it worked out.

Hanton was giving her a wonderful, professional opportunity. Creating a whole unit from scratch. In ways, it would be more challenging than vice. She would be dealing with much more serious, personal crimes.

The unit was to be housed in the Justice Center. Lucie drove into the underground garage and took the elevator up. She walked into the big, empty room. As she looked around, her vision forming in her mind, she thought, How do I want to do this?

21

St. Joseph's Calendar

990. Lucie turned on WCLV, classical music. It was a gray, muddy winter day. Rain was in the air. Lucie was due at the range for her annual firearms training—Oh, fussberries! I forgot my gun. She always had a gun in her purse, but she liked to bring her department issue gun to the range. It's bad weather anyway, I'll postpone it. Teas lined her kitchen shelf: Raspberry Patch, black currant, jasmine. She was in a black currant phase, but mornings were for caffeine. She drank her coffee from an FBI mug. She dressed in her favorite colors, a multicolored patched turtleneck sweater, with swatches of red, pink, purple, black. A matching skirt. Pink lipstick—"Romance" by Prescriptives. She fed Max, the Manx.

Opening her sliding glass kitchen doors, she checked on her three squirrels, Max, Max, and Max. Their bushy red tails twitched and bounced as she poured the corn and nuts mix. One Max scampered from a tree, the limb hanging into Lucie's small, fenced-in backyard. One ran over the fence. The third Max climbed the wood steps up to the small deck in front of the doorway, toward the bowl of feed. Lucie watched him, worried. Is he really eating, or is he just taking the stuff out of the shells and leaving it there? Food splattered over the bowl's edges as Max nibbled.

Lucie decided to buy her own place several years after separating from Eric. She felt as though she were too much of a transient in apartments. She looked at condos first. She didn't really want one, but she thought she should look.

Finally she bought a three-floor, century-old farmhouse, which had been gutted and redesigned. She lightened the decor by hanging paintings, a large abstract in pastels in the living room, a Georgia O'Keeffe print behind the dining room table. She arranged four-foot Chinese fans along the walls, gathered while on Eric's business trips to the Orient. She placed oriental vases on the furniture, draping them with long, silk scarves. Her twenty-odd teddy bears surrounded her bed, upstairs.

In the small study off the kitchen, she set up her word processor, arranging pictures of her family and her books, including a complete Sherlock Holmes with reproductions of the original drawings. She was in the middle of reading a book on dream interpretation and a Tony Hillerman mystery. Velvet sleek Max elegantly roamed the terrain, his wise eyes surveying the environment.

In the house behind hers, a lawyer, John Nolan, lived. John's favorite character in the whole world was Lucy on "I Love Lucy." The fact that his new neighbor's name was Lucie and that she was a redhead struck him in a positive light.

John introduced himself as Lucie moved in. "If you need anything, let me know."

Lucie took him up on the offer when she needed help and returned the favor by bringing over dishes she had fixed. They started talking. She told him she was a cop and working in sex crimes.

OK, John thought. She's tough. She's smart. She's succeeding in what has been a man's world for a long time. They got along instantly.

John invited Lucie to a barbecue he was having over the weekend. He was feeling his way along. John was gay. With each neighbor he had to be careful. How was Lucie going to react? How cool was she going to be?

At the first barbecue there were twenty-five gay men and Lucie. Lucie had fun. John realized that Lucie was OK with any type of person.

With her new neighbor and his pals, Lucie was able to re-create a small-town atmosphere right in the middle of the city. In the summer, they had Saturday barbecues at Lucie's house. In the winter, they did Sunday pancake breakfasts several times a month. Lucie made the first batch, anyone who wanted seconds was on his own. They decorated their Christmas trees together. She introduced Eric and Brad to them.

John became a lawyer "probably because Gregory Peck in *To Kill a Mockingbird* was the most noble character in my whole life." The reality of student loans dictated his first job—corporate law. He worked at two of the three biggest Cleveland firms and hated it. He quit, and Lucie helped him with job hunting. Every letter would start out: Dear So and So, Lucie Duvall suggested that I talk to you. He landed a job at the AIDS commission for a big cut in pay—but he loved it.

Lucie set off to work in her brown Daytona Dodge, with its sunroof and bumper sticker on the back PEACE THROUGH MUSIC. She turned on her car radio. Music was one way she had maintained her sanity during the past eighteen years. Music, art, friendship, laughter.

She drove into the Justice Center underground parking garage. It was always packed, officers left their keys in the ignition. If she had to go anywhere, she had to move three cars out of the way. Well, if I get fired, I can always be a parking lot attendant.

Up the elevator crowded with bailiffs, cops, lawyers, visitors. The elevator opened on the sixth floor.

The sex crime/child abuse unit, SCU, was through a locked door, next to homicide. Fifteen detectives split two shifts, handling every felony sex crime reported in Cleveland. The office was bustling. Typewriters were clattering. Phones were ringing. A detective led a child into the interview room, decorated with a Muppets poster. The anatomically correct dolls were piled on a table.

Lucie tried to make coffee, but she forgot to change the filter and old grounds. The water steamed through, the coffee dripped yellow. Oh, no. She grabbed the coffee pot away, which only made things worse. Water spurted everywhere. She yelled, "Anderson!"

Tim Anderson, her office man, took the coffee pot and changed the filter. "Good thing you have a man around to do the domestic stuff," he kidded her.

His shift was from six in the morning till two in the afternoon. His job—doing all the personnel-related paperwork. He kept the unit running from day to day. "Without him I would be in administrative chaos," Lucie commented. He was far beyond an office man; he was the core of the unit. A clearing house of information. If she wanted to change a procedure or someone's job, Lucie ran the idea by him before implementing it. "He's my alter-ego." His easy manner and dry sense of humor provided her with relief and support.

Anderson was an alcoholic. Having a kid die in his arms while he was on patrol started his downward cycle, then there were years of working vice. He had gone through the stress unit and quit drinking twelve years before, staying on to counsel other cops and their families in trouble. Now he liked being an office man. He had had his fill of dealing with the public.

After rescuing the morning coffee, he returned to one of the unit's two old computers. A detective sat at the other computer and brought up the computer-tracking system that stored details on crimes—the MO, license plate, suspect description. A detective could enter "tattoo" in the data base and come up with all the offenders who had a tattoo on certain parts of their body. Or offenders who wore ski masks, or drove a particular car, or carried a knife. The system helped track serial rapists.

"Hey, we got the alibi of the year," Lucie joked with the detectives as she drank her coffee, "a stepfather who says it was the cat that molested his nine-year-old stepdaughter. Fortunately, the cat has a purr-fect alibi."

Detective Pat Evans walked in, dressed for day shift in a blue suit. "How are you?" Lucie asked.

"I'm finer than frog's hair," he said as he sat at his desk.

"There is no such thing." Sergeant Ruth Lanier's sweet smile changed to pursed lips at Evans's joke.

"I know that," Evans insisted. On his desk was a thank-you note from a rape victim. Her internal injuries from the attack were so severe she had to have surgery.

Sergeant Lanier sipped coffee from a mug that said THE BEST MAN FOR THE JOB IS A WOMAN and returned to reading the day's reports from the Ohio Central Registry of Child Abuse and Neglect: a family friend played with four-year-old child in her private parts ... five-month-old white female suffered a skull fracture and expanding hematoma, mother had no explanation ... seven-year-old black female put out of home by father who drinks excessively ... mother observed father in six-month-old child's crib, child taken to hospital found to have been bruised in vaginal area.

Detective Andrea Zbydniewski, whom everyone called Zeb, strode in, dressed in sweat pants, gym bag in hand. She had won medals in the National Law Enforcement Olympics for racketball and javelin. Children's drawings were hung on the side of her desk, next to a manila envelope with subpoenas sticking out of it. A bottle of Evian was near her desk calendar, which noted her upcoming court dates and interviews. A case she had been working on had just been lost: an eleven-year-old learning-disabled boy who accused his school cab driver of molesting him. "I'm not going to lose any sleep over it," Zeb said tersely, checking her messages. "It was a weak case. I told the prosecutor that. But they like to make a fool of me."

Zeb was excellent at interviewing children, Lucie thought. "If you've got a young child, and you want to get something out of them—if anybody can do it—she can." Zeb had been in the unit since its inception. Lucie had a reputation for being hard on women who worked for her. Nevertheless, her unit was usually one-third to one-half women, in a department which was now 13 percent female. Over the years only four women had been assigned to homicide: Sandra Ramsey had been the first, achieving her goal in 1979.

Zeb was on the phone with another victim. "Did he touch you ... did he pull his pants down ... I see ... was anyone else there ... do you want to prosecute ... it will have to go to juvenile court."

Detective Rich Martin escorted a rape suspect from the jail to the office. The man's clothing was confiscated for possible evidence and he was dressed in the city jail's outfit, a blue paper top and pants; he shuffled along in paper shoes. He sat down at Martin's desk, his scraggly dirty blond hair falling over his forehead.

Martin, a former tool and die maker, came on the job in 1969 because he was tired of reading blueprints. With his dark, slicked-back hair and a constant cigarette dangling from his mouth, a half-jaded look hid his sensitivity.

Martin felt one of his qualifications was that he was a father. He had dealt with child abuse from the beginning of his career in the Fourth, answering a call to find a man who had killed his six-month-old girl and cut her head off. The head was boiling on the stove. His year-old daughter was cooking in the oven. The little boy and the mother had been stabbed. He had held them for about three days before the mother managed to break away and call the police. Martin and the other cops had to protect the scene. He learned that you can't allow yourself to get emotionally involved. You can't become inhuman, but you can't allow yourself to feel so sorry for the child that you are overcome by it.

Martin wheeled over a typewriter (the detectives had to share the old electrics) and informed the suspect of his rights.

"They did that already," the man said, a whine in his voice. "Sure, I'll tell you anything you want to know."

"Age?" Martin asked, beginning to type.

"Twenty-eight." The man was accused of raping his girlfriend.

"Do you want a cigarette?" Martin offered.

"Sure do." The man shifted uneasily in his chair. He took a deep drag on the cigarette. "I've been living with this girl for two years. This is unbelievable."

"She is eight months pregnant," Martin said.

Martin's partner, Jonathan McTier, was sitting nearby. Heftier than during his days in the Fourth, with a protruding belly and a roll of muscle on the back of his neck, his scalp-tight Afro was now speckled with gray. His eyes were still kind after twenty-one years on the force. Suddenly, he spoke. "Isn't it a fact you assaulted her a-a-anally?" McTier had a slight stutter.

"I didn't assault her," the man retorted, angrily.

"I'm just asking the question." McTier's manner was calm. He turned the page of his newspaper as Martin continued typing. Lucie had great respect for McTier. "Joe is a legend. He's just a real good all-around detective—good at dogging people's trails."

McTier had worked with Lucie in Fourth District vice. Back then, McTier didn't think Lucie had what it took to be a police officer. She was too soft, too concerned. Too caring. He still saw in Lucie the same qualities. She had compassion for victims. "She wants to right the wrongs." He could mention a case to her, and then come back a couple of weeks later and she'd remember it.

After the suspect gave his statement and was taken back to his cell, McTier took the paperwork to the city prosecutor's office. "I'm a right-now person. I don't like: we'll do it later." He had already checked to see if the victim had a record—something he had learned in his long years in the detective bureau. And had she charged him before? This was a bad case, hard to prove. He walked through the halls, on the way to see the prosecutor, greeting people as he went in his friendly, full hey-how-ya-doing voice. The prosecutor said, Let the case go to the grand jury. By that time, the victim will probably drop the charges.

McTier went into the jail, the entrance was right next to the sex crime unit. He checked his gun in a locker and was buzzed through. He released the suspect, explaining about the grand jury and warned him, "Don't go near her."

Evans was on the phone with a young victim who was nervous about going to court. "Your mom says you're worried ... you were three when this started, right. It carried on for a number of years, it happened a lot. We know at that age, you don't keep a diary of everything. When you came in, we narrowed it down to a year." Evans's voice was gentle. "Don't worry about the defense attorney trying to make you a liar. You are as accurate as anyone could be. You did great. It's tentatively set up for the ninth. Don't worry, you'll do fine. Enjoy your weekend. Let us do the worrying, that's our job. OK?"

Lucie sat at her desk. Her job was supervising the detectives, overseeing the investigations, fighting to keep them supplied with cars and other equipment, dealing with the media—she didn't want detectives talking to the press—keeping her finger on every aspect of the unit's functioning. On her right hung her teddy bear calendar and a sign that said, HAVE YOU HUGGED YOUR TEDDY BEAR TODAY? Behind her desk was a small table with her personal engagement calendar and a polished rock that said HOOKERS DO IT AND DO IT AND DO IT. Her walls were lined with certificates.

On her desk was a stack of computer printouts from the crime report center. Another horrible child abuse case. A nineteen-year-old mother tried to drown her five-month-old baby in the bathtub. The mother's sister took the blue baby to the hospital, where the doctors performed a tracheotomy and put the infant on a respirator. It was still alive. Lucie wasn't sure if that was good news or bad news. They were using the term neurologically devastated. The mother was in a psychiatric hospital. Lucie tried to give the case to homicide, but they didn't want it. It was the second case in one week that might end up in homicide. The second infant hanging between life and death.

A mother called. Her daughter had been raped. What's happening? Lucie checked—her unit had never gotten the crime report. The crime report center was a mess, an archaic computer system—about five hundred reports behind, and they couldn't get overtime to catch up. The mother explained that the suspect was a juvenile, she had called juvenile court, but they told her the investigation had to come through sex crimes.

"I'm sorry," Lucie said, pushing her index finger against her forehead. "We screwed up. The report got lost in the system. I promise, I will assign it by the end of the day." She started tracking down the report. Lucie fielded a call from the newspaper. This is not a good day for me to go tap dancing with the media.

Lucie shifted from phone call to phone call without missing a beat. An officer called from the Fourth District. A zone car had stopped a motorist for a traffic violation and found out there were other traffic warrants on him. After they arrested him, his common-law wife called the station and told the officers he had been molesting her daughter. The officers were not able to talk to the child and the information was sketchy.

"If we book him on a white, he's going to get bonded out," the officer said to Lucie. "What should we do?"

"Where is the man living?"

"He is living in the house with the wife and child."

"Book him on a pink," Lucie responded without hesitation.

After the conversation, Detective Al Walton came in to Lucie. A tall black man with a peaceful manner and graying Afro, he had been the one to forward the call to her. He wanted to know what Lucie had advised and why.

"Is there a problem?" she asked him.

"No. It is just interesting to me how you make decisions."

Lucie had to stop and think. It reminded her of the process she went through in her decision-making class at the FBI National Academy. Her response to the officer's query had been fast, but she had actually thought it through.

"Technically, we don't have enough to book him as a felon. But if he gets out on bond, he could go home and have access to that kid. In a situation like that, you are never wrong if you err on the side of protecting the child." She pulled the ruffled twister from her ponytail and wrapped it back around her hair as she talked.

Martin typed a report as a young, blond woman described her assault by her mother's landlord. "I tried to stop him." She held her hands up in front of her, making a pushing gesture as she explained the sexual act forced upon her. She flushed and burst into tears.

In East Cleveland, a woman was home when her ex-boyfriend kicked in her door, kidnapped her at knife point, took her to his apartment in Cleveland, and raped her. The East Cleveland police refused to take a report, though that was where the crime originated. "I don't see how they can get away with that." Lucie shook her head. She assigned the case to Detective Mike Cipo. Cipo arrested the man and charged him with rape. He was released on bond and then didn't show up for the preliminary hearing.

Now, Lucie learned, the suspect had kidnapped the victim's three-year-old daughter and called her over and over again, telling her to drop the charges. Lucie coordinated from her desk, Ohio Bell traced the calls, and Lucie dispatched a zone car. The officers reported back: they knocked and got no answer.

Lucie answered a hysterical call from the victim's mother. The man had called her and told her the police were at his door. Lucie calmed the mother down and called ROPE—repeat offender program enforcement unit—to reinforce the zone car men. No answer. She called her supervisor, Commander Angel J. Morales. "Do you know where the ROPE unit is?"

More calls back and forth. The suspect was finally arrested, the three-year-old rescued.

Lucie's coffee was cold.

Detective Derrline "Dee" Fragomeni burst into Lucie's office and plopped down in the swivel chair facing Lucie's desk. Dee called herself a hothead. She was lean and fit. Her short curly perm ended with a "tail" at the back of her neck. Her mocha complexion deepened with anger. "This lady is still complaining," she said. Dee needed to steam off. An alleged date rape case that was driving her nuts. The prosecutor had reviewed the case and said there was nothing to it—which was Dee's opinion. The girl's mother was still calling and complaining. "She says something should be done. Blahblahblahblah ..." Dee had twelve other cases on her desk.

Dee had been the victim of an attempted rape when she was a young girl. Kathryn Mengel, then with the Women's Bureau, had handled her case, and Dee was so impressed with Mengel that she decided to become a policewoman. She joined the force in 1981 and the sex crimes unit after about seven years in basic patrol. She wasn't sure which was more stress-ful. "In the zone car, you can be personally shot or cut or stabbed and you're terrified, paranoid of everybody and everything. Then you come in here and you're still paranoid because you see what people actually do to little kids."

When she joined the unit, Lucie told her she had to be impartial. Dee was training, riding with two other detectives, when they went to the hospital to see a one-year-old boy. "This guy had taken the kid by the feet and swung him up against the wall and his brain had shifted in his head. He had this tube stuck down his head, and his head was about three times the size it should have been. I'm supposed to be impartial!" Dee ran to the bathroom and barfed. "This is not for me," she decided.

But she hung in. She worked hard on her cases. "I dig and dig and dig." Dee admired Lucie's ability to separate her emotions from the job. "I try to learn from her, but it's very difficult for me."

Lucie kept tabs on the cases. "Why is this case still open?" Lucie asked.

"Why is this case still open?" Dee words were charged with pent-up frustration. "It's open because I haven't finished it," her voice cracked into a laugh. "And you keep giving me all this other stuff." A case a day landed on each detective's desk. You're frazzled every day you walk into this joint, Dee thought. "I got THIS and I got THIS," she told Lucie. "Come over here and look at my desk—"

Lucie went to the outer office with Dee and looked over the cases. "Do this one," she told her. "Try to get to this one next."

Lucie returned to her desk, to her pile of crime reports and endlessly ringing phone. She called the range to reschedule a time for her annual Chapter Ten firearms training. "Let me remember to bring my gun," she mumbled to herself and opened the desk drawer. "Here it is, carefully concealed with the pantyhose," she said, laughing, hanging on to her humor no matter what.

September 1985. The hectic pace of the sex crimes unit began the day it opened. One of the first callers was the director of a mental health clinic on the West Side. He introduced himself and asked if he could run something by her.

"Sure," Lucie said easily, indicating that she had all the time he might need.

He told her about a woman under psychiatric care at the clinic who kept talking about her male roommate who got letters from people all over the country, and the letters described sex with children. "This is a woman with problems," he said, "but—does any of this make sense to you?"

"Yes," Lucie said. "That makes a lot of sense to me. Why don't you find out who this man is—"

"I've got his name right here," the director said. "It's George Devlin."

Lucie drew in her breath. Her eyes widened and shone. Thank you, God, she thought, for sending Devlin back to me. "I've been looking for him for six months," she said. "This is wonderful."

She swung into action. Detectives Eddie Gray and Zeb went to talk to the woman, *Nancy.* She told them she shared a common dresser with Devlin and that she had four letters and envelopes that had been written to him. Last year she had seen five photographs of Devlin's girlfriend, Susie, on a couch. Several of the photos included Susie's nephew, who was ten months old. He was nude. The photographs were Polaroid shots; Devlin had a one-step camera.

Devlin worked as a telephone solicitor somewhere in the Arcade. Zeb and Gray discovered which bus routes he took home and when he arrived. Lucie called Hartman at Postal and told him the good news. Gray and Hastings conferred with Lucie and then talked to a prosecutor about obtaining a search warrant from the judge.

Before they left, the director of the mental health clinic called and told them that Nancy knew they were going on a search and was going home to destroy any letters and photographs Devlin had.

Lucie, Hartman, Eddie Gray, Mark Hastings, and Andrea Zbydniewski piled into their detective cars and sped off toward Devlin's home.

It was September 4, 1985, two days after the official inception of the sex crime and child abuse unit and two days after George Devlin's fifty-second birthday.

If the director had made his call a few months before, there would have been no sex crimes unit to call. If he had talked to anyone but Lucie, they would not have known about George Devlin. If he had talked to someone unfamiliar with how pedophiles work, they might not have taken the call seriously or given it top priority.

After the Women's Bureau was disbanded in 1975, rape investigations were assigned to district detectives, detectives who also handled robberies, burglaries, and other crimes. A Sex Crimes Unit existed for a short time in the seventies, consisting of about six detectives, who took only certain rape cases. The unit was disbanded after a few years and only gathered statistics. Rapes were once again handled by district detectives, who were not specialists in sex crimes or child abuse. During the seventies and eighties the women's movement catapulted rape into the headlines. Laws were changed and services developed. Cleveland's Rape Crisis Center conducted training sessions with the police. Though all crime lends itself to good basic detective techniques, sex crimes and child abuse required special skills. The fields were new, expanding with information. The skill of the detective was crucial to the investigation and could have a major impact—positive or negative—on the victim's emotional recovery.

The age-old struggle between the police and the city council continued. In 1985, the city council wanted a sex crimes unit. In March 1985, after two young girls were raped and murdered, Councilman Jeff Johnson introduced emergency resolution No. 260-85, calling upon the safety director and Chief Hanton to establish a citywide sex crime and child abuse unit. Letters urging the establishment of the unit poured into Chief Hanton.

"It is time that Cleveland put the safety and dignity of its women and children on a par with stolen cars," wrote one Lakewood resident who worked in the city.

From the board of the Clark-Metro Local Development Corporation: "The establishment of such a unit would give these crimes the publicity and priority they deserve."

"The fear of rape and violent assault is ever present in the minds of most women—and it is certainly justified by the danger we face," wrote a woman who lived in Berea and worked in Cleveland. "Women and children make up perhaps two-thirds of the population and their needs should not be the last priority."

The mother of one of the murdered young girls wrote, "If you would only consider my cause ... and allow the unit to become in existence, you can count on me to type, file, get coffee, run errands, or just be there for support for wearied-eyed detectives."

While Councilman Johnson wanted Captain Richard McIntosh to head the new unit, women's groups were pressuring for a woman. The idea of a sex crimes unit had already been brought to Hanton by officers within the department. He didn't think someone with the rank of captain was necessary for the new unit. He gathered recommendations, and Lucie was one of the names put forward. She was a good supervisor and she worked well with community groups.

Lucie was already involved in child abuse while running vice. She had joined IFSAP, Intra-Familial Sexual Abuse Project, conducted training in child pornography, and attended conferences that disseminated the latest information about child sexual abuse. When Lucie went to the National Academy in 1984, Hanton had mentioned to her the possibility of starting a sex crimes unit.

In charge of the new unit, Lucie wrote an anticipated assignment. She was not necessarily looking for investigative experience. She was looking for people who had sensitivity and a willingness to be trained. She wanted a balance—black and white detectives, men and women. She required officers to have a minimum of five years' experience on the force. However, she would consider a college degree in lieu of two of the five years. "A degree in sociology, social services, psychology, or related fields." She also gave preference to officers who had specialized training or work experience in crisis intervention, social work, family counseling, or had experience in microcomputers, or child sex abuse investigations. Sixty-four people applied. Not at all similar to Lucie's experience in vice, when few were willing to work for her. Sex crimes and child abuse investigations were no longer shuttled off to the Women's Bureau, whose functions were disparaged as social work, or handed to district detectives to be dealt with amidst their other cases. Lucie was in charge of a prestigious new unit handling felony crimes. People wanted in. Badly. She had to follow union guidelines. "I've got to pick half the people on seniority and half the people on ability, and hopefully sometimes it'll be the same."

Andrea "Zeb" Zbydniewski was working a zone car in the Third District when the anticipated assignment came out. She didn't know of any other assignment that requested college in lieu of actual years on the job. Zeb thought rewarding education was good. People had specialties, this gave them the opportunity to use them. She had come on the job in 1981, the third academy class where women went out on patrol. She had taken psychology and law enforcement classes in college.

She had no problems working a zone car, but she was ready for a change. Investigations interested her. Starting from zero and getting to something.

Zeb is an intense, serious woman with a sudden smile. Of Polish descent, she grew up in Slavic Village. She exudes confidence, her build is muscular, her stride strong. She had been into sports all her life, and it showed. She went to college on an athletic scholarship and had played on the Cleveland Brewers, a women's football team, as a running back. Zeb had no trouble thinking women were strong. "I'm telling you, women can hit."

Lucie partnered Zeb with Eddie Gray, an experienced detective who had investigated numerous sex crimes. Zeb was pleased with Lucie's choice for her. Gray taught her about investigating, court preparation, corroboration. He was thorough. She couldn't have asked for a better teacher and partner.

She was still learning the basics when she was swept into the search of George Devlin's house.

Lucie told the detectives what to look for at Devlin's house, the letters she had written to him under a pseudonym, photographs of nude children. Since Devlin had already sent a photograph of a child to a postal inspector in Indiana they had enough to get an arrest warrant as well as a search warrant.

The landlady let them in, and they trooped inside his house. Under

Devlin's pillow, they found a pair of boy's underwear. They found the letters Lucie had written to him under an alias.

On Devlin's dresser, they found a photograph of a nude boy. It had been torn, as if it was the corner of a larger picture.

They found a photograph of a baby girl lying on a couch, her pants pulled down to just above her knees, her shirt pulled up. The photo was taken from above. The child's dark, teardrop-shaped eyes stared directly into the camera. Other photographs were of an infant girl lying on her stomach, her pants pulled down; a baby on a checkered quilt, pants down. A toy was visible in one of the pictures. They found a copy of *Moppets*.

In the middle of the search, Devlin came home. The detectives arrested him. He was eager to talk. He told the detectives that he had correspondence and pictures stored in the basement. He claimed he was gathering them for the postal inspectors and FBI to assist with a pedophilia investigation.

Mark went down to the basement. The door was partially open. Through it, Mark saw a book with nude females on the cover.

The basement was not a part of the house covered in the search warrant. Lucie called the assistant police prosecutor and asked if the search could be expanded. She gave Lucie the go-ahead. Mark went into the basement and found a large-size book of professional photographs, the kind people keep on their coffee tables. A legitimate book, Lucie said. Mark leafed through it. One of the photographs had the lower corner torn off. The photo was of a large room. Mark took the jagged tiny picture of the naked boy they had found in Devlin's bedroom and held it to the corner of the large photograph. The pieces matched. Devlin had ripped the nude boy from the photo and kept it with him in his bedroom.

Lucie noticed the St. Joseph's calendar on the wall. "Let's look at this," she suggested. She knew pedophiles kept diaries of their experiences. They began reading through the numerous, cramped entries that filled almost every day's box on each month of the calendar.

They found the entry for April 7, 1984. "Amy, aged six months, sucked and licked me." Lucie thought Devlin had gotten mixed up. Surely, he meant that he had sucked her—not the other way around. How would a six-month-old infant do that?

They took Devlin back to the Justice Center. He waived his rights. He wanted to confess to Eddie Gray. He told them his history, how he had been charged with child rape in 1976 and was sent to the Western Reserve Hospital. He had worked in the mail room.

The mail room! Lucie couldn't believe it. They assigned a pedophile to work in the mail room! Like putting a kid in a candy shop.

Devlin explained that in 1979 he had made up his mind that he was going to chase out all child molesters. He ran an ad in a swingers' magazine and began corresponding with those interested in pedophilia. The Cleveland area is the number one spot for Ped. clubs in the United States, he told Gray. He had read literature about children for sale—pay a fee, travel, food, lodging, and have a child come stay with you.

Gray typed as Devlin talked. He tried to make Devlin as comfortable as possible. To make their case, the detectives needed specific information about the photographs. Gray showed him the photograph of the little girl, and Devlin said it had been taken at his girlfriend's house.

"Now is your chance to tell us about it," Gray said. "Why did you take this photo?"

"It was my Ped. instincts."

"What do you mean when you refer to the word *ped?*"

"Pedophilia. That is the short term for that word. It means a person who has a desire for children, a love for children," Devlin answered.

"Have you on any occasion had any sexual contact with the children in these photographs?" Gray continued.

"Yes," Devlin admitted. "But never no penetration, no act of penetration. I'm a Ped. I have had oral contact, rubbed my penis around the mouth, vaginal, and anal area."

Devlin talked for hours. "All of these sexual contacts were recorded by myself on a calendar as a diary like. There were times that I would look at the pictures and masturbate, reliving my past sexual experiences with the children."

Gray read from the calendar. "'Amy, aged six months, sucked and licked me.' What do you mean?"

"I mean that my penis was around the mouth area but not in the mouth."

Pedophiles have a code of acceptable behavior. Oral sex may be more acceptable than penetration. Anal penetration leaves the child still a virgin.

Gray kept pushing. Finally, Devlin admitted more. "I held my penis up to the baby's lips while she had sucking action on the tip of my penis. I didn't ejaculate."

Zeb was sitting nearby. Shocked. This was her first week in sex crimes. This was like—whoa. Open your eyes real quick.

She was impressed with Gray's techniques. When you hear something like that—with such a little kid—you want to jump up and strangle the person.

The six-month-old girl Devlin wrote about in his calendar was now almost two years old. Hastings showed Devlin's pictures of Amy to her mother, who identified her and said she had not given permission for the photos to be taken. Amy and her mother were Laotian. The mother barely spoke English.

Gray and Zeb interviewed her again. She identified the place in the photos. It was her neighbor, Susie's house, and Susie's boyfriend, George Devlin, was allowed to babysit for Amy there. The mother could not pinpoint exact dates or times.

It was a nightmare case, Lucie thought. She didn't think the mother really understood what had happened, and the family seemed afraid of the police. Maybe they were afraid of being sent back to Laos.

Devlin's saying he did it, Lucie thought. But there's no proof. Did he fantasize it? I don't have a victim to put on the stand or parents to substantiate any of it. There was not a helluva lot to go on. She was worried.

Devlin was charged with four counts of rape and illegal use of a minor in nudity-oriented material. The court date arrived. Devlin's defense attorney said that the calendars were not specified in the search warrant, and he wanted them thrown out as evidence. A suppression hearing was scheduled to decide which evidence was admissible. If anything was wrong on the search warrant, the case could be blown.

The expertise Lucie had carefully developed over the past years and her attention to legal process paid off. She testified as to her knowledge about pedophiles and child pornography. She said she felt the calendars in this case were used as a diary. Diaries had been specified in the warrant.

The judge ruled in her favor. The calendar qualified as a diary and was admissible. Devlin's lawyer decided to plead George guilty on two counts of rape, one count on Amy and one count on the ten-month-old boy. Devlin was sentenced to a mandatory ten to twenty-five years. He would not be eligible for parole for ten years.

Thank God, Lucie thought.

22

THE HOPPING PENIS

Three days after Christmas the case came in. A sixteen-year-old girl told her mother that her gray-haired grandfather had molested her on his boat when it was docked at the Lakeside Yacht Club on the shores of Lake Erie. He had also molested her at his home in Lyndhurst. The mother had had enough. The man was her father, and he had also abused her when she was a child. She wanted something done.

Lucie went after the case with a vengeance. The Department of Human Services was involved. The mother was referred to Witness/Victim for counseling. The daughter had been molested in Cleveland, and in the suburb of Willoughby. Lucie finagled having the case handled by her unit. She was concerned that the suburban police would botch it up. She assigned it to Hovan and Hastings.

Joe Russell, Lucie's partner from the Fourth, had dropped by to see her. He asked her who she was putting into her unit.

"I don't know. Are you interested?" she asked him.

He wasn't. But he knew someone who was. "What about Arnie?"

Arnie Hovan was Lucie's field-training officer from the Fourth, the big man with the booming voice who took her up and down Buckeye Road, in and out of the bars with the wild Hungarians.

"Arnie wants to put in, but he's afraid to," Russell said. "He's been in the Fourth twenty years, he's gotta get out."

"Tell him to put in for it," Lucie said. "I have no problems with Arnie as long as he doesn't embarrass me."

Russell assured Lucie that Arnie had calmed down. Despite his hot

275

temper and antics, she thought he was a good policeman and good worker. He was streetwise. He knew the city and he knew people. Arnie
Hovan became part of the new sex crimes unit.

Hovan and Hastings interviewed the teenager. She described her
grandfather's sexual abuse. The assaults had happened a while ago. She
wasn't sure when, only setting the time as after her mother's husband had
walked out on them. The grandfather had warned her, If you tell, no one
will believe you and they'll think you're bad.

The grandfather refused to talk. The prosecutor issued papers authorizing his arrest for rape and gross sexual imposition, and three days later,
on January 17, SWAT and the Willoughby police moved in and tried to
pick up the suspect, but they couldn't find him. Hovan and Hastings kept
after him, and two days later they made the arrest. A grand jury returned
indictments against the yachtsman on January 21.

Boy, I am so happy to get this guy, Lucie exclaimed. This was the second generation of his abuse. It was about time he was stopped.

On January 30, the suburban police answered a suicide call. The
grandfather had put a pillow over his face and shot himself. He was
depressed over the indictments, the police were told.

Lucie's joy at catching him withered into self-condemnation. That
one sure didn't turn out, she thought. She wasn't sorry he had committed suicide. But it certainly wasn't going to help the family at all. The kids
are going to be much worse off. The girl had been removed from her
grandfather, it wasn't as if he had access to her anymore. Now, not only
did she have the problem of being abused by him to get over—but she
also had to cope with guilt over his suicide.

Lucie slumped back in her chair and chewed herself out. "You really
did a great job, Lieutenant. You really did a wonderful job. The whole
damn family will be in therapy now. You put them all right over the
brink."

Nothing was simple dealing with child abuse. Sometimes she wondered if she was doing the right thing.

Over at Cleveland Metropolitan General Hospital, Lucie's friend and
colleague social worker Gerald A. Strom was wondering the same thing
about his own cases, cases that no one wanted to talk about.

Strom and his team began a sexual abuse clinic at the hospital in
1985, just as Lucie was setting up her unit. Strom is a small, thin man
with light brown hair. He is insightful and caring.

He came into conflict with the medical staff over the treatment of
child sexual abuse victims. The OB/GYN got the calls, came in with the
protocols, and Strom tried to intervene. Children needed time and preparation for the examinations. In most cases, the type of exam was determined by the child's story. If a child said he or she was fondled, the child

was given a physical examination, but there was no need for a full pelvic exam with a speculum or an anal exam. Strom wanted to make sure children weren't subjected to procedures that weren't necessary. Any time a child complained of a pain, or there was discharge or bleeding, there would be no question—the medical reasons overrode everything else.

The doctors always took anal, vaginal, and oral cultures to check for sexually transmitted diseases. Children didn't always have a choice about whether they would be examined, but they could have a choice about the type of swabs used for the cultures. "Thankfully," he said, "for most of the penile and vaginal cultures, the swab only had to go in just a little ways." Strom was not in favor of putting children under general anesthesia to perform the exams, another source of struggles in the emergency room.

Support for his sensitivity came from an initially unexpected source—Lucie.

Lucie and Strom first met at the Intrafamilial Sexual Abuse Project (IFSAP) in the early eighties. IFSAP was holding weekly meetings in an effort to develop a communitywide approach to child sexual abuse. He had never worked closely with police officers and was astonished that he and Lucie spoke the same language. They struck up an immediate and lasting friendship. He had more respect for Lucie than anyone else he knew in the field: "She's a professional's professional, but she is also a person's person. She cuts across those lines."

"Yes, we need the evidence," Lucie said, "but the kids are very important too." They found out that in only about 5 percent of the sexual abuse cases was there strong physical evidence. It wasn't like physical abuse, where there was evidence in 95 percent of the cases, a burn, a broken bone. At first they were losing cases.

Lucie and Strom switched the emphasis. They looked at the investigative interview, using what the child said, trying to bring as many of those cases through the legal system, so as eventually to set precedents. The more cases that got into the system, the greater chance down the road that people would plea bargain. Strom was very much in favor of pleas: "Trials aren't fair fights for kids."

Lucie and Strom's concerns sparked their formation of the Second District Project, so named because Metro Hospital was located in the Second District. They wanted to save child victims from having to go through interview after interview—with the police, hospital personnel, social workers.

Strom and Lucie developed an interview protocol. They worked in teams—one detective, one member of Strom's staff, one Department of Human Services (DHS) employee—and learned to do investigative interviews using the anatomically correct dolls. The child would only be subjected to one interview, the other two people watching through a one-way mirror. Then they would decide how to handle the case.

In cases of incest, the goal was to remove the perpetrator and leave the child home, if possible. With Lucie's support, that was happening. The detectives were arresting the suspects on the spot, so the child did not have to be removed from the home. Lucie consulted on a training video that demonstrated the interview techniques. Produced by the Child Guidance Center of Cleveland and the Metro Hospital Medical Center, the video won an award from the American Psychiatric Association.

Lucie helped Strom with court preparation and in surviving the cross-examination. "The more the defense attorney hammers away at you, the more you're doing a good job," she told him.

Strom didn't know whether that was true or not, but it was helpful advice. "When I was grilled over the coals, I sat back and said to myself, Gee, I must be doing a good job, because Lucie said they only bother you if you are."

Lucie's exuberance helped Strom deal with a difficult field. "You can live off her excitement and enthusiasm," he said. "Her energy level is amazing."

Early on, a case went to court which, Strom thought, was a good one. They had documentation. He thought they had what they needed. They lost. He was pissed off at the court system.

Lucie pulled him out of the dumps. "You win some, you lose some," she said. "You can't get down, 'cause the next case is coming. It's a good thing we have this kind of court system that really looks at both sides, and looks to see that justice gets served. We'd rather have some people go free that are guilty than one innocent person go to jail."

Her next words stuck with Strom. "Put yourself in the position of the person being accused. How would you like to be treated by the system? That's what you've got to keep in mind. You collect as much material as you can, and the court needs to make the final decision."

Lucie's advice helped Strom in the years that followed. He tried to remember not to hang his hat on every single case because he would burn out.

Lucie and he continued the "lunch bunch" tradition that began at IFSAP meetings. She knew people everywhere. They were walking in the Flats one day for lunch, and she knew the two men building a bar. She took him into an old broken-down hotel on Prospect Avenue.

"Lucie, where are you taking me?"

"Don't worry about it. You'll have the best lunch you ever had," she assured him.

They walked into the abandoned-looking building. The waitress came up to Lucie and said, "I haven't seen you in years."

It was a Middle Eastern restaurant and after his first venture in there, Jerry Strom went with Lucie many times. She was a Damon Runyan-type character, he thought with a smile.

They did training sessions for suburban police departments. Strom wanted the suburbs to refer cases to Metro Hospital for interviews as well as medical exams. But when he walked into the suburban departments, they didn't want to hear from a social worker. "They could care less." He told Lucie the problem. She agreed to go with him. What a difference walking in with a lieutenant! She had a good reputation with the departments.

Strom asked Lucie to be a guest teacher in his class, social work with child abuse, at the Mandel School. They traveled around the state, conducting training sessions on setting up programs like the Second District Project. They spoke to social agencies, police departments, school systems, anyone who would listen. They thought their approach was working, and they wanted to share it. They made presentations together at a judges' conference in Columbus. And on that trip, they had dinner with Strom's daughter, who was at Miami University. Strom watched Lucie and his daughter. They really hit it off. Beneath Lucie's sometimes gruff exterior, Strom saw a very feeling person.

He wished he had as many social workers who had the same kind of passion that she did. Lucie's attitude was, Let's just do it because it needs to be done. And she didn't mind sharing the limelight. "Between Lucie and me—we didn't think there was a limelight in sexual abuse."

Janice Rench, director of the Cleveland Rape Crisis Center, had testified at the city council in support of the formation of the sex crimes unit. Less than 10 percent of rape victims reported the crime to the police, Rench estimated. They were afraid of the treatment they would receive. She had dealt with a lot of police officers, men and women, who were called to the hospitals to interview rape victims. She found them "rather ugly people."

The Rape Crisis Center had done training sessions with the police over the years. Attitudes were changing, Rench felt, but were nowhere near where she wanted them to be.

Rench took the initiative. She called the sex crimes unit to establish contact with the new lieutenant in charge. She expected Lucie to be tough and hard.

She was very surprised. Lucie's voice was quiet and polite. Rench asked her to come speak at a volunteer training session for rape crisis counselors. Lucie was receptive; she was eager to establish coordinated efforts between different groups.

Lucie came to the volunteer training session both as participant and presenter. Janice learned a lot. The problem wasn't only the police officers. It was that the rape crisis workers didn't understand the role of the police.

Lucie made that role crystal clear. "I'm not a victim advocate. I'm a police officer. That's the bottom line. It's not to say that we don't care about victims. I do—but my primary job is solving crimes and doing criminal investigation. We need to develop ways to do that so we don't further victimize the victim. I don't want to hurt this person either—but let's not forget, I've got a defendant I've got to worry about, too. I've got to worry about the suspect's rights and everything else."

Strom, Lucie, and Janice Rench had lunches together, and out of those came a venture for their own consulting business. Later, Carolyn Oppenheimer joined; her specialty was handicapped victims. They conducted programs on sexual abuse prevention for interested agencies.

Lucie placed high priority on education. Sergeants Christ and Lanier attended a two-day seminar on juvenile court procedures. Lucie was a contributing author to the manual *Responding to Sexual Abuse: A Multi-Disciplinary Approach,* developed by IFSAP. She gave each detective a copy of the comprehensive training handbook.

She worked with Prosecutor Henry Hilow and streamlined the unit's dealings with the prosecutor's office and the grand jury. He attended several of their training sessions as speaker or participant. In their first month, Lucie's staff was afforded five days of training.

It wasn't easy to get Ressler and Lanning from the FBI behavioral science unit to come and conduct training. They were booked, but Lucie got them.

Ressler was glad to do a school for her unit. He didn't know of any other woman heading a sex crimes unit. He still hadn't heard of any in 1991. Ken Lanning had the same impression. There were plenty of women around the country investigating sex crimes, men were only too glad to let women take them on. It gave them another excuse not to handle the unpleasant cases themselves. Women talk better to kids, let them do it. But a woman actually running the unit?

Lucie took Ressler to the Flats and showed him how Cleveland had improved since he had left in the seventies. But he still felt its police department was very traditional. An old-time big city police department. Old hat. Here Lucie had popped up with this progressive approach. She was dragging Cleveland along.

When Ressler held his school for Lucie's unit, hardly anyone from homicide attended. Those that did attend, ho-hummed. Lucie was a breath of innovation. She was part of a new era of policing. He thought she would make a good chief.

Chief Hanton thought the biggest point in Lucie's favor was that she was people-oriented. "She dragged me to meetings," he said. She took him to one at Charity Hospital that concerned sex crimes against children. He thought she wanted to impress each group that the department was really interested.

She joined with the American Bar Association and succeeded in getting legislation passed in Ohio so that children's testimony could be videotaped. Marcia Dettelbach, of the American Bar Association Target Site Sexual Abuse Legislation Reform Task Force, called Lucie's efforts monumental and said that the closed-circuit provision was among the best in the country. But Lucie was disappointed by the legislation; it had been watered down.

"People hear the term videotape and they think this means the child never has to go to court, and they do the whole thing on tape, hand it to the jury—closed case—but that has nothing to do with it." The new legislation allowed for videotaped testimony only during the preliminary hearing. "We don't even bring kids to the preliminary hearing in Cleveland!"

Lucie kept her perspective. She thought it was a bad idea when police or counselors gave out their home phone numbers to victims and said, call me anytime. "You can't give one hundred percent one hundred percent of the time. If you diffuse yourself too much, you never step back and revitalize. Plus—when I am out of my work environment, in the midst of doing something—I'm not in that mode. Those victims aren't getting our best.

"Victims have to get a subtle message from anybody that is helping them, that the bottom line is: something terrible has happened to you—but you are ultimately the person who has to deal with it."

Lucie held on to her personal life—books, ballet, theater, parties. Lucie, John, and six friends went to see *Forbidden Broadway* together. The show is a cabaret, a spoof of Broadway shows, with tables up on the State Theater stage. They were all laughing aloud. After a spoof of *Cats*, one of the cast members placed a note on their table. It said "You are such a puuuurrrfecct audience, members of the cast would really like to meet you after the show, please come backstage." John, Lucie, and the others waited after the show, wondering if the cast really wanted to meet them. An understudy told them they were wanted backstage. You guys made our night, the cast told Lucie and her friends.

Lucie befriended Linda Strasser and others in the cast and took them places, out to lunch, over to her house. They had been on the road for months and hadn't seen anything of Cleveland except the inside of shopping malls. Lucie loved showing people her city. The cast taught John, Lucie, et al., Celebrity Password, which became their "drug of choice." They played for eight hours at a stretch. When the cast left, they threw their Cleveland friends a party.

When John rented part of his house to his friend Christian Halstead, Lucie and Christian became friends. They went together to *Don Pasquale* and *Les Misérables*. John had How to Host a Murder parties. Lucie played Florence Wing Brook—otherwise known as Flowing Brook—the Far Eastern Shadow Girl. One winter, Janice Rench talked Lucie into taking acting classes at the Cleveland Playhouse. Lucie studied her Stanislavski and did a scene from *The Subject Was Roses*. "But Broadway never called," she joked.

Lucie brought her sense of fun and adventure to the unit.

She was planning a Christmas party for her detectives. One night, while she was out at the Watermark in the Flats, she had an idea for the party. A hopping penis game. She had seen an ad for hopping penises in a magazine. She called a friend who owned a novelty shop. He said he didn't normally carry that particular item.

"I want forty of them," she told him. "Can you order them and give them to me at cost?"

"I'll donate them if I can come to the party," he replied.

Lucie talked to Tim Spencer, who agreed to give her the PLAYDIUM for the night and provide cocktail waitresses, bartenders, and drinks at happy hour prices. She invited all the detectives and their spouses— "wives, girlfriends, sex crimes groupies." Jerry Strom and other friends and colleagues were also invited. Everything was set. Now she only had to figure out what kind of game they were to play.

The hopping penises were plastic, pink, and about four inches tall. Wind them up and they hop. Lucie giftwrapped them.

She gave out the packages at the party. "Don't open them until I tell you to," she instructed her guests.

She drew circles on the floor. Then she took the microphone.

"We're going to have a hopping penis contest," she announced, laughing. They opened their gifts.

"Everyone—put your penis in the circle," she continued. She was kind of amazed. They did just what she said.

"The penis that hops out of the circle first wins first prize for speed. The penis that hops the longest wins for stamina," she said.

Hysteria broke out. Little pink penises popping up and down.

"So many penises, it was like a gay bathhouse," Spencer chortled.

Jerry Strom's wife won for stamina. Jerry liked the game so much he tried it at a few of his own parties.

Detective Rich Martin growled when asked later what happened to him. "I lost. She gave me a defective penis."

Sometime later, McTier and Martin caught the case of rapist Alphonso Calhoun, aka Perry Willis. A woman went to buy cocaine from him, and he accused her of stealing some. He forced her to take off her clothes, strip-searched her, and made her perform oral sex on him. He yelled at her that she wasn't doing a good job and threatened to kill her.

"That was Calhoun's mistake," Martin smiled, his cigarette bobbed up and down as he took a long drag and described the situation: afraid for her life, she bit—like a pit bull—and tore off his testicles. She ran out and got to a hospital. He wrapped his balls in a handtowel and, bleeding profusely, drove to another hospital—farther away.

"He knew where the victim would go," Lucie said. Testicles in hand, he walked into the emergency room, and the story went around that the nurse passed out. The medical staff tried but could not reattach them. The doctor was supposed to determine how they had been removed but couldn't. "How much experience do they have?" Lucie said, laughing. The testicles could have been cut off. The rapist offered several stories. The victim cut them off. His girlfriend cut them off in a jealous fit. The medical reports and testicles were both subpoenaed from the hospital as evidence, and Martin and McTier had to bring them to court for the rape trial.

They were kept in a plastic container, in the small refrigerator in the sex crimes office where the detectives stored their lunches and snacks. Right next to all the deli food. They marked the container DO NOT EAT. The afternoon shift always poked around, eating the day shift's leftovers. When it was time for court, McTier carried the jar through the halls up and down the elevators into the courtroom. Jokes were inevitable.

"Hey, Lieutenant," someone called to Lucie as she walked out of the office. "We always knew you wanted some. Now—you have your own set."

There was jealousy of Lucie in the department, and anger. Lucie felt Hanton placed her in sex crimes because he was retiring and wanted her protected. She had made enemies in her rise through the ranks. Her latest appointment had made more enemies for her. She bounced detectives out of her unit if they weren't doing their job. "If you have a unit of people who are all working really hard, to watch one person sit and do nothing was devastating to morale." Lucie could not tolerate disloyalty or laziness. She had given one detective a warning during his ninety-day probationary period in the unit. When he then refused to help another detective transport a prisoner, Lucie was furious. She told him she was transferring him. He was enraged—she thought he was going to pull his gun and shoot her. She had never seen anybody so angry with her in all her life.

No matter how much resentment it caused, she preferred to lose a detective—who might not be replaced—than have someone whose performance or attitude was unacceptable.

But even before she bounced that particular detective, grumblings from "police sources" reached the press about other transfers she had effected. Despite the camaraderie cops paid homage to, some were all too willing to complain publicly—if anonymously. "Problems handcuff police sex crimes unit, say critics," a *Plain Dealer* headline announced on March 24, 1986. The article criticized Lucie. Four detectives had left the unit within the first four months. Anonymous police sources claimed it was because of Lucie's rigid management style. "I think I'm pretty easy to get along with as long as the job is getting done the way I want it done," Lucie told the *Plain Dealer.* The article attacked her on grounds of her lack of expertise. Councilman Jeffrey D. Johnson said that if Richard McIntosh had been named to head the unit, it would have been a model for the nation. Johnson charged that Lucie was chosen because she was a crony of Chief Hanton. The accusation caused quite a stir in the department.

Hanton felt that Johnson took all the credit for forming the unit and deserved none of it. He stood by Lucie. "When someone like Lucie does her job, it creates a lot of resentment," he contended, "because a lot of people can't stand to see people work." He thought Lucie was one of the finest cops on the force. "Lucie's credit is all hers. Nobody else's."

The article reported that critics said Lucie didn't have media savvy. That she lacked coordination with social services. In fact, she excelled in these areas. She was well informed and experienced in every aspect of sex crimes investigation, and she had already developed both local and national contacts to further her unit's expertise. A year earlier, the *Plain Dealer* had run a series on child sex abuse citing what was needed in Ohio. Lucie had already been working in the areas mentioned.

Letters from social service people who worked with Lucie arrived at the mayor's desk and the chief's desk, complaining about the slanted article.

But it wasn't the press that concerned Lucie most. Hanton retired in April of 1986. She lost the man who had mentored her, given wing to her talent. Her experience with the next two chiefs—Howard Rudolph and Edward P. Kovacic—would be a whole different ball game.

23

THE MADAM

L ieutenant Duvall," Lucie answered the phone in her chipper voice. The caller was Postal Inspector John Campisi, who had taken over the prohibited mailings assignment from Paul Hartman. He was working on an adult obscenity case: the suspect, *Perry Orcutt,* was distributing pornographic films through the mail. He wanted to bring out as much information as possible. How were these films being produced. Where were they being produced. He had no idea. He had been writing to Orcutt and ordering tapes using the name Sue Bates, the female half of the couple charged with child pornography back when Lucie was working with Paul Hartman. Campisi referred to himself as "A Boy Named Sue," as in the Johnny Cash song. Now he wanted to make phone contact. But there was one problem—he was a man.

He had never carried out an assignment like this. "I was real new." He knew he had something, but he wasn't quite sure what it was. He had heard from an FBI informant, whose information was secondhand, that there might be child porn involved. "I'm not going to convict anybody on that information," Campisi asserted. He had to have a very solid warrant.

"Could you possibly jump in and become Sue Bates for me?" he asked Lucie.

"No problem, John," Lucie said, thinking she would make a couple of phone calls and be done—not knowing she was about to reprise her role as undercover cop and help crack Northern Ohio's first successful obscenity case in about eighteen years.

Campisi's sandy mustache, long face, and lean build were not his most attractive attributes. Most striking were the kindness and intelligence shining in his brown eyes. He had been a mailman for ten years before becoming a postal inspector. He had no background in law enforcement when he attended the postal inspectors' training academy in Potomac, Maryland, for the eleven-week course. Postal inspectors had kept a low profile over the years. There were popular shows on the FBI—but postal was actually the country's oldest federal law enforcement agency.

John Campisi did not believe in censorship. In fact, he kept a Soviet flag on his desk. A good friend of his was a high-ranking member of Buffalo's Communist party. He didn't agree with his friend on everything— but they were still friends. "That's why we live in America." Campisi smiled behind his long mustache.

No, he didn't believe in censorship. But the material Orcutt was distributing was so degrading. People defecating on one another and rubbing it in, people drinking urine. It was horrible. Animals of all kinds. Not just dogs and horses—which were more typical in pornography—but mice, eels, gerbils, snakes. "How do people think of this stuff—it hurt my head sometimes trying to figure it out." A trailer on one of the films featured a sex change operation being performed live in Singapore. It was done like an informational video, with a commentary about Oriental men trapped in women's bodies. They actually showed the operation. If this is a show, Campisi thought as he watched, it was a helluva show. It was gruesome.

Orcutt wasn't transmitting the videotapes through the mail. He was using United Parcel Service. "A slight ruse like that isn't going to throw off an investigation," Campisi said.

Orcutt was getting a ton of mail—checks and money orders—coming in to his two post office boxes, rented at two different locations.

"Orcutt had a great idea," Campisi said. "The kid was bright as far as cash flow. He knew there was very little enforcement on adult obscenity. Because—what is it—nobody knows what it is."

Orcutt was forty, the same age as Campisi, and was a college graduate. He was something of an eccentric, who might be in his bathrobe at two in the afternoon. He didn't have a driver's license. He was isolated and seemed to have no friends. He was living at home with his parents, who owned several chains of businesses. They were successful members of the community.

Campisi set up an extensive surveillance at Orcutt's residence. He watched Orcutt's mother take the UPS deliveries into the house, watched his father and brothers pick up the mail and go to the bank. Campisi subpoenaed bank records. Orcutt was paying household bills with the money from his business ventures and giving money to his brothers and parents.

They are wealthy already, Campisi thought, at least compared to me. One brother repaired Orcutt's VCRs when they broke. Campisi was certain the family knew what Perry was doing. They all seemed like normal people. His brothers worked in the family businesses. Perry just stayed home. He was the family recluse. Orcutt seemed to like alliteration. His long list of dba's (doing business as) included Innovative Industries, Prancer Productions, Serendipity Services, and Inventive Incentive.

Perry was a bizarre fellow, Campisi concluded.

Lucie and Campisi talked and laughed and came up with the idea that Lucie, as Sue Bates, would pose as a madam interested in perhaps having some custom videos made for her clients.

Campisi had met Lucie earlier, shortly after he came to Cleveland, during a reverse sting operation set up by Postal, Customs, and the Cleveland Police.

In some cities the local police would warn suspects that Postal was looking for them. Campisi never would have called Lucie if he didn't have confidence that he would not have a problem.

Besides, Sue Bates had red hair and so did Lucie.

Lucie came over to Campisi's office on December 7, 1987. She sat in the big chair opposite Campisi's desk. He set up the tape recorder for recording phone calls. Lucie dialed the number of Perry Orcutt at Starlite Studios.

Starlite Studios was in Orcutt's home, a one-story brick and frame single-family residence with an attached two-car garage. In a corner of the dining room was a desk with a computer on it. Turn the corner, and there was a copy machine blocking the hallway. The room beyond it was filled with videotapes and banks of VCRs. Forty-eight VCRs. Beta and VHS to copy tapes for distribution.

Perry answered the phone.

"Hi, Perry," Lucie said cheerfully. "This is Sue Bates calling."

"Hi," Perry said.

"How are you?" she asked. No matter who she was talking to Lucie always took time to ask how they were.

"Pretty good," Perry said.

"I was very pleased with the shipment," Lucie said, beginning the process of buttering him up. "And I did want to talk to you about possibly ordering some more films. I'm interested in getting a variety of subjects, and I did like what you had although"—Lucie paused—"do you have anything in English?" she said with a laugh.

"Not from Europe we don't," Perry said. "Hopefully this week, I should be getting all kinds of European stuff, but it won't be in English. It's in German."

"Well, I may have to adjust," Lucie said.

"You know," Perry said, beginning to reveal a quirky sense of humor, "those kind of tapes, it really doesn't much matter."

"True." Lucie rolled along with him. "The message is there."

"You could sorta figure it out, huh," Perry teased.

"What I'd like to do," Lucie continued, "is become more or less a regular buyer. I've been looking for someone in the area that has this type of thing available. It's not easy to find, and I do have a business clientele—"

"What kind of business clientele?" Perry asked.

"It's an entertainment-type business." Sue Bates revealed her true occupation. "And I'm not interested in producing any of this stuff myself."

"I don't care. Everybody else takes it and copies it." Perry laughed.

A lot of the films were foreign. Orcutt was not a producer. He was a reproducer. There was much more freedom in obscenity in Germany and the Scandinavian countries. Orcutt was getting hold of the films and editing them. Sometimes he had portions of two or three films on one videotape. He named it, priced it, put out a list, advertised, and sold them. The videos were obviously amateur productions. Compare "America's Funniest Home Videos" to "L.A. Law"—that was the contrast between professional and amateur pornography.

"I really have neither the time nor the desire to get in that part of it, quite frankly. Do you have any complete lists of films available?" Lucie probed.

Perry needed his memory refreshed as to what exactly she had ordered.

"Some was the lesbians with the brown and golden showers," Lucie explained, "and there was some transsexual."

"What about fisting? Was that part of it?" Perry asked.

"No—but I probably would be interested in that down the line." Lucie paced the conversation.

Perry started giving her some of the details she was after. "'Cause in fact, we even got girls doing custom service stuff. It's like a specific, tailor-made tape."

"Oh, I see," Lucie said. "You give them the scenario and they make the tape?"

"Right. More or less. Yeah. That's the way it is."

"What?" Lucie exclaimed. "Did you dabble in film directing? No, I'm just kidding." She was laughing, while egging him on.

"There will be no laughing because we're doing that with some other guys," Perry remonstrated. "We sorta serve as a middle man." Perry told her his brand-new offerings: "Golden Fisting." A film with pregnant women. "Enema Cocktail."

Lucie said that sounded interesting. "Unfortunately, what I've been able to get so far is a lot of pretty standard stuff. S&M, that kind of thing. That's why I need to branch out, because I'm getting some clients who say they see that at every stag party." She added that she wasn't interested in amateur productions.

Perry rose to the bait. "My guy that does the stuff in Ohio—he has a brand-new Super VHS camera, which is really high quality. It tapes better than live broadcast TV."

"Oh, really," Lucie said. "See, I'm not real technically oriented."

"Oh, me either," Perry commiserated, explaining that the producer had picked up the camera at a consumer electronics show. He told her the upcoming production plans. In January, seven girls were going to be taping. "All kinds of stuff. Fisting, golden showers, girl-girl, everything. It's gonna be as good a quality as you'll ever see, anywhere," he bragged.

Lucie played it up. "I don't want some of these things that look like somebody made it in their basement with second-class stuff. I want decent quality."

Perry reassured her, and they chatted some more. Lucie kept asking if he had a list of his films, and finally Perry said he would send her one.

He boasted again about the quality of his film. "It's not junk stuff. I mean, maybe the background is like regular background." There were no sophisticated sets. "But who cares about the background? The action's there. The quality's there."

Lucie tried to get more. "What about the possibility of getting together with you sometime and looking at some of this stuff. Then I could just take a whole bunch of it. Do you ever do that kind of thing?"

"Never." Perry was firm. "And don't take that personally."

"No, I'm not."

"The one rule we have is never, ever meet with people. Simply because we don't know who's watching who. It's just a bad thing. You shouldn't do it either."

"I agree," Lucie said, changing tactics.

"You shouldn't even trust me. I might be some sting operation. You gotta be careful," he advised, and then laughed.

"I'm pretty careful." Lucie was laughing. "Believe me. I've been around for quite a while, Perry."

"Like—I'm the teacher here. OK, my student. I'm telling you to be careful now." Perry laughed.

"Well," Lucie laughed again. "I appreciate your concern."

"We've been around here about three years, and we hear a lot of stuff. Some of my customers get in trouble because of stupid things like kiddie porn. And I keep telling them, don't mess around. There are people who are out there watching. Maybe we never do it, but we might pick up some customer and they go, 'Ah ha,' and they think we're linked to it. Do you know what I mean?"

Lucie certainly did.

"That's why we just have to be really careful that we don't rock the boat. 'Cause we're not into that. We don't want to mess around with it."

Lucie asked more questions about the custom videos. Orcutt told her the prices and said there was a girl named Velvet who made custom tapes of herself with an Irish setter.

"Some people are offended by it, but I say, as long as no one is getting hurt here," Perry said, explaining his philosophy.

The conversation slowly wound to a close. Take it easy, he said to Lucie as they hung up.

Perry had fallen for her, hook, line and sinker.

The next call was January 6, 1988. This time, Perry answered the phone with another of his alliterative business names, Innovative Industries. Lucie asked him how his holidays were and apologized to him for not getting back to him sooner. "Sue Bates" had just received Perry's order form. Lucie explained, "Rather than just send in the thing, I thought I'd just give you a quick jingle, because I have a couple of questions. I want to order 'Fisting Fems.'" She also wanted "Pregnant Pretties."

Perry prodded for information. "You don't have to answer, but I'm just curious. It isn't like I'm going to come down and raid you, but what do you—you say you're in the entertainment industry. Is this above ground. Or is it something you don't want to talk about."

"We-ell," Lucie hesitated. "Some people might think it was a little less than legit."

"I'm not going to push you."

"Now, you were the one that cautioned me about talking to people," Lucie volleyed. "So you just use your imagination."

They discussed the film selections, Perry offering suggestions. He mentioned a film with a baby being born.

"Well, I mean kinky is in the eye of the beholder," Lucie laughed as she placed her order.

"Yeah—it happens every day. What the heck," Perry said.

They bantered back and forth. Perry tried to add up the price of the order. "I mean I could get my calculator, but you're smarter than me in math."

Orcutt told her about an upcoming production date. Six girls coming together to do some tapes. From January 25 to 31. Girls might be coming from Georgia and Florida. A pregnant girl was coming in from Illinois.

"I'm telling you this because maybe you can fit into some kind of situation with what you're doing," Perry offered.

This was a big break, but Lucie acted as if she was cautious. "I may have to give that some thought. I've got some girls that are—you know—kinda ..."

"Kinda what?" Perry helped her along.

"Work with me. They are real exhibitionists. And I think some of them might be interested in doing some films. How do they get into that?"

"It's not hard," Perry assured her. He began to stutter as he explained. "This is a guy I work with all the time. He's a real good guy, reliable and trustworthy." Perry detailed the production plans. "You don't see this every day, you know, five girls doing fisting tapes."

Lucie agreed. "No, you don't." Lucie made faces to Campisi as she wound the phone cord over her shoulder and rocked in the chair. The contortions her lips went into were like Lily Tomlin's telephone operator.

"I'm just running up the flag pole, this is something you might want to know." He tempted her further. One girl, a nurse, was coming in from Pennsylvania. She had been in the December issue of *Hustler,* the Beaver Hunt issue. "Can we talk here?"

"Yeah, go ahead," Lucie encouraged.

"There's going to be a German shepherd, just for the one girl from Pennsylvania."

Bestiality in videos made an obscenity prosecution easier.

"I don't know whether your customers would—" Perry asked.

"Oh, yeah," Lucie said quickly. "Listen, I've got people that will, you know, I swear to God, Perry. It never ceases to amaze me how kinky some people can be."

"You don't have to tell me," Perry said to his new chum. "I don't know where you guys draw the line, but a lot of guys want violence, and we don't want to do violence. Well, dogs, I don't care about that."

"Well," Lucie said, always ready with a quick comeback. "You're not going to get AIDS from a German shepherd."

"I don't even know if he's compatible, but he's not a vicious dog."

Lucie confided her business plan. "I've got a couple of things in mind, some scenarios to have filmed. Some of these clients, they fantasize. And to be able to provide them with their fantasy in person is sometimes not really appropriate, sometimes the fantasy on film is better for them because they can't really frequently perform in person, if you get my—"

Perry distributed films with a woman blindfolded and handcuffed, men having anal intercourse with women, women with objects inserted in them—pool balls, a metal mallet, electric toothbrush, a model airplane.

In one, a man inserted a metallic device in a woman's vagina, and Campisi noted in his affidavit that it apparently caused the actress mild discomfort.

But Orcutt told Lucie he had specific guidelines for the custom tapes. He didn't want to put the girls in jeopardy. Girl-dog, girl-girl was one thing. Guy-girl stuff was the worst seller. "What I'm trying to tell you here is there's certain things that might sound interesting to do—well, it makes me a little nervous."

"The easier and more conventional things are things we can handle on a personal basis." For investigative purposes, Lucie needed to know about the kinds of activities that made an obscenity prosecution easier. "It's some of the more unusual, quote unquote kinkier things that we're better able to deal with from the film standpoint. I do have some girls that are real exhibitionists, and what I'm saying is that if you ever need people—I think I might have some girls that might be interested. But you would have to trust me enough that you have to tell me a little bit about what's going on, because I'm not going to put anybody in a bad situation."

Perry tried to interest her in having her girls make their own films, using a video recorder on a tripod. He would distribute them. Lucie was concerned, once again, about quality. Perry kept trying to convince her. "Our customers don't care if it's an Academy Award direction with special effects ... that's the charm of the amateur stuff. As long as it's not horrible, and they don't put it on a pogo stick, and it's real out of focus ..."

Lucie and Perry's conversation had run to the end of the first side of the tape. Campisi needed time to turn it over.

"Hold on a minute," Lucie improvised. "I'm going to sneeze. I caught cold over Christmas."

Campisi flipped the tape.

"I'm sorry," Lucie said. "I tell you this weather, I've really been busy, I just run myself down here."

"There's something I think I can help you with. Do you want to get better?"

"OK."

"I'll give you a kiss." Perry kissed Lucie through the phone.

She laughed. "Thanks." Campisi could only hear Lucie's side of the conversation. She was rolling her eyes. The faces made it fun for him.

"I was with this girl the other day, and she came down with pneumonia. No more of that."

"If I get worse, I'll call you for sure," Lucie teased.

Perry told Lucie that the upcoming production was scheduled for a city in southern Ohio. "It's not like you can go on your lunch break."

"That's no problem, it's not that far away," Lucie said. "Would he have a problem if you gave me his phone number?"

Perry said OK, but then couldn't find the number. He couldn't find Lucie's number either; she gave it to him again. He was a successful businessman, but some organizational details eluded him. "I'll just transfer it into my book—if I can find it."

Perry said he didn't think there would be any problem with the producer taping Lucie's girls. They would get paid a hundred dollars per tape. And they could get a copy of the tape, no charge, so they would have it for their own records.

"Yeah," Lucie quipped. "Memorabilia."

"They can show their grandchildren, right?" Perry said, laughing.

"You're something," Lucie said. "That sounds good."

The discussion continued. Making plans was a slow process. Perry finally decided he would call the producer, *Donald Hyde,* tell him about Sue Bates, and then leave his number on Sue's machine.

"These girls are somewhat attractive, right?" Perry asked.

"Yeah. These are not the dogs," Lucie giggled.

"Funny. Funny." Perry seemed to want to keep talking. "Did I ever tell you about the guy with the monkeys? He used to work for the Shell Oil company in South America. He had a plane which he flew private. He brought over thirty hours of stuff—amateur film with a Spanish girl with a dog and a monkey."

"Oh, good Lord!" Lucie exclaimed.

"If anybody's interested in monkeys, which I'm sure there will be thousands, and they have something to trade."

"I'd like to see those monkey tapes myself," Lucie laughed. She told him she'd get her money order off for the tapes she was ordering and call him in a few weeks.

"Thanks for calling," Perry said,"and take care of your cold."

Their second conversation had been almost twice as long as the first. Perry had kind of fallen for Lucie, Campisi thought. He was starved for people. He's an outgoing guy, stuck in his house. Lucie was real easy to talk to, she was putting on a good act. It was like a flood, as if Orcutt was talking to an old friend.

The next call was January 21. Perry asked Lucie how her cold was.

"Oh, I'm fine," Lucie said.

"See—it worked," Perry laughed.

"Yeah," Lucie laughed with him. "It was you thinking about me, I know."

They talked for a while about various film choices and then Lucie said she "got an idea that I'm playing around in my mind."

"I love to hear them ideas," Perry said.

"I'm thinking maybe some of these clients would like to see some of the girls that they know through me in the films. If I would have a girl that we could film with a dog—you mentioned before that he has access to a dog—I mean I wouldn't have to find my own dog."

"Here's the situation. There is this girl who has a purebred German shepherd. But—she sorta had a nervous breakdown, like a couple of weeks ago."

"The owner—not the dog, we're talking about," Lucie joked.

"Yeah. And she's already out of the hospital. He thinks it will be OK," Perry said, referring to the producer, Hyde. "Now it's tricky finding these dogs. I mean, I got girls all over the country who want dogs," Perry said. He told her there was a man in L.A. who said he traveled and showed people how to find dogs, but that was too much trouble.

Lucie agreed that was a little much. She ordered more films.

"So, OK. Well, listen, I got a little ... sort of a little party planned here for a little later. So ..."

"How come I wasn't invited?" Perry asked. Sucked in.

"Huh?" Lucie laughed. "Well you never know, you might show up here. So I have to get going. But if you would send out that 'Golden Showers Kink,' I will get that money to you in the mail the first thing in the morning."

The plan was going well. Lucie used the number Perry had left and called Hyde several times. She gained his confidence as well. She told him she was running a clean operation and wanted to make sure his was a well-run setup before she let any of her girls be part of it. Hyde invited her to come watch the filming.

Preparation for the sting began. The case crossed division lines; southern Ohio was under the jurisdiction of the Cincinnati division. Campisi called Postal Inspector Brad Reeves, his Cincinnati counterpart. "We got a guy for you. We're coming down, we're going in undercover."

Lucie would go in with Campisi's supervisor, Stan Wood. She would introduce Wood as her manager. There were a lot of preliminaries to all this. Campisi said, "You just don't pull up in front of a house and start recording."

They had two unmarked vans, one was from Cleveland's postal division and the other from Cincinnati. They had to be in range for the transmitter. They used a Magnavox system, which was built into a suitcase with an antenna. They went down ahead of time to find the best location for the setup. The best location might be in front of the residence, but was there parking? They needed to check the equipment in advance, to make sure of its range. The recording equipment worked from a greater distance in a suburban, residential neighborhood than one with a lot of brick and steel buildings.

It was midwinter and cold. The postal team checked to see if the heaters in the van were working.

They used a backup recorder. Wood had experienced instances where the batteries didn't work or the microphone wire was frayed. The equipment was delicate.

Stan Wood, as manager for Sue Bates, madam in charge of an exclusive call girl service, could hardly have been playing a role further from his true personality. An extremely serious man, with black hair and dark eyes, Wood held strong beliefs about obscenity. He had been an inspector about fourteen years and had worked in Bristol, and Richmond, Virginia, Miami, and Memphis.

Hyde knew what kind of video Lucie wanted, though he did not know why. They wanted one that was actionable for an adult pornography case. Bestiality helped. The northern district of Ohio had not had any successful adult obscenity prosecutions since the seventies, when Cleveland native Reuben Sturman, the world's pornography king, was found not guilty. The jurors stated that they felt the government had no business being involved in that type of investigation. Wood believed Sturman's pornography had gotten much worse since. He declared, "Society in general was in a constant downward spiral. Man, given to his own evil being, will digress to his lowest point."

Wood was particularly outraged by child pornography. "We laugh about it and we call it kiddie porn. It's not kiddie porn. We shouldn't window dress it. It's victimizing children." Child pornography was Postal's main concern in pornography investigations. Campisi and Wood were fairly certain by now that Orcutt was not involved in child pornography. His brochure stated that he wasn't, and he had told Lucie the same thing. But they still wanted to take action on the adult films.

Wood had reviewed the films, and the worse they became the more adamant he became about testing the system with another adult obscenity case. The laws were a quagmire. Cases went by the three-pronged Miller test. Based upon contemporary community standards, the average person must find the sexual conduct depicted in an offensive way; the work as a whole has to appeal to the prurient interest; and it must lack serious artistic, political, literary, or scientific value. Campisi and Wood ran into trouble. Some of the assistant DAs said, Absolutely not, these are consenting adults.

"They are endangering the lives of those dogs." Wood was emphatic. "I'll take it to state court. Can we charge them with abusing animals?"

He also argued that a decision made in the seventies should not keep setting the standard. Pornography had gotten much worse since then. Wood didn't think the material should be available. And the government certainly should not be used to carry it out—via the mail. The climate of the times had become more conservative. Since the mideighties, the U.S. attorneys had been willing to go after pornography. "It's the Reagan administration. Thank God for that," Wood declared.

Finally, an attorney had agreed to prosecute Orcutt.

Lucie wore a tailored V-necked black jumpsuit and borrowed a Toyota Supra from one of her Midtown Corridor business buddies for her debut as a madam. She drove down in the afternoon, listening to music on the radio. This was a nice break, she thought. It was exciting to be going undercover again.

Campisi and Wood were having fun, too. They got into their roles with a relish and went into a drugstore and bought two fake diamond pinky rings.

But Wood did have concerns. He had never worked with Lucie. He had never worked undercover with any woman. He had confidence in her background, that she would be cool, that she could handle herself, but he didn't know what was going to happen or how she would react. "Maybe it's just my male desire to protect, but there's always this fear when you are working with a female—if something goes down and she gets hurt, it will be you that has the trouble." He wanted this to go off well.

What if something went wrong, what kinds of problems would it create between the Cleveland Police Department and the inspection service? The police department was doing them a great service allowing her to help. They had to write a formal request for Lucie. It was unusual to be able to take a local police officer clear across the state unless it was a joint investigation.

Wood wore dark wool slacks and a pink oxford shirt with a buttoned collar, and a sports jacket. He had a sweater on; he was uncomfortable. He was concerned that with the transmitter and his gun it was too bulky. He started to wear a shoulder holster, but he hated them. He took it off and wore his gun as he normally did, on his side. His sports coat was tight. What would happen when he got inside? It could be very hot, and he would want to take off the coat, so how could he conceal the holster.

Hyde's neighborhood was being renovated. It reminded Wood of neighborhoods he had seen in Washington, D.C., in the early seventies, with the brick row houses being revamped. Campisi and Wood had noticed some of the furniture on the videos, particularly a plaid couch.

Campisi was parked in front of Hyde's house in the Cleveland van. He was cramped, cold, and tired. Wood knew he had the fun part, being inside with Lucie.

Wood was wearing the wire. What if somebody realizes I have a wire on. What if the wire isn't working. Such worries always went through his mind. He wore the wire in his inside coat pocket. It was a small recorder with an external microphone, which was also a transmitter. They weren't using their best equipment for Hyde, the best was being used somewhere else that night.

Lucie and Wood walked into the house. Hyde wasn't there. The man who let them in was wearing a patrolman's jacket.

How did he fit in?

Lucie and Wood made small talk, waiting for Hyde. They could smell grass. The girls, *Princess* and Twinkles, were in the other room, smoking.

"What's the story?" Wood asked the man. "Why do you have that coat on?"

The man told them he used to work for a Florida police department and before that had held a security position in a Michigan auto plant.

Hyde was an independent businessman, a computer consultant for hospitals and other organizations. When he came home, Lucie introduced Stan as her manager. "Quite frankly," Sue Bates said, "I don't really do the hands-on thing. I just wanted to see the operation, but from now on you would be working with Stan."

She figured they were thinking she had a big operation.

Hyde took them upstairs. The second floor was one big room with a cathedral ceiling and spotlights. And the plaid couch.

Hyde took a liking to them and started talking. He gave them computer printouts. He explained how his computers worked, showing them that all his actors were on the computer and that he sent them 1099 forms. He showed them the consent form that he had them sign, a declaration stating they were older than eighteen. How much they were paid. His file was computerized so that if he ran an actress's name through it, he could bring up a list of all the films she was in. His cabinets were full of videotapes.

He was like a kid in a toy shop. Excited, he led them into the bathroom, proudly showing them how he had redone it with new ornate fixtures. He salivated constantly as he talked.

Princess was from Pennsylvania. She was a health technician, and was there with her husband. She had made several videos for Hyde's company, Den Video. A couple of local women showed up. The pregnant woman from Illinois never came.

Twinkles announced that she did not want to film in front of Stan and Lucie.

From the van, Campisi could see the spotlights on the second floor; the curtains were open. He was listening to the discussion inside Hyde's place. Twinkles will sell the stuff to any mope who sends fifteen or twenty bucks, he thought, but she doesn't want to do it in front of Lucie and Stan. The security of the camera, I guess. Campisi shrugged.

Lucie and Stan had to leave before filming started. But Hyde had given them his whole operation. "Talk about stupid," Lucie grimaced.

They all went out to the Red Lobster for dinner and had a riotous good time.

Campisi and Reeves executed simultaneous search warrants on Orcutt and Hyde. Orcutt had mail from all over the world. Campisi had to review each and every videotape confiscated from Orcutt's. He fast forwarded through, but didn't find any child pornography, not even a hint. Orcutt said he refused people on that. He had nieces and nephews, and harbored no ill will to children.

They retrieved about two thousand pieces of mail from Orcutt's box after they froze it. Campisi read all his correspondence. There was nothing about children.

Campisi knew in his heart that Orcutt's family was aware of Perry's activities, but there was no question when he walked into the house and saw the photocopy machine, forty-eight VCRs, and a room full of videotapes. The family lived in this house. Their house was filled with pornographic films and videotape machines. Plus—the father went through the mail and the mother paid for Perry's advertisements from his big business checkbook. They were definitely cooperating.

The family employed a top-flight defense lawyer, Carmen Policy. Policy was the general manager and general counsel for the San Francisco 49ers. "We're not talking they hired some bum down the street. Carmen Policy is big, big, big," Campisi exclaimed as his eyebrows arched upward.

Campisi went to the meeting with the lawyers. Policy "had two Superbowl rings on with enough diamonds in them to satisfy any five women I know," Campisi recalled. "His suit cost more than my car."

"You really don't want to indict all five of these people, do you?" he asked Campisi.

"No, I don't," he said. "But if I have to, I will."

The father, mother, and brothers had nothing to do with it, the defense asserted.

"Carmen, if I didn't think they had anything to do with it I wouldn't have said they did. I have videotapes of surveillances. Read my report. All I want to do is stop this thing. Perry is the major offender here. I don't want to send his mother to jail. I'm not an animal. But we need to deal with the problem. The problem is Perry, the videotapes, the money."

Shortly afterward, Perry Orcutt pled guilty. Campisi felt good. Policy was no lightweight. "He knows every trick in the book, and he knows everybody in the book."

The plea agreement called for Perry to forfeit all the equipment seized, plus a fine of a hundred thousand dollars. There was a hundred thousand dollars in the Starlite account. The idea was to hurt the violator in the pocketbook. "It would have been real, real mean to send Perry to prison, and I'm not a mean guy," Campisi said. "We're not out to destroy anybody. He wasn't a violent criminal."

Campisi found Perry pleasant, lively, well educated, and alert. "But something back there—there's a short fuse in there somewhere."

The investigation had taken thirteen months. Eventually Hyde pled guilty as well. Orcutt's copy machine is now in the post office. The VCRs were distributed to divisions all over the country. Lucie was given two of the VCRs for her office. The detectives used them to go through pornography tapes they confiscated looking for child pornography.

M. D. Moore, inspector in charge at Postal, sent a commendation letter to Chief Howard Rudolph and to Safety Director Mitchell Brown, citing Lucie's work on the Orcutt case.

The letter read in part, "Lieutenant [Duvall's] unfailing cooperation and professional expertise were vital to the successful completion of this investigation.... Using an assumed identity Lieutenant [Duvall] assisted in taping five telephone calls which did irrefutable damage to any defense possible to our target.... You must be very proud to have such dedicated officers in your department."

24

SERIAL RAPISTS

Kelly Kachinsky lived in Lakewood, but in mid-December 1987 she
drove to her fiancé's home on Rocky River Drive in Cleveland to
wrap Christmas presents and his birthday present. She was going to
bake him a cake. The next day was his birthday. She brought in all
the gifts and boxes from her car.

She made herself something to eat. She sat in the family room; the
Christmas tree lit the room. She turned the television on and started to
wrap up the gifts.

About six o'clock Kelly thought she heard some noises out on the
patio. Animals often crossed in their travels; she turned the television
down and listened. Quiet. She assumed it was just an animal and turned
the TV back up.

Someone forcefully grabbed her by the hair. A hand covered her
mouth. Instinctively she turned and fought. Sitting on the floor, she
struggled to stand. Once on her feet she got away. But just long enough
to yell.

She was hit in the face. Twice. With a fist. She was knocked to the
floor.

He sat on top of her chest and grabbed for the scissors Kelly had used
to wrap her gifts. He hit her with the scissors across the face. She continued to yell. He hit her again. Then another time. Once again. Her nose
was cut and bleeding. She thought she would black out.

He told her to shut up. He told her he would kill her.

She could see stars. She didn't want to black out. She decided to stop fighting him.

"Don't look at me or I'll kill you." His baseball cap was on the floor. He had topped his own hat with one of her boyfriend's from the clothes tree. He had on a pair of sunglasses. "I want money," he told her.

"I only have two dollars."

"I know that. I've already been through your purse. I don't believe you." He constantly told her not to look at him.

"I don't have any money," she answered.

What about her bank account, he wanted to know. But she'd already spent her paycheck. He wanted to know if there was any money in the house. She didn't know. "I don't live here on a permanent basis." He grabbed her by the hair again. He told her he wanted to leave.

Kelly thought, I'm lucky. I'm going to get out of this. She started to walk to the doors they normally used to exit the house.

"No. Not that door," he stated. "The side door."

She had never opened that door. It was in the stairwell to the basement. He pushed her up against the door. Open it, he ordered. It had a couple of locks and she wasn't familiar with them. She couldn't get it open.

He swung her around with one hand. The scissors still in the other hand. She landed in the corner. He managed to open the door. Now his escape route was planned; he wanted to know when her boyfriend got home.

He seemed to have information about her. That she was not married, that this was a boyfriend and not her husband. She suspected he thought her boyfriend would arrive any minute. He would have. Normally. She knew he wasn't going to be back that evening. But she told him the usual time her fiancé arrived home. In fifteen minutes. Anytime now.

He told her to take off her sweater. He took the scissors and cut off her bra. Her back had cuts and punctures from the scissors. He unzipped her pants and pulled them down. He told her to take them off. He asked her to turn around. Then said, "Move."

Her back was toward him; she was naked. Pressed against the wall. He tried to push his penis into her anus.

"Please. Don't." She begged.

He told her to sit down on the two steps that led to the kitchen. The scissors were at her throat. "Don't look at me or I'll kill you," he repeated. He wanted her to cover her eyes with her hands or turn her head. Or close her eyes. He told her to spread her legs.

Kelly wouldn't.

He took his other hand and spread her legs. He asked if she was on her period. She was. He told her to hold her breasts together. He masturbated between her breasts.

He told her to perform oral sex like she did on her boyfriend. She
couldn't.

He masturbated between her breasts until he ejaculated.

He said he was leaving. He was going out to the car to get more
money, because he had seen her car. It was a silver Toyota. He said he
would watch her through the window. He knew the first call she would
make. If she made that call—she would not have a Christmas. He would
be back to kill her.

Kelly ran through the house. Grabbing a blanket from the couch, she
wrapped it around her body. She tried to find where he had gotten in.

The door to the master bedroom was open. It was never open. She
shut it and ran downstairs. She called the police.

Her eyes were both black when SIU crime photos were snapped.
Later her face got worse. Both blackened eyes swelled. A large lump rose
on her forehead about the size of a tennis ball. Her lip swelled. Her nose
was cut from the scissors.

There had been other rapes by this suspect. The first report had come
into the sex crime and child abuse unit two years earlier, the same day
Lucie completed her first monthly activity report, October 9, 1985.
Detective Edward Gray looked at the report. The rape was very similar to
ones he and other detectives had worked on in the Second District before
the inception of the centralized sex crimes unit. Two months later, another rape. Same suspect. Zeb and Gray were assigned the case.

Chief Hanton asked Lucie, "Do you want Matuszny?" Detective
Robert Matuszny had also worked on the rapes in the Second District.

"Well, it would be helpful, 'cause I don't know that much about it,"
Lucie said. "They can just pick up on it."

Lucie had inherited a serial rapist.

The rapist had struck in the suburbs also. Parma, Parma Heights,
Middleburg Heights, Fairview Park. Matuszny, Gray, and other Second
District detectives had arranged joint meetings with suburban departments. There were identifying traits, common denominators. The victim
was the only adult home. The apartments were in secluded or wooded
areas. All the victims described the suspect about the same way. Five foot
eight, 130 to 150 pounds. He usually gained entry by cutting a window
screen; then he crawled through it. The screens were cut with a knife.
The sexual acts were similar: penis between the breasts. Fondling. Sometimes ejaculating on the victim's chest.

Keep your eyes closed. I'll be back. Don't make any noise or I'll hurt
your child.

One woman vomited.

Many were forced into the bathroom—told to stay there for an hour. I'll be back.

Some of the victims were related to cops. One victim had a newborn infant, another was a grandmother.

He had dark feathered hair. Olive skin. He was lean. In his early twenties. White or Hispanic.

Some of the women said he had a bump on his penis near the head.

There were rapes the detectives attributed to the same rapist as early as 1983. Over thirty possible cases. The same guy. Two years. They had hundreds of possible suspects. None of the meetings produced solid leads. There were no breaks in the case.

Matuszny stayed with the sex crimes unit working on the case with Gray for ninety days. But the rapist didn't hit again. They covered a lot of leads—they didn't come up with anything. Matuszny went back to the Second District.

Now, Kachinsky. It was becoming the longest serial rape case in Cleveland history. Eight days after Kachinsky, he raped again.

He held a knife to *Jeanne*'s throat. He said he knew her. Don't call the police. I'll be back. His threats were not idle. He had returned in several previous cases. It had been two years since Lucie's unit had inherited the rapist. Four years of his rapes.

Lucie was appalled at some of the investigative techniques that had been used before her unit took over the case.

Some of the suspects had been asked to drop their pants to demonstrate they didn't have bumps on their penises. Lucie wanted things done right. "Like how about warrants to examine their penises. What had happened was guys were actually down at the Stadium and anybody matching that description, they were taking them in the men's room and making them drop their drawers," Lucie exclaimed.

The idea of asking people to drop their pants was, to Lucie, extremely unprofessional. Not only was it unprofessional, she could also see that if it ever got down to court testimony, number one, you'd look like a bunch of jerks, and number two—"What in God's name could you testify that you saw? It just to me was insane that they were down there doing this random gee-there's-a-guy-who-looks-like. They're not doctors, they can't—" Lucie's voice rose another octave. "Policemen have to understand that they're policemen. We are not lawyers, we're not doctors, we're not counselors. That was just an irresponsible way to try to find this person. Nobody who works for me will ever consider trying anything like that."

Lucie started doing some research on these warts to try to figure out what they might be. She had talked to one of the doctors in the medical unit. She was concerned because not all of the victims described the bump the same way. She found out that, number one, it comes and it goes, and number two, it wasn't the hot clue that originally everybody thought it was. It would be a helpful clue if they could establish the rapist had such a wart, but it was not evidence like a fingerprint.

The sex crimes detectives used a "penis composite," asking victims to draw the bump or scar or nodule as it was variously described. The victims couldn't liken it to anything.

Public pressure grew. People wanted a composite. Lucie just didn't like to bend to that pressure. Eyewitnesses were the weakest corroboration. "What if the composite doesn't look like him? What if, by drawing a composite, it tainted the investigation? So you've tunnel visioned everybody. While you may have generated a lot of false leads, you just may have cut off some really good leads. Then, what if you get the person, and you have good substantial evidence, maybe fingerprints or something that he did at the crime, and he doesn't look like the composite. Now you've got a defense attorney that's going to say, Now you're saying that this is the person who did it. But, Lieutenant, two months ago weren't you on the six o'clock news saying that this was the picture of the guy who did it?!"

Lucie had a number of witnesses who had gotten a pretty good look at the rapist. She asked an artist from one of the television stations to draw a composite in color because so many victims described his olive skin.

"I was confident that it was a good likeness," she said. "There was the paperboy who had seen someone coming down the street. When they can *collectively* agree, then you know you've got a pretty good likeness."

Lucie stared at the color composite on the wall in her office. Every day. "You're somebody," she said. "And we're going to find you." She thought every policeman felt that way. They were all looking for him.

The composite of the rapist was shown on television and in the newspaper. The *Plain Dealer* referred to him as the West Side rapist.

There were not many suspects that had enough elements for a court order. But they had enough on one man to get a warrant and take him to the doctor. He was from Parma and worked at a restaurant open all night. An early FBI profile had indicated a restaurant as one possible place of employment for the suspect. A cook or a dishwasher. His work hours fit. He matched the description. They searched his apartment, looking for something that belonged to the victims, to tie him to the crime. They didn't find anything.

Two years after they inherited the serial rapist, Gray was transferred to SIU. Zeb was left with the bulk of the West Side rapist's numerous cases to solve, along with her other cases. A new case or two every other day. Manpower had been diminished within the unit; they were all really stretched. Zeb would continue to work without a partner for almost two years.

"If I'm in the middle of the West Side rapist case and you put something that could be really hot on the desk and I can't get to it, who knows." Zeb's usually expressionless face enlivened with an edge of anger. "By the time I get to it, it's gone possibly. I got a victim, I got a suspect—I got to do *something*. That victim is entitled for something to be done. Just like all the West Side rapist victims."

Zeb tried to find privacy to interview victims. "Sometimes she'd be at the scene, sometimes she'd be at the hospital." There might be a zone car there. SIU at the scene. A couple of bosses. Sometimes the media. "How is she going to tell me everything when all these people are walking by?" Zeb wanted to make her as comfortable as possible. She often took the victims back to the office.

They would go through their natural reactions. Crying, shaking, upset. Not all of them—some were more composed than others. "I've had girls giggling who were raped. It happens for a reason. I don't find that particularly unusual." She'd seen all kinds of reactions. If they're going to cry, let them cry. Support them. If they wanted to talk, she listened. They lost a sense of control. You got to give them that back in a way. But no matter what, Zeb definitely would get them privacy.

Zeb asked, What did *he* make you do? How did *he* force you? She tried to show some empathy, tried to feel for them. Sometimes she told them, "I'm sorry it happened."

They asked, Why me? Some felt shame. The not knowing—is he going to come back? In one suburban case he did find the victim again. Even though she had moved. He raped her again.

Zeb keyed in on the common denominators when she recognized one of the West Side rapist's cases. Words that were said. What were you doing? How did he seem to you? Was he nervous? Was he confident? Was there a knife? How did he hold it? She made charts of all the crimes and the common traits. Suspect. Weapon. Method. Time. Point of entry. Assault. Words spoken. Orders given.

He always went in at a time when the victim was vulnerable. "When you would be the least alert—you're never ready for anything like that, but at the worst time. Shower time and morning time. He had control, total control in those situations. If he had picked a different person ..." Zeb paused. "It would have been a fight to the end with me. Ain't no way. No two ways about it.

"In the beginning, getting into the unit, listening to all these women tell me about all the different situations, the thought of somebody coming into *my* house when *I'm* there. I'm not going to say I was paranoid, but boy, it was like, phew! But after the first couple of years in this unit it wore off. I'm always alert. I take my gun everywhere, because I'm not going to be a victim."

Lucie told the detectives to have victims fill out FBI VICAP questionnaires. She wanted the FBI to try a second profile. The VICAP questions were very specific. The profile was gathered from behavioral data, not the physical evidence.

Another year began. Another string of rapes. A knife to her throat—he wanted cash. He forced her to perform oral sex, raped her vaginally, ejaculated in her mouth, and ordered her to swallow it.

Zeb tracked down leads. The rapist had taken a bank card from one victim and used it, a possible break in the case. But the lead led nowhere. The bank didn't have a camera at its automatic teller station.

It was getting to the point where it seemed that this was all anybody in the unit was working on. But Lucie couldn't allow her detectives just to drop everything else.

Lucie called Inspector Wood at Postal and asked him for help. The rapist seemed to have access to some buildings. Could he possibly be a mailman, a letter carrier with a key to gain entry through the front door to get to the mailboxes? Wood circulated the picture to managers of the postal stations. He knew Lucie was taking a lot of heat and the police department was getting adverse publicity. "The *Plain Dealer* is very powerful, particularly when it's the only show in town." He could sympathize with that pressure, but you couldn't solve a crime just because of the newspaper pressuring you.

Lucie was getting pressure from all sides. Hers was a day-to-day existence. Another rape in December. Two in January, another in February. All the leads that didn't pan out. All the shuffling through information. Members of the victims' families called. The press called constantly. The *Plain Dealer* now named him the West Park rapist due to the high concentration of rapes in the West Park community.

Tips came in from all of the suburbs and from all over Cleveland. The sex crimes unit looked at everyone, from robbery suspects to voyeurs—anyone that was a possibility. Any lead had to be checked out.

In March of 1988, the West Park rapist hit again. This time the suspect wore a bandana. He had worn a variety of coverings to distract the victims from what he looked like. A ski mask, a pair of underpants, a mesh T-shirt over his face.

He was targeting and studying his victims. He used information about them to intimidate them. It was eerie. "I watched you through the window give head to your husband. I want you to give me head the same as you gave him."

Commander Bob Bolton handled some of the media calls and relayed them to Lucie. He got calls from different districts. They guaranteed this was the guy. He got calls from out-of-state media and out-of-state police agencies. There was a rape in Detroit. Could he be somebody on the freeway? Who knows. He tried to help keep the media on track.

The pressure on Lucie was always present. When are you going to get this guy? "We are just doing everything we possibly can," she answered.

Pressure from the chief, the community. She spoke to community groups. People asked, When are we going to see some results? Is it true you got some fingerprints at the scene?

"I'm not here to discuss the specifics," she told them.

The public thought that once you had a fingerprint, you had a suspect. SIU did lift fingerprints from the scenes. But whose prints were they? They didn't have a computerized system for matching prints. The only way to compare a random print with the prints on file was to go through the almost two hundred thousand cards by hand and compare them under a magnifying glass. Even if that was feasible, it would only help if he'd been arrested and printed before. And if he had been arrested for a theft in Cleveland or a suburb, no one would know he was a rape suspect. How could the department match the prints of everyone arrested for theft, rape, or voyeurism with every other print on file?

SIU lifted a palm print from one crime scene. Whose palm had left enough sweat on the windowsill so the runman could lift its impression? Palm prints were rarely helpful. Usually the whole palm print had to be lifted from the scene in order to make a match. Unlike a partial finger-print, a partial palm print was rarely good enough. And most of the time, a partial palm print—perhaps the heel of the palm—was all the suspect left behind.

If it was a safety issue, Lucie would let out some facts to the public. She advised people to lock their doors; he was entering through open screens. Some things she lost control over, some victims had talked to the media. The fact that he was using bank cards came out. Lucie felt it was better if the victims didn't talk to the media. The victims didn't know all the details. She was very concerned that the investigation not be compromised in any way.

Lucie had the victims called into the sex crimes unit to brainstorm. Were there any similarities in the patterns of their lives?

"We tried to have them think back to see if there was some common denominator in their lives that would give us some insight into where to look. If they frequented the same places or went to the same stores. Or had the same dentist. Something," Lucie said. "Some commonality. If they all went to the same gas station—anything." Lucie sighed. "It didn't help."

She referred some of the victims to counselors she knew. "This guy left a trail of devastated women."

She shared her frustration with her friends. Judy heard about it. "In installments over time. It was taking forever." Lucie told Judy about all the pressure from the administration and the media, and the most frustrating part—that they had cut her staff.

For each case, Zeb had to interview neighbors. Paper delivery people. Utility people. Lucie wanted the trash department employees' work schedules checked. What time did they start? Maybe someone saw somebody. There were tips from bars, from traffic cops. What was the weather? Would he have left footprints in the snow? In one case someone saw a man leave the scene on a motorcycle. That meant tracking down motorcycles through the Registry of Motor Vehicles.

Zeb talked to bank personnel. Bank transaction records were obtained, and she hunted down customers who had used the bank at the same time the suspect did. At one of the banks, the suspect parked his car, left it, and walked to the machine—even though it was a drive-through.

Sergeant Jackie Christ arranged with Lucie to take one of the bank customers to a policeman who was trained in hypnosis. Officer Bob Kahl had worked with Lucie back in 1979 when the strike force made its first big crackdown on prostitution. He was the hypnotist.

Kahl drove to the bank a couple of days before the first session. He wanted to be familiar with the location. It was a drive-through with a steep ramp. It was kind of odd that this guy would park his car and walk up to use the ATM, Kahl thought.

Kahl had a list of questions that the sex crimes unit wanted asked. Primarily, they were interested in the plate number. Second, a good description of the car. And a description of the guy. The first session was all preparation. Any questions? The subject was about twenty-five. She could hardly remember anything, and she was very skeptical about the hypnosis. They didn't give her any information about the investigation.

The sessions were videotaped. Kahl knew it was a desperate move because of the constitutional questions that could be raised in court concerning hypnosis. Everything gleaned from the session would have to be corroborated.

The induction he did with her was called "merry-go-round." It dealt with going to kindergarten and early childhood memories. The objective was to build successes out of each memory. If you could remember something in the past, how about what happened only two weeks ago.

Kahl's deep voice filled the small room, the quiet click of the clock in his office seeming to stand out in space and time as he continued. "You've got your head down for a nap and your mind wanders out of the room and goes to the kiddie park and there's where the merry-go-round is and it goes up and down and around and round and up and down and around and around and I can't hear the music and I can't see the people ..." Confusion worked the best.

He didn't want to put her to sleep—just to keep her in that gray area where she would feel no emotion for what she recalled. She would see it as if on a TV screen.

The next day Kahl began again. He would try for information now. She was more comfortable. She knew what to expect. He began, "With every breath that you take, every word that I speak, I'd like you to go deeper and deeper. More and more relaxed. Every click of the clock with every word that I speak, every breath that you take."

The bank customer began to talk. She saw layers of clothing. She could tell what each layer was. She saw his sneakers and even the brand name.

Kahl took the tape to Lucie. Lucie found it fascinating—but the customer had not been able to recall the information they needed.

Lucie had a lot of respect for Detective Mike Cipo. He had been in her academy class, and she thought he had turned out to be one of the best detectives in the department. He was tall and he had dark brown hair with a receding hair line. He had blue-gray eyes and a long nose that wasn't quite straight. He wore dark charcoal three-piece suits; his handcuffs looped over his belt in the back, and a string of bullets clipped on the right front side of his hip along with his pager.

"He will start with nothing and start picking away at it," Lucie said. She thought she was good at her job but that Cipo was a better detective. She recognized a good detective and laughed. "That's why I'm a lieutenant." She felt law enforcement didn't allow officers to be good detectives anymore. They weren't given the time to stick to a case. But she did get aggravated with Cipo. Often he didn't report back to her and keep her up-to-date on cases. "He's a loner."

Cipo caught the bus stop rapist case. His partner, Andrea Markus-Mace, worked on it with him. The first victim had been on West Twenty-fifth Street waiting for a bus. It was early in the morning before daylight. The assailant came up behind her and asked, "What time is it?" He pulled her into the car, drove her to the East Side, and raped her. She saw a billy club in his car. Some women were grabbed and got away from him. A few days later another rape. Same MO. Early morning. Over to the East Side. Now the victim saw a policeman's hat. The pattern was repeated. Each time there were more indicators, a flashlight, navy blue pants, black shoes. The suspect grabbed another victim on the East Side, a fourteen-year-old girl who was kidnapped and raped. Each one had a little piece of information. He was pockmarked where his beard grew, black, about thirty. He had jheri curls and a slight mustache. Five ten to six feet tall.

Cipo and Markus-Mace were putting it all together. Markus-Mace said, "He either lives east or lives west and works in the opposite direction. He's on his way to or from work." They thought he was a security guard.

One victim had given them information on the suspect's car. "One of our supervisors screwed up and told the media that this broken window has plastic," Markus-Mace recalled. She thought you can't say that, that's all the suspect needs to hear. He'll get it fixed.

Cipo waited outside the courtroom. He was late. He didn't want to go in and have the jury think he didn't care about the case he was there for, so he waited for the recess. He was sitting talking with the deputy when he observed a man get off the elevator. He saw he had on security pants. Cipo looked at his face and thought, God that's the guy that's been raping all these women. Cipo stared at him, this has gotta be the guy. He had to be the bus stop rapist. The suspect was on the wrong floor. He walked over to the deputy and asked for directions. Cipo watched. Then got the guy's name, Lapetto Johnson, through the deputy. Cipo knew he didn't have probable cause to arrest, he didn't want to ruin the case. He needed more information.

He came into the office and told Lucie about it. Is this possible?

She said, check it out. Anything's possible. What a break.

He went to the record room, but they didn't have anything on him. So he went to the sheriff's department. Cipo got Johnson's picture. He and Markus-Mace selected a victim to look at the photo spread. They chose the victim whose case involved the fewest charges. They were still being cautious, so they wouldn't take a chance of screwing up the other cases, if there was any problem with the identification process in court later.

The woman started shaking when she saw the photo spread. She pointed to Johnson. "This is him."

Markus-Mace and Zeb got the warrant and went out to arrest him. Cipo had to return to court. Lucie wanted to pick up Johnson right away. Zone car backup followed. Markus-Mace had her gun out as she entered Johnson's workplace. She said, "Put your hands up." She laughed, later. "You see a woman with a gun—I think this guy almost had a cow. It was pretty funny."

They got a warrant for the car. The window had been fixed, but there were still signs from where the tape had been. Cipo got the receipts for the body work. Lucie was thrilled. "Really, hell of a case," she said. She put Cipo in for the Police Officer of the Month award. It was his for May 1988.

One of Johnson's victims was under thirteen. Conviction on that charge carried a mandatory life sentence. The prosecution offered to drop that charge in exchange for a plea. At first, Johnson refused. Then the day after his trial was scheduled to begin, he changed his mind.

As he pled guilty to twenty-six crimes, the victims waited in the Justice Center, prepared to appear. Some sobbed in relief when they learned that they would not have to testify and that Johnson could serve up to fifteen years before being eligible for parole. Assistant County Prosecutor Patricia Cleary said, "We had some responsibility to spare the women from testifying."

Later, Johnson was sentenced to 96 to 235 years.

An elderly couple, *Wilbur* and *Sophie,* were watching "Harry and Son." It was about half past midnight. Suddenly, he was there. Six foot one. A Halloween mask covering his face, white and orange, black around the eyes. With an eight-inch bowie knife, he sliced at Wilbur's and Sophie's clothes, cutting Wilbur's skin. He forced the couple to perform oral sex on each other.

Why are you doing this? Wilbur asked.

He wanted all their property. He forced the naked couple to look for things he demanded. When he couldn't find their car keys, he slashed their mattress.

Another serial rapist had hit the West Side. He began in the spring of 1988. This rapist was black; he attacked elderly white women in their homes. The victims could not see his face. He was tall and extremely strong, with a soft voice that sputtered profanities. He slipped into houses without a sound. He was called Creepwalker.

This is one scary guy, Lucie thought. Violent and unpredictable. She wasn't worried about the West Park rapist murdering his next victim. But she was worried about the man in the mask. She expected his next victim to be killed. This faceless, anonymous man was leaving a trail of horror in his wake.

"When you think of an elderly couple having their clothes cut off and being forced to perform oral sex on each other while he watched ..." Lucie's voice swelled as she talked about it.

Kathleen Brandt was sixty-five years old. He raped her anally and vaginally, tied her with rags, battered her into a coma, and then called EMS from her phone. She was put on a respirator. When she regained consciousness, she still suffered brain damage.

Lucie had no idea what this man was going to do next. The crime reports reeled in on the computer. A Monday in May. A Friday in June. One in July. One in August. Jesus. Every time he hit it was worse than the last one. "Talk about somebody we just really have to get off the streets."

He was an extremely good burglar, and he left no fingerprints. He wore gloves and dark blue clothes, work pants and work boots described as "ugly," or a jogging suit and tennis shoes. He went through the victims' whole house, piling up their possessions to steal. He took his time with the victims, taking time to terrorize them, taking time to cut their clothes off, put pillowcases over their heads. There were indications he had been in several of the homes quite a while before even waking the victims, because their belongings were already heaped by the door for him to take as he left.

Lucie assessed him as calm, sophisticated. He had what it took to stay in a house and methodically go through every room in the dead of night while the people were home.

He told one victim, "Jason is here, Freddy is back," referring to the horror movie characters. After raping another woman, he made sure she would be able to untie herself when he left. "I'm sorry," he told the sixty-three-year-old victim. "You're a sweet old lady."

Lucie listened to the victims talk about seeing him with this Halloween mask on, and she thought, How would I feel if I looked out a window and saw that looking in?

Pat Blackmon and Lucie went out to dinner. Talk was of serial rapists. "It was like every other minute, you'd look up and a new guy would pop up," Pat exclaimed. "This black guy in the midst of all of this—he goes on a spree. It was just amazing."

Lucie looked for the patterns. She photocopied the portion of the Cleveland city map that covered the area of the rapes and used a yellow highliter to mark where he had struck. Poring over the crime reports, she marked the items stolen with a blue underliner. He stole some of the victims' cars, but apparently he couldn't drive a stick shift. Unlike the West Park rapist, he didn't know how to use an ATM card. He asked several victims to take him to the bank but then didn't follow through. He took their VCRs. He robbed them of jewelry—from one he took a watch that was a twenty-fifth anniversary gift.

Lucie made a chart with the crime, date, day, and hour, and property stolen. She took sheets from a calendar and marked the days he had struck. He was hitting on and around the weekends. Thursday, Friday, Saturday, Sunday, or Monday. He was wearing a Halloween mask. Maybe he would hit on Halloween.

The cases that fit the Creepwalker profile were assigned to detectives Mike Cipo and Andrea Markus-Mace. Both had been in the unit since its inception. Markus-Mace had a ready laugh, a lively step, long, swinging brown hair and large, vivid green eyes.

She decided she wanted to be a cop in high school, in 1974, when she heard about women—Lucie and her fourteen female classmates—

going out on patrol. Her grandfather was a traffic cop in Europe during the twenties and thirties. He was killed on duty, by a cable car, before Markus-Mace was born. Her father was a detective. His job had been to track political dissidents before World War II in his native Yugoslavia. Her mother was Austrian. Markus-Mace still lived in the old neighborhood where she grew up, the Slovenian-Croatian community.

She received her BA in social work, but her concentration was in law enforcement. She thought about being a veterinarian, about teaching. But the one thing she really wanted to be was a cop.

She spent four and one-half years on patrol before coming into sex crimes. She liked the unit. She got to follow through on cases, go to trials, and see the whole system at work.

The Creepwalker certainly wasn't her first serial rape case and she didn't get emotional about it. It was something she wanted to solve. It was exciting to piece things together. Some of the cases were routine, when the victims knew their suspects. It wasn't that those crimes were not legitimate, but technically, she wasn't doing detective work on those cases. She was just a paper shuffler. The Creepwalker was much more of a challenge.

Markus-Mace and Cipo went to every scene. They needed to see how this man entered homes, what was similar about the houses, what made him choose a particular residence. They did not have time to go to the crime scene of every rape they handled. Markus-Mace sometimes had to say that in court. "Oftentimes the jury just looks at you in surprise—but it's better to be honest. We don't have the time."

Not all the victims were elderly. One victim who was in her thirties said the man had cut off her clothes but hadn't raped her. "Sometimes they don't tell us," Markus-Mace said. "Why would he go that far and not do whatever he usually has done." Sometimes the victim would rather not talk about it. The older victims were not difficult to interview. They seemed fairly comfortable talking, and they were eager to help. But none of them had seen his face.

It was a July night in 1988; Rich Martin was the IRD—initial response detective—when he was beeped over to Brookside on a rape and arrest. A Second District zone car had cruised through the park and found a couple they thought were having sex. Martin found out the girl had been kidnapped from North Ridgeville. She was eighteen. The man, Darryl Durr, was in the process of raping her. Martin came out to the scene. The victim was the same age as his daughter. When he had been married, he had lived just a few blocks away from the victim. "The case struck home."

Martin started working on it right away. Durr had a record. In 1982,

he had been convicted of felonious assault after he stabbed a woman customer at the gas station where he worked. The victim said he told her
that he didn't appreciate a woman telling him what to do. He served
ninety days in jail. Now, he was charged in the rape, and while he was free
on a five-thousand-dollar bond, he raped and stabbed a fourteen-year-old
girl. Lucie gave Martin the new case, since it was the same suspect. The
victim told Martin that Durr's girlfriend had been at the apartment while
Durr raped her. Martin and McTier interviewed the eighteen-year-old
girlfriend, *Elizabeth*. Working on her. Sure enough, she was there at the
time. Martin could tell she was scared, but "she was staying with this
scumbag, allowing him to bring victims into the home."

Elizabeth had a baby. Martin took a shot in the dark. "Unless you
can help me, I'm going to have the county take away your baby," he told
her. He thought the suspect was involved in other things. Maybe he was a
drug dealer.

Judge Shirley Strickland Saffold set Durr's new bond at a hundred
thousand dollars. Elizabeth knew Durr couldn't make that high a bail.
She made a decision. She called Martin. She sounded very upset. "I have
to talk to you," she told him. "I have something to tell you."

Martin went in and talked to Lucie. "I'll go with you," Lucie said.
Elizabeth was terrified. She came from the Elyria area, where she had
lived near a sixteen-year-old girl named Angel. Back in January, Durr had
come to pick her up one day with Angel in the back of the car. Angel was
tied up, pleading for help.

"I'm going to rape and kill this girl," he told Elizabeth. "And you
better keep your mouth shut."

In the past, Durr had brought Elizabeth a pair of jeans, a pair of
panties from his other victims and made her wear them. A memento of
what he did. Now he brought home Angel's clothing and jewelry. And
Angel had disappeared.

Durr told Elizabeth he had strangled Angel with a dog chain and
stuffed her body into barrels.

As she talked, something clicked for Martin and Lucie.

In April, the body of a young woman had been found near the zoo,
hidden in two construction barrels laid end to end. The body was so
decomposed the girl could not be identified. Her prints had been sent to
the FBI lab in Washington.

Was the body the girl, Angel, who had disappeared?

It was. Angel was identified through her medical records. She had
been reported missing in Elyria; her mother had been searching for her,
following leads across the country.

"We solved a homicide," Lucie said. At least one serial criminal was
off the street.

Elizabeth was a key witness at Durr's trial. She said she had been afraid to come forward while Durr had been free, afraid for her life and for the life of her baby daughter, whom Durr had named Angel. Darryl Durr was convicted of murder and sentenced to death.

Mid-August 1988. The West Park rapist struck again. Another cop's daughter. There was a print, and a break in the case.

Minutes after the rape he had used the ATM card. They were able to get a photo. In the picture from the bank he wore unusual white sunglasses and a denim jacket.

Lucie had Crimestoppers run the bank photo on the evening news. Tips started flooding into the unit. The tips were assigned secret numbers to keep it clean when paying out the reward money. Lucie and her unit followed the leads. Some were impossible to track—a look-alike riding down I-71 two months ago on a motorcycle. But anything could develop.

The detectives jotted their notes on scraps of paper: where was victim when home? Could suspect have already been in the apartment? What were her recent activities? Were there workers in the building? Deadbolt lock. Installed by whom? What time mail delivered? They scribbled notes as information came forth: suspect called one victim back—he had used her card, he complained, not enough money in the account. Indicates he knew victim and had been watching. The crime scene evidence was processed. No breaks. Another victim's boyfriend was going to start his own investigation. A mother called, her daughter not interested in prosecuting.

A tip said the suspect worked for LTV Steel. And owned glasses like the one in the photo. His name was *Gary Stanley*.

Lucie had Stanley's work records checked. She called the personnel department at LTV Steel. She checked the hours that Stanley worked. Where he lived. "Which was right smack in the middle of all the crimes."

Lucie talked to his supervisor. "His boss, who had been his supervisor for ten years and knew him well, looked at the bank photograph and said he was about ninety percent sure it was Stanley." They had enough for a search warrant for his locker at LTV Steel. Lucie went out with a detective from the First District strike force. They didn't find anything. Someone they talked with at the plant said it wasn't uncommon for workers to have more than one locker. "So we really don't know," Lucie concluded.

She subpoenaed all of his employment records. Two of the victims worked at LTV Steel. The only crime that had not occurred on the West Side was right down off Fleet Avenue. Right by LTV. Right in that area. "Everything really fits," Lucie said.

Pat Blackmon said, "You've got him. You've got him." She was convinced. "I'll give you a warrant for him right now." She knew Lucie's hunches were good. Lucie picked a time when he would be at work, when his wife would be at home to let them in. Otherwise they would have to break down the door.

Lucie took everyone working that shift, Markus-Mace, Cipo, Zeb, Martin.

Markus-Mace found the glasses. The same distinctive glasses in the bank photo. They had thick white frames with square slots in the arms. Stanley came home from work in the midst of the search. He said he had bought them three or four years ago.

They arrested him. His wife was upset. "No, no, no," she kept saying.

But Lucie had more than enough to get him indicted.

The detectives interviewed his neighbors. His brother called Lucie. Lucie told him she was being as fair and thorough as she could be. "We've got a lot of crimes here, and we've got a lot of evidence that points to him. We have to get this straightened out, and that's what we're going to do."

Lucie made a plus column and a minus column. Plus: sunglasses. Minus: looks older. Plus: Stanley admitted going to the bars, alone. Partying. Some victims had frequented bars, gone home, fallen asleep, and then been attacked.

His prints didn't match any of the prints they had picked up at the crime scenes. Which didn't mean anything. "We don't know whose prints we have," Lucie said. She arranged a couple of lineups. "But the victims had told us they didn't get a very good look at the person." The lineups were a last resort. She didn't think the victims would be able to pick the person in the lineup. No one picked Stanley.

Lucie began to get a feeling that maybe he didn't do it. Her detectives were grumbling that it wasn't him. Zeb thought he looked too old. Lucie thought the evidence still weighed in favor of holding him.

"Number one, what you *think* is not good enough. You can't just say, 'I don't think it's him' and discount all the stuff that pointed to him. That's irresponsible. What if he is the guy?"

Pat Blackmon said, "It's him. It's him. Let it go, Lucie—you got him."

Lucie just couldn't be satisfied with that. Everything was circumstantial. "We don't have that one positive thing that satisfies me. If we've got the wrong guy, not only have we screwed this guy up—the right guy is still out there."

Lucie decided the only thing that was going to satisfy her was a DNA test. She obtained a court order for a blood test. She walked Stanley over to the doctor's. Let the DNA be the deciding factor.

She decided to let him go in the meantime. She couldn't keep him in jail for two months. The DNA test would take a long time. There were only a few labs in the country to process the sample.

She called Pat and told her, "I'm letting him go and I'm not charging him with anything. I just can't." But she was nervous. It might be him.

On September 24, thirty-six-year-old *Gabriela Diaz* was watching television with her two children. He entered. He had leaned one of the children's bicycles against the house and pried open a window. It was unbelievable how swift he was. Gabriela heard a noise at the kitchen and then he was there. He seemed like a superman, as if he had flown in. He had a black mask over his face with openings for the eyes and mouth, a foot-long pipe in his hands and a knife in his pocket. The pipe was a metal blue-gray rod with a V-shaped point at the end. It was like nothing Gabriela had ever seen, and she was sure it could easily kill someone.

He hit her with it. He grabbed her two children and put them in a closet and continued beating her with his fists, cursing at her and threatening to kill her children. He ripped a macramé planter right out of the ceiling and tied her to the bed with the ropes. Gagging her with one of her children's pajama bottoms, he raped her and ransacked the house, repeatedly asking her where her gun was, saying he wanted to put her out of her misery. He drove off in her car.

The Creepwalker had hit again. Markus-Mace and Cipo decided not even to try to interview her children. They had watched their mother being beaten. "What would be the point," Markus-Mace said. "She had done a fine job on her own telling us her ordeal." And she had given them a big break. When he first attacked her, she yanked off his mask and caught a glimpse of his face. "She was a fighter."

He was light-complected, Gabriela said, with a thick voice and a thin mouth, a skinny nose. He had an unclean smell, as if he didn't bathe.

Four days after Gabriela was raped, at one-twenty in the morning, a patrol car observed a car speeding on East Seventieth, just a short distance from the Dunham Tavern Museum, a nineteenth-century building and historic landmark at the top of the Midtown Corridor. The driver sped onto Euclid; the patrol officers activated their red and blue light and followed. The driver took off, whizzing northbound on East 71, westbound on Chester. The cops ran the plate through radio, and the dispatcher informed them that the vehicle was stolen and was concerned with an aggravated burglary, felonious assault, and rape. It was Gabriela Diaz's car.

The rapist spun into a U-turn and screeched off in the opposite direction. The zone car zoomed ahead, one officer continually broadcasting their location over the radio, eastbound on Chester, northbound on East Seventy-ninth. The suspect careened west on Decker, firing a shot at the officers.

The police raced toward East 71, yelling "Shots fired" into the mike. The suspect pumped out two more rounds as he drove past an abandoned brick building, and the Eliza Bryant Center. The officer driving aimed his gun, shooting diagonally across the intersection. The suspect hit the gas, circling and looping through the city blocks, along Wade Park, north on East Seventy-ninth, over to East Seventy-first, onto Superior, down East Seventy-fourth, where he slammed into a bus parked in front of the Come Home Baptist Church. He leapt out of the car and raced west through yards along Lockyear, carrying a small blue steel revolver.

He escaped.

The West Park rapist investigation continued. They checked suspects with B & E arrests and suspects with drugs. He'd asked a victim for drugs.

Superintendent Victor Kovacic, head of SIU, followed the case with increased interest. One of the victims was the daughter of a detective in SIU. Kovacic put a large map on the wall marking all the locations of the rapes. He was determined to find the West Park rapist. Like Lucie's unit, Kovacic's units were centralized. The evidence from all crimes in every district went through his forensic lab. That was the advantage of having a centralized unit.

The pressure to catch him was becoming unbelievable. Internally personalities clashed. Competition increased under stress. Everybody wanted this guy.

There had been two rapes near Chief Howard Rudolph's home. He was Lucie's new chief. He had taken Hanton's position in April of 1986 and was weathering his own pressures.

A drug scandal exploded, eventually making national news. In 1985, when Rudolph was head of narcotics, narcotics detectives made the biggest drug bust in Ohio history, netting a Florida supplier. The public's accolades were short-lived. The narcotics unit's informant, Arthur Feckner, claimed that the detectives had sanctioned his running a drug house to raise the nearly half a million dollars they needed to finance the Florida sting. An undertermined amount of money from the operation, perhaps several hundred thousand dollars, was missing—and was never recovered. Drug trafficking indictments were brought against five of the narcotics officers, but the judge dismissed the case. Feckner also claimed that one of the narcotics detectives told him that the whole operation was engineered to make Rudolph chief.

"Howard Rudolph did get to be chief," Lucie commented. "The saddest thing was, it put a horrible cloud over the Cleveland Police Department. We all looked like fools. Howie Rudolph, let's face it, was in charge at the time—used at best extremely poor judgment."

Rudolph didn't talk to Lucie much, not directly. Word got to her though. Lucie heard rumors that Rudolph was threatening to disband her unit if she didn't catch the West Park rapist.

"They just want anybody. Get somebody. You can't do that. I just keep plugging along. We are on the news every day. All the time. Then when he hits again—the calls come. Do you have him yet? Do you have him yet?"

Everybody felt the pressure to catch the West Park rapist. But catching him was Lucie's responsibility. The task of making sure no one screwed up the investigation or tainted any aspect fell on her shoulders.

Kosits, now Lucie's commanding officer, thought Rudolph would use Lucie when he needed to use her, but he didn't think the chief liked her. "I think the only reason he left her alone was because of Hanton. Because he respected Hanton, and in fact Hanton got Rudolph the chief's job. I think that's the only thing that saved Lucie."

As Lucie's unit tracked the West Park rapist, Creepwalker, and over 1,500 other cases, plus reviewing 5,000 referrals from the Department of Human Services, the cutbacks continued.

They started in the summer of 1987. By the fall of 1988, Lucie was down to eight detectives officially. Zeb recalled at one point there were only six detectives. Meanwhile, sex crimes increased by 15 percent during that year. The detectives could not keep up with their policy of interviewing rape victims within twenty-four hours of the crime report. Interviewing children took twice as much time. And children comprised half of all sex crimes victims. Often they were down to two cars, one for Lucie and one for all the other detectives. They had a hard time getting supplies, like medical forms. They had to show up at the prosecutor's office with their notes written on scraps of paper. "Makes you look like an ass," said one detective. Then the prosecutors thought they were lazy. Prosecutors had complained about the unit's performance on investigations.

But at city hall, drugs were the top concern. Councilman John E. Barnes prepared a resolution calling for an additional fifty to sixty cops to be added to narcotics. "Drug crimes are our priority," Barnes said. "When you curtail drug crimes you will see rapes go down." Marty Flask, now lieutenant in charge of narcotics, didn't see the reasoning in that theory. He said no connection could be drawn between drugs and sex crimes. Despite the problems the sex crimes unit faced, Chief Rudolph had agreed to add ten detectives to the narcotics unit by February.

Lucie went to Kosits, but there wasn't anything he could do for her, except sympathize. He knew she couldn't get the job done with the cuts.

As her commander, Kosits took his marching orders from Chief Rudolph. He didn't question why. But Kosits thought the cuts to her unit had been done on a personal level. They devastated her. And he knew there was animosity even among Lucie's so-called friends, some of Kosits's own core group, which included Lucie. When they needed something, they wouldn't hesitate to go to her; but there were always snide remarks made behind her back. There were a lot of people who would have loved to see Lucie fall.

They were no closer to catching Creepwalker or the West Park rapist or even knowing who they were. Lucie was more and more concerned. She utilized her extensive network within the department. Then she went further. She called *Clint Decker.*

Clint Decker was young and black, with a velvet voice and liquid brown eyes. He wore a black leather wide-brimmed hat; his smile glowed. He was exceedingly polite, referring to suspects as gentlemen, holding doors open for women. Confronted with danger, he changed in an instant. His clothing concealed a .357 Magnum, his quiet manner a will of steel.

When he was not disguising his identity, he announced himself with a James Bond flair. Clint Decker. Bounty hunter.

Gangs dominated the projects where he grew up. "They held up a preacher and kicked him over a lousy fifty dollars." Decker knew who did it. One day Bigfoot George Deli and two other officers stopped and talked to him. Decker decided to tell them who the assailants were. They told him there might be a reward. Then they suggested he go to a private police school and become a bounty hunter.

He took their advice and attended fifteen months of classes, studying a curriculum similar to the police academy's. He became a bounty hunter. He was twenty-one years old.

He worked for Thomas McGuire, bail bondsman. The work was free-lance. No health coverage, no guaranteed salary. If someone jumped bail, and about 20 percent did, McGuire called in Decker, and if Decker was successful in returning the person, McGuire paid him a commission.

The work made Decker feel good inside. "You getting them creeps off the streets. You never know when it might happen to you. It might happen to someone in your family." Clint's mother was his main support.

Decker never had to shoot anybody. "I try not to. No matter what they do, I don't think you should take a human life unless they are about to take yours." With a hint of Steve McQueen, he added, "We like to bring them in alive."

Decker volunteered his time working for police and the FBI. Lucie considered Decker a friend, a "real, nice guy." Some of the bounty hunters were goofy, but Clint was bright and articulate. Street savvy was his stock in trade. Lucie called him from time to time just to keep up her street contacts. She knew his work was dangerous, that he often got shot at. People ran him off the road and took contracts out on him. What a helluva way to make a living.

She told him about the Creepwalker and the West Park rapist. These guys were thieves as well as rapists. Someone might know something. Rapists had been known to brag. But Clint got nowhere on the West Park rapist.

Bigfoot George Deli was working under Roger in the strike force by then, and Dennerll and the strike force and Decker rode around at night trying to catch Creepwalker. He was operating in such a small area they thought eventually they would spot him. Night after night, sometimes in pouring rain, they searched the neighborhood. No luck.

Then, McGuire sent Decker on some business into that area, and Decker picked up information that a man named *Tigue* knew about the rapes. The people in the neighborhood were scared, they wanted the attacks stopped. Decker had grown up with Tigue. Next thing he knew, his luck broke. He ran into him. "Do you want to buy a VCR?" Tigue asked him.

"You're sure you're going to have it?"

"Yeah."

"I'll come back later on and buy one," Decker said. He arranged to meet Tigue in the parking lot of the Sno-White Donut Shop. Decker called Lucie. She notified Roger, and they set up a sting. Bigfoot, Roger, Decker, and Lucie met near the parking lot, and Lucie gave Decker a hundred and fifty dollars to purchase the VCR.

Decker waited in the donut shop parking lot. Tigue didn't show. They decided to call off the sting, but then Decker suggested they ride past Tigue's house. He caught Tigue out in front.

"What happened to the VCR?" Decker asked.

Tigue called *Randall*. Randall brought over the VCR, but he thought that Decker was a policeman.

"Are you still in the business?" Randall asked.

"No," Decker said. "I retired."

Randall agreed to sell him the VCR. He wanted one hundred dollars for it.

"Fifty," Decker bargained.

The deal was struck.

Lucie and the other officers watched as Decker came out of the house and got into his car. They arrested Randall.

Tigue and Randall were charged with aggravated burglary and put in a lineup. None of the rape victims could identify either suspect. One of the victim's friends came forward and said he had seen Tigue breaking into homes. Cipo and Markus-Mace went through the computer and checked the burglaries in the area of the rapes. They found a store that was selling some of the stolen property. Some of the crimes were tied to Tigue and Randall.

There was speculation that Creepwalker worked with other people who robbed the homes while he committed the rapes. But Lucie saw him as a loner. Randall admitted to committing burglaries but insisted he had nothing to do with the rapes. Lucie and the detectives executed a search on Randall's home, but they found no evidence to connect him to the rapes.

On October 15, Creepwalker raped another woman. Lucie formed a task force with Cipo, Markus-Mace, and First District detectives. They met in a computer room down the hall from the sex crimes unit. They shared information; the First District put out a special attention notice for the area of the rapes. The task force members all carried pagers. If a crime report came in that sounded like the rapist, one of them would be called to the scene. Markus-Mace shelled out her own twenty bucks for one. She hated pagers.

Saturday, October 29. Two days before Halloween. Three forty-five in the morning. A *Plain Dealer* carrier, Curtis Beckman, noticed a black man coming down a driveway, carrying a piece of patio furniture. When he saw Beckman, he ran off. Beckman thought that was strange—maybe the man had been trying to break into the home. Beckman called the police.

Fifteen minutes later, a seventy-two-year-old woman heard a scratching at her front door. She turned on her porch light and saw a huge man with a red and yellow mask over his face. A few seconds later, she heard her side window break. She screamed. He ran away. She called the police.

First District officers Alex Farkas and Douglas Regrut answered the call. They saw a man in a car fitting the assailant's description at a nearby gas station. The officers took off after him, lights and siren. The man slammed on the gas and sped onto Route 71. The officers raced in pursuit. The suspect pulled over, jumped out of his car, and fled on foot. The officers raced after him. This time he was caught.

The young man was sweating profusely. His clothing was soaked. He was six foot one and carrying a knife and nunchakus.

None of the sex crimes detectives were called to the scene. The man was interviewed at the First District. His name was Johnnie Lee Knight. His street name was Creepwalker. He was eighteen years old and already had a long record. His last arrest had been in January of 1988. He was sent to a halfway house and in May was permitted weekend passes. That was when the rapes started.

But where was the mask the woman had seen? He didn't have it on when he was arrested. Knight told a sex crimes detective he had put it in his pocket and then kicked it under the seat of the zone car. They called to find out which zone car had conveyed him to the Justice Center and told the district to send the car over immediately. They found the mask right where Knight said it was.

"It was a miracle it was still there," Lucie said, relieved. She looked at it. It was one of those masks that you pull over your head, it had white hairs sticking out of it. Really scary.

When interviewed, Knight explained that he had once attended a "prejudiced" school in Parma and was bitter about his third-grade female teacher who was "prejudiced, as was the white city of Parma."

He was caught by a fluke, Markus-Mace said. But that is the way it usually is. She gave a lot of credit to the zone car officers who caught him.

Gabriela Diaz picked him out of the lineup. Lucie ordered a DNA test from the lab in Maryland. Markus-Mace and Cipo took him to the Thomas F. McCafferty Health Center for the blood sample. He was no longer the agile superman. He walked slowly, confined by shackles and wearing the blue paper pants and shoes given to prisoners when their clothes were confiscated for evidence. He was so big he needed two paper gowns to wrap around him.

His manner was subdued. They escorted him down to the police garage via a special elevator used for conveying prisoners and placed him in their detective car. Usually, Cipo did not let Markus-Mace drive, but this time he did, and he sat in back with Knight. On the way over, Knight asked how his girlfriend was. Hmm, Markus-Mace thought. He is actually showing concern.

Knight's girlfriend called Lucie frequently over the next few months. She was shocked—she had thought Knight was ten years older than he was, closer to her own age. He seemed a nice, caring person. She just couldn't believe her boyfriend had done such horrible things.

Lucie was also surprised Knight was only eighteen. She had pegged him for an older man, the way he calmly ransacked the houses, the expertise with which he committed the burglaries. But when she saw his juvenile record, she realized why he seemed like an expert. He was. Over forty burglaries. He had been caught as a juvenile through a fingerprint match, and after that wore gloves. He had started early and had gone from being a burglar to being a rapist. He had been incarcerated in various places, a hospital, a detention home. The DNA test established a genetic fingerprint linking Knight to one of the rapes. After being found competent to stand trial, he was convicted on twenty-three counts and sentenced to 224 to 545 years. Lucie was very relieved. It would have just been a matter of time, she was certain, before he would have killed somebody.

The West Park Community Council asked Lucie to send someone to speak to them. They were concerned about all the rapes in their area. She sent Mark Hastings. They found him informative and interesting, but were concerned about the cuts in her unit. The group passed a resolution on November 6 and sent copies to Mayor Voinovich and Council President Forbes, urging them to increase Lucie's unit back to its fifteen detectives.

On November 26, the West Park rapist hit again. He had visited the woman's home a month earlier, masturbated by the window at four-thirty in the morning, and then left; she had seen him. Her father, a police captain, started watching the house. But the rapist got in anyway. Like many of the victims, she lived on the first floor.

He entered through the bedroom window, his face covered with a nylon—the holes cut for his eyes. He jumped on her back and straddled her while she slept. He called her by name. He knew the cops had been watching. He held the knife to her throat. He knew her boyfriend had left her earlier that year.

Again, he used the victim's bank card after raping her. This time he was photographed entering the kiosk with a newspaper in front of his face. He had parked his car outside, but the camera caught the car in its view.

Zeb went to the bank. She had to interview customers who had been before and after him in line. It took time getting hold of every person. Someone described the car as a "semirusty American clunker" and added that it was probably a full-size car with a big motor.

After receiving the VHS tape from the First Federal of Lakewood Bank, Hastings met with Robert Dunn of Ameritrust downtown. Dunn was with the bank's security department and could use a machine to take sequential photographs from the tape.

But the grainy picture of the car was too out of focus to discern much. Martin and Hastings drove out to Cleveland's NASA Lewis Research Center and met with Howard Slater.

NASA did everything from motion picture production to video production to typical photo-finish work to scientific work and high-speed imaging. Slater had been at NASA eight or nine years. A transplant from New Jersey, everybody back east thought he'd slowed down too much, and everybody in Cleveland thought he was still too hyper.

Slater had heard about the West Park rapist. He was glad to help. He led Hastings and Martin down a hall lined with large color photos taken in the famous zero-gravity facility. The ATM tape had been played over and over by the police department. It was of very poor quality. It was an extralong play time-lapsed recording, taking images every three seconds.

Slater worked with the tape, but it was no use. Tapes were fine-tuned to the deck they were recorded on. He asked Hastings to see if he could get the original deck from the bank. They brought the deck to Slater.

Slater took the bank's tape deck to the communications lab, located in the basement under the supersonic wind tunnel, where space shuttle designs were tested. Now he had the deck the tape was designed for. It was like putting a key into the right lock. He reproduced the tape and expanded it, about ten seconds in the original lasted about a minute. He slowed it up, step by step. The movements were very smooth. Now he could grab a particular area of interest. The images were fed through a computer, and using Image Pro, off-the-shelf image-processing software, Slater asked the computer: "What's the edges? What's the shape." He wasn't looking for a pretty picture, something to hang on the wall or something that looked correct to the eye.

It was really just pattern recognition and image enhancement. Slater looked on the suspect's jacket, for fabric identification, for a logo. The suspect's hand was up. Slater traced across the arm. It shifted and changed across the wrist. Something that didn't have the same reflection pattern. Slater zoomed in on it. He outlined the edges. It was a watch. "We can't tell you what kind of watch, but it's a metallic watch—that's our best guess." It was added information. The suspect was wearing a ring, but he was not able to tell if it was a wedding ring. He appeared to have a mustache.

He instructed the computer to look at ranges of tonality on the car. All of a sudden rust spots started to appear. Slater was excited.

"Just look at a very select area of contrast range, maybe two tones, and maybe drop everything else out. The image pops up. Now you see patterns, very ragged, strong tones right in this area, that's the wheel well—rust." He found a big tear that showed up in the vinyl top. They had clear identifying marks. The car was a two door, with a light color top, with damage to the right front fender. There were mag wheels on the rear and different wheels on the front.

Hastings and Martin now knew the car was a 1975 Monte Carlo with certain areas of damage. They couldn't get the plate. But it might be enough to spot the car.

Slater felt terrific. To know that he was involved. "That's why I came to work for the government," he said, beaming, "to make a difference, to make an impact and get a real sense of satisfaction." Each night on his way home he found himself driving in the area of the crimes. He didn't live in the area. He was looking for a Monte Carlo with rust spots. He was looking for the West Park rapist.

Superintendent Victor Kovacic was also out of the area where he lived and off duty when he spotted a car he thought looked like the one in the photo. His unit had also enhanced the photo. He had reproduced copies and passed about a hundred and fifty of them around. On December 20, he saw the car in a parking lot. Kovacic circled it. He sketched a drawing of the car, marking the damage. There was a temporary tag in the rear window. He got close enough to record the number.

After tracking down the plate number through a call to police radio he had a name. Ronnie Shelton. He obtained Shelton's Social Security number and went through the records and got a description. It matched the description many of the victims had given.

He notified the sex crimes unit.

Everything started coming in at once. Kovacic had gone back to the scene with a camera, but the car was gone. Lucie sent her detectives over to the apartment building to see if anybody remembered the car.

She knew who they were looking for but not where he was located. Shelton's car was registered to his father's home address. The police were notified to watch the house.

The suburban Brooklyn police department called. "They had arrested this same person for public indecency," Lucie said, "and so we thought, Now, this is our guy." Shelton had had three sets of keys for apartments in the Floridian Apartments Complex when the Brooklyn police had arrested him.

Lucie and Jackie Christ drove out to Shelton's parents. After a day of watching the house, Lucie said, "This is stupid. We've got to do something. We're going to talk to his father." They asked him if he knew where his son was. "I want to talk to him because I think he might have witnessed a crime." There had clearly been some dissension in the family, Lucie observed. The father did not have any information. His son had not lived at home for a long time. He had last lived with a friend off of Fleet Avenue.

No permanent address. A name. A face. A license. Soon prints would be matched to his card on file. But where was he?

Hastings questioned the manager of the apartments. He knew Shelton. He didn't live there, but he came and stayed with a friend. The friend was being evicted and was supposed to move out over the weekend. Lucie was sure Shelton would show up to help with the move. She already had an arrest warrant.

Hastings and Hovan were on the afternoon shift the day that everything came down. Lucie had made arrangements to get them an undercover car. Their orders for the evening were, Sit there.

"Wait for him to come back in the car. If you'll stay there, he'll come back," she insisted. "He's got to help his friend move. He's got to come back. I don't care if you have to stay all weekend. Just go out there and wait."

Lucie didn't feel certain that Shelton was the West Park rapist. But there was definitely more on him than all the others. She felt better about this one.

Hovan was sick as a dog that night, he had a bad sinus infection. He really didn't even want to be at work, but he and Hastings *were* the afternoon shift. The other detectives were working days. He couldn't leave Hastings alone to pick up Shelton. Sick or not, he had to go along. Water was running out of his nose. He looked like Rudolph the Red-Nosed Reindeer. His eyes were bleary. When they arrived, they sat perched in the parking lot of the apartment building. Thank God for Hastings tonight, Hovan thought, because I'm not seeing real well. He couldn't see halfway across the parking lot. It was a dank, rainy night. It seemed like hours to Hovan, but it was actually about half an hour when they saw movement.

They saw a blue Chevy Nova pull into the parking lot. Two males were in the car. As the car passed them, Hastings thought the man in the passenger seat looked like Shelton. When the passenger got out, Mark was sure it was the man in the composite, the man in the photos. He wore a waist-length black leather coat, blue jeans, and high-top white tennis shoes.

Hastings said, "That's him."

"Mark, you're out of your goddamn mind," Hovan sniffled and blurted out, "that ain't Ronnie Shelton."

"I'm telling you it's him. It's him." Hastings was ready to make his move. "It's him." Hastings was behind the wheel. He leaped out of the car.

"Mark, you're gonna blow this whole goddamn thing." Before he knew it, there Shelton was. Guns drawn, they threw him across the hood of the car. Hastings and Hovan were twice Shelton's size.

Hovan saw a marked police car from Brooklyn, coasting into the scene. This "old codger" came walking up. They had Shelton thrown on the car, with their guns in his ear. They were screaming at him. Hovan thought, Well, this is a fiasco, but a fiasco to say the least. From an outsider's point of view, it looked like they were getting ready to assassinate Shelton. They were in an unmarked car, dressed in leisure clothes. Hovan knew they looked like two hit men. He figured, Any smart copper is gonna pull out his gun, shoot, and ask questions later. He sure as hell didn't want to get shot.

But the Brooklyn cop didn't pull out his gun. "Hey, what are you fellas doing?"

Hovan thought, If we were hit men, we could turn around, smoke him, turn away, and he wouldn't know what hit him. "We're detectives." Hovan was more scared than the old copper.

"Who you got there?"

"We got Ronnie Shelton."

"Oh, well, you gotta turn him over to me."

Hovan said, "He's ours."

"You're in my city."

"I don't give a shit if I'm in Chicago," Hovan blared back. "He's ours, we got an arrest warrant for him." They got into a shouting match.

"No." The Brooklyn cop wasn't giving in. "I got a phone call from some Second District detectives today. They told me, if we grab Ronnie Shelton to turn him over to them."

Hovan knew there was in-fighting within the department. Everybody else wanted the recognition. "I'll tell you what"—he punctuated the t's like pin pricks, "I don't give a shit who you talked to. You ain't getting him from me."

"I'm going to have to do something. I'm gonna have to call my chief." The Brooklyn cop persisted.

"I don't care who you talk to, you ain't getting him from me." Hovan thought, Shelton, he don't know what the hell is going on. He doesn't realize that we are the people getting ready to put his ass in the can. Somebody like a Shelton, ain't no way I'm going to turn him over to somebody else to start to question him. They'll screw up our investigation and we're responsible. Lucie'll chop our balls off and have them for supper if we turn Shelton loose.

Shelton told them his car was at his parents'. Hastings went over to the driver of the car Shelton had arrived in and talked to him.

Hastings found out Shelton's car was not at his father's house, it was at West Sixty-eighth street. They drove over and found the car. It was the one caught in the bank photo.

Hastings asked Shelton if he wanted a cigarette. "Marlboros, right?" Hastings ribbed him. Marlboros had been found at one of the crime scenes.

"We hooked his car," Hovan said. "It was like he lived out of his car. It was just a real garbage can. Hastings was with the tow truck and all these people, watching the property so that none of it disappeared. It was a big job.

"As sick as I was," Hovan said, "I stayed in the car and watched him because we had no screen. It was a damned white El Dorado that we got from narcotics."

They brought all the evidence back to the Justice Center. It had to be tagged. "We didn't even get finished that night, we were tagging for two days." There were two sets of binoculars in the front seat, women's bikini underwear and a switchblade, a stiletto-type knife. In the rear was a variety of jewelry, necklaces, rings, and watches. There were numerous flashlights of assorted sizes and shapes. They all worked. Some were Kel lights, which were small and easily concealed. There were numerous VHS videotapes, including *Breaking Away, Back to School, Grease, Super Bowl Bondage,* among others.

A stolen VCR recorder and a boom box were recovered, and they traced them through serial numbers to a house located near two of the rapes. Shelton had a couple of cameras and—a pair of white sunglasses. Ordinary white sunglasses, not the distinctive ones with the square slots.

The trunk of the car was locked. Zeb went down to the police lot with a search warrant. There were more knives, kitchen knives, a jewelry case with an Eisenhower silver dollar and three Susan B. Anthony dollars, and some change. And one black denim zip-up jacket. Zeb recognized the clothing Shelton wore the night he was arrested. Some of the victims had previously described it. Shelton's fingerprints matched the ones recovered from at least six scenes.

They never found the slotted sunglasses. They were, Lucie said, "another great clue that didn't go anyplace."

On December 23, Shelton was interviewed at the jail by Zeb and Martin. Lucie asked Martin to go along, she didn't want Zeb interviewing him alone. Zeb introduced herself. She started on questions about his background.

"Where were you born?" She wanted to put him at ease and get him talking.

California, he replied.

She followed through his history, places where he had lived. He claimed he did carpentry work—remodeling. She thought he seemed a little immature. She surmised that he was hot with the ladies. He was cocky and had a quick temper—he had gotten in many fights over the years. He told her he had lots of girlfriends and that he had normal sexual relations.

Shelton told them he had an injury four years ago—a joist beam had fallen on his head. That he got headaches from the surgery. Zeb felt he was trying for sympathy. He was trying to con them.

He began to incriminate himself on the use of credit cards and indicated he might have problems with drugs, not alcohol.

Martin was looking for something he could pick up on—something that would break him. He was intelligent, sharp. A nice-looking kid. He wasn't a scumbag off the street. Martin detected something and started to ask him about being abused as a child. Shelton broke down and started crying. Bleary-eyed, he wiped a tear from the corner of his eye.

Zeb confronted Shelton with the hard evidence. He denied he raped anyone. She showed him the bank photos. Shelton stared at them and turned pale. He wouldn't talk with them after that.

Lucie walked through her backyard over to John Nolan's. He was having his annual pre-Christmas party. She burst in through the door, carrying her two-dollar anonymous gift to go under the tree. John's aunt, Marge Scheel, enjoyed her nephew's holiday events. She just never knew who she was going to meet, there were always such interesting people— actors, writers, cops. Lights blinked on the tall tree. Music played. People were munching on hors d'oeuvres. Marge was standing near Lucie.

"We got him." Lucie began talking rapidly. "We got the West Park rapist."

Marge's eyes widened.

"Bank photo ... his face covered with a newspaper ... took it to NASA ... printed pictures of the car ... spotted the car ... we had a name ..."

Marge worked in a bank, and now Lucie was saying the breaking lead came from a photo from an ATM machine. Marge was excited.

Lucie's words spilled out. "Went to his father's house ... he hadn't been there ... talked to his father ... apartment house ... he'll come, I know it ..."

Someone brought Lucie a glass of wine. Marge hung on Lucie's words.

"He drove up in another car ... recognized him ... we made the arrest."

With just that little bit of information they solved the case, Marge thought. What good police work. Marge knew about the West Park rapist. The case had been on the news all the time. And her sister, John's mother, lived in the West Park area, where many of the rapes had occurred. Now that worry was gone. And Lucie—she couldn't believe how excited and relieved Lucie seemed.

Lucie sipped her wine. She could take down the color composite in her office. She wouldn't have to wonder every day, Who are you? The longest-running serial rape case in Cleveland history—a case that had burdened her since the second month her unit started—was finally over.

After the holiday, the victims were brought in to make their identification of Shelton. Zeb, Christ, Markus-Mace, and others observed the numerous lineups. Some, who had never gotten a good look at him, picked out his voice. Others identified him right away. One of them wasn't sure. It was just a feeling—but she picked out Shelton. After leaving the room without making a choice, another victim said, "It was number one, wasn't it." She hadn't wanted to say it while she was in the room with the prosecutor and the defense attorney.

Little by little, the case locked into place. Zeb still followed leads down and interviewed roommates and others pertinent to the case. Lucie got wind of the fact that Ross Santamaria had seen Shelton as a client at some point. She met with Santamaria and asked him to share any insights he could without violating professional confidentiality. She also asked him to check the dates that he had seen Shelton. That could place Shelton in Cleveland at the times of certain crimes. She was trying to figure out where Shelton was when; he had used his parents' address on his driver's license and other records, even when he was living in Colorado.

Lucie went over to the lab with a list of the crimes she thought were attributable to Shelton and asked Joe Serowik, in the forensic unit, to go through the evidence and the rape kits. "Look at what we've got. See if they're good enough to submit for DNA." For a good test, the specimen had to have sperm in it, not just seminal fluid. Lucie had had one case where the perpetrator was too young to produce sperm in the seminal fluid. The specimens were sent off to Maryland to Cellmark Diagnostic Laboratories. Stanley was cleared through the DNA test. Shelton was not. He matched.

It was a media blitz. Everyone was taking credit, now that he was caught. "It wasn't a fluke," Lucie said. "It was a lot of goddamn hard work. Sure, there's not an investigation in the world where luck doesn't play a part. Sometimes you make your luck. It was fortunate that Vic Kovacic spotted the car. He did at least call my office."

Lucie wasn't about to tell reporters the problems she was having with the prosecutor on the Shelton case. Assistant County Prosecutor Timothy J. McGinty criticized Lucie. A lot of people did. Why didn't you catch him sooner. Now McGinty was going to run the show. McGinty would go for the highest sentencing he could get. A record number of charges.

"It was clearly overkill. We had him, dead bang." Lucie was concerned about the victims. By the time the case came to trial, it would be six years since some of the women had been raped.

Lucie tried to suggest to McGinty that Shelton cooperate with the FBI. Over the last ten years, the FBI had been compiling data on serial murderers and rapists from all over the country. The data was beginning to provide new insights into the mind of the criminal and new tools for investigating serial crimes. It could mean faster apprehension of serial rapists like Shelton. His attorney had indicated that he would be interested in a plea. "My feeling was, and I may be wrong, but if Shelton would plea and we could make sure that he never got out of jail, but if we kept him receptive to the idea of interviewing him, it would be very beneficial."

McGinty just refused.

McGinty was telling her things that he was going to do and how they were going to be done. He had decided to run the investigation. Lucie had to ask him to leave her office. She said, "Nobody talks to me in my office like that." She found him to be very difficult. She finally said, "Here's the investigation. Do whatever you want."

Lucie often dropped by trials to watch, but she didn't go to Shelton's trial.

Over 230 counts had been charged. Thirty victims were involved for crimes occurring over a period of six years. The trial was so packed, a special room was set aside for reporters. The trial was videotaped and the tape played in the reporters' room as they jotted down notes. Cameramen and technicians milled around. Zeb stayed outside with the victims. She'd busted her butt on the case, handling all her other investigations as well as the Shelton cases. Without a partner most of the time. Now she calmed the witnesses, gave them support, answered their questions. She told them, "If you need to cry, cry. I'm not telling you to do that, but if that happens, it happens. This is your chance to tell everybody what he did to you."

Zeb counted twenty-five Cleveland cases out of the thirty. She thought she had worked on seventeen of them. There were so many victims. Zeb didn't care about who took credit for it. "Give me my paycheck. Hey, he was caught, I don't care who says what. It's finished. I don't have to hear about him anymore." That's what she was happy about.

Detective Matuszny sat at the prosecutor's table. It was a long and tedious trial. Channel 8 news reported, "Shelton pleaded not guilty by reason of insanity. The psychiatrist is expected to testify next week that Shelton suffers from compulsive rape syndrome, a disorder not widely recognized in the mental health field."

Lucie laughed. Compulsive rape syndrome. "Cops call it career criminal."

Shelton was convicted. A few counts were dropped. The jury found him guilty of aggravated burglary, aggravated robbery, felonious assault, gross sexual imposition, intimidation of a crime victim, interfering with telephone messages, rape, and theft. A total of 219 counts. He was sentenced to 3,195 years.

The victims formed their own ongoing support group.

Long after the case was over, Lucie was still not convinced it had been handled properly. She felt the victims had been manipulated. "I think we had enough, we could have gone in and gotten a very substantial plea. True, it might have knocked off two hundred years. What difference does it make. After fifteen, he can ask for parole anyway." When the parole hearing came up, the prosecutor could say, we had x number of charges we didn't pursue because of this. The parole board would be fully aware that there were other victims.

Shelton appealed on June 27, 1991. The Eighth District Court of Appeals ruled on his case. One area of the appeal charged prosecutorial misconduct had prejudiced the case. Specifically, the treatment of the defense expert, Dr. Emanuel Tanay. McGinty called him E.T. and injected his own opinions about Dr. Tanay's character.

The judges found that the case had been proved "in light of the overwhelming evidence of guilt." However, they found that "the prosecutor's egregious conduct and disregard for established Constitutional values and guarantees would have worked a great public and judicial disservice by requiring all thirty victims to relive the horrors of their individual criminal attacks as a result of a new trial."

Lucie had been so afraid that kind of thing would happen. The thought horrified her. "If they had overturned it—can you imagine. God."

25

UNDERMINED

June 1990. Lieutenant Wayne Torok walked into Lucie's office. Torok's gold badge reflected the overhead fluorescent light. His bearing was military; he had chosen to wear his uniform—starched, short-sleeved white shirt and dark blue pants. He was tall, lean, fit. "Hi, Lucie," he said.

Torok was in charge of field inspection. One of his jobs was investigating administrative screwups.

"The chief asked me to look into the workload." His deep voice was smooth and resonant.

Lucie was wide-eyed. "What are we doing?" she asked. It was obvious to her the chief thought she was lying about the number of investigations she had. Oh, they wouldn't come right out and say that was what this was about, but obviously they didn't believe her. Why else would Wayne be standing in her office?

The reality was she couldn't get the department to put two walls up for an interview room. She'd written about a half-dozen reports saying: You know, we can't treat victims this way. Detectives can't concentrate amidst chaos, expecting people to talk.

Lucie thought, Do they care? Hell no, they don't care.

Lucie had been moved out of her own office nine months earlier, and the arson unit moved into her office; she moved into what had been her unit's interview room. She was left with only six detectives for nine months of the year. How were they supposed to handle 1,600 investigations? There were enough investigations to keep fifteen detectives overloaded with work—when she had them, when detectives weren't snatched away and detailed out of her unit.

The humor was bleak in the sex crimes office. Tim Anderson said, "Hey, we've been cut by a third. I've got an idea. Every third victim that calls, hang up."

The community was pressuring for more cops on the street, an issue that came up with the change of each new administration. All the specialized units were getting cut. The press got wind of the cuts.

A reporter called Lucie, asking, "I hear you're really swamped with work."

She didn't know where he'd gotten his information. "We're busy."

"I hear you've lost a lot of people," he pried.

"I've lost a few," she said. The department had gagged officers from talking about the cutbacks.

"Are you going to talk to me about it?" the reporter pressed.

Lucie stopped the interview. "You'll have to talk to Commander Morales."

After she hung up, she called her immediate superior, Angel Morales, commander of the bureau of special investigations. Morales asked Lucie to work up some figures for him. For some reason, the first two weeks of June had double the usual number of crimes. It was just a fluke, it happened every once in a while. "It puts the stats up unbelievably," Lucie said.

Morales wanted the information that day.

"OK, we'll do it today, but it's been real busy. They want them accurate." She sent the commander the figures.

"Well, they were horrified," Lucie exclaimed. Especially when she gave them comparable figures for the year before. She knew it was way up. She tried to explain. "I know it's going to even out."

Lucie figured they powwowed around about whether or not to talk to the media. Later, Marty Flask called her. He was now working in the chief's office. "The chief wants you to do the interview," he told her. "Do the best you can. We have no choice. Don't lie, but if there's any way you can …"

"Don't worry," Lucie assured him.

Lucie thought she whitewashed it pretty well. Yeah, they were busy. But it would level out. She didn't even say how many people she had lost. She really didn't say all the stuff she could have, like, "Heh! this is what they really think about women and children."

But here was Torok, with his sergeant, in her office. She had whitewashed the cutback issue. She kept it low-key. But apparently not low enough.

"I talked to Commander Morales before we came down here," Torok told her.

"What did he say?" Lucie said.

"He said, 'She keeps awfully good records.'"

"Well, you know, obviously you don't believe my activity reports."

"It's not that he doesn't," Wayne countered.

"Yeah, sure." She flushed crimson. She was defensive. This was an attack on her integrity. She took the investigation personally.

On a state and national level, Lucie was at the pinnacle of her career. In 1987, FBI Supervisory Special Agent Ken Lanning had sponsored a conference for people he considered the fifty top experts in the child pornography field. He chose Lucie as one of the participants. The group gathered at the Xerox Center in Leesburg, Virginia: each expert made presentations, and they all shared information.

In 1989, Lucie was given a prestigious appointment to the Children's Trust Fund, a statutory board that oversaw child-abuse prevention funding for the entire state. She was appointed by Governor Richard F. Celeste, under the sponsorship of Senator Lee I. Fisher, who in 1991 became Ohio's attorney general. Gerda Freedheim, Lucie's colleague and friend from IFSAP, recommended her; Freedheim was on the local advisory board. Every other month Lucie traveled to Columbus for the meetings with state representatives and senators and other Trust Fund members. The Trust Fund was the largest funding source in Ohio; in 1991 available funds totaled over two million dollars.

But on a city level, Lucie felt she was in a more tenuous position. A new mayor—Michael R. White—had been elected. He had appointed a new chief, Edward Kovacic. Voinovich had always been supportive of her, so she had felt somewhat protected even under Chief Rudolph. Now, she didn't know what to expect.

About a year before the investigation, under Chief Rudolph's administration, she had lost Detective Markus-Mace. One of the commanders in the chief's office had called Markus-Mace at home. "How would you like to come and work for us?" he said.

"I'm happy where I'm at," she answered.

"We need somebody up here," the commander said.

"Can I think about it?" Markus-Mace didn't know what to do. She figured, it's one of the commanders from the chief's office, how can you say no? She talked to her husband. "What the hell am I going to do?"

He told her she couldn't say no.

"But I'm happy, I have a good partner. I like what I'm doing."

Markus-Mace received the call on a Friday. On Monday morning she was gone. She was working for the chief's command staff.

Markus-Mace asked the commander who had called her, Who's going to tell my supervisor, Lieutenant Duvall?

He answered, Now, this is between you and me. Keep your mouth shut. Then he told her he would take care of it.

No one told Lucie the truth. She believed Markus-Mace wanted to leave the sex crimes unit.

Rumors built in the unit.

The detectives grumbled. Why did she let her superiors take detectives out of the unit? Homicide didn't lose as many. How come they have more detectives and we have the bigger caseload? How come we don't get any equipment? Any cars? Detectives blamed Lucie, she was their boss. Talk was—the chief didn't like her. Morale was low.

Lucie was being undermined. Was it a power play to oust her as lieutenant-in-charge of a specialized high-profile unit? No matter how many years she had on the job, nor how much expertise she had developed, how much state and national recognition she had received—she could be transferred at any time back out to a district to supervise a platoon.

But Lucie fought for her detectives. In the fall, she had written a memo saying in part, "Investigation of felony sex crimes and child abuse is frustrating, complicated, and depressing. Few officers are willing to conduct these types of investigations, and even fewer possess the personal traits necessary to deal with the traumatized victims of these sensitive crimes and remain objective and thorough in their work. The unit has members who have remained dedicated and hard-working despite the continual lack of vehicles and equipment. As a supervisor, I am concerned that this added burden increases the rate of burnout and stress in those officers—officers who have developed considerable expertise in this field."

Dee Fragomeni brought her own son's toys in to use in interviewing children. "We had nothing here. With children, you have to get down on the floor and color and play house, you have to gain their trust." When they went out to crime scenes, they often had to buy their own film to take pictures. Dee didn't blame the problems on Lucie. She appreciated Lucie's backing of her when questions came down from the top brass. "She knows how I work. You need to know that you're working for someone who has backbone and is able to stand up to whoever—even if it's the chief or the mayor." Lucie would check before just reprimanding. "I would think it's hard being Lucie Duvall," Dee reflected. "She's got to put up with a lot of shit, not only from us, but she's gotta take it from all kinds of directions."

If there was ever a time Torok felt like the big bad meanie this was it. He and Lucie had made sergeant the same year and had been rookie sergeants in the Fifth District together. Their job was supervising the administrative functions of the platoons.

Torok knew the attitude of most policemen: women were just there to collect the paycheck. Women didn't view police work as a career. Torok himself felt the ultimate responsibility fell on the man to take care of the family. "The husband views the job in a different light. This gives meaning to his life." That was his belief when he met Lucie.

But Lucie impressed him. What struck him the most—not to put the other guys down—was that Lucie went above and beyond what was the normal course of business.

Maybe she was trying to prove herself to him, Torok didn't know her at all well, but she obviously wanted to do a good job. Because she was a woman her behavior made a greater impression on him. More than anything, he thought, she's intent upon doing the right thing.

Over the years Torok had periodic contact with Lucie—on a Hi, how are you basis—but not much more. Now he had to deliver her a horrible professional blow. Despite the impression she had made on him during their few brief meetings, he could not refuse the direct order of the new chief, Edward P. Kovacic.

Torok had conducted smaller investigations, where officers were working part-time without permission, minor violations of departmental rules. But this was the first time he had to investigate an officer of equal rank, or an officer in charge of a unit. Lucie was both. The stress of having to investigate a fellow officer weighed heavily on him. Have I changed to the point where the chief is sending me down to investigate her as a head hunter? To find something wrong so the chief will have her head on a platter?

"Here's the assignment books," Lucie said. "We'll go through them line by line."

After a cursory look at the records during the first day Torok mapped out a plan. He called Marty Flask, who served as Torok's liaison to the chief. "I'll give the chief a statistical overview of the personnel that she had at the time, the number of arrests, the number of clearances, the number of reports, compare the two frames. Ask the chief if this will be what he wants, because anything else would be more arbitrary. If you want to get into, Is she doing a good job, what's a good job? It's all relative—more of a personal opinion." Torok was protecting himself. He didn't relish getting into that trap, having heard all the rumors that were floating around. He set out to do his own job.

Torok watched Lucie as they went over her records. He saw fear in her eyes.

Lieutenant Flask talked to the chief and told Torok his plan was sufficient. Torok breathed a sigh of relief. Now he knew the format in which he could work.

But even though he knew he was going to give a strictly impartial, unemotional, unbiased report to the chief on the data, there was no way for Lucie to know that. He looked in her eyes. Lucie was not relieved.

He wanted to say, This woman doesn't deserve this. But he didn't. He continued his job.

Torok brought his sergeant with him. The sergeant was more computer literate. He worked on the graphs, statistics, and charts, the year-to-year comparison, percentage changes. Torok would write the written part of the report.

Lucie was extremely upset. She met Pat Blackmon at the Olive Garden. Pat was busy campaigning for a position as judge; she wanted to become the first black woman judge on the court of appeals. Usually they had fun together. Often they went to the symphony or a play.

The point was to clear their minds and have a good time. But now Lucie seemed devastated.

"They think I go home at night and dream up these people," Lucie stated in complete frustration. "The work is there."

Pat wondered if this move against Lucie was coming from the prosecutor's office. It was so uncalled for, so unnecessary. It was low-down sneaky garbage.

Torok's sergeant was very cold, very hard, very statistical. As the second day proceeded, poring over the books, case by case, Torok looked up and saw tears well up in Lucie's eyes. She sat across from him. She tried to break the ice. "I'm guilty," she said. "Type out the confession. I'll sign it." Her hands moved nervously, her cheeks and neck flushed red.

Torok watched the tension build in her each day. She was terribly distraught. They worked over the weekend.

"How much personnel did you have at this time?" Torok's sergeant asked.

She explained very matter-of-factly what the unit had done.

Torok tried to be a little lighter, but it seemed the lighter he tried to be, the heavier his sergeant got. Lucie was getting mixed signals. He felt like the grand inquisitor.

There were a lot of things he and his sergeant didn't understand. Lucie explained the procedures and policies for handling the volume of suspects and referrals that came from county on cases of possible criminal child abuse. Her voice cracked with emotion under the strain.

She had never felt more defensive. She was scrupulous about her records. If they were concerned, why hadn't they come down and talked to her. Give her the benefit of the doubt. Why don't they say, If these stats are right, this woman is overwhelmed. Let's give somebody some support, but oh-h no-o that's not the way the police department works. Lucie was bitter.

Women weren't going to be given their due. Talk in the ladies room among policewomen was women will never get anywhere under this administration.

Lucie's friend Ron Kosits had been her commander during the Shelton case under Chief Rudolph's administration. When Kosits had become commander of the bureau, he had twenty-six units and 452 people under his command. Lucie was the only lieutenant he didn't replace. When he was trying to decide whether to centralize the bureau he asked Lucie, "Among all the other things you're doing, how'd you like to do a little research for me?" Lucie said sure. She helped Kosits put together a plan for reconstruction of the bureau. "She had excellent ideas I didn't even think of. That is the type of person she is." He knew she scared a lot of people. If they felt threatened by her, fine. He thought she was an ideal role model because of her drive, knowledge, and abilities. If he had a dozen people like her, there wouldn't be anything he couldn't get done.

Now Kosits encouraged Lucie. She could handle the pressure. He thought the department was hitting bottom. He called it retrenchment management. You could only cut back so far. He saw the new police administration as being very weak, even though he thought of the chief as a friend. "I don't think Kovacic can handle the job, and I don't know if he's trying," he said with a sad frustration in his voice.

In spite of what Lucie was going through he didn't think she'd want to do anything else. Kosits knew that she could, and she'd had outside offers. "She always comes up with an excuse not to take it. She loves being a cop."

Lucie went out to lunch with Bob Cermak and was on the verge of tears. Under normal circumstances, Cermak felt that Lucie dealt with frustration very well. But this was too much. First, her unit was cut, and now, to have her integrity challenged. She just didn't know what to do anymore. "I was just a shoulder to cry on and somebody to talk to and vent her frustrations with," he said. "I don't think I did any good, but at least I listened.

"The bureau of inspection isn't like internal affairs—handling serious criminal accusations. But it doesn't mean that the inspection unit can't screw up your career, 'cause they can. They could conduct an investigation that could ultimately destroy you for the rest of your career."

Cermak thought the investigation was a crock of shit. The straw that broke the camel's back. Lucie was so flustered. There was nothing she could do to control it. It made no sense to Cermak; he was also frustrated with the new chief. They both talked about quitting.

Torok's investigation was complete. The three-day grilling was over. He tossed the five-page report on the chief's desk. He didn't give the chief a glowing report. What he gave him was statistical data. Numbers don't lie.

The chief looked at the report and asked Torok, Aside from this, what is your opinion?

"Well, Chief, I think she's doing a hell of a job. You might be able to find somebody in the police department to replace her, there are other qualified supervisors, but it would take you probably five to seven years to put somebody into that position. They would have to be as dedicated as her in seeking out the knowledge to educate themselves about that position to get to the point where she is now. Could someone go in there and do the job? Yes. Could it be done as well? No."

Flask backed Torok, and Torok felt relieved. Flask had known Lucie longer. Torok didn't know Lucie personally, she might have all sorts of character defects, he wouldn't know. But from what he had seen, he liked her as a person and as a police officer, and that was a combination he hadn't run across often.

It would be over a month before Lucie would hear anything of the results. Even then the report would be confidential. She would never see it. Torok couldn't tell Lucie anything. But he had renewed respect for her. The success of her unit was based upon her leadership. He got the same impression he'd gotten years before. She wants to do the right thing because it's the right thing to do. Period.

26

THE ETERNAL BELIEVER

Chief Kovacic never talked to Lucie about the investigation, but within a few months her unit was back up to its full complement of fifteen detectives, though one each month was detailed to the jail unit—while their cases sat, unattended, on their desks.

Torok was made lieutenant in charge of a new unit—youth gangs. He had to set up the unit from scratch—much as Lucie had done. Now he asked her for advice. Lucie was happy to help. Upset as she had been about the investigation, she certainly didn't hold it against Torok. She liked him. And she understood the chain of command.

Chief Kovacic began establishing a cordial working relationship with Lucie. He took her with him to community programs and asked her to speak to the men and women of the local naval reserve about rape avoidance. Lucie was impressed with the way he related to community groups; he seemed genuinely concerned. Lucie took the relationship with Kovacic in stride. Well, she thought, if he felt he had to do that investigation, at least he was willing to accept Torok's report.

At the opening ceremonies of Stop Rape Month, a representative from Mayor White's office gave a speech citing Lucie's national reputation.

Lucie talked to Chief Kovacic about an issue she had become very concerned with—date rape. It was an issue many people misunderstood. She knew some of her own detectives didn't consider date rapes "legitimate" crimes. Lucie explained to Kovacic, "If a man and woman go out on a date, they have dinner, drinks, they go dancing—there is an emotional impetus. But if the woman doesn't want to take it further, if she doesn't want to have sexual contact and the man persists, then the emotional impetus stops—and sexual contact becomes a control issue." She told the chief that victims describe how the man suddenly changes, a Jekyll and Hyde transformation from someone they trusted to someone threatening, cold, violent.

"If everything goes well on a date," Lucie told him, "the woman doesn't go to the emergency room at the end of the night. That's how I look at it."

Lucie worked on bringing the issue of acquaintance rape to the public, doing radio shows and conducting training seminars for university security forces. Big campuses had independent police forces, they handled their own investigations but were not trained specifically about sexual assaults. "Historically, universities have back-burnered acquaintance rape," Lucie said. Roger Dennerll, now director of public safety at Bowling Green State University, arranged for Lucie to address their officers. She explained the law, how acquaintance and stranger rape investigations differed, and what the needs of the victims were.

She chaired the rape committee of the Task Force on Violent Crime, a citywide organization. Their current campaign was an awareness drive about date rape.

Lucie walked into the Justice Center conference room for the monthly meeting. Ex-prosecutor Tom Buford served on the committee. He and Lucie had conducted many organized crime raids together. He had handled numerous rape cases while working in the county prosecutor's office—and he had gotten to the point where he hoped for a murder case. Murder victims were out of their agony. When he was a prosecutor, there was no centralized sex crimes squad, and cases were often inadequately prepared. To say the least. He was glad Lucie was running the unit. He was now a civil attorney, but his commitment to helping rape victims continued.

People walked through the conference room. The committee member from Witness/Victim apologized to Lucie—she was too swamped to attend. A police officer in uniform walked by.

"Do you want to come to the meeting?" Lucie teased.

"My idea is to transport them all in a microwave bus," he grinned. "By the time they get to prison, they'll be real small. Or tie 'em in a room and give the victim a baseball bat. You don't want my ideas."

"I like that idea," Lucie said, laughing.

She called the meeting to order. She had a lot of experience chairing meetings. She believed meetings should last one hour or less—that way people were willing to come.

They planned billboards for buses, videotaped public service announcements, and a brochure. The Cleveland Institute of Arts video class volunteered to do the tapes as a project. Dennis Sadowksi, the director of public information for the task force, Lucie, and Buford discussed the slogan: Dinner Plus Drinks ≠ Sex. Date Rape Is a Felony.

Lucie preferred the term acquaintance rape. Date rape conjured up a relationship in progress. "That's not the majority of cases. It's often an acquaintance situation—the victim says, 'Yeah, I saw him at the bar a couple of times, I saw him in the student union, he knew some friends of mine.'"

But for the purposes of a public awareness campaign using billboards on buses, the term acquaintance rape wouldn't work. "The bus would be gone, and people would be still trying to read the message," Lucie joked. She was always practical.

The only problem was funding. They needed twelve thousand dollars for the campaign. They discussed the possibilities—which groups and corporations to approach.

"We are going to put date rape on the map," Lucie said. She laughed lightly, but her intent was serious. Her eyes glowed with an electric blue intensity.

The meeting adjourned.

It was while she was working on the date rape campaign that Lucie arrested Cleveland State University basketball player Roy Z. Williams after a CSU student, Debby, accused him of raping her at a fraternity house party. Lucie found out Williams was convicted of murder as a juvenile and was a suspect in the murders of two young women in California.

Williams was indicted on the Cleveland rape charge, and then he jumped bond. When Lucie heard that he had disappeared, she got right on the phone to the police in California and to attorney Richard Caplan, who was representing the family of murder victim Lina Aldridge.

Lucie was worried. The fugitive warrant for Williams had to be processed by the Cuyahoga County Sheriff's Department, then through the FBI. The paperwork took time. Lucie wanted to make sure they found Williams. For three weeks, there were numerous calls, back and forth to California.

Then Caplan called Lucie and told her Williams had been spotted at his mother's house. Lucie called the police, and Long Beach detectives arrested Williams and held him on the Cleveland rape. Simultaneously, the two California homicide cases fell into place.

Williams was charged with both murders and made his first court appearance on May 1, 1991. Friends and relatives of the victims attended the hearing. Katie Aldridge, Lina's grandmother, wore a black suit and T-shirt featuring a picture of her granddaughter beneath the words: JUSTICE FOR LINA ALDRIDGE.

A twenty-three-year-old Compton woman watched the Roy Williams story on television. She recognized him. Two years earlier, when she was twenty-one and pregnant, she had been raped by two men. She had reported the attack, but the suspects had never been found. Now she saw one of them on television. Roy Williams.

The men had raped her five times. Then, one of them began choking her. As she gagged for breath, the second rapist yelled, Roy, man, don't.

The one called Roy replied, I'll kill you if I go back to jail for this.

After seeing Roy Williams on television, she called Compton police. New charges of attempted murder, rape, and kidnapping were filed against Williams.

All three cases would be prosecuted together in Los Angeles County. The prosecutors said they might go for the death penalty. Attorney Richard Caplan had worked hard to force the police to reopen the Lina Aldridge investigation. The Cleveland rape case was a key element, Caplan felt. "The cases never would have been solved without that chain of events."

It was ironic, Caplan realized, because there probably wouldn't have been a conviction in Cleveland. "The jurors would figure, she was intoxicated, she had it coming," Caplan said. He had run the case by friends and relatives, and they said, She was asking for it.

But Caplan was confident about the murder cases. Maybe he'll plead, Caplan thought, to avoid the death penalty.

"If those cases had occurred in Ohio," Lucie said, "Williams would already be on death row." She was relieved he was finally going to face trial. She knew if you looked at the Cleveland rape as an isolated case, people would not be overly concerned. No one would have suspected him of being a killer. You never know, Lucie thought. She had learned long before never to second-guess criminals.

"Everyone said it was a bullshit case," Lucie said wryly. "Except me. The eternal believer."

It was the spring of 1991, just over eighteen years since Lucie had come on the job. Another new academy class was coming in. When Lucie was a rookie, there was no specialized training in child abuse and rape. Now, she was doing the training for the recruits, and the academy was under the direction of Commander Kathryn Mengel, who supervised the bureau of human resources, which included the budget, personnel, and staff planning units.

Before Lucie joined the force, women had been relegated to the

Women's Bureau. Lucie had no female supervisors, no female veterans out in the Fourth to show her the ropes. Several years ago, Sergeant Jackie Christ noticed that there were more father/daughter police teams than father/son for the first time in the history of the Cleveland Police Department.

Two high school girls wrote Lucie letters for a class project. What is it like to be a policewoman? What has your career entailed?

On the second floor in the strike force office, a patrolwoman readied herself for a john detail. On the force just a few years, she had heard of Lucie. She's an inspiration, the woman said. Her accomplishments are something I can aspire to.

Law enforcement had come a long way since 1973, Lucie reflected. She had tried to make a difference. "If I can't make it better than it was eighteen years ago, I might as well have quit this a long time ago. There is no point in staying in any company, whether it's Huron Road Hospital or the Cleveland Police Department, if you're gonna leave it the same way you found it."

Lucie went to the Justice Center cafeteria and picked up her standard eat-in lunch—egg salad on multigrain bread with pickles. She rode the elevator up to the sixth floor and passed classmate Michele Kratzer's office on the way to the sex crimes unit. Kratzer was captain in charge of the jail. Another classmate, Valerie Wilson-Jones, was now commander in charge of the report center.

Back in her office, seated next to her teddy bear calendar, Lucie started to read her crime reports as she ate her sandwich. A thirteen-year-old girl said she got out of school early. At eleven-thirty, five black males grabbed her at the bus stop and took her to the park and raped her for five hours. She could not provide any description of the men. She went to the hospital and refused to talk to the rape counselor.

Hmm, Lucie thought as she chewed her pickle. She always was a little suspicious when a kid who was supposed to be in school came up with something like that. The park where the alleged rape took place was a well-traveled area. For five hours? The kid could have been cutting school and then had to come up with a story. Kids get trapped. "I'm not saying it didn't happen," Lucie mumbled. She assigned the case. As always.

Pat Blackmon called. In the fall, she had won the election, becoming the first black woman judge on the appellate court. She was calling Lucie to make social plans. "How about seeing *Dances with Wolves?*" Pat suggested.

"Oh," Lucie said, "here's the thing. I'm scheduled to see that tonight. But if I like it a lot, I'll go back. You know how I lust for Kevin Costner. I might be able to take six hours of him in the same week."

Lucie giggled, her left dimple appearing deep in her cheek. A sapphire earring sparkled in one ear.

She later changed the plan. She did love Costner and thought the sexiest scene she ever saw was in *Bull Durham,* when he painted Susan Sarandon's toenails. Outrageous. But *Dances with Wolves* gave her nightmares. Fingerprinting the severed arm of Danny Greene was no problem, bloody homicide scenes faded from her memory. But the wanton slaughtering of the wolf and buffaloes did her in.

Her phone rang constantly. The mother of a rape suspect called. Her son was in a district jail. When will he be released? What happens? Lucie explained the system. He still has to be charged.

"Even when he is charged, he has to have a bond hearing before he can be released. Don't sit there." Lucie's voice was kind. "He won't be leaving right away."

A rapist was in jail awaiting a lineup. Another serial criminal. He had been convicted in 1973, but he was now out. He had grabbed a seventeen year-old, stabbed her through the cheek, staked her to the ground, and then ran her over with the car. She was so mutilated they couldn't even tell if she had been sexually assaulted. He was educated, good-looking. "A guy most women would date," Lucie said. He used simple tricks to get close enough to his victims. One woman was jogging. When he asked her the time, she stopped and he grabbed her, threw her on the ground, and started to rip her clothes off. But other people saw the attack and she escaped. She picked him out of a mug shot. He was suspected of numerous rapes over the years. Lucie hoped to clear up a string of rapes when victims identified him in a lineup.

Some victims from the nearby suburb of Lakewood did identify him, clearing up Lakewood's cases. But the Cleveland victim picked Detective Pat Evans instead. Which meant Evans was teased unmercifully—and also meant there was yet another serial rapist on the loose.

Channel 8 called Lucie, wanting to tape a segment for the six o'clock news. A judge in juvenile court released a teenager who had raped two eight-year-old girls. Once out, he raped another child. Will Lucie comment?

Lucie grew tense as the afternoon progressed, her sandwich only half eaten between calls.

A twelve-year-old rape victim was scheduled for an abortion at Metro Hospital. Lucie needed a DNA test run on the fetal matter to determine paternity. With a victim that young, paternity was evidence of rape. Metro Hospital gave Lucie the name of the lab in Denver that usually handled their tests on fetal specimens. Lucie called the police department's budget office.

There was a problem. The lab did not have a contract with the city.

The test was seven hundred and fifty dollars. Anything over five hundred dollars had to be put out for a competitive bid.

A competitive bid? Lucie rubbed her fingers against her forehead, thinking, I don't have time to go through a bidding process. The soon-to-be aborted fetus would be in college by the time we got through that. The phone cord was wrapped under her right arm. She clamped her arm over it, catching the receiver between her left ear and shoulder. She took a deep breath.

"You don't understand. I have this twelve-year-old. She has to have an abortion on Tuesday. It's Friday. We don't have time," Lucie emphasized.

"Can't they use the lab we normally use?"

"Metro is used to working with the lab in Denver. This is not the time for a learning experience. Just tell me how to do it," Lucie insisted, tossing humor at any disaster.

The woman told her. Lucie had to have the lab fill out forms stating they had never contributed to Mayor White's campaign. If they were campaign contributors, and the story got into the paper that something that should have gone out for a competitive bid was given to a contributor to the mayor, well, who knows what would happen.

Lucie called the lab in Denver. She felt like a total jerk. She told the lab she was sending them a three-page form that they had to sign and have notarized, swearing that they never gave any money to Cleveland's mayor. The lab was very responsive. They faxed the forms right back, the originals would follow.

The prosecutor called. They needed a court order to obtain blood from the suspect.

The next dilemma was who would pay for the Fedex. The fetal matter had to be sent immediately after the child had the abortion.

As she picked up the phone, Lucie muttered, her deep blue eyes blazing, "I hope somebody is thinking about this twelve-year-old."

ACKNOWLEDGMENTS

When we decided to write this book, there was no book about the career of a woman law enforcement officer, and no book about an officer who was still on the force. We owe a special debt to FBI Supervisory Special Agent Kenneth V. Lanning for recommending Lucie J. Duvall, and to Lucie, for having the courage and perseverance to see this project through to the end.

We are deeply grateful to our literary agent, Sandra Elkin, for having faith in us as a writing team, for her profound understanding of process, and for unremitting support and guidance each step of the way. Our editor Janet Goldstein of HarperCollins believed in this work from the beginning. She offered sharp insight, as if focusing the lens of a camera, so that we could see our work with new perspective. We thank Bruce Cook for a detailed chapter by chapter critique; and copy editor Shelly Perron for her careful attention to the spirit of our work. We appreciate assistant editor Peternelle van Arsdale, production editor Mark Hayden, attorney Matthew Martin, and the design team for their outstanding efforts on behalf of this book.

We thank the city of Cleveland and Chief Edward P. Kovacic for departmental authorization; and in particular, Lt. Martin Flask, Executive Assistant to the Chief, for facilitating our research.

We are grateful to Kathryn T. Mengel, Commander of the Bureau of Human Resources, for patiently responding to our numerous requests for information.

Every single interview contributed to this book. Many interviewees also gave us additional assistance. Thank you: Lester Adelson, M.D., Det. Timothy Anderson, Thomas C. Buford, Det. Robert Beck, Patricia Ann Blackmon, Booker Bledsoe, Robert L. Bolton, Det. Robert Borsuk, Lt. Lloyd Bratz, Off. Timothy Bright, Det. E. Gail Buddie, Det. Michael P. Burger, Shirley Aley Campbell, Postal Inspector John G. Campisi, Richard Caplan, *Carmen,* Sgt. Robert J. Cermak, Sgt. Jacqueline M. Christ, Det. Michael A. Cipo, Jean Clayton, Judith Cooke, *Matthew A. Corbett,* Det. Muriel Craig, Off. James Davidson, Richard Davis, *Clint Decker,* Det. George Deli, Carl Delau, Roger J. Dennerll, Mary Louise (Jill) Jayne Dunn, Andrew Bradley Duvall IV, Sgt. James C. Erne, Det. Patrick Evans, José C. Feliciano, Howard Filler, Jr., Lt. Martin Flask, Det. Derrline Fragomeni, Gerda K. Freedheim, Off. Robert Galaszewski, Off. Gregory Gamble, Dana Garcia, Sgt. Thomas R. Gaul, Off. Tom Guenther, Charles Gurtsak, Lynn Hammond, William T. Hanton, Postal Inspector Paul M. Hartman, Det. Mark Hastings, Lt. Frederick P. Hafner, Christian Halstead, Sgt. John Horvath, Det. Arnold V. Hovan, Cmdr. John C. James, Cmdr. Valerie Wilson Jones, Off. Edward Kelly, Det. James Kennelly, Sgt. Kenneth Kirchner, Off. Robert G. Kahl, Carla Kole, Ronald S. Kosits, Capt. Michele Kratzer, Off. Frank Krob, Dennis J. Kucinich, Sandra M. Kucinich, FBI Supervisory S.A. Kenneth V. Lanning, Madonna C. Lewis, Jacob John Loeffler, Kenneth J. Lusnia, Det. Andrea Markus-Mace, Rev. Paul Marshall, Det. Richard Martin, Marilyn Mason, Thomas McGuire, Det. Jonathan McTier, Cmdr. Kathryn T. Mengel, Carl Monday, Cmdr. Angel J. Morales, Margaret L. Murphy, the late Wilma L. Neubecker, *Nikki,* John M. Nolan, Violet E. Novak, Sgt. Robert J. O'Brien, Mr. Odell, Susan Pack, Jane M. Picker, Isabelle Katz Pinzler, Sandra L. Ramsey, Maryanne Kingzett Ras, Det. William L. Reese, Det. William Reiber, Janice E. Rench, Robert K. Ressler, William A. Riedthaler, Janet Riedthaler, Charles Rominski, Ross Santamaria, Det. Bienvenido Santiago, Marge Scheel, *Eric Schmidt,* Linda Smarr, Howard Slater, Cathy Smith, Tim Spencer, Gerald A. Strom, *T,* Sgt. Phyllis Trappenberg, Lt. Wayne Torok, *Treetop* Andi Udris, Lt. William Vargo, Ann Marie Wieland, Michael L. Walker, Melody A. White, Postal Inspector S.J. Wood, Raymond Zander II, Det. Andrea Zbydniewski, Off. Bruce Zuchowski, and others who remain anonymous. We thank the staff at numerous establishments who talked with us about the community and police.

We are extremely grateful to the unit personnel who allowed us to accompany them on tours of duty and provided technical information: Range: Sgt. Thomas R. Gaul; Fourth District: Cmdr. William Stanley, Sgt. Sharon Lawrence, Officers James Chura and Joselito Sandoval; Strike Force: Sgt. Charles W. Lane, Dets. William Leonard, William Reiber,

John Rozack, Helen Parries, Charles Thomas, Anthony Sandora, Manuel Roman and Off. Shelley Patena; Third District Vice: Sgt. Michael Thomas, Dets. Bienvenido Santiago, Robert Preston, James Kennelly, Ernest Graves; Technical Operations Section: Supt. Victor Kovacic, Sgt. George Walter, Dets. Richard Wilson, Bonnie Rudolph, Edward Prinz, Mitchell Wisniewski, and civilians Cynthia Mund, Tina Wolff, Jill Ryan, Joseph Serowik, Charles Sikora and other staff members; also the staff at the Cuyahoga County Morgue. Thank you to Sgt. Phyllis Trappenberg for a tour of Communications; and to Cmdr. Valerie Wilson Jones for a tour of the Record File Section. A special thank you to the Sex Crimes Unit: Sgt. Ruth Lanier, Dets. Albert Walton, Steven Stacho, Arnold Hovan, Jonathan McTier, Richard Martin, Muriel Craig, E. Gail Buddie, Gregory King, Derrline Fragomeni, Andrea Zbydniewski, Andrea Markus-Mace, Michael Cipo, Timothy Anderson, Mark Hastings, and Patrick Evans.

For assistance we also thank the Task Force on Violent Crime Rape Committee; Ohio Children's Trust Fund; and Northern Ohio Women Police, particularly Det. Mary Ann Rusnov, Det. Sue A. Sazima, Sgt. Katherine E. Schlegel and Off. Deborah Stoner; the Cleveland Police Patrolmen's Association; Gerald A. Strom and the Mandel School of Applied Social Sciences at Case Western Reserve University; Supt. Harry K. Russell and staff at the Lima Correctional Institute, Lima, Ohio; John Coyne and Mary Ellen Huesken of the Cleveland *Plain Dealer;* A. Nicholas Groth; and the following members of the New York City Police Department: Det. Lucille C. Burrascano, Det. Lillian Braxton, Pres., Policewomen's Endowment Association, Det. Kathleen Burke, Regional Director, International Association of Women Police.

Thank you for making our home away from home in Cleveland: Jerome H. Schmelzer & Associates, the Toma family, Tim Spencer, John Nolan, Thomas Buford, Don Hart, Tom Bonda, Christian Halstead, Pat Evans, Mark Hastings, Steve Sharrock, Gladys and Norman Hosansky, Doris Fogel, Dr. Lily Pien and Ruth Anne Witteman.

Our deep appreciation to those back home: Seda A. Sparling, whose unflagging support made this book possible. She allowed her home to be turned upside down into a writer's retreat and provided financial backing. She read, proofread, researched, prepared footnotes and bibliography and performed assorted tedious tasks through rewrite after rewrite. Thank you: Sona Aronian and Geoffrey Gibbs, for financial support, enthusiasm for the creative process, and soul food for writers; Anne Hosansky, who despite her own hardships came through with encouragement, books and financial aid; David Hosansky for sharing his journalistic expertise, and listening with a writer's ear; Steven Sparling, for his optimism and faith in us; Nancy and Bob Cleveland for legal advice while on vacation and

Nancy Cleveland for follow-up consultation; Fran Boyce, for being a go to the wall friend, whose insight at unexpected moments helped us find the perspective we had lost; Laura Moskowitz for flexibility, strength and safety; Lois and Howie Camber, for taking care of Yoda and home as if they were their own; Michele Padula, for bunny sitting; and Judy Surette for home and plant sitting.

We are extremely grateful to the Cleveland Police Historical Society, Inc., Anne T. Kmieck, Museum Curator, particularly for the Wilma Neubecker and the Violet E. Novak Collections. We greatly appreciate access to court documents in the possession of the Women's Law Fund, located at the Fair Employment Practices Clinic of Cleveland Marshall College of Law at Cleveland State University. We also thank the Cleveland Press Collection at the Cleveland State University Archives; Cleveland Public Library; John Carroll University and Prof. Alan R. Stephenson for access to Channel Five archives (now called WWS News Channel Five, an ABC affiliate); WJW-TV8 (a CBS affiliate), Phyllis Quail and Carl Monday for allowing us to view file footage; Convention & Visitors Bureau of Greater Cleveland; Kenneth Andras at the Civil Service Commission, Melinda McIntosh and Steve Shraison at University Library, University of Massachusetts at Amherst; Freedom of Information Center at University of Missouri School of Journalism; Fitchburg Public Library; Freiberger Library at Case Western Reserve University; Federal Bureau of Investigation; United States Postal Service; Bradford County Historical Society in Towanda, Pennsylvania; the Broome County Public Library, Binghamton, NY.

We are indepted to the following newspapers and magazines: Cleveland *Plain Dealer, Cleveland Press,* and *Cleveland Magazine;* we read numerous articles spanning over twenty years for background and information. We also read selected articles in the *Boston Herald,* the *Cleveland Call & Post, Columbia Journalism Review, Detroit News, FBI Law Enforcement Bulletin, Ladies' Home Journal, Lake County News-Herald, Long Beach Press Telegram, Mademoiselle, McCall's, MS., National Centurion, New York Times Magazine, Newsweek, Playboy, Providence Journal, Today's Health, USA Today, US News & World Report,* and *Woman's World.*

We consulted film footage from: ABC, June 24, 1982, transcript of "20/20" segment entitled "Women on Patrol," with correspondent Geraldo Rivera. Fox Network, Fall 1990, "America's Most Wanted," segment on William Riedthaler. WJW-TV8 (CBS affiliate), 1982, series on the crackdown on prostitution along Prospect and Euclid avenues, with Bill McKay; August 7, 1984 and December, 1985, series on Stage Door Johnnie's with I-Team reporter Carl Monday; September, 1989, news segment about the trial of Ronnie Shelton. WKYC-TV Channel 3 (NBC affiliate) January 7, 1984, "The Dick Feagler Show." WWS News Channel 5 (ABC affiliate), news coverage of the following events: December 15, 1978, Cleveland goes into default; January 15, 1981, shooting of William Riedthaler; August 1981 *Richard Palmer* death; December 17, 1982, police promotion ceremony.

We also consulted the following books: Edmund H. Chapman, *Cleveland: Village to Metropolis,* the Western Reserve Historical Society and the Press of Western Reserve University, 1964; George E. Condon, *Cleveland: The Best Kept Secret,* Doubleday & Company, Inc., New York, 1967; Willa Mae Hemmons, Editor, *The State of Black Cleveland,* Urban League of Greater Cleveland, 1989; Eric Johannesen, *Cleveland Architecture 1876–1976,* the Western Reserve Historical Society, 1979; Hank Messick, *The Silent Syndicate,* Macmillan Co., New York, 1967; Carol Poh Miller and Robert Wheeler, *Cleveland: A Concise History, 1796–1990,* by Indiana University Press, 1990; James Neff, *Mobbed Up,* Dell Publishing, New York, 1989; Charles O'Hara and Gregory L. O'Hara, *Fundamentals of Criminal Investigation,* Charles C. Thomas Publisher, 1988; "The Jayne History," compiled by Lillian Jayne Dull and Ruth Jayne Hardy, 1960; *World Book Encyclopedia,* Field Enterprises Educational Corporation, 1959 and yearly supplements; *Role of Commercial Banks in the Financing of the Debt of the City of Cleveland,* hearing before the Subcommittee on Financial Institutions, Supervision, Regulation and Insurance of the Committee on Banking, Finance and Urban Affairs, House of Representatives, July 10, 1979; *Final Report of the Attorney General's Commission on Pornography,* Rutledge Hill Press, Nashville, Tennessee, 1986. A special thank you for the following book, which makes writing about Cleveland a researcher's dream: *The Encyclopedia of Cleveland History,* compiled and edited by David D. Van Tassel and John J. Grabowski, published in association with Case Western Reserve University, Indiana University Press, 1987.

Index